To Mike

I it was a
pleasure meeting you
Atlanta. Be careful

Sam

# Drug Interdiction

Partnerships,
Legal Principles,
and Investigative
Methodologies for
Law Enforcement

## George S. Steffen
## Samuel M. Candelaria

## CRC PRESS

Boca Raton   London   New York   Washington, D.C.

## Library of Congress Cataloging-in-Publication Data

Steffen, George, S.
    Drug interdiction : partnerships, legal principles, and investigative methodologies for law enforcement / George S. Steffen, Samuel M. Candelaria.
        p. cm.
    Includes bibliographical references and index.
    ISBN 0-8493-1252-3
    1. Drug traffic--Investigation--United States. 2. Narcotics and crime--United States. 3. Narcotics, Control of--United States. 4. Drug abuse--United States--Prevention. 5. Law enforcement--United States. I. Candelaria, Samuel M. II. Title.

HV8079.N3+                                                                                              2002031439

**Visit the CRC Press Web site at www.crcpress.com**

© 2003 by CRC Press LLC

No claim to original U.S. Government works
International Standard Book Number 0-8493-1252-3
Library of Congress Card Number 2002031439
Printed in the United States of America        2  3  4  5  6  7  8  9  0
Printed on acid-free paper

# Foreword

The much-debated "war on drugs" has fostered many initiatives that seek to reduce the availability, distribution, and use of drugs through education, aggressive law enforcement, prosecution and incarceration, and treatment for those who abuse drugs. Law enforcement officers and, in fact, most people in the United States, understand that conquering the substance abuse problems that face our society entails a multifaceted approach through cooperative efforts. This book, *Drug Interdiction: Partnerships, Legal Principles, and Investigative Methodologies for Law Enforcement*, does not address society's ills in the psychological or social context but simply provides a real-world view of law enforcement efforts geared to making a difference in fighting the "war on drugs."

Our role in this effort is best served by developing effective enforcement practices and tactics that are based on sound logic, experience, and are within the confines of the law. Scrutiny of our actions is thorough and, while sometimes frustrating, is necessary, because professional law enforcement values require total accountability. Ethics and integrity are principal values in the successful investigation of drug-related cases. Our experience shows that sometimes the best evidence in a drug case is the word of the investigating officer. So many cases involve one-on-one contact between officer and suspect that integrity is paramount. Once an officer loses that integrity there is no going back. The most efficient way to maintain integrity is to use the best practices available. This book provides that guide.

The challenges facing officers today are different than when the open drug culture emerged in the 1960s and 1970s. If we look at illegal drugs from a historical perspective, we know that abuse in the United States has been a problem since the 1800s, and addiction was rampant during the Civil War when doctors fought to control the pain of the thousands of soldiers wounded during the conflict. Heroin was first used in the late 1870s as an alternative to morphine and was viewed as an effective way of reducing pain and addiction. We now know that heroin is not the cure-all it was intended to be. Simply put, one form of addictive drug replaced another.

The rampant and open use of marijuana, D-lysergic acid diethylamide (LSD), heroin, and the other drugs of choice during the 1960s caused a

iii

change in how police officers enforced the law. Having policed during that era, I observed that views toward substance abuse changed dramatically during those years. The drug abusers of then are among the leaders of today.

The use of drugs has also affected the personal lives of police officers. Early on, it was unusual to hear about officers using illegal drugs. Today most law enforcement agencies have reduced their intolerance of drug use by prospective officers. This has occurred not because administrators believe that illegal drug use by officers is tolerable, but by the reality that such use affects every stratum of our society. According to the Centers for Disease Control 1999 Youth Risk Behavior Surveillance System, 47.2% of high school students surveyed nationwide had used marijuana and 9.5% had used a form of cocaine during their lifetimes. Our hope is that drug use by those prospective officers has been kept to a minimum and has not affected their perspective on illegal drug enforcement.

Much of today's law enforcement efforts is guided by reaction to the events of September 11, 2001. American nationalism and commitment to maintaining a free democracy are at a fever pitch. The terrorists attacked the symbols that help define the American way of life — our economy and our military power. However, there is no greater threat to our economy than the damage done by illegal drug use and trafficking.

On January 23, 2002, John P. Walters, Director of the Office of National Drug Control Policy (ONDCP) released a study detailing the economic damage caused by this illicit industry. The study, entitled "The Economic Costs of Drug Abuse in the United States, 1992–1998," revealed that drugs sapped $143.4 billion from the U.S. economy in 1998 and projected the loss for 2000 at over $160 billion.

According to the study, illegal drugs cost the economy $98.5 billion in lost earnings, $12.9 billion in healthcare costs, and $32.1 billion in other costs. Crime-related costs involving goods and services lost to crime, property damage, work hours missed by crime victims and those incarcerated, and criminal justice system costs amounted to $88.9 billion. Projected costs for 1999 and 2000 amounted to $152.7 billion and $160.8 billion, respectively. These figures are truly sobering.

There are always those who challenge the need to engage in aggressive drug enforcement. The economic impact and the affect of substance abuse on the youth of America supports tough enforcement. Substance abuse among youth has been linked to delinquency. While abuse does not directly cause delinquency, there is a strong correlation. Such antisocial behavior brings about school and family problems, and some argue will eventually bring down our American way of life.

Officers are best prepared when they learn from their peers, and this book by Samuel M. Candelaria and George S. Steffen will have a tremendous effect on how law enforcement officers accomplish their goals in fighting drug trafficking and associated crime. Drug enforcement cannot be measured but must be aggressive and a major part of community efforts to maintain public safety. Anything less is not acceptable.

**Gilbert G. Gallegos**
Chief
Albuquerque, New Mexico Police Department

# Preface

The intricacies and complexities of criminal investigation have become commonplace, certainly in the area of forensic science, technological advances, and criminal procedure. Profound changes in law enforcement have occurred in the past 25 years. However, what clearly remains the same is that law enforcement relies on training, experience, and expertise to identify criminal conduct as it relates to illicit narcotic activity and criminal behavior in general.

This book breaks from traditional criminal investigation texts in a number of ways. It provides a simple but comprehensive examination of proven investigation methods in the areas of domestic drug interdiction and consensual encounters for law enforcement officers and investigators. The way we approached the material in the book is from a "cop's point of view." A great deal of the information presented to the reader is directly related to the authors' experiences in the field and in the courtroom setting, where the nuances of domestic drug interdiction are learned.

There are several principal themes in the book that are emphasized throughout. The central theme is the importance of safety. The safety of the officer is critical in all interdiction environments. Emphasis should be placed on training, proper preparation, and planning. The investigators should conduct themselves properly and within the scope of the law. We urge law enforcement officers participating in domestic drug investigations to be professional and conduct themselves appropriately. We stress throughout that the foundation for our work is based on case law, whether federal or state laws. Attention is given to this because we do not want to create an environment in which we lose the benefit the courts have afforded us in combating the drug trade. The majority of courts are clearly on the side of law enforcement with respect to criminal conduct and narcotic enforcement. Collaborating with the business community is another fundamental principle that is explored. Law enforcement must look to the community to create viable solutions to combat the drug dilemma.

The 21st century is upon us; law enforcement faces many challenges ahead with the war on terror, the criminal element, and drugs within our society. These battles will not be won any time soon; however, we do have a number of tools at our disposal to combat them effectively. Effective law enforcement is essential for reducing drug-related crime in the United States. One of the tools is recognizing the way criminals behave while engaged in criminal conduct. Proper training will help in identifying individuals involved in drug trafficking. This is the ultimate goal of this text. We hope that we have accomplished this objective in an effective fashion.

# Acknowledgments

We are indebted to many individuals who contributed to the preparation of this book. Their valuable assistance and expertise have been extraordinary. First, our professional police agencies — the Albuquerque Police Department in New Mexico, and the Pinellas County Sheriff's Office, Largo, Florida — for providing us the opportunity to work in the great profession of law enforcement. We want to thank them for the training and freedom to explore our creativity during our careers. Without their support, this project would not be possible. We have worked with some of the finest, most skilled, professional law enforcement officers in the country.

We thank Chief Gilbert G. Gallegos, of the Albuquerque, New Mexico Police Department, the immediate past National President of the Fraternal Order of Police, for his splendid foreword to this text. Chief Gallegos is nationally recognized as a leading law enforcement professional. We were deeply honored that he accepted our invitation to write the foreword for the book.

We extend our appreciation and gratitude to the Multijurisdictional Counterdrug Task Force Training program of St. Petersburg College, St. Petersburg, Florida. Their leadership has provided us with an opportunity over the past several years to render much of the information contained in this book to thousands of federal, state, and local law enforcement officers throughout the United States.

The most sincere respect and thanks to Special Agent Kevin Small of the Drug Enforcement Administration's Albuquerque, New Mexico District Office, with whom Sam Candelaria had the honor of working for 11 years, and who provided the initial insight and development of the Consensual Encounter training class, which was used as a guide for this book.

The preparation for this text would not have been possible without the expertise of professional law enforcement officers. We owe a great deal of gratitude to Frank R. Campbell of the Pinellas County Sheriff's Office, Largo, Florida, canine section, for his assistance and guidance in the preparation of the "Use of the Drug Canine" chapter and overall domestic investigation information for this text. His dedication to drug canine development and training is nationally recognized. Additionally, we thank L.T. "Tom" McCabe

ix

of Schlim, McCabe and Associates. Their purpose is to provide drug training for law enforcement (1-800-490-DRUG). Tom McCabe and John Schlim's information concerning the "Knock and Talk" technique was extremely valuable in the preparation of this text. Their many years of law enforcement experience and training are certainly evident.

Still others, who were generous with time, advice, guidance, energy, and information include James Sheridan, retired detective with the Albuquerque, New Mexico Police Department. Our appreciation goes out to Albuquerque Police detectives Steve Flores and Art Lucero, and Agent Jonathan Salazar of the New Mexico State Police, all of whom gave their time and effort to contribute to this project. The guidance and expert views of nationally recognized author Rudolfo Anaya, the uncle of Sam Candelaria, proved most valuable.

We extend our gratitude to Assistant U.S. Attorney Larry Gomez, U.S. Attorney's Office of New Mexico and Sergeant David Chester of the Albuquerque, New Mexico Police Department, Central Narcotics Unit, for their positive reviews and critiques of the material for this text. Because of the assistance, insight, and recommendations of these talented individuals, the topic coverage is stronger, more complete, and more accurate.

We thank Kathi Liadis for her professional work in the clerical preparation of several portions of the text.

Appreciation goes out to the many men and women of law enforcement who work in interdiction groups throughout this great nation. Their efforts combating drug trafficking on a daily basis continues to make a difference. We salute them all and thank them for their contributions toward counterdrug enforcement.

We thank our families, the Candelarias and Steffens, for their patience and support. Without our strong family foundations, our lives and law enforcement careers would not be nearly as successful.

**George S. Steffen, MPA**
Pinellas County, Florida


**Samuel M. Candelaria**
Albuquerque, New Mexico

# The Authors

**George S. Steffen** is a captain with the Pinellas County Sheriff's Office, Largo, Florida, a progressive law enforcement agency located in the Tampa Bay region of west central Florida at the Gulf of Mexico. He earned a Bachelor of Arts degree in Criminal Justice from St. Leo College, St. Leo, Florida and a Master of Public Administration degree from Troy State University, Troy, Alabama.

Lieutenant Steffen has been a law enforcement officer in Florida for over 20 years — as a patrol deputy, criminal investigator, and supervisor in several capacities including Patrol Operations, Internal Affairs, Criminal Investigations, and Child Protection Investigations, and has over 12 years of Narcotic Enforcement Investigations experience.

Lieutenant Steffen is a certified law enforcement instructor in the state of Florida. He is a nationally recognized expert and instructor in domestic drug interdiction and narcotic enforcement. He travels extensively throughout the United States instructing local, state, and federal law enforcement professionals in domestic drug interdiction and narcotic investigation.

**Samuel M. Candelaria** is a 22-year veteran police officer of the Albuquerque Police Department, Albuquerque, New Mexico. He worked narcotic investigations for 17 years, working in an undercover capacity for 6 years and with the Albuquerque Drug Enforcement Administration's Interdiction Detail for 11 years. The group focused on all forms of public transportation, such as airport, bus, and train interdiction, and on hotel and parcel interdiction. The detail specialized in the Amtrak passenger train system.

Candelaria, a nationally recognized expert, has instructed nationally and internationally with the Drug Enforcement Administration's Jetway Program and with the International Narcotics Interdiction Association (INIA). He has also instructed law enforcement programs throughout the country on consensual encounter techniques.

Candelaria was selected Albuquerque Police Department's Detective of the Year for 2001 and was the recipient of the INIA's Distinguished Lifetime Achievement Award for 2001. The interdiction detail to which Candelaria was assigned was also selected as the HIDTA Interdiction Detail of the Year for 2001 by Asa Hutchinson, administrator of the Drug Enforcement Administration.

# Table of Contents

# Introduction to Drug Interdiction

**1**

The focus of our effort is to provide a simple, insightful, but comprehensive "how to" text for law enforcement professionals who are interested in learning specific investigative techniques to identify and deal with criminal activity, specifically narcotic trafficking. The book targets law enforcement officers who want to create new initiatives, innovative programs, and strategies to combat the drug problem in their communities by using domestic interdiction investigations and consensual encounters. The use of community-based solutions in partnership with the business community is the cornerstone of this text. It will provide the reader information from the authors' experiences and the expertise of hundreds of investigators from around the country from which the reader can learn and benefit. This includes the wise use of experiences to attain goals and to keep officers safe in the drug interdiction environment.

The illicit drug market in the United States is one of the most profitable in the world. It attracts aggressive and sophisticated drug traffickers and organizations. Many diverse groups from around the globe distribute and traffic narcotics through a variety of methods. Narcotic trafficking is a global issue and the United States government has put into place strategies and programs to combat the problem. We are spending billions of dollars (Figures 1.1 and 1.2) on initiatives such as prevention, education, treatment, research, and disruption of drug availability. Interdiction efforts, eradication, and bilateral cooperation with other countries as well as domestic law enforcement initiatives are being deployed. It is a massive undertaking to battle this conflict.

International and national interdiction efforts are conducted by a variety of agencies, such as the United States Coast Guard, United States Customs Service, and the Drug Enforcement Administration. According to the Office

Fiscal Year 2003 President's Request, by Area
Total Resources: $19.2 Billion

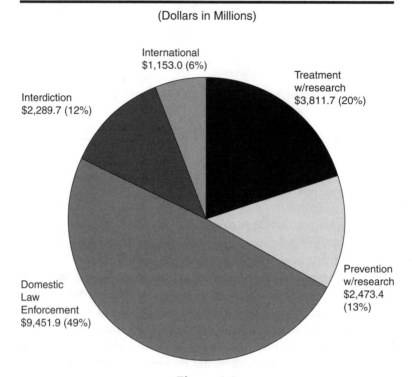

(Dollars in Millions)

International
$1,153.0 (6%)

Treatment
w/research
$3,811.7 (20%)

Interdiction
$2,289.7 (12%)

Prevention
w/research
$2,473.4
(13%)

Domestic
Law
Enforcement
$9,451.9 (49%)

**Figure 1.1**

of National Drug Control Policy in a presentation in March 2002 known as "Data Snapshot: Drug Abuse in America — Office of National Drug Control Policy," indicates that interdiction must be included as an essential element in a comprehensive approach. Targeted interdiction based on solid intelligence data will have the greatest long-term impact. This is also true in the domestic interdiction arena within the borders of the United States, by federal, state, and local officials. It is important for agencies to put strong investigative emphasis on drug traffickers and couriers transporting drugs and operating within our borders.

The chart prepared by the Drug Enforcement Administration (Figure 1.3) shows the major corridors into the United States from the source zone, transit zone, and arrival zone. It illustrates the primary drug flow from the 60% rate through Mexico and the other 40% flow through the Caribbean corridors. The drug flow then becomes a localized issue that must be addressed by state and local law enforcement.

The Federal Drug Control Budget Has More Than Quadrupled
since ONCP Was Established in 1988

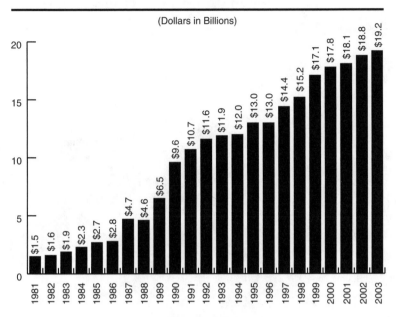

**Figure 1.2**

To date, more than 300 domestic drug interdiction groups exist in the United States and are growing due to the demand for counterdrug efforts in a variety of settings. These initiatives started because drug couriers and drug organizations facilitating the transportation of narcotics first used major commercial airports. They branched out to other transportation methods to include commercial bus systems, such as Greyhound; train systems, such as Amtrak; and parcel package freight systems such as Federal Express, United Parcel Service, and the United States Postal Service. Since the mid-1970s, counterdrug efforts have been performed from major transportation areas and have been expanded to other areas such as hotels/motels, storage units, and rental vehicles.

We are passionate about the material we present in this text; we strongly believe in the programs and techniques outlined. We know from personal knowledge and the experiences of other drug interdiction investigators from a variety of law enforcement agencies across the United States that these methods have proven to be extremely effective investigative options for the drug enforcement officer.

The text will outline step by step the selection process of an interdiction officer, how to initiate specific domestic drug interdiction programs, and how

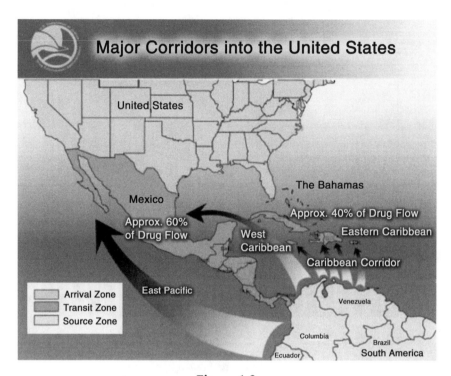

**Figure 1.3**

to use the business community to assist law enforcement in identifying potential violators who use legitimate businesses to facilitate the drug trade.

Domestic interdiction, investigation, or interception programs refer to the interception of illegal contraband within the confines of the United States. It targets the interception of drugs prior to sale on the street. Drug traffickers use a variety of techniques to facilitate their trade. They perpetually search for creative mechanisms to prevent law enforcement from detecting their illicit contraband. Drug trafficking organizations will exploit any means possible to shield their drug shipments from detection.

We want the reader to be aware of the distinction between domestic interdiction as opposed to highway interdiction. When law enforcement officers hear the term "drug interdiction," most associate it with highway interdiction. Highway interdiction, as controversial as it is, is an effective method of combating drug trafficking. Experienced highway officers who work interdiction look for certain behaviors of the drug courier. Although we do not address highway interdiction, much of the theory outlined in the text is similar to what the highway interdiction officer looks for during a highway encounter — certain characteristics that couriers display when transporting narcotics.

Law enforcement has identified a variety of legitimate businesses that are used by individuals and drug organizations in the drug trade, such as hotels, commercial bus systems, commercial airlines, storage unit facilities, commercial parcel services, the U.S. Postal Service, trains, and rental vehicle companies. Business owners, managers, and staff essentially participate in a "business watch program" and are volunteering to be the "eyes and ears" for law enforcement. Staff from these businesses are trained by law enforcement to identify suspicious behavior of individuals who may be involved in criminal conduct, namely drug trafficking. All programs are voluntary. The processes of searching for anomalies and separating legitimate guests, passengers, and individuals from drug traffickers are the focal points of these programs. The businesses then contact law enforcement to report suspicious activity. They act only as reporters of information. Each of these businesses has been identified as a conduit for drug traffickers to transport, store, and facilitate flow of narcotics.

Drug traffickers and couriers are compelled to travel and behave in a particular manner, due to the nature of the drug business. Last-minute travel is common among drug traffickers; they cannot make travel plans too far in advance because they do not know the exact times when drugs will be procured by their source of supply. A supplier will contact the buyer to tell him that the drugs have arrived and to be at a certain location at a certain time, generally that day or the next. The trafficker or courier will consequently exhibit certain behavior and conduct which, if properly observed, can be identified by an officer. This book will prepare the investigator to identify and investigate the behavior that a drug trafficker may display in a particular setting. The investigation will focus on how to conduct a consensual encounter if the opportunity presents itself. In addition, the text will delineate the use of other investigative strategies, tools, partnerships, and resources, such as trained drug canines and how to best use a drug canine team to enhance the effectiveness of an interdiction group.

Consensual encounters are approaches and conversations with suspected couriers, traffickers, or drug dealers. If the opportunity presents itself, law enforcement may approach an individual, without having reasonable suspicion or even probable cause, to make an inquiry. The degree of suspicion required to conduct a consensual encounter is *zero*. One type of consensual encounter is known as a *knock and talk*; this technique is exactly what it implies: it is knocking on someone's door and talking to them. This technique is a last resort effort on the part of law enforcement when information is received that someone is trafficking in narcotics from their residence or business. Officers contact the suspect and ask for a consent search of the premises or if the suspect would surrender any drugs to investigators. These requests are voluntary and subject to refusal and termination of the encounter by the individual at any point.

We will deal with investigator report writing and courtroom presentation and testimony. It is important to thoroughly document the officer's observations and actions in the interdiction investigation process. Articulating these critical facts can and will be used in testimony, to include motions to suppress evidence hearings, depositions, and ultimately criminal trial. Defense attorneys have sadly resorted to repugnant tactics in the last several years in defense of their clients. These tactics are affectionately known as the CAL ("cops are lying") defense. It seems that if defense counsel cannot effectively attack the facts of the case, he will attack the officer's integrity by accusing the officer of setting up the client, either by lying about a consent search or planting drugs on the person. The old conspiracy theory rears its ugly head again. That is why law enforcement must be totally professional in interdiction efforts. To meet the challenges of a professional law enforcement investigator, preparation and documentation are essential.

The selection process of an interdiction officer is a significant component to the success of these programs. Temperament, flexibility, creativity, patience, resourcefulness, assertiveness, and the ability to speak to people are some of the attributes essential to the individual who aspires to be a successful interdiction officer. Hand in hand with the selection of an interdiction officer is the selection of a drug dog handler and a trained narcotic canine. It is important that the canine team be able to work in a variety of demanding environments including large, crowded, or noisy settings, and to deal with a medley of odors. The supervisor's role in an interdiction group is equally important. He or she must be prepared to meet the challenges concerning a variety of operations, such as instituting an interdiction program, briefings regarding the execution of search warrants, knowledge of search and seizure issues, and related case law.

The programs can be modified and tailored for a variety of enforcement groups. Traditionally, interdiction groups work from a police agency's narcotics division or bureau. They tend to be successful, because drug interdiction is the sole responsibility of the team. Other parts of the agency such as traditional patrol officers and street crime units can work these programs. Each faces unique challenges and pitfalls.

The programs and ideas presented are not all our own; we owe a great deal of gratitude to the men and women of law enforcement interdiction groups before us, who were creative and innovative enough to combat drug trafficking in a non-traditional fashion.

As law enforcement professionals, we feel compelled to address the issue of *profiling*, specifically the terms *"racial profiling," "race-based policing,"* and *"bias-based policing."* Racial profiling occurs when an individual is targeted based solely on that person's race, ethnicity, or national origin. These practices invoke much contempt for the police, especially in minority communities. Racial profiling is one of the most controversial issues confronting law enforcement today. We do not know of any law enforcement agency or training group in the United States today that teaches that race is a characteristic of a drug trafficker or courier. We want to discuss the issue because it is extremely important. The debate rages among law enforcement professionals, government, and civic leaders. As authors of this text and as law enforcement professionals for a number of years, we would encourage strong policies to eliminate the practice of racial profiling. Individuals cannot and should not be targeted based strictly on their race or ethnicity in narcotic investigations. We do not condone or encourage it, and we fundamentally oppose the practice of racial profiling under these circumstances.

We do, however, strongly endorse the use of behavioral recognition of those individuals who engage in narcotic and other criminal activity. This practice focuses on the individual conduct of the person; race, national origin, and ethnicity should not play a role the decision to focus on an individual. Drug traffickers, couriers, and dealers are forced into certain conduct by virtue of the drug business itself. They will inevitably behave in a certain fashion as a direct result of their criminal conduct. A law enforcement officer or investigator, based on his or her training, experience, and expertise, will recognize the behavior and be able to articulate it. However, based on the recent terrorist events of September 11, 2001 at the World Trade Center in New York, the Pentagon in Washington, D.C., and the downed plane in Pennsylvania, it would be difficult to not profile certain ethnic groups who have been identified as part of terrorist networks. We should not do this at the expense of innocent individuals, but have in place a strong policy for identifying terrorist networks and their participants. Law enforcement must constantly adapt to new circumstances and situations. Cooperation between agencies with the sharing of intelligence and information is key to effective drug control strategies.

The objective of this book is to enhance the law enforcement investigator's ability to investigate criminal activity, specifically narcotic activity. We stress proper conduct by the investigator when participating in the programs outlined in the text, along with consistency and a "do it right every time" mentality, in accordance with current law. The courts, including the U.S. Supreme Court, support consensual encounters and the domestic drug investigation programs outlined. An abundance of case law exists acknowledging law enforcement in the practice of utilizing behavior and conduct as instruments to proceed further in investigations, providing a legal foundation for programs such as the ones described.

Law enforcement at the national, state, and local levels has developed strategies for detecting and apprehending terrorists. As a direct result of the terrorist attacks on our country on September 11, 2001, the issue of profiling once again has become prevalent in our national discussion on how to identify potential terrorists at our nation's airports and consequently prevent future terrorist attacks. Boston's Logan Airport has recently hired a security consultant to try to identify subjects flying out of Logan who may be involved in terrorist activities, using a technique known as Behavioral Pattern Recognition (BPR). The fundamental process of separating legitimate passengers from passengers who may be engaged in terrorist activities, based on their behavior, is the focus of this type of technique. This is not dissimilar to what we will be describing in this book as it relates to domestic drug interdiction investigations, focusing on the drug trafficker's behavior.

Each chapter includes relevant case law concerning the particular program described. The foundations of all of the programs outlined are firmly entrenched in the law, whether dealing with consensual encounters, search warrants, or the use of trained drug canines.

A strategic plan must be put in place to aggressively target drug traffickers and their organizations based on solid investigative efforts. We must remember that criminal and drug trends constantly change, but human behavior remains essentially the same when individuals are engaged in criminal activities.

# The Consensual Encounter

**2**

In this chapter, we will explore the consensual encounter and how to use it for our benefit in initiating and conducting investigations lawfully and safely. Officer safety should never take a back seat in police work, especially in a consensual encounter type setting, and it must always be at the forefront of any encounter we initiate. In this type of setting, we are always approaching the unknown. There will never be a dope load, money load, or bad guy worth getting ourselves, our partners, innocent citizens, or even the offender hurt. Conducting a consensual encounter should always be based on a person's conduct and behavior and never on his race, age, gender, or national origin. What does a courier or a person involved in criminal activity look like? There are no boundaries; we have encountered every imaginable type of person, with no limits on age, race, or gender. The youngest person in our combined experience has been 13 years old and the oldest 78 years old. There have been entire families, mother–daughter teams, husband–wife teams, brother–sister teams, and so on. There was the 17-year-old Canadian girl traveling by herself across the country from Los Angeles to Toronto, Canada with 3 kg of cocaine. Each kilogram of cocaine was concealed inside a separate box of laundry detergent in her suitcase. There was the 70-year-old couple traveling from Los Angeles to New York with 1.8 million dollars of U.S. currency in six suitcases. They had picked up the money from one son in Los Angeles and were taking it to their other son in New York. What was consistent about these two separate cases was the conduct and behavior displayed by the people involved.

How many of us would have approached a 70-year-old couple who looked like they were on vacation? But based on their conduct and behavior, the 70-year-old couple were contacted and the U.S. currency was discovered and seized. In conducting consensual encounters, we need to remove the blinders and rely on our training and law enforcement experience. The people involved in criminal activity may not be obvious to us in many cases, but their conduct and behavior will usually raise a red flag. If a person is involved in some type of criminal activity, whether transporting drugs or money, robbing banks, or using stolen credit cards, certain behaviors will allow you to identify him. You may look at a person and second-guess yourself, and make excuses as to why you do not think that a particular person could be involved in criminal activity. But if you focus your attention on his conduct and behavior and not on race, age, gender, or national origin, you will encounter the 70-year-old couple or the 17-year-old girl to engage in conversation and determine if, in fact, they are involved in criminal activity. How many times have you looked at someone and for no other reason than what he looked like or who he was, decided that it "couldn't be him" and walked away, allowing him to continue with his criminal activity. Criminals hope that we will be lazy and stereotype them.

You will ignore gender, age, race, and national origin when encountering a person and rely on your law enforcement training and experience and your observation of the person's conduct. You need to be consistent in your approach and try to adopt the same method each time. You need to treat people the same. We are not telling you to disregard officer safety, for that should always be your priority. The authors are advocating that your approach and questioning be consistent and you should not be deferred because of a person's age, race, gender, or national origin.

You will use certain vocabulary while conducting a consensual encounter; the words "approach and contact" will be seen throughout this book. The word "*STOP*" will *never* be used in the same sentence, report, or during testimony to describe a consensual encounter. You might as well exclude the word "*STOP*" from your vocabulary if you work in an area where you will be using consensual encounter techniques as a basis for your investigations. Undoubtedly your boss, co-workers, prosecutors, and especially defense attorneys will ask you what you did when you "stopped" a subject. If you answer that question, especially to the defense attorney, without correcting him with the answer "I did not stop the person," you will have used that word *STOP* to describe your consensual encounter. The defense attorney will almost always began his cross examination of you with that simple question about what you did when you "stopped" the suspect, and the defense attorney will be your best friend while he is asking the question: "Officer Jones, you are a 10-year veteran of your law enforcement agency; you have a number of years of great experience in the area of narcotic enforcement, isn't that correct? And, as a matter of fact, you are often relied on by junior officers and detectives to assist them in these types of investigations; isn't that correct? So when you *STOPPED* my client, he was very cooperative and agreed to speak to you, and even gave you permission to search his suitcase; isn't that correct?" If the answer to that question was "yes," we just gave that defense attorney a reason to ask the next question. "Well, Officer Jones, what reason did you have to *STOP* my client?"

In this book, we will explore terms such as *reasonable suspicion* and *probable cause*, which we are sure any law enforcement officer is familiar with from reports and testimony.

- Definition of Reasonable Suspicion: Reasonable suspicion, which will justify an officer in stopping a defendant in a public place, is a quantum of knowledge sufficient to induce an ordinarily prudent and cautious man under these circumstances to believe criminal activity is at hand.
- Definition of Probable Cause: Probable cause is having more evidence for than against. It is a reasonable ground for belief in the existence of facts warranting the proceedings complained of. It is an apparent state of facts found to exist upon reasonable inquiry (that is, such inquiry as the given case renders convenient and proper), which would induce a reasonably intelligent and prudent man to believe, in a criminal case, that the accused person had committed the crime charged or in a civil case, that a cause of action existed.

What must be present for a law enforcement officer to detain a person? The answer, of course, must at least be reasonable suspicion. If the initial contact with an offender in a drug case was described as a consensual encounter, then the suspect could be approached without reasonable suspicion or probable cause, and on the witness stand, you must justify contact with the offender to keep from losing the case. "Well, defense attorney, I really didn't stop your client." This answer will lead to the next question from that defense attorney. "Officer Jones, I just asked you if you had *STOPPED* my client and you answered YES to that question." As you sit on the stand contemplating that question and what your answer will be, a scene every law enforcement officer has experienced on the stand will begin to play out in your mind — a scene that shows the officer doing the backstroke in a large pool of water with no end in sight. Therefore, the word *STOP* will never be used in a sentence, report, or on the witness stand to describe a consensual encounter. By the way, the answer to that defense attorney's question, should have been "Sir or Ma'am, I did not STOP your client." End of answer! That will be another chapter.

"Hi. I'm a police officer. May I speak with you?" This is one of the easiest phrases that police officers can use, both uniformed and non-uniformed, but it is one of the most difficult for many. As a police officer, you talk with people every day in the performance of your duties. You have people coming up to you asking for directions, you talk with people as witnesses, you talk with people about their neighborhoods. You have to maintain a continuous dialogue with people because of the job you do.

Every person in the United States is protected by the Constitution. One of the most important amendments is the First Amendment to the Constitution, which guarantees every person freedom of speech. The First Amendment did not exclude those of us in law enforcement. It is one of the most basic rights that we as citizens (including police officers) use every day. Nowhere in that First Amendment did it describe that every citizen of the United States, except for police officers, was entitled to free speech.

So why don't we use this more to our advantage? For many of us in law enforcement, just talking to people is difficult. You know that people will ask you for help and that you must be able to communicate with them. You know you must investigate crimes and be able to ask people when they are at their lowest point for important information. You know that you must ask witnesses to crimes to describe certain information that will enable you to perform your duties as a law enforcement officer. So why is it so difficult for some of us to use this basic right to initiate a conversation?

Let us break down the words consensual encounter and define them. Consensual means existing or made by mutual consent without intervention or any act of writing. Encounter means to come face to face. You as a police officer can approach and speak with people anywhere, anytime you choose as long as you have a legal right to be there. You might think to yourself, "I'm a police officer; I can go to any location or contact anyone I want, because I'm the police." In a consensual encounter setting, the Supreme Court of the United States protects and supports you in this situation. Supreme Court case law also defines for you what circumstances must be present and how you, as a law enforcement officer, must ensure the persons you are contacting or approaching that those factors are present. In a consensual encounter, the courts will scrutinize your every action, from the minute you approach or contact a person to the last second of contact until you terminate the encounter, or until you make an arrest or seizure. Having the legal right to be at a certain location in a consensual encounter will be a very important factor in the court determining whether or not the encounter was lawful. Was the law enforcement officer there lawfully? These are questions you must define before making the encounter, for surely the courts will define it for you and it could be a determining factor in your case.

There are three types of police–citizen contacts. The first and most intrusive is an arrest of a person by a police officer. To arrest an individual, you must have probable cause. You learned the term *probable cause* early in your career; this is one of the first subjects taught in most police or law enforcement academies. When you make an arrest, you must have facts or specific circumstances to arrest a person. What is probable cause? Probable cause is having more evidence for than against; reasonable grounds for belief in the existence of facts warranting the proceedings; an apparent state of facts found to exist upon reasonable inquiry. That is, such inquiry as the given case renders convenient and proper, which would induce a reasonably intelligent and prudent man to believe, in a criminal case, that the accused person had committed the crime charged or in a civil case, that a cause of action existed. As you see in this definition, the courts used the example of a reasonably intelligent and prudent person to determine whether the facts supporting the charge of an accused person existed.

The second, less intrusive police–citizen contact is when a law enforcement officer detains a person. For a law enforcement officer to detain an individual, certain circumstances must exist. A law enforcement officer must have reasonable suspicion in order to detain or stop a person. Reasonable suspicion is another term taught in law enforcement academies that you use every day in your career. Reasonable suspicion, which justifies an officer in stopping a defendant in a public place, is a quantum of knowledge sufficient under the circumstances to induce an ordinarily prudent and cautious man to believe that criminal activity is at hand. As we see in this definition, the degree of facts and circumstances that must exist are greatly reduced in order to detain a person to further investigate criminal activity at hand.

The third and least intrusive police–citizen encounter is a consensual encounter. You need not have reasonable suspicion or probable cause to contact or approach a citizen. The degree of suspicion needed is zero. Although no legal justification for approaching a person is required, you should not approach or contact an individual based on impermissible factors such as race, age, gender, or national origin. In most situations, you will approach a person because of particular actions that are suspicious to the trained law enforcement officer.

The Supreme Court defined that police officers can conduct consensual encounters anywhere and any place they choose as long as they have a legal right to be there. (Case law defined.)

Consensual encounter techniques can be used by uniformed and non-uniformed law enforcement. Consensual encounters can be used for investigations of violent crimes, speaking to witnesses, or canvassing an area where a crime was committed. "Hi. I'm a police officer. May I speak with you; do you live or work in this area; did you hear or see anything occurring this morning?" Consensual encounters can be used in sex crime cases, property crime cases, white collar crime cases, and, of course, in narcotics investigations. The use of consensual encounters in transportation cases, i.e., airports, bus stations, train stations, parcel facilities, rental car counters, and storage facilities will be the primary initial investigative technique. A consensual encounter can enhance any investigation in which you want to gather intelligence. You are not interested in an arrest or seizure at this time in your investigation, but you want to find out about the players involved in a particular organization. Whether that organization is a three-member drug street dealer group working a particular area or a sophisticated money-laundering group, gathering intelligence can be accomplished by a simple encounter or contact with a person of that organization in a neutral area. The consensual encounter can assist your investigation if you are attempting to identify people, such as in the example of the three-member drug street dealer group. Which one of those persons is the leader of the group and controls the level of drugs being dealt? Which one is the "enforcer," responsible for carrying weapons and inflicting harm on any other rival drug organization or for warding off "rip-offs?" Who is the person who will stop law enforcement from disrupting the group's business? Of course, an officer's level of safety would be lowered when approaching this person. Which person in the organization is responsible for maintaining the drugs or money?

The consensual encounter will enhance your investigation if you are attempting to make seizures and effect arrests, such as in transportation cases. You are working in one of the areas previously mentioned. The phrase, "Hi. I'm a police officer. May I speak with you?" will help initiate contact with a potential drug or currency courier. The consensual encounter will assist you in seizing property and currency, again as in the transportation case. Money couriers will almost always use the same routes and modes of transportation as the drug couriers. Even though in most cases concerning the seizure of currency or property an arrest will not be made, the consensual encounter will allow you time to interview the person concerning the property or currency. In law enforcement and for many of us in our jurisdictions, we have the option of not arresting an offender if we choose. The consensual encounter will allow you an opportunity to establish confidential sources.

Let us look at what the consensual encounter is not! The consensual encounter is not a seizure; for a seizure or investigative detention to occur, you must have at least probable cause. The consensual encounter is not an arrest; you must have probable cause to arrest a person, and in a consensual encounter setting, probable cause is not a requirement to make an approach or contact a person. A consensual encounter is not a traffic stop, although many traffic stops have been turned into consensual encounters when the driver of the vehicle was made to feel free to leave.

When can you use a consensual encounter? A consensual encounter can be used anywhere and any time as long as a law enforcement officer has a legal right to be where he or she is. A consensual encounter can be used at a residence; although a law enforcement officer will more than likely have some reason for approaching a house, it does not have to be reasonable suspicion or probable cause, but perhaps some information concerning the residence has come to the officer's attention. Of course one of the main factors in conducting a consensual encounter at a residence is to obtain the resident's permission to speak to them and to enter the residence. A consensual encounter can be used in a hotel or motel setting; people involved in criminal activity often use hotels and motels so as not to bring attention to the areas in which they live. A consensual encounter can be used on the street, especially in an area where open air drug markets are prevalent. Consensual encounters can be used at commercial places of transportation, such as airports, bus stations, and train stations. Consensual encounters can also be used at privately and government-run parcel facilities; for example, the U.S. Post Office in cooperation with the U.S. Postal Inspector's Office, Federal Express, United Parcel Service, and DHL, with the permission of that parcel facility. Consensual encounters can be conducted at places of employment as well.

What can be learned from a consensual encounter? It can be a great source of intelligence-gathering, such as identifying people for later contact or identifying people to associate with a long-term investigation. No arrests or seizures are planned during this type of encounter; its purpose is only to identify persons involved and what their possible role is in an organization — identifying ownership of property. Again, this can be used for later seizure of assets or currency. "Hi. I'm a police officer. May I have permission to speak with you; is that your house; is this your car; do you bank at this branch; who else owns the boat with you; how long have you owned these apartments; is this your money; whose money is it?" Or, you may just want to identify people and what role they play in an organization: leader, financier, enforcer, workers, dealers, lookouts, and heads of organizations.

Consensual encounters can also be utilized to effect arrests for narcotics violations. They can be used in areas where law enforcement is present in commercial transportation areas — airports, bus stations, and train stations. They can be used to effect arrests of persons who possess illegal weapons or are in areas where weapons are not allowed. Consensual encounters can be used to contact or approach persons transporting currency that was obtained from illegal means or is to be used to facilitate the flow of illegal drugs. Consensual encounters can also be used in effecting arrests where people have outstanding warrants: identifying persons, and arresting them for warrants.

An approach by a non-uniformed officer is the most common method of consensual encounter, especially in commercial transportation scenarios. Working in plain clothes is useful for many investigators and detectives. There are certain factors that the courts will consider about a consensual encounter. First they will want to know what type of clothing the officer was wearing during the encounter. The defense attorney will attempt to make the choice of clothing seem intimidating or coercive. This will be a factor with a uniformed officer. Whatever your style of clothing is, it should be described in court. It is only necessary to state in your reports that you were in plain clothes fashion. The important factor for non-uniform dress is to have a way to conceal your weapon and any other tool, such as handcuffs, mace, or collapsible baton, that you might use in the course of your duties. The reason for concealing your weapon, handcuffs, mace and collapsible baton is to minimize the show of authority. On the other hand, your reason for having these items easily accessible is for officer safety (Figures 2.1 through 2.3).

The courts are concerned with the defendant and whether he was intimidated or coerced by the show of any weapons when consenting to the contact. Of course, display of your badge or law enforcement identification is essential in identifying yourself on initial contact. A defense attorney will attempt to show that if any of these items or tools was exposed, their client was coerced or intimidated into speaking with you. Depending on the location where you work, the time of year, and the typical style of clothing for your area, concealing these items might be difficult. For example, if you work in a tropical climate, or during the summer months, shorts and t-shirts might be the dress of the day. You need to be cognizant of your weapon, handcuffs, and any other tool you have with you (Figure 2.4)

In order to be safe and prepared, not only do you need to know where the weapons or tools you might need are, but you also need to be proficient in gaining access to them. When walking through a crowded airport or bus terminal, you do not want these items in plain view. One of your biggest assets in conducting a consensual encounter is the element of surprise. This way, the offender is not prepared with a story. If you give the offenders time to react, not only will it decrease your chances of a successful encounter, but it could also be very dangerous. When you make contact with a person, you have no idea what that person just did or was planning to do. Did the individual just rob a bank or kill someone and you encounter him as he is attempting to flee? The individual knows what he just did, you do not! So why give the person the chance to react to you. Sometimes an officer may want the individual he is going to approach to know that law enforcement is present. This gives the law enforcement officer time to watch the individual and observe any nervousness or fear.

In any case, the courts will undoubtedly consider your manner of dress during the encounter. In the jurisdiction where you present your case for prosecution, whether in the federal, state, or municipal court system, time will elapse from when you made your arrest to the time you present your case in court. Will you honestly remember what you wore 1 $1/_2$ years ago and where your weapon was as well as your handcuffs and mace. This will be a

**Figure 2.1**

**Figure 2.2**

**Figure 2.3**

**Figure 2.4**

question the defense attorney can ask to make the point that his client was intimidated when observing your weapon. Let's not give a defense attorney any ammunition to work with in attempting to discredit you on the stand or make you look incompetent. The manner in which you were dressed and where your weapon was and how it was concealed should be in the body of your report, so that there is no doubt when you testify.

If your dress of the day is a uniform, you must consider certain factors when conducting a consensual encounter. The most important is how you will minimize the show of authority. This is difficult but can be overcome. Describing how you were dressed and not hiding the fact that you were in uniform will be important. You will need to describe how you approached the suspect, where your weapon was, and if it was still in the holster and snapped. Where was your hand that normally holds your pistol? For example: "As I approached the person from the right side, I stood approximately 5 feet from the person. I stood at a 45 degree angle, keeping my weapon side from view of the person. My right hand was down near my right thigh touching the bottom of my pants pocket. My hand was not on my weapon and my weapon was firmly secured in my holster with the thumb strap still attached to it. I identified myself as Police Officer Jones of the Small Town Police Department and I asked the person for permission to speak to him." Would you remember a year from now which side you approached the individual from and where your hand was at the time? Again, this will be a critical factor in determining if the contact was free to leave or if the suspect was coerced. We want to give the defense attorney the least amount of surprise questions they can ask us. If your prosecutor fails to ask you about your dress and where your weapon was, the defense attorney surely will!

Always have a plan prepared for any consensual encounter type case. Whether you always work with a partner or if you are working with someone for the first time, make sure you have a plan before beginning the encounter. You should not perform a consensual encounter with less than two investigators, detectives, or officers. In many jurisdictions this is a luxury and not the norm, and many of you work alone all the time. We can only stress that your level of officer safety be at its highest peak. Having a plan before any consensual encounter will enhance your chances of going home that night.

Decide who is going to do the talking and who is going to do the observing before making the contact. It does not mean that whoever does the scanning or observing cannot speak, but that person's primary responsibility should be as a backup officer who is aware of the surroundings and all persons in the area. The roles can change — the scanner can take up the position of the person talking and the person who was talking can take the role of scanner. But the two law enforcement officers involved should not be talking at the same time. If this happens, the concentration of both investigators is on the individual they contacted and not on the person approaching from behind with a weapon. To maintain that level of officer safety, one investigator needs to do the talking and one has to maintain a surveillance point and act as a backup.

The backup officer has to be aware of all persons in and around the scene and watch for any furtive movements or gestures from other persons. He must also be observant of the person with whom the conversation is being conducted. Does the backup officer observe any unusual bulges or weapons protruding from the person's waistband, pants leg, purse, or torso area? It is the responsibility of that backup officer to notify the investigator conducting the conversation that the backup officer observes something he is uncomfortable with. It is also the responsibility of the backup officer to intervene with any other person attempting to intercede in the conversation.

Criminals involved in illicit activities will often attempt some type of diversionary tactic to draw attention away from the possible drug or money courier. Criminals have also rehearsed what will happen in the event law enforcement disrupts the illegal activity.

The backup officer should also be the note-taker and the time-keeper. Time is an important factor in determining whether an encounter is valid. If you have been talking with the person for 30 or 45 minutes and no action has been taken by this time, the courts will consider whether the encounter was valid. A consensual encounter should be somewhere in the time frame of 6 to 8 minutes, before asking for consent to search an item, house, or hotel room. You will probably know within the first 2 to 3 minutes of conversation if the person is legitimate. If the person is legitimate, then it is time to end the encounter and move on.

The backup officer should note what time the partner made contact with the person. The next time indicated should be when consent to search has been asked. That time frame, as previously stated, should be between 6 and 8 minutes. There are times when that time frame could increase due to certain circumstances and factors, such as the case when a consensual encounter was being conducted at the airport and a passenger was contacted as he walked away from the luggage carousel with a large piece of luggage. The passenger told the detective that he would talk with him but that he was in a hurry. The detective thanked the passenger for agreeing to speak with him and walked next to the passenger as the passenger proceeded out to the rental car lot to retrieve his car, approximately three blocks from the main airport terminal. That encounter was approximately 15 minutes long. Circumstances will determine the length of the encounter, but keep in mind that the courts will be scrutinizing the length of time the conversation took.

Pre-planning your encounter should also include deciding who is going to handcuff the suspect — the talker or the scanner. "Excuse me sir, could you stand up and face my partner." No mention of putting the suspect under arrest was made in that statement. We want to keep the person unaware of what is going to happen until it actually does. When making the arrest or seizure, the two partners should act as a team and approach the suspect together. If your encounter is going to result in a possible search of a piece of luggage, hotel room, house, or car, your plan should define who is going to search. Will the talker conduct the search while the scanner takes up the role as talker? Keep the conversation flowing.

There are different schools of thought on who should do the searching. The talker has been conducting the conversation and is aware of all statements made by the individual including the reason for traveling or being at a particular location. The backup officer may not be privy to all parts of the conversation; therefore, is he the one to conduct the search? He may overlook certain items that would have importance to the officer who had conducted the conversation. For example, if a person was contacted at a train station and agreed to speak to the officer and told the officer she was traveling back from a friend's wedding where she was the maid of honor. The person tells the officer she spent a week and a half at her friend's house and now was traveling back home. If the talker were the one to search the suitcase, he would expect to find items consistent with this person having been to a wedding: appropriate clothing, shoes, and memorabilia. If the officer who conducted the interview did the search and found two pair of shorts, a t-shirt, and some toiletry items, this would increase his suspicion. If the officer who was scanning and playing the role of the backup conducted the search was unaware of the supposed wedding scenario, finding items inappropriate for a wedding would not be of any significance.

The other school of thought is that the officer who conducted the conversation with the suspect should continue the conversation and allow the backup officer to search. The officer who conducted the conversation has already established rapport with the person, and a break in that conversation could give the offender time to react. Whichever method you and your partner use, make sure that it is defined before making the contact. If the partner is going to conduct the search, as soon as permission to search has been given, the backup partner should begin the search of the bag, suitcase, house, or hotel room. The backup partner should not hesitate and should not look at the initial officer for approval to begin searching — this should be worked out before making the contact.

The roles of the officer conducting the conversation and the backup officer can also interchange. If the officer who conducted the initial contact senses that there is a problem, that officer should allow the backup officer to step in and continue with the conversation. If the backup officer senses any problem between the officer conducting the conversation and the person, then the backup officer should step in and change roles with the initial contact officer. Your plan should also include where the backup officer or scanner will take his position in relation to the person being contacted.

Many jurisdictions recommend a one-on-one encounter, with the person being contacted unaware of a second officer. Some jurisdictions feel comfortable with two officers making the initial approach, with the contacting officer standing slightly ahead of the backup officer. If a one-on-one type encounter is preferred in your jurisdiction, then positioning of the backup officer or scanner will be very important. The backup officer should maintain a position where he can view the contacting officer and the suspect, of course, but the backup officer should also be able to scan the entire area and view other persons or other activity occurring in the area. The main focus should be on the officer conducting the conversation and the person involved. The scanner should be aware of anyone in the area paying close attention to the encounter. Just because your partner is encountering one person does not mean that others in the area are also involved.

We see in numerous transportation type cases that a "mule" is given a load of dope and then a second person, of whom the mule is not aware, travels along with the mule to ensure that the load arrives at its destination. If the mule is arrested, that information is relayed back to the source by the second person, in case the mule cooperates with police and attempts to conduct a controlled delivery or attempts to return the dope to the source. The backup officer should pay close attention to anyone who is watching the encounter. A consensual encounter is a very low-key approach and only the person being contacted should know that police are present. If the source or recipient is in the area of the contact, he will be suspicious and will also conduct "counter surveillance" of the encounter.

Many times in this situation, the source or person responsible for ensuring delivery of the dope or money will attempt some type of diversionary tactic. Creating a disturbance of some type, a fight, or antagonizing the officer conducting the conversation; for example: "Hey man, why are you picking on that guy? He wasn't doing anything." This will be a distraction for the officer conducting the conversation. It is now the responsibility of the backup officer to intervene and quell any disturbance or distraction other persons might be trying to initiate. The backup officer should be aware of any danger signs and the use of counter surveillance. A danger sign might be an unusual bulge or outline of a weapon on the person with whom the conversation is taking place. The backup officer should signal the initial officer of the danger signs, or, if appropriate, he may take action at this time and step into the scene to address the situation. "Excuse me sir, but I'm going to pat you down for my own and my partner's safety." Do not hesitate in this area; if the backup officer feels the need to intervene, then the initial contact officer should be aware that the backup officer is stepping into the scene because of something he observed or anticipated.

One of the most important factors in having a plan before initiating contact with a person is having a predetermined signal or code to alert of a seizure or impending arrest. The two officers involved need to be on the same sheet of music if a seizure or arrest is going to be made. The backup officer has to know if the officer conducting the search located contraband; however, this should not be broadcast to the person whose luggage, house, or hotel room they are searching. The suspect does not have to be told that the contraband, dope, guns, or money was located; however, if there are any other police officers in the area, it should be made known to them that these items have been located. A signal, verbal or nonverbal, or a code word should be agreed upon before making contact with the individual. There is nothing worse than attempting to arrest a person and having your backup officer concentrating on another person he observed paying close attention to the encounter. It might only be a few seconds, but those few seconds could allow an offender to react or get the upper hand on the arresting officer. If contraband or dope is discovered, the officer conducting the search should alert the backup to the discovery with the predetermined signal or code word. For example, you may be searching a suitcase and you locate the dope that the offender thought they had concealed so well. So now you jump up and yell out, "Hey, I found it," and you look over and your backup officer has become distracted by a second subject. Now you have the dope and the bad guy knows you found it, which gives him an opportunity to run or fight. Or maybe, you locate the contraband and look over at your backup officer and give your pre-arranged code, which was a verbal code, such as "What time is lunch? I'm getting hungry." But as you look over, you see that your partner is having an encounter with the second subject. You now wait until you have your partner's attention, and you tell him again "Hey, what time is lunch? I'm getting hungry." The suspect still does not think you found the dope, and now he believes you are more interested in going to lunch than dealing with him. You wait for your partner to approach, and you and your partner can now take the subject into custody, placing handcuffs on him in a low-key manner. Of course your backup partner will still be observing any actions from others in the area. Your partner may not have known what or how much you found but due to the signal he received, he knew a seizure had been made and arrest was imminent.

If the signal you have worked out before making contact with the person is a nonverbal signal, make sure that you give the signal when you have your partner's attention. Have both a verbal and nonverbal code worked out. Having a plan will increase the chances that you and your partner are going home that night.

This may seem simple, but identifying yourself as a law enforcement officer is very important when making your contact. There should be no doubt in the person's mind as to who you are. With badge or credentials displayed in hand and visible to the person, "Hi. I'm a police officer. May I speak with you?" Again, no doubt about who you are — you are not the local security guard, you are not the neighborhood watch coordinator, you are not a concerned citizen; you are a police officer. Leave no doubt in that person's mind. You may wonder why this is so important. Many police officers around the country have been seriously hurt and even killed because the offender thought the officer was there to rip him off, or hurt him. The offender did not recognize the officer as a law enforcement official, and the officer did not clearly identify himself, leaving a doubt as to who the officer was. In many cases, we have seen offenders escape conviction on the charge of battery or aggravated battery on a police officer. There is no loyalty among thieves, and dopers ripping off dopers is a common occurrence.

When making contact with a suspect, never touch him or put your hands on him. Any type of touching, such as placing your hand on the shoulder of the offender, can be construed as a detention, where the person you contacted felt they were not free to leave. This is a major factor the courts consider in determining whether the encounter was valid. Some officers feel comfortable in shaking hands on the initial contact, a brief gesture and a international sign of greeting. For most people, this is a friendly gesture and it might put the suspect at ease. If this is your style of initiating a contact, and it is a good technique, be sure to indicate this in your report and include which hand was shaken.

Have your conversation planned before making contact, such as what type of crime you are investigating and what type of questions you will be asking. In a transportation type case, there is a series of basic questions. Each of us has our own style of questioning. By already knowing the answers to your questions, you will be able to identify when the person is being deceitful or dishonest. You can capitalize on these points and follow up on questions that you know the person is answering untruthfully. The dishonest person will begin to show signs of nervousness. Ultimately you want this person to lie, if he is involved in some type of criminal activity. In transportation type cases, some of the important questions to ask are the following:

- Hi. I'm a police officer. May I speak with you? (Always the initial question).
- Where are you traveling to?
- Where are you coming from?
- How long do you plan on staying? or How long were you there?
- Was this a business or pleasure trip?
- If it was pleasure, were you visiting friends or family?
- What is your name?
- Do you have any identification with you, and may I see it? (You might be asking for an airline, bus, or train ticket in conjunction with this question.)
- How many pieces of luggage do you have with you?
- Is all the luggage yours?

Followup questions may be asked after each of the initial questions; we will look at these a little further on. If you just observed the individual come off of a flight from Los Angeles, you already know the answer to one of your questions, "Where are you coming from?" Again, knowing the answers to your questions will greatly increase your chances of determining if the person is being untruthful or evasive. Anything you do before encountering the person may also lead to questions in the conversation, such as presurveillance, any information received from other sources, and information received from documentation or records.

You have selected a person you are going to approach and talk with. Remember you can approach and talk with anyone anywhere as long as you have a legal right to be there. If someone is standing on a street corner and you want to engage him in conversation, you have a legal right as a law enforcement officer to be on that street corner. However, if you want to speak with someone as he exits a commercial bus, did you have previous permission to be on the property of the commercial bus company? Did you have permission from the management to conduct law enforcement activities and to engage in contact with their passengers? Having permission to be on private property is necessary in order to conduct law enforcement activities. This issue will be brought out in court and will be a necessary factor in the courts determining whether the encounter was valid.

What do basing our contact on a person's conduct and behavior entail? Although we do not need reasonable suspicion or probable cause to approach a person, our goal is not to approach and talk with everyone. We want to narrow it down to the person we believe is involved in some type of criminal activity or acts in a suspicious manner. For example, we enter a bus terminal filled with passengers — is it our goal to approach everyone in that bus terminal and speak with them, hoping that one of our encounters will result in a seizure and arrest, or is it our goal to observe these passengers and use our law enforcement training and experience and narrow it down to the person we believe is involved in some type of criminal activity?

How will this be accomplished? As you stand in the terminal attempting to identify persons acting in a suspicious manner, these same individuals will also be looking for law enforcement. It is a cat-and-mouse game; you are looking for them and they are looking for you. Many times as you are observing people, the person who displays unusual behavior has probably identified you and will also be conducting counter surveillance. This should be noted in any document that you prepare for your case. Describing what the person was doing that caused you to approach him will defuse any defense attorney's attempt to show that you approached his client based on age, race, gender, or national origin. For example:

> As I entered the bus terminal, I began a counterclockwise view of all pas-
> sengers waiting in the passenger waiting area. I observed a person standing
> in line preparing to board the eastbound bus to Chicago. As I observed him,
> I noticed that he was looking around the bus terminal area; he was scanning
> the front doors to the bus terminal, watching all persons who were entering
> the terminal. The subject was clutching a small red duffel bag under his
> right arm and appeared to be protecting the red duffel bag. As I entered the
> terminal, I observed that the subject looked directly at me and then focused
> his attention on the maroon-colored fanny pack attached to the front of
> my body. As I walked to the north side of the terminal area, near the chairs
> equipped with television sets, the subject continued to watch me. As I
> stopped and turned toward the line in which the subject was standing, he
> was still watching me. As I looked at him, he quickly looked away from me
> and stared at the floor in front of him. I then observed him switch the red
> duffel bag from his right side to his left side, again clutching it under his
> arm. The subject then stepped out of line and proceeded to a set of public
> telephones located near the west end of the bus terminal. He stood in front
> of one of the public telephones and picked up the receiver. As he did this,
> I noticed that he began to speak into the telephone. The subject never dialed
> a telephone number on the keypad, and I was close enough that I did not
> hear the telephone ring. As the subject was talking into the telephone, he

continued to look at me and then would look away immediately whenever we made eye contact. He remained on the telephone for approximately 2 minutes, continuously talking and looking around. As he placed the tele-phone receiver back to its original position, he continued talking. The subject remained standing in front of the public telephone area for another minute. He then walked away from the area of the public telephones and stepped into line for another bus, not the same line he was in originally.

Based on this person's conduct and behavior, an approach to conduct a conversation with him would be warranted. Even though I do not need reasonable suspicion or probable cause to approach a person, this subject's suspicious activity allowed me the opportunity to identify him as a person I wanted to speak to.

As you approach the targeted subject, take into account his size in com-parison to your size. You must account for every action you take. If you have the luxury of having additional officers or agents in your unit, attempt to physically match up the person doing the encounter with the subject being contacted. If the subject is a female and you have a female in your unit, attempt to allow her to do the encounter. Many times this is not an option, but take into consideration what the defense attorney will attempt to show if the person being contacted was small and the person conducting the encounter was much bigger. The defense will attempt to show that the mere presence and the stature of the officer conducting the encounter was intim-idating so that their client felt impelled to agree to the encounter.

You pick the location of the encounter. If it is in a public location, attempt to keep the encounter there; do not move the subject to a less open and public area. Do not say, "Can we step into the bathroom?" or "Would you like to go to my office to continue this conversation?" This would allow the courts to determine that the person was being seized at this point, or that the person was not free to leave. If the area of the initial encounter is not safe for you or the subject, ask if moving to a safer location would be okay with her. "Excuse me, miss, we're in the street here. Would it be okay with you if we moved over to the curb?" If you are inside an airport terminal, bus station, or train station, be aware of the exits and entrances. Where could the subject flee to in the event of an escape? Where can other persons involved with the individual approach?

As you approach the subject, do not stand directly in front of him. This is a tactical mistake; placing yourself directly in front of the subject would allow him to strike out at you more easily. Standing in front of the subject would make him feel he was not free to leave or terminate the encounter. You would be blocking the subject's egress from the point of contact. A safer and legally more advantageous placement would be to stand slightly to the right or left of the subject. This would allow you reaction time if he attempted to strike out at you or flee. You should have your weapon side away from the subject. The court's concern will be for the defendant and whether he felt he was free to leave or terminate the encounter (Figures 2.5 and 2.6).

Once you have made your approach, the backup officer should take up a position close enough to react to any overt actions on the part of the subject. The backup officer should also be able to scan the area from his position and be able to watch other persons in the area, to see if anyone else is with this person, while staying away from the encounter. The backup officer should be aware of anyone approaching the site of the encounter in an attempt to

**Figure 2.5**

**Figure 2.6**

intervene or distract the initial officer. Your jurisdiction and the interpreta-tion of the law will determine how many officers approach the subject. Some jurisdictions will allow a two-officer-to-one-suspect type of encounter. Other jurisdictions suggest that a one-officer-to-one-suspect encounter is best. In such a case, can we have many backup officers in the area to assist? Yes, as long as those officers were not made known to the person being contacted. The courts will consider intimidation or coercion, based on the number of persons conducting the encounter.

The number of persons to be contacted determines the number of officers to have present during the encounter. If you are going to approach two persons who are traveling together, there should at least be two officers conducting the approach and contact.

As you approach, have your badge or law enforcement identification out and ready to be displayed. This can be done in two ways. One is by displaying your badge or law enforcement identification and identifying yourself. "Hi. I'm a police officer. May I speak with you?" Another approach is to attempt to solicit a response with a greeting: "Hi," with your badge or law enforcement identification not displayed, in your hand. You have initiated a greeting and, in most cases, the subject will respond to that greeting. It is hard for a person not to acknowledge you. Once you have received the response, then you can display your badge and ask for the subject's permission to speak to him.

"Hi." (response)
"How are you doing?" (response)
"I'm a police officer. May I talk to you?"

Your tone of voice should be friendly and conversational and not overbear-ing or authoritative. The old saying "you can catch more flies with honey than with vinegar" applies here. If you are too overbearing and authoritative, that will set the tone of your encounter, your success rate will decrease and when you get to court, this will be a factor. The defense will attempt to show that their client was intimidated or coerced into talking with you just by the tone of your voice. There have been cases where a defense attorney was able to subpoena witnesses who were in the area and bring them in to testify. Those witnesses would be asked to describe your actions and your tone of voice as you made contact with the suspect. When you testify, your prosecutor should ask this simple question, because if he does not, the defense attorney will. You should describe your tone of voice as friendly, nonauthoritative, calm, nonthreatening, or conversational. Describe to the attorney that your tone of voice was exactly as you are speaking now on the stand; conversational. In the encounter you should allow the subject to respond, and continue from there. The response does not have to be verbal. The subject might just nod his head in a positive response. Why would someone respond with a nod of the head and not answer verbally? Your biggest asset in any consensual encounter situation is the element of surprise. The person you are contacting does not have a story prepared and may not have been anticipating any law enforcement personnel while they are in a train or bus station or in their hotel room.

As you ask the subject for permission to speak to him and you see that his only response is a gesture, such as the head nodding in an up-and-down manner, would this be a positive response for you to continue to speak to him? Yes, but you would want to clarify this gesture. "Sir, I see your nodding you head in an up-and-down fashion, giving me permission to speak to you, is that correct?" Give the person time to regain his composure. You have approached him unexpectedly; give him time to answer. Once you have received permission to speak to him, you can continue with your conversation.

In your report you want to articulate all actions on your part as well as those of the subject. Describe his head movements, describe how his eyes widened as he saw your badge, how his eyes were riveted on your badge, and how his only response at that time was a nod of the head. Describe how you asked a second time to obtain a verbal response, although you had defined the positive gesture. This should all be in your report. This is going to be a conversation with the subject, remember that. When you get into court, the defense attorney is going to describe your encounter with his client as an "interrogation." This will always be a conversation and never an interrogation. We are approaching and contacting these people to engage them in conversation. Never let a defense attorney describe your encounter as an interrogation. Use the word "conversation" in your report and testimony. Some like to use the word "interview," but that word can sometimes appear to be strictly a question-and-answer session.

If the subject answers you verbally, and in most cases he will, remember their initial response. If he answered "Sure," "Yeah, go ahead," "Okay," "Yeah, what about," "Yes," or an other positive verbal response, indicate this in your report. Remember to keep the questioning simple: "Hi. I'm a police officer. May I speak with you?" What if the question was asked, "Hi. I'm a police officer. Do you mind if I talk to you?" What type of response would you receive if the subject agreed to talk. The correct affirmative answer would be "No, I don't mind if you talk to me," but we do not talk like this. The subject might just answer "No," indicating they would talk with you. What if the person answered that same question "Yes." A yes to that answer would be "Yes, I mind if you talk to me," indicating a negative response to your question. It is all a matter of semantics, but those semantics could cause some difficulty in court. Keep the questions simple so that when you ask the question, "Hi. I'm a police officer. May I speak with you?" a yes means yes and a no means no, with no room for interpretation.

What if the subject says "NO!" Can you continue with the encounter? NO. If the person does not want to speak to you, then there will be no conversation; you must terminate the encounter at that time. Can you insist that the person speak with you? Can you ask him "Why don't you want to talk to me?" NO. You must terminate the encounter at this time if you have no further facts or circumstances you can make use of. What would allow you to continue the encounter even without the subject's permission? You must be able to articulate reasonable suspicion at this time. If you had a certified narcotic detection canine alert to a suitcase or to a hotel room door, this would give you reason to detain. It does not provide a reason to advise the subject that he must speak to you now, but if you could articulate your reasonable suspicion, you could seize the item or secure the area for the issuance of a search warrant.

An important question frequently asked is "At what point must I advise them of their *Miranda* rights during this conversation?" Must we always give a *Miranda* warning, and what circumstances must be present to advise some-one of his *Miranda* rights? During a consensual encounter, it is not necessary to advise a person of their *Miranda* rights. This person is not being detained, he is not being arrested at this time; you are merely having a conversation with him. Just because a person lies to you does not mean you have to advise him of his *Miranda* rights, and just because you have developed reasonable suspicion during your conversation does not mean you need to advise him of his *Miranda* rights. The only time we need to advise someone of his *Miranda* rights is if we are placing him under arrest or if our questions become accusatory. Even if we arrest someone, unless we ask them questions concerning the crime, we do not need to advise them of their *Miranda* rights. A question such as "Are you a drug dealer?" might warrant advising him of his *Miranda* rights.

Talking with the person you have approached and asking for permission to talk to him seems simple, but for many law enforcement officers this can be difficult. You want to have your conversation planned so that it flows smoothly. You do not have to tell him what you know; you do not have to give him any information you have about his background, or if someone has given you information on him, or if you had a prior canine alert to his luggage, or if you know he is lying to you. Stay away from pointed questions such as "Are you a drug dealer?" Ask the subject where he is traveling to, and if you sense hesitancy or observe nervousness as he answers, ask the question again later in the conversation. Is his answer the same or did he change it; is he more nervous now?

You must keep your head in the game at this point. You must become proficient at observing whether the person you are dealing with is nervous. Are his answers also becoming inconsistent with what you already know? You must watch the subject's behavior and listen carefully to the answers to your questions. One of the questions should be, "What is your name?" Along with that question, you should ask for identification. If the person does not have identification, ask him how to spell his name. If a person is using a fictitious name, he may hesitate while spelling the name, or look to you for confirmation that he has spelled it correctly. If he is using a fictitious name, he may spell it incorrectly or stutter while spelling it. Watch his behavior as he is spelling the name for you; watch his actions.

If he has identification, ask to see it. Watch his reactions as he removes his wallet or purse for you, and watch his behavior. Can he find his identification or drivers license, especially when it is visible to you? If you see his identification and he is so nervous he passes it by, let him look for it for a few seconds, and then point it out to him. "Oh, is that your identification right there?" Once he turns his identification over to you to look at, do not remain in possession of the identification any longer than necessary. The courts will consider this a factor in determining if the subject was being detained or seized. Look at the identification, maybe repeat some of the information on the identification to the person, and then return it immediately. If you hold onto the identification for the entire length of the encounter, the courts will determine that you detained the subject, and that he was not free to leave or terminate the encounter while you were in possession of his identification. If you detain or seize someone, you must have at least reasonable suspicion to accomplish this legally.

When you describe this portion of your encounter in a report or in testimony, make sure you describe the entire scene; for example, what the person did as he removed his wallet or purse, and how long it took him to find his identification, or how many times he passed the identification as he looked for it. Were his hands shaking as he was holding his wallet? Were his hands trembling as he removed the identification article from his wallet or purse? Watch the subject for a few seconds as he hands you the identification, watch his hands to observe any shaking or trembling, do not take the identification from him immediately. This will allow you time to observe his behavior. Do not be in a hurry! Once you have inspected the identification and asked questions, such as "Do you still live at the address on the identification card? Is this your current address? Where do you live now?" Other questions may come to mind as you look at the identification article.

What should you do with the identification once you have had an opportunity to look at it? Should you give it to your partner or should you put in your pocket? If you answered "yes" to one of these questions, then you have just detained or seized the person by merely holding onto their identification. The courts will consider that the person was not free to leave or terminate the encounter. If you detain someone, you must have reasonable suspicion to do so, and you must be able to articulate your reasonable suspicion. If you have none at this point in your encounter, then you will have lost anything you do past this point. So you must return the identification article immediately after you have viewed it; therefore, the person is free to leave and he is free to terminate the encounter. When you describe this in your report or when you are testifying on the stand, articulate what you did. "As the subject handed me his identification, I looked at it briefly and then returned the document to him." You should be able to make a mental note to remember names, streets, or locations in a brief time span of about 15 to 30 seconds. Once the document is returned to the subject, observe what he does with it.

If the subject has no identification but you can see the outline of a wallet in his hip pocket, ask "Is that a wallet in your back pocket, and is there anything in that wallet with your name on it? It does not have to have your picture on it. May I see it?"

You can ask people anything you want as long as they consent to it! As you continue your conversation, remember to keep in mind your questions, but more importantly the answers you are hearing. Keep your questions simple but remember to ask follow-up questions. If you asked the person where he was traveling to and he told you he was going to visit family in New York, ask who the family is. If he states he is going to see a cousin who lives there, ask for the cousin's name. If it is family he says he is going to visit, he should know first and last names. If it is friends, again, he should know first names and last names. These follow-up questions will determine if the subject is being evasive about the nature of his trip. If he tells you he is going on vacation ask him how long his vacation is and what will he be doing there, does he have family there, etc.

This is just a conversation you are having, and you want it to flow smoothly. As you are listening to the answers, observe the subject's body movements for any signs of nervousness. When you use the word "nervous," you should be able to articulate in great detail what that entailed as far as the encounter. The word "nervous" can mean many things, both verbal and nonverbal, and articulating this behavior on a report or during testimony will establish your reasonable suspicion or probable cause. Following are some phrases or words to describe indicators of nervous or unusual behavior.

## Nonverbal Cues

- Trembling
- Rubbing or touching part of body
- Shaking
- Playing with mustache

- Tugging on ear
- Covering the ears or eyes
- Excessive blinking
- Darting eyes
- Closing eyes
- Evasive eyes
- Staring
- Patting cheek
- Yawning
- Licking lips
- Biting lips
- Appearance of goosebumps
- Sweating (especially where weather does not warrant it)
- Fingernail biting
- Fidgeting
- Swallowing repeatedly
- Fainting
- Visible palpating of the carotid artery
- Grooming hair repeatedly
- Fidgeting with fingers or items in pockets
- Toying with jewelry
- Clutching onto items (solids or moveable)
- Wiping hands off due to profuse sweating
- Vomiting
- Running

These are only a few words and phrases to describe nervous behavior, but whatever you observe, articulate the actions or behavior.

## Verbal Cues

- Shaky voice
- Voice cracking
- Stuttering
- Tooth grinding
- Deep sighing
- Hesitant speech
- Repeats question with a question (What's my name?) — this is a stalling tactic
- Answers a question with a question (You asked me what my name is?)
- Asks you to clarify question (What do you mean, where am I going?)

- Answers with unrelated information (You ask the question "where are you traveling *to*" and he tells you where he is traveling *from*)
- Inability to answer (our greatest asset is the element of surprise; a subject is often ill prepared with a story, and he freezes)
- Reluctance to answer (make sure this is not a language barrier rather than nervousness).

## Vocabulary and Phrasing

- "To be perfectly honest ..."
- "To tell you the truth ..."
- "I wouldn't lie to you!"
- "I swear!"
- "To the best of my knowledge or recollection ..."
- "Honestly!"
- "Truthfully!"
- "Believe me!"
- Says "No," then looks away
- Says "No," then closes eyes
- The 5-second "No"
- Repeating "No, no, no, no!"
- Says "No," then crosses arms and legs
- Says "No," with an empty look
- Says "No" with hypnotic glance

These are only a few examples of signs of nervousness; articulate in detail how the subject behaved. What did he do to bring you to the conclusion he was nervous during your encounter? You must be able to articulate what caused you to have reasonable suspicion.

If the encounter is going to result in asking for consent to search the subject's suitcase, hotel room, or house, must you have reasonable suspicion to ask for permission to search? NO. There may be times when you have conducted your conversation with the subject and you are not able to artic-ulate reasonable suspicion. The person you were talking with may have been calm, with no signs of nervousness. You may nonetheless ask for consent to search his property or articles. Some drug and money couriers have been at this type of work for a long time and may not display the nervousness or evasiveness you are looking for; you may still ask for consent to search.

Asking for consent to search will be the next step in your conversation if you think it is warranted. You must determine whether the items to be searched are in the subject's control. A second party cannot give consent to search someone else's property or possessions, so you must determine whether the subject is in control of the items at that time. Were they entrusted with the items to be searched? For example, a courier was given a suitcase at the airport and told to take the suitcase to Detroit, where someone would meet him, and he was to turn the suitcase over to that person. The courier has therefore been entrusted with the suitcase, so he is in control of the item.

Continue to keep the conversation simple, but leave no doubt as to what you are asking. The word *search* will be used when asking for permission to search. You might think this word will lessen your chances of obtaining permission, but it is the only word that should be used because this is what you plan to do: *search*! If you ask to "look," "look around," or "take a peek," in the eyes of the court there is a distinction between searching and looking. A reasonable person giving you permission to look inside his suitcase would not feel comfortable watching you open containers or remove all of his clothing from the suitcase to check the lining. If you ask for permission to *search*, then there is no doubt about what your intentions are; you are going to open containers, remove clothing, and search through clothing articles. You must use the word *search*!

There are several different ways to ask for permission to search someone's suitcase, hotel room, or house. "Sir, would you voluntarily consent for me to search your suitcase?" "Would you allow me to search your suitcase?" "I'm asking for your permission to search your suitcase." "Is it okay with you if I search your suitcase?" Whatever style of asking works for you, use this same question each time you encounter someone and ask for permission to search, being consistent with your questioning.

Must you advise the subject that he has the right to refuse the search of his items, hotel room, or house? NO. The Supreme Court does not require that this warning be given. In the eyes of the court, this would be a plus, but it is not required. However, many state and local jurisdictions require this warning. Are you required to have a Consent to Search form signed before conducting the search of a person's luggage, hotel room, or house? The Supreme Court does not require written permission, but many state and local jurisdictions do. Your department's or agency's policies might also require a Consent to Search form before conducting a search. This, of course, would be a plus in the eyes of the court, although it is not required.

Do not use threatening language when asking for consent to search; for example, "If you do not give me consent to search, then I will get a search warrant." This might be true, but phrasing your statement in this manner would be considered threatening or coercive by the court. Be careful of your questioning in this phase of your conversation. If the subject asks what you are looking for, depending on what type of investigation you are working, tell them. A good term to use is "contraband;" this word can mean many things, including guns, drugs, money, property, or anything illegal. The consent must be unequivocal and free of coercion or intimidation. If you ask for permission to search and the subject says, "Well, I really don't want you going through my personal items, but I guess you can search as long as you don't mess anything up," would this statement be considered permission to search that person's personal items? The consent must be unequivocal. The first part of that sentence would taint the permission to search: "Well, I really don't want you going through my personal items." A confirmation from the person would be warranted. "Sir, the decision is up to you." Make sure there is no doubt in the subject's mind that he is giving you consent to search. If the subject nods his head in an affirmative manner, such as in an up-and-down motion, confirm this gesture. "I see you are nodding your head in an affirmative manner. Are you giving me permission to search your suitcase?" "I see by the extension of your right hand that you are allowing me permission to search your hotel room. Is that correct?" Whatever phrase the person uses to give permission to search, make sure to use that phrase, such as, "Sure, go ahead," "Yes," "Yes, here is the key to the luggage," should be used in your report.

Once you begin your search, if your partner was not directly in the initial contact, the subject should be made aware of the your partner's presence at this time. Bring the backup officer into the scene, "Sir, this is my partner and he is going to stand by with us." If the subject had any ideas of attempting to hurt you or possibly fleeing, he might reconsider. Begin the search immediately and remember that the person can withdraw consent for the search at any time. The backup officer should continue to talk with the subject as you search. Never allow the subject to search the suitcase for you; this is a *major officer safety issue*. The item to be searched is now in your control and you will search the item or place, not the subject. If it is a suitcase and it is locked, ask the subject where the key is. If it is a piece of luggage with a combination lock, let the subject unlock the suitcase. This will show that the subject is cooperating voluntarily, but do not let him conduct the search. He knows what he has in the suitcase and where it is concealed. If a weapon is in the suitcase, that will be the first place he will go to. Do a complete and thorough search; there is nothing worse than walking away from an encounter and feeling that you have missed something because you did not search in one particular location or one particular item. Do not make a mess of all the subject's clothing and personal items; be careful of how you remove things and where you place them if you remove everything from the suitcase. Look inside lotion bottles, baby powder bottles, and any unopened containers.

Couriers may conceal drugs or money in obvious places, betting on us not looking in those areas. Inspect any unopened food containers, such as cookie bags or canned items. Feel the weight; smell the item. Are the weight and smell consistent with what the label identifies is in the container? If it is a can of pork and beans, shake the can to make sure you hear a sloshing sound. If it is an unopened bag of cookies, check the openings to make sure the package has not been opened and then resealed. Check unopened canned items to ensure that lids have not been resealed. There is controversy in this area as to whether an unopened food container or unopened container in general can be opened. The question in this type of scenario is whether we need to ask permission again from the owner to open the separate container.

Conduct the search in the area where the encounter took place; do not move the individual to a different or secluded location. If contraband is located, do not broadcast the discovery to the target or to anyone else except your partner; the code word or signal should be used at this time. Wait until you and your partner both have your attention directed at the target. If an arrest is going to be made, you and your partner should be moving in unison to avoid the target attempting to escape or strike out at you. Be aware of anyone else entering the scene — is there a coconspirator attempting to intervene? Make the arrest as quietly as possible; there could be more people to contact, so you do not want to yell out, "Put your hands up and face the wall!" Keep it quiet: "Sir, stand up and place your hands behind your back." Whatever procedure you must follow according to your department's guidelines or whatever is comfortable for you and your partner should be adhered to, but do not advertise the arrest to anyone else.

If you have searched the suitcase and you do not find any contraband, what should be the next place to consider as a possible concealment area? The person, of course! Many couriers body-pack drugs or money. Do not take it for granted because you contacted someone coming off of a 2-day bus ride that they would not be body-carrying the contraband. Ask the subject for permission to pat him down or search his person. If you are given permission to search, then conduct a complete search. Pat and search the groin area. For women, think of the areas on their bodies where they may conceal drugs or money. What does your department's or agency's manual state is permissible when searching females, especially if you do not have a female officer or agent available? How would you conduct a pat-down or search of a female you suspect of body-carrying drugs or money? One thing you can do is use the back of the hand for a pat-down, or use a pencil or pen to run along the subject's body to check for unusual bulges. Another thing you can do is have the subject pat herself down. Have the female subject start at the top of her torso and smooth the clothing out starting at the arms, upper torso, legs, and, if she agrees, ask her to remove her shoes and socks. Again, we can ask people to do anything we want as along as they consent.

The target denies your request for consent to search. Now what? You have just spent several minutes talking with the target — were you able to establish reasonable suspicion during this time? What was his behavior like? Are you able to articulate his behavior? How many times did the target lie to you, and how many times was he hesitant in answering your questions or evasive about the information? This is "reasonable suspicion," and you can articulate it. If the subject denies consent to search, then you must rely on your training and law enforcement experience to establish reasonable suspicion. If there is no reasonable suspicion, then you must terminate the encounter, as hard as it may be. If you can articulate reasonable suspicion, then you can detain the item to be searched and, in some jurisdictions, you can detain the individual. It is important that you are aware of Fourth Amendment search and seizure. In this type of scenario, you do not have time to call your prosecutor — you must make your decision right then and there. You cannot ask the target, "Can you wait here a few minutes while I call my local prosecutor and advise him of what I have?" You have to live and die by the decisions you make on the street.

Another tactic is to ask the target if he would allow a canine to examine his luggage in the event he denies you consent to search it. Many couriers think they have masked the odor of the product they are transporting and think the canine will not alert to it. Once the canine alerts to the item, then you have probable cause to detain it and the target and seek a search warrant.

If you seize an item, such as a suitcase, based on reasonable suspicion, or if you have probable cause, as in the case of the canine alert, or if you can smell the odor of a drug such as marijuana, cocaine, heroin, or 1-(1-phenylcyclohexyl)piperadine (PCP; be careful with this one — PCP is usually in liquid form and is harmful if inhaled or touched). There are several steps you need to take when seizing an item:

- Explain to the target what is going to happen. "Sir/Miss, I am seizing your luggage based on reasonable suspicion." (Briefly explain your reason for seizing the item.)
- If you are able to seize the target, this should be done for your safety before seizing the item. If you are not seizing the target and only the item, such as a piece of luggage, explain to the target what is going to happen. "Sir/Miss, I am going to seize this piece of luggage. I have a canine en route and that canine will be given an opportunity to examine the suitcase. You are not under arrest and you are free to leave. If you choose to stay until the suitcase has been opened, that is your choice. If the canine alerts to the suitcase, I will prepare a search warrant for the suitcase and open it. If the canine does not alert to the suitcase, where can I send the suitcase back to you?"
- Ask for an address or location where you can send the suitcase to the subject and tell him how long it is going to take to obtain a search

warrant. Let him know that in the event there is nothing in the suitcase, you will forward the suitcase in the quickest manner possible.

- Ask again for identification, and record the information.
- Ask the subject if you can take a picture of him. Explain that this is to ensure that if someone else comes back to retrieve the suitcase, he will be the only person the suitcase will be released to.
- Provide the subject with your business card and a receipt for the suitcase.
- Ask the subject if he has any questions.
- In many jurisdictions, if you have reasonable suspicion to seize the item, seize this person also.

How do you deal with a subject who will not allow you to take his luggage and becomes hostile and argumentative? You must be assertive and inform him that you are going to seize the luggage and if he interferes with this process, he will be arrested for interfering. If he does interfere and you arrest him, can you search the suitcase incident to arrest? NO, you must treat this incident separately. He is being arrested for interfering with you in your lawful duties. You must still apply for the search warrant for the suitcase.

Another scenario to be aware of is where the target abandons the item, such as the suitcase. What can you do with an abandoned suitcase? The target can abandon the suitcase at any time and we must allow him to do this. Then we must determine that the suitcase is in fact abandoned. We have developed several questions to deal with this situation.

- Is this your luggage?
- Do you know whose luggage it is?
- Did you pack this luggage or do you know who did?
- Do you care what happens to this luggage?
- Do you have any interest in this luggage? (Very important question, if it's the only question you ask.)
- Does anything inside the luggage belong to you?
- Would you voluntarily consent for me to search this luggage?

Usually by the last question, the target is yelling at you, telling you the luggage is not his. You might feel this is a bit of overkill, but it will demonstrate to the court that the target fully abandoned the suitcase. Once the suitcase is abandoned, you can open it. You can tell the target at this time that he is free to leave, and you can open the suitcase immediately. If contraband is discovered in the suitcase, you must now tie the suitcase to the target. If you had previously observed the target holding the suitcase, this will make it easier for you, but if the target was standing next to the suitcase and you did not see him in actual possession of it, you must find a way to tie the suitcase to the target. If you contact the target on a bus or train and the luggage is in the overhead luggage rack and he denies ownership, a very common occurrence, you must be able to associate the suitcase with the target. When searching the suitcase, look for items to connect it to the target:

- Clothing — Does the clothing in the suitcase match the size and style of what the target is wearing?
- Shoes — Are the shoes the same size as what the target is wearing?
- Any receipts or documents that might have the target's name, or a location that the target may have told to you during your conversation.
- Are there photographs in the suitcase depicting the target?
- Look for identification articles.
- Look for hotel receipts or receipts from stores or restaurants. Couriers always keep their receipts so they can be reimbursed by the source.
- Cellular telephones can also be used to connect a person to a suitcase. You can contact the cellular telephone company and ask for subscriber information.

You have to be creative in this area to connect the person to the suitcase. This will not always be possible; sometimes there is nothing in the suitcase to connect it to the target. If this is the case, you have at least removed the drugs, if that is what was located, from the streets or from reaching their final destination. The target will also arrive at a destination without his product, and this is probably a greater danger for him than going to jail. If the target is searched, most courts hold that detaining a person for a search warrant is a seizure if the person has not given you permission to search him. You must be able to articulate your facts as to an exigency. If you can do this, you can search the target right there and then. The decision to search based on probable cause is usually suppressed by the federal courts unless your exigency was great. The consensual encounter is over — the courts hold that the burden of proof is on the government to prove that the encounter was voluntary. The courts will scrutinize your every action from the moment you approached the target until you discovered the contraband in his luggage. Every detail will be put under a microscope to ensure that you did not violate any rights of the target under the Fourth Amendment. One of the main issues that will be scrutinized is the approach and the consent for the conversation. The manner in which you asked for consent to search will be scrutinized. You have heard the term, "totality of the circumstances;" in other words, the entire scenario. It is not important what the target believed — whether he thought he was under arrest, whether he thought he was free to leave, or whether he thought he had to give consent.

The test will be what a reasonable and innocent person would have believed in the same situation. These are some of the factors the Supreme Court looks at to make a determination of voluntariness. Our state and local jurisdictions can be more restrictive about how we conduct ourselves in a consensual encounter, but they cannot be less restrictive than what the Supreme Court tells us we can do. These are factors that the court will consider in determining voluntariness of a consent to search:

1. The court will look at the number of officers visible to the target. One to two officers is advisable. We can have many, as long as they are not seen by the target.
2. Dress of the officers conducting the encounter: whether the officers were in plain clothes or uniform. An encounter made by uniformed officers will be scrutinized more closely than one made by non-uniformed officers in determining whether the encounter was consensual.
3. If in plain clothes, all items such as weapon, handcuffs, mace, and any other tool should be hidden from the target's view. The target might *assume* you have these items on you, but you want them concealed. If in uniform, make sure your hand is away from your weapon, and do not appear overbearing and authoritative.
4. The officer's approach and tone of voice will be scrutinized. Use a casual approach and a friendly tone of voice, which is nonauthoritative and nonaggressive.
5. The court will look at the physical surroundings in which consent was given, public or nonpublic.

Remember, you do not need probable cause or a warrant to search a suspect and their belongings if the suspect voluntarily consents to the search. The burden of proof is on the government to prove the consent to search was voluntary. The courts will conduct a test. The test will be a look at the totality of the circumstances in determining the voluntariness of the consent. Factors that show coercion include the following:

- The presence of many officers
- Display of weapons and handcuffs
- Tone of voice
- Physical surroundings in which consent was given
- Suspect's capacity to give consent, whether the item was in his or her control
- Suspect's knowledge of the right to refuse; although this is not necessary, the court will look favorably upon you if you give this advice
- Whether the consent was the fruit of a prior illegal act

- Threatening to obtain a search warrant
- *Miranda* warnings; they are not necessary before asking for consent to search

The scope of the search is defined according to the scope of consent. If the target advises that you can search one suitcase and not another one, then the scope is confined to the one suitcase. If the target tells you to search only his pants pockets and not his jacket pocket, then the target has defined the scope of the search.

The consensual encounter is one of law enforcement's greatest techniques. We are supported by the courts in every aspect of the consensual encounter, and the United States Supreme Court has defined for us our plan of action. Although the consensual encounter is not used as frequently as it should be, it can be used in any type of investigation, any time, with or without probable cause as long as you have a legal right to be there. The consensual encounter allows law enforcement to utilize friendly, noncoercive conversations and settings to create investigative opportunities. A well-prepared law enforcement officer can greatly enhance his investigation by using the rights guaranteed to everyone under the First Amendment.

## Related United States Supreme Court Case Law Supporting Consensual Encounters

### *U.S. v. Mendenhall*, 446 U.S. 544 (1980)

On February 10, 1976, Drug Enforcement Administration (DEA) agents at the Detroit Airport arrested Sylvia Mendenhall for possession of heroin. The agents observed Mendenhall deplane from a flight that originated in Los Angeles. After asking to see Mendenhall's airline ticket and identification, determining that the ticket did not bear Mendenhall's name, and observing her extremely nervous state, the agents asked if Mendenhall would accompany them to the DEA office to answer some additional questions. After reaching the office, the agents asked Mendenhall if she would consent to a search of her bag and person. The agents also indicated to Mendenhall that she had the option to refuse such a search. Mendenhall agreed to the search, which revealed an airline ticket used by Mendenhall to fly to California. A policewoman subsequently arrived to search Mendenhall. The policewoman ascertained from the agents that Mendenhall had consented to the search. The policewoman then asked Mendenhall for her consent to the search, which Mendenhall gave. The policewoman indicated to Mendenhall that she would be required to disrobe as part of the search. Mendenhall then responded that she had a plane to catch. The policewoman explained to Mendenhall that she would have no problem catching the plane if no narcotics were discovered; at that time, Mendenhall removed two small packages of heroin from her undergarments, which she then gave to the policewoman. The issue at hand is whether the circumstances of the stop, search, and subsequent arrest of Mendenhall violated the Fourth Amendment. In reasoning, the government took the position that a valid consent occurred in this case. Therefore, the Court addressed the issue of whether any police conduct violative of the Fourth Amendment occurred before Mendenhall's consent, which would have affected its voluntariness. The Court found that no seizure occurred in this case and that no objective reason existed for Mendenhall to believe that she was not free to end the conversation she had with the agents on the concourse. In so doing, the Court made what has become a frequently quoted statement regarding the seizure of persons:

> We conclude that a person has been "seized" within the meaning of the Fourth Amendment only if, in view of all of the circumstances surrounding the incident, a reasonable person would have believed that he was not free to leave.

The Court also cited circumstances that might indicate that a seizure occurred even though an individual did not attempt to leave:

> The threatening presence of several officers, the display of a weapon by an officer, some physical touching of the person or the citizen, or the use of language or tone of voice indicating that compliance with the officer's request might be compelled.

The Court concluded that no unlawful seizure occurred during the initial encounter on the concourse between Mendenhall and the agents. The Court then discussed whether a Fourth Amendment violation occurred when Mendenhall went to the DEA office. In assessing this question, the Court turned to the "totality of the circumstances" test that was previously established in *Schneckloth v. Bustamonte,* and found that a review of all of the facts surrounding Mendenhall's decision to accompany the agents indicated that she went voluntarily. After concluding that the search revealing the heroin had not been "infected by an unlawful detention," the Court then addressed the question of whether Mendenhall's consent to search was invalid for any other reason. The court then analyzed the voluntariness of Mendenhall's consent, finding that it was valid. In reaching its conclusions, the Court reversed the decision reached by the Court of Appeals, and remanded the case back to that court for further proceedings.

## *Reid v. Georgia,* 448 U.S. 438 (1980)

On August 14, 1978, Reid arrived in Atlanta on a morning flight from Fort Lauderdale, Florida. A DEA agent working at the airport noticed that another individual on the same flight had a shoulder bag similar to Reid's. While the men did not walk together through the terminal, Reid occasionally looked back toward the other man. The agent approached the men outside of the terminal building, identified himself, and asked to see their tickets and iden- tification. After the men agreed to the agent's request to reenter the terminal for the purpose of a consent search, Reid began to run from the agent. Reid abandoned his shoulder bag, in which agents later found cocaine, before being apprehended. The trial court granted Reid's motion to suppress the cocaine because the agent had made a seizure without any articulable suspi- cion that Reid had narcotics. The Supreme Court ultimately vacated the Georgia Court of Appeals' reversal of the trial court decision. The issue was whether the agent lawfully seized Reid outside of the terminal. In reasoning, the Georgia Court of Appeals based its decision that reasonable articulable suspicion existed to stop Reid on the following factors: Reid had arrived from Fort Lauderdale, which the Agent testified was a principal place of origin of cocaine sold elsewhere in the country; Reid arrived in the early morning, when law enforcement activity is diminished; Reid and his companion appeared to the agent to be trying to conceal the fact that they were traveling together; and they apparently had no luggage other than their shoulder bags. The Supreme Court vacated the Georgia Court of Appeals' decision. The court concluded that, as a matter of law, the agent could not have reasonably suspected that Reid carried narcotics on the basis of what he knew about Reid when he approached him outside of the terminal. Therefore, because the agent lacked reasonable suspicion at the time he stopped Reid, no lawful seizure could have been made under the existing circumstances.

## *Florida v. Royer,* 460 U.S. 730 (1983)

On January 3, 1978, two Dade County, Florida detectives observed Royer in the Miami Airport. Royer bought a one-way ticket to LaGuardia and checked two suitcases, upon which he placed an identification tag bearing the name of Holt, with the destination of LaGuardia. After observing a number of other characteristics typically associated with individuals engaged in transporting narcotics, the two detectives approached Royer in the airport concourse and identified themselves. Royer agreed to speak with the detectives and produced his ticket and driver's license on request. Royer's driver's license bore the name Royer, but his ticket was issued in the name of Holt. Royer explained that a friend had made his reservations in the name of Holt. Royer became increas- ingly nervous during the course of the conversation with the detectives. The detectives then informed Royer that they were narcotics detectives and they suspected him of transporting drugs. The detectives retained Royer's ticket and license and asked him to accompany them to a nearby room. Royer did not verbally consent to the request, but did accompany the detectives to the room, which was later described by one of the detectives as a large storage closet. At this point one of the detectives, using Royer's claim tickets, retrieved Royer's checked-in luggage and brought it to the room. Royer had not consented to the retrieval of the luggage. The detectives then asked Royer if he would consent to a search of his suitcases. Without verbally consenting to the search, Royer produced a key to open one of the suitcases. Royer indicated that he could not remember the combination to the second suitcase. However, Royer also said that he did not mind if the detectives opened the second suitcase. The detectives pried open the second suitcase and found marijuana inside it. The trial court denied Royer's motion to suppress. The court found that the warrantless search of Royer's luggage was both voluntary and reasonable. In reversing the trial court decision, the District Court of Appeals held that Royer's consent was tainted by the unlawful involuntary detention of Royer in the room, which went beyond the scope of a permissible *Terry* stop. The issue was whether the detectives' detainment of Royer exceeded the limited restraint permitted by *Terry*, thus violating the Fourth Amendment and invalidating Royer's consent to search his luggage. In reasoning, in affirming the Florida Court of Appeals decision, the Supreme Court made six preliminary observations in this case:

1. The validity of Royer's consent depended upon whether it had been freely and voluntarily given.
2. Law enforcement officers do not violate the Fourth Amendment by approaching an individual in a public place and asking him or her questions. Similarly, an encounter does not become a seizure merely because an officer identifies himself. An officer may not even momentarily detain an individual without reasonable objective grounds to do so. The refusal of a citizen to answer or listen to questions posed to him or her by an officer does not provide a reasonable, objective ground for detention.
3. The Terry decision makes it clear that probable cause to arrest is not necessary in every seizure of a person. As the Court noted: *Terry* created a limited exception to this general rule: certain seizures are justifiable under the Fourth Amendment if there is articulable suspicion that a person has committed or is about to commit a crime.
4. The Terry case created a limited exception to the rule that seizures of persons require probable cause to arrest. Absent probable cause, detentions that are "investigative" may still violate the Fourth Amendment.

In discussing this concept, the Supreme Court made it clear that "the scope of the detention must be carefully tailored to its underlying justification." While noting that the scope of a detention will vary with the facts of each case, the Court also stated that "an investigative detention must be temporary and last not longer than is necessary to effectuate the purpose of the stop." The state has the burden of demonstrating that the detention was sufficiently limited in scope and duration.

5. If statements are a product of an illegal detention, are made during the detention, and are not the result of independent free will, they are inadmissible.

6. Royer's consent was tainted because his confinement went beyond the scope of the limited restraint permitted by *Terry* and its progeny.

The Court then outlined the three arguments presented by the state regarding the legality of Royer's detention:

1. *Royer was not being held against his will and the encounter was consensual.* The Court rejected this argument on the basis that under the circumstances, a reasonable person would have believed he was not free to leave.

2. *Reasonable, articulable suspicion existed to justify a* Terry *stop, the bounds of which were not exceeded.* The Court agreed that the officers had adequate grounds for temporarily detaining Royer and his luggage to ascertain the validity of their suspicions. However, the Court stated that when Royer produced the suitcase key, a more serious intrusion on his personal liberty occurred. The Court then discussed three reasons why the detention was more intrusive than necessary:
   • The officer retained Royer's ticket and driver's license and did not tell him he was free to leave.
   • The officers' motivation in getting Royer into the room appeared to be to examine his luggage, something they did not discuss with Royer before entering the room.
   • The government failed to explain whether there would have been a more expeditious way to examine Royer's luggage, such as a dog sniff.

3. *There was probable cause to arrest Royer at the time he gave his consent.* The Court rejected this argument and agreed with the District Court of Appeals' finding that no probable cause existed at the time Royer gave his consent.

## U.S. v. Place, 462 U.S. 696 (1983)

Law enforcement officers observed Place as he waited in line at a ticket counter at the Miami Airport. The officers approached Place after he left the counter and asked to see his ticket and identification. Place showed the ticket and identification to the officers and consented to a search of the luggage he had just checked in. However, because Place's plane was preparing to depart the airport, the officers decided not to search the luggage at the airport in Miami. The agents called DEA in New York regarding the information they had obtained about Place. DEA agents at LaGuardia Airport watched Place deplane and approached him after he had claimed his bags and called for a limo. The agents informed Place of their belief that he might be carrying narcotics. Place indicated to the agents that the officers in Miami had already searched his luggage and subsequently refused to consent to a search. At this point, an agent told Place that they were going to take the luggage to a magistrate to try to obtain a warrant. The agents offered to have Place go with them, an offer Place declined. Place did accept a paper containing a telephone number where the agents could be reached. The agents took Place's luggage to the Kennedy Airport to conduct a canine sniff test. The narcotics dog alerted positively to two of Place's three bags 90 minutes after the initial seizure of the luggage. At issue: did the temporary detention of personal luggage on the basis of reasonable suspicion that the luggage contained narcotics violate the Fourth Amendment? In reasoning in *Place*, the Court initially discussed the general principles relating to the seizure of personal property. The Court began its discussion by stating that a warrant issued upon probable cause and particularly describing the items to be seized is necessary to validly seize personal property. The Court then noted that law enforcement authorities may seize property until a warrant is obtained if probable cause exists that the property contains evidence of a crime and exigent circumstances exist, or some other recognized exception to the warrant requirement is present. The Court stated that the principles in *Terry* are applicable to situations involving personal property. In reaching this conclusion, the Court balanced the law enforcement interests allegedly justifying the intrusion against the individual's Fourth Amendment interests. The Court agreed with the government's contention that law enforcement has a substantial interest in briefly seizing luggage to pursue an investigation based on specific and articulable facts indicating that the luggage may contain drugs. While acknowledging that a seizure of personal property can vary both in its nature and extent, the Court stated that some brief detentions may be so minimally intrusive that where the government interest is strong, a seizure based on specific articulable facts may be justified. The Court then summarized its reasoning by stating:

In sum, we conclude that when an officer's observations lead him reasonably to believe that a traveler is carrying luggage that contains narcotics, the principles of *Terry* and its progeny would permit the officer to detain the luggage briefly to investigate the circumstances that aroused his suspicion, provided that the investigative detention is properly limited in scope.

The Court then concluded that a canine luggage sniff is not a search within the meaning of the Fourth Amendment.

After discussing the basic principles governing personal property seizures, the Court then addressed the question of whether the seizure in *Place* required probable cause, or whether it fell within the *Terry* exception. The Court concluded that the conduct of agents in *Place* exceeded the bounds of a permissible *Terry* stop. In reaching its conclusion, the Court noted that the length of time the individual's Fourth Amendment rights are invaded is an important factor in determining whether a detention can be based on reasonable suspicion. While the Court flatly refused to establish an outside time limitation for a permissible *Terry* stop, the court did definitively state that 90 minutes was too long. Thus, in finding the seizure in *Place* was unreasonable under the Fourth Amendment, the Court affirmed the Court of Appeals decision, which had overturned the District Court's denial of Place's motion to suppress the cocaine found in his luggage.

### *Florida v. Rodriguez*, 469 U.S. 1 (1984)

On September 12, 1978, a Dade County Public Safety Department officer noticed Rodriguez at a ticket counter in the Miami Airport. The officer became suspicious of Rodriguez and his two companions during his observations of them when leaving the counter. Two officers then followed the three men through the terminal and to the escalators, where Rodriguez's companions spoke to each other and repeatedly looked back in the direction of the officer. At the top of the escalator, one of the officers testified that he heard one of Rodriguez's companions say "Let's get out of here." Rodriguez then attempted to move away from the officers and apparently began to run in place. The officer identified himself to Rodriguez and asked Rodriguez if he would talk. Rodriguez indicated that he would talk to the officer and agreed to accompany him to where the other officer was talking to his two companions about 15 feet away. While Rodriguez was unable to produce a ticket or identification upon request, one of his companions produced a cash ticket with three names on it. The officers then identified themselves as narcotics officer and asked to search Rodriguez's luggage. Rodriguez initially indicated that he did not have a key, but later produced one when one of his companions told him that he should let the officer look in the luggage. The officers then searched the luggage and found three bags of cocaine inside of it. The trial court granted the defendant's motion to suppress, a decision later upheld by the District Court of Appeals. The Supreme Court reversed the District Court of Appeals' decision and remanded the case for further proceedings. The issue: should the cocaine found in Rodriguez's luggage have been suppressed? In the reasoning of addressing this case, the Court initially examined the basic legal principles governing this area of law. The Court cited Royer for the proposition that if there is a reasonable articulable suspicion that a person is committing or is about to commit a crime, then certain seizures may be permissible under the Fourth Amendment even if there is no probable cause. The Court stated that the initial contact between the officer and Rodriguez was a consensual encounter with no Fourth Amendment implications. Even assuming that the movement of Rodriguez to the location where his companions and the other officer stood and where the consent search occurred was a seizure, the Court held that "any such seizure was justified by articulable suspicion." Finally, the Court indicated that it could not determine whether the trial court's opinion regarding the voluntariness of the consent search would have been the same if the proper Fourth Amendment principles had been applied.

### U.S. v. Sokolow, 490 U.S. 1 (1980)

Passenger Sokolow went to the Honolulu Airport and purchased two open return date tickets to Miami with $2100 in $20 bills from a large roll of twenties. The ticket agent noticed that Sokolow wore a black jumpsuit and gold jewelry, that he was about 25 years old, and that he appeared nervous. The ticket agent also noted that neither Sokolow nor his female companion checked any of their four bags. The ticket agent subsequently contacted the police and gave them the telephone number left by Sokolow. Police called the number, and the ticket agent identified the voice on the answering machine as Sokolow's. The telephone number was listed to Karl Herman, who was Sokolow's roommate. The police found no telephone listing for Andrew Kray, the name Sokolow had given the ticket agent. The police later determined that Sokolow and his companion had made return reservations from Miami with stopovers in Denver and Los Angeles 3 days later. DEA agents in Los Angeles observed Sokolow during his stopover there upon his return trip. The agents described Sokolow as appearing very nervous. Upon arrival in Honolulu, agents observed Sokolow deplane wearing the same black jumpsuit he had worn 3 days earlier. Sokolow and his companion had not checked any bags on their return flight, but proceeded directly through the terminal, where they were approached by four DEA agents as they attempted to hail a cab. Upon approaching Sokolow, one agent displayed his credentials, grabbed him by the arm, and guided him to the sidewalk. Sokolow indicated that he did not have identification or an airline ticket to show the agents, but that he had been traveling under his mother's maiden name of Kray. The agents then escorted Sokolow and his companion to the DEA office, where a narcotics dog alerted to Sokolow's shoulder bag. The agents obtained a warrant for the bag. Upon opening the bag, the agents found documents indicating Sokolow's participation in drug trafficking, but no narcotics. At this point the agents had the drug dog reexamine the remaining bags. The dog alerted on another bag, but it was too late to obtain another warrant, so the officers kept the luggage but let Sokolow go. The next morning the agents obtained a warrant and found cocaine in the bag. Sokolow entered a conditional plea of guilty to the charges against him after the trial court denied his motion to suppress. The Ninth Circuit Court of Appeals reversed Sokolow's conviction on the grounds that "the DEA agents did not have reasonable suspicion to justify the stop." At issue: did the DE agents have a reasonable suspicion that Sokolow was carrying narcotics when they stopped him outside the Honolulu Airport? In reasoning, the Court initially addressed the Fourth Amendment requirement that a stop must be made on "some minimal level of objective justification." The Court subsequently stated that the level of suspicion required for a *Terry* stop is less that probable cause. The Court went on to reject the two-part analysis developed by the Ninth Circuit in deciding this case. Instead, the Court stated that "in evaluating the validity of a stop such as this, we must consider the 'totality of the circumstances — the whole picture.'" In applying the aforementioned principles to the facts in *Sokolow*, the Court concluded that the facts indicated that reasonable suspicion existed. The Court acknowledged that each factor describing Sokolow's behavior, when taken alone, would not be indicative of illegal activity and would be consistent with innocent travel. The Court rejected Sokolow's argument that the agents were required to use the least intrusive means available and should have just spoken to him to dispel their suspicions instead of detaining him. With respect to this issue, the Court stated that "the reasonableness of the officer's decision to stop a suspect does not run on the availability of less intrusive investigatory techniques."

### *Florida v. Bostick,* Cite to 111 S. Ct. 2382 (1991)

In 1989, Bostick boarded a bus in Miami. Two police officers in Miami boarded the bus during a stopover in Fort Lauderdale and, with articulable suspicion, asked to inspect Bostick's ticket and identification. After finding Bostick's ticket and identification to be in order, the police requested consent to a search of his luggage. Bostick consented to the search, and the police found cocaine in one of Bostick's bags. Bostick pled guilty to charges of trafficking in cocaine and reserved the right to appeal the trial court's motion to suppress. The District Court of Appeals affirmed the trial court's decision, but certified a question to the Florida Supreme Court. The Florida Supreme Court reversed the trial court and suppressed the cocaine found during the course of the search. The issue: does the rule permitting police officers to randomly approach people in public places to question them and "request consent to search their luggage, as long as a reasonable person would understand that he or she could refuse to cooperate," apply to encounters occurring on a bus? In reasoning, the United States Supreme Court reversed the Florida Supreme Court, stating that the court had erred in adopting a per se rule that "prohibited the police from randomly boarding buses as a means of drug interdiction." While the Court declined to decide whether a seizure occurred in Bostick, the Court did articulate a rule to be used in determining whether a specific encounter with the police constituted a seizure. Therefore, the Court stated that to determine whether a particular encounter constituted a seizure, a court must consider all the circumstances surrounding the encounter to determine whether the police conduct would have communicated to a reasonable person that the person was not free to decline the officer's request or otherwise terminate the encounter. The Court noted that the rule applied to encounters that occur on a bus as it would apply to encounters occurring in other public places. In reaching its decision, the Court explored a number of cases addressing police encounters and questioning. The Court noted that since *Terry*, mere questioning by the police has repeatedly been held to not constitute a seizure. The Court rejected Bostick's argument that a police encounter within the confines of a bus is much more intimidating that a normal encounter in a public place. The Court found Bostick's assertion that a reasonable person would not feel free to leave a bus indistinguishable from previous cases permitting such questioning.

## Key Terms

| | |
|---|---|
| Agents | Dog sniff |
| Approach | Egress |
| Baggage | Encounter |
| Briefly | Examination |
| Canine | Fictitious |
| Canine alert | Freedom to leave |
| Case law | Freedom to terminate |
| Casual | Indicator |
| Characteristics | Ingress |
| Consensual encounter | Innocent |
| Contact | Law enforcement experience |
| Court of Appeals | Luggage |
| Detain | Nonaggressive |
| Detectives | Nonauthoritative |
| Detention | Officer friendly |
| District Court | Officer safety |

Officers                          State Court
Ordinary                          "Stop"
Probable cause                    Supreme Court
Prudent                           Terry stop
Reasonable doubt                  Testimony
Reasonable man                    Tone of voice
Reasonable suspicion              Training
Reexamination                     Unusual behavior
Refusal                           Vocabulary
Right to refuse                   Voluntariness

*Florida v. Bostick,* Cite to 111 S. Ct. 2382 (1991)
*Florida v. Rodriguez,* 469 U.S. 1 (1984)
*Florida v. Royer,* 460 U.S. 730 (1983)
*U.S. v. Mendenhall,* 446 U.S. 544 (1980)
*U.S. v. Place,* 462 U.S. 696 (1983)
*U.S. v. Sokolow,* 490 U.S. 1 (1980)

# Knock and Talk Technique

# 3

Law enforcement officers, specifically drug enforcement investigators, are always looking for innovative ways to combat the drug trade. Historically, drug enforcement officers have utilized traditional methods of narcotic enforcement, such as the use of informants, undercover operations, surveillance, wire intercepts, and reverse sting drug operations. Never did the drug enforcement officer imagine that merely knocking on a drug dealer's door and asking if he or she would surrender drugs to police officers or allow the police to search their residence for drugs would really work. In the early part of our careers, never did we think that this would be an option, much less a reality.

The technique now known as a *knock and talk* is an effective law enforcement tool, not only for drug investigations, but also in other criminal investigations. The method is a consensual encounter as described in Chapter 2. This is one type of encounter that starts with the consent of the individual. The difference here is that we are going to the person's residence or business and asking for a consent search. A consent search is one of the exceptions to a search warrant.

This technique is believed to have started in the early to mid-1980s and has developed today into an excellent investigative option. It is creating previously unimagined investigative opportunities. Before this technique, drug enforcement units would receive information regarding drug traffickers dealing or possessing drugs in their homes and businesses, but really did not know what to do with the information. Investigators would rack their brains to think of a way to "get in" to the residence or business to try to make a drug case. If no informants were available or surveillance was either impractical or failed to produce the desired results, that information would probably be left in a file cabinet somewhere. Intelligence information regarding drug activity was handled in that fashion before this technique.

Criminal intelligence should be collected by law enforcement; however, if we do not act upon the information, it is essentially worthless. The knock and talk technique provides an investigative avenue for law enforcement to act on information and intelligence. According to L.T. "Tom" McCabe of Schlim, McCabe & Associates, "the method is simple and straightforward." McCabe is a former California law enforcement officer, and he and his associates teach the technique throughout the United States. The knock and talk enhances a law enforcement agency's ability to combat crime with minimal expense and resources. Whether the police agency is small and rural or large and urban, the knock and talk program can be used with success.

## What is a Knock and Talk?

In this chapter, we will explore a number of areas regarding this investigative tool. We will define the nature of knock and talk investigations, identify when it would be most advantages to use this technique, as well as learn the steps of this process. We will emphasize the safety concerns surrounding knock and talk investigations.

The term *knock and talk* simply means what it infers: knocking on someone's door, talking with him, asking for consent to search the premises — the subject's home, apartment, or business. The knock and talk technique does not require probable cause or a search warrant to allow law enforcement to make contact with an individual and ask for a consensual search of the premises. Many courts provide a definition of a consensual encounter. In the case of *U.S. v. Werking*, 915 F.2d. 1404, 1410, 10th Circuit (1991), the court stated that "a consensual encounter is simply the voluntary cooperation of a private citizen in response to non-coercive questioning by a law enforcement official." In *U.S. v. Cormier*, 220 F.3d. 1103, 9th Circuit (2000), the court indicated "the general rule regarding 'knock and talk' encounters is that there is no rule which makes it illegal per se, or a condemned invasion of the person's right of privacy, for anyone openly and peaceably to knock on the front door of any man's 'castle' with the honest intent of asking questions of the occupant. There is no evidence to indicate that was anything other than consensual and no suspicion needed to be shown in order to justify the 'knock and talk.'"

Skeptics of this technique will say that a drug dealer is not going to let you into his home to search for drugs. That may be true under certain circumstances. However, it is absolutely astonishing how many times a drug trafficker provides consent to officers to search his premises. In many cases, the drug dealer surrenders narcotics to the officers.

You never know what can happen in a knock and talk; but if you do not try, nothing will happen anyway. The technique calls for being assertive and trying something new. Many police officers say to us, "That stuff won't work in our area. They won't let us in their houses." We say that may be true; however, one never knows until one tries.

### Case Study

An investigator in the south part of the country asked a knock and talk detective to make an arrest for him. The investigator, who was an undercover officer, had purchased a small baggie of marijuana from a suspect several weeks earlier. The investigation had come to a standstill and he was ready to arrest the suspect. The agency had a knock and talk section, and the detective volunteered to arrest the suspect for the undercover officer and ask for consent search of the suspect's residence.

The detective arrived at the residence and spoke to the suspect. He told the person he was conducting a narcotics investigation; however, he never told the person he was a suspect or that he was under arrest. The detective and his partner asked the suspect for a consent search of his home, which was given. The search revealed 200 pounds of marijuana in the garage of his home. The undercover investigator was certainly surprised when he heard what was found in the suspect's home.

What typically happens with the information that law enforcement receives about a person dealing drugs? Generally a police agency receives information via a "tip" from an informant or other source of information that a particular individual is trafficking narcotics at their residence or business. Information may be received through a tip line, set up by the police agency to receive information about drug dealing in their community. Many police agencies take this information and act upon it. Much of the information received via a tip line is anonymous, and many of the people providing information about drug dealing prefer to remain anonymous. Information received through a tip line is often generic, something like "Cars are coming to the house and leaving a short time later. I think the guy is dealing drugs because he doesn't work." Other tips may be more specific as to what is occurring at a location, such as "the person is dealing cocaine from his business and keeps the drugs in a safe in his office." Historically, this information was too generic to act upon if no other investigative avenues were available, such as an informant. Today, we can and should act upon just this information. As law enforcement we have an obligation to act upon information regarding drug dealing. Certainly there is an element of risk involved in the decision of doing a knock and talk. We may get nothing at all; the person may slam the door in our faces and refuse to allow us to search. At least we tried to do something and show the community that we are acting on the information. We put people on notice and advise them we are aware of their activities. Yes, the person may move from the area, and some would argue that we are just displacing crime. That may be true; however, at least we tried to act upon this very serious problem we call drugs.

An investigative group or analyst will do some background work on the individual, and there may or may not be information concerning their narcotics activities. At this point, depending on the police agency, the information may be provided to a detective for further follow-up investigation.

The investigator may drive by the residence or business to see if there is any activity and what vehicles are at the location. He or she may conduct some surveillance at the location. There may or may not be any activity observed at the location that would indicate that drug trafficking could be occurring. Once all of the investigative efforts have been exhausted and there is no active informant or other information, the investigator may either close the investigation or try to obtain further information at a later time. The knock and talk may be an option at this point.

The investigator and his or her partner travel to the location, knock on the door, and ask to speak with the occupants. Investigators at this point should ask consent to enter the premises to discuss some concerns regarding information they have received. A consent may be considered coerced if the investigator uses some sort of trickery or is untruthful about his true purpose. The officers can tell the subject that they have received information concerning drug dealing, or they can be more generic about specific information. The individual is provided with an opportunity to discuss the information. The investigators either ask the individual to surrender drugs if there are any narcotics in the residence or consent to a search of the premises. The drug traffickers may surrender narcotics or the investigators may search the premises and find drugs, at which point the subject will be charged criminally. It sounds simple, does it not? It does not always work this way, but there are numerous documented cases in which this technique has been extremely effective.

This particular method is a versatile program for all types of law enforcement. Criminal investigators, such as robbery investigators, homicide, and property crime detectives can use this technique. In addition, uniform officers can use this process to obtain evidence in a particular crime. Individuals who are most successful in conducting the knock and talk are those who are most comfortable speaking with people. They are officers who know proper procedure and are familiar with search and seizure (Fourth Amendment) in particular. The investigator should display a good presence and demeanor when making contact with individuals in the knock and talk process.

Does the knock and talk work? It certainly does, and the key is to gain entrance to the premises first. It is cost effective for law enforcement agencies that have limited resources. Many agencies are not in the position or do not have the resources to place officers on long-term surveillances or long investigative efforts. The knock and talk is an effective method in dealing with situations of drug trafficking under these circumstances.

There are, of course, safety issues and concerns with this technique. The biggest concern for the officer is entering the unknown. It can be extremely dangerous when the officers enter a location where they are not familiar with the surroundings, do not know how many individuals are at the location, and do not know if there are weapons or firearms present. The purpose of this technique is to verify that a subject or subjects are violating the law, then to obtain a legal consensual search of the premises. Investigators must be aware that false and slanderous information may be provided to law enforcement for a variety of reasons. Some of those reasons include, but are not limited to, domestic situations and child custody issues. A background investigation must be completed before conducting a knock and talk; it may flush out any issues such as false information.

## The Use of Tip Programs and Processing

Many agencies throughout the United States have now implemented successful drug tip information telephone lines. These tip programs provide law enforcement with additional assets to obtain information relating not only to drug trafficking, but also other types of crimes such as violent crime, including homicide and robbery. Typically a tip line is operational 7 days a week, 24 hours a day and handled either by law enforcement or other designated groups. The information provides intelligence information to law enforcement regarding a number of crimes and there may be opportunities for rewards for information provided by citizens. Many agencies have a protocol for collection and documentation of the information. The documentation process should include a standard form for the information obtained via the tip program. The tips should have some numerical order and be easily accessible for tracking purposes. A typical tip form should include information such as the name of the subject being reported on and as much biographical information as possible with respect to gender, race, age, date of birth, weight, height, hair color, and eye color. Information regarding the subject's residence, telephone number, business or occupation, and vehicle information should also be included, if available. Any information concerning the family, relevant intelligence information such as the types of drugs being sold or possessed, the location of dealing and any associates that may be part of an organization, and any other additional information that may be pertinent to the tip should be included. Also include the caller addresses and telephone number if the caller chooses to provide this information. This is helpful for possible future contact of the caller by an investigator.

Many of the tips received by agencies are anonymous. It is important to acquire the caller's motive for providing the information. Motive is important because it lays a foundation as to why an individual would be reporting on a drug dealer. The caller could be a concerned neighbor or friend, or it could be the drug trafficker's competition, although the caller will certainly not admit to the latter. The documentation or tip form should indicate who received the information so the investigator may go back to obtain further details. If this information is to be provided to an investigator, a background check should reveal any open cases on the person to whom the tip was referring. The tip information should be provided to the case agent with the open case for further review. Overzealous investigators do not always do a proper background check, and may do a knock and talk when other investigations are being conducted on the subject. This can cause problems for the existing case and investigator.

All local databases should be examined for local criminal history and any narcotic intelligence. A national search should be conducted to further examine the subject's background. The form should include the name of the investigator to whom the information is routed. It is suggested that a monitoring system be included in this process so that the information can be tracked. If the information results in an arrest and seizure of narcotics, this information should be tracked as well, for statistical purposes. Any other information such as negative results (no arrest or seizure of drugs) or no action taken should also be documented.

Much intelligence is collected with respect to drug traffickers and their activities. Using a tip processing system to document information should be a part of a narcotics intelligence group. Some agencies have full-time tip squads that respond to tip complaints. The technique they deploy on most occasions is the knock and talk. These successful programs are a tribute to this method. Once all the investigative options have been explored and exhausted with respect to either a tip complaint or other information, consider the knock and talk.

## Reasons to Use a Knock and Talk

It is essential that investigators investigate information or intelligence as thoroughly as possible, and use a number of investigative options. If other options "run dry," the knock and talk is a viable alternative. If the investigator has no probable cause for a search warrant or arrest and surveillance fails to produce information where probable cause can be established, the knock and talk can be considered. This technique is a last resort when there are no other investigative leads and no informants who can either provide information or be able to take an active role in the investigation.

Investigators should not use this technique as a shortcut for their cases. If probable cause does exist for a search warrant to the premises, by all means, draft a search warrant and execute it. Some investigators use the knock and talk as a shortcut when they do have other investigative options. In the case of a knock and talk, there are only two things that will happen. You will get into the residence or you will be refused entry. In a search warrant situation, there is no question that investigators will enter the premises and conduct a search. With the knock and talk, there is no guarantee.

## Why Do People Consent?

There is an ongoing debate concerning police–citizen encounters and the consent issue. A number of court interpretations exist with respect to consent. The Fourth Amendment to the Constitution of the United States provides individuals the right to be free from unreasonable search and seizure of their persons, houses, papers, and effects. In the past several years, police–citizen encounters in various venues, including public transportation areas, has dramatically increased. These voluntary searches have provided law enforcement with an additional tool to combat and prevent crime. What the courts debate and have begun to examine more closely are the conditions under which consensual encounters are conducted, and whether a person's consent to the police search was in fact voluntary.

There are number of rational reasons why people would consent to a search by the police, and these are recognized by some courts in the United States. Certainly, there are many psychological implications with respect to what an individual believes is occurring during the consent search. Many people believe that evidence in their home will be overlooked, that the officer will not really search; they wish to appear cooperative and think that if they do not consent they will look guilty. A subject may consent to a police search thinking that if drugs are found, he can explain its presence or deny knowledge. A person may think that he simply has been caught, and give up. In providing a consent search, a person may believe that consent will make him appear not to have knowledge. The logic is, "why would I let you search if there were drugs in my house? It doesn't make sense." A subject may believe that the narcotics or contraband is so well concealed that law enforcement would never find it. This is what we call "wrapping 101." Drug trafficking organizations and individuals use a number of masking agents or conceal-ment areas in a variety of locations. Whether it is in a parcel, a vehicle, home, or on their person, they may feel secure enough to provide law enforcement with consent. There is much discussion between traffickers as to what to use to eliminate the odor of narcotics or to conceal it in a fashion such that they believe it will never be found. Traffickers may build false compartments in the walls, floors, and ceilings of their homes. Many other elaborate conceal-ment areas have been used in homes and businesses. Law enforcement must educate prosecutors, judges, and juries concerning consent searches and how they are a viable mechanism for criminal investigations.

In many instances, unfortunately, law enforcement backs away from individuals who appear to be cooperative. We call this the "lazy cop syn-drome." Many officers justify in their minds that if the subject gave them consent, maybe that person does not have anything to hide. If an individual provides the officer with consent to search, the officer should always do a thorough and complete search. If the officer went to the trouble of asking an individual to conduct a consent search, why would the officer not complete that search?

A consent search is one of the exceptions to a search warrant. Other exceptions include incident to arrest, the plain view doctrine, exigent cir-cumstances, abandonment, and the open fields doctrine, where there is no reasonable expectation of privacy in open fields. The U.S. Supreme Court provides homeowners with a great deal of protection, and rightfully so.

An abundance of case law related to consensual encounters exists. One of the premier Supreme Court decisions with respect to this issue is *U.S. v. Bostick*, 501 US 429 (1991). The key phrase in the Court's opinion with respect to a consent search is: "a reasonable person would feel free to decline the officer's request or otherwise terminate the encounter." This phrase is important when law enforcement deals with a consensual encounter such as a knock and talk situation. A person can refuse a search of his premises at any time. The courts have said that law enforcement can conduct a consti-tutional search without a warrant if they receive the consent of the individual whose premises, effects, or person are to be searched.

## Knock and Talk as an Investigative Technique

Once investigators and officers have exhausted all other investigative options and decide to conduct a knock and talk, a number of factors should be taken into consideration with respect to planning and execution of the technique.

The investigator should have as much information as possible concerning the individuals before making contact at a premises or business to ask for a consensual search. You should know as much as possible about the criminal activity you are dealing with, and know the answers to your questions before you ask. It is absolutely essential that a background investigation be done on individuals who can be identified in the residence. Do not go into the knock and talk blindly; it is dangerous. Criminal histories, warrant checks, drivers license checks, and violent tendencies should all be explored.

Know the type of narcotics that is being distributed from the premises. This is important not only for safety, but for health issues. When individuals are operating a clandestine laboratory, this information is crucial to the planning effort. Other information to take into consideration before the knock and talk commences is whether there are any prior tip complaints or intelligence information regarding the individuals at the location. Have a plan before entering a location and consider how many investigators should be taken to a knock and talk.

Once a plan is in place, typically two investigators or officers will go to the door. There is a reason for two officers; one is for safety reasons, and the other is that one of the officers should talk as the other one scans. This is typically called the "talker" and the "scanner." The talker initially makes verbal contact with the individual, as the scanner scans for things that can hurt them, such as a weapon or firearm. In addition, the scanner is looking for items in plain view, such as paraphernalia or narcotics. One officer or more than two should not commence a knock and talk. Going to a knock and talk alone is dangerous. Three or more at the door becomes a coercive and intimidating situation, and the officers may lose the search under these circumstances.

If other officers are available, a plan should be in place to position them as backup at the exterior perimeter, watching for suspicious activity inside as well as outside the residence. Often in these situations, people may approach the residence to purchase drugs. Those individuals can be encountered and possibly used as witnesses.

When the exterior perimeter investigators are in position, two officers should approach the door and make contact with the individual(s). Once the contact is made, the officers should identify themselves with their proper police credentials. Officers should then ask if the person has a moment to speak, and if he would allow officers to come inside. The officer should speak calmly and not be authoritative or accusatory. The object is to get inside of the residence to be in a position to possibly see items in plain view. The element of surprise is a factor in knock and talk, so the suspect will not have the opportunity to hide or destroy evidence or have a plan of response for the detectives' questioning.

Investigators have a variety of options as to what they can wear when conducting this technique. As a plainclothes investigator, casual clothing is an option. As a uniform officer, that is the dress of the day and what the officer would be wearing. In a situation where the officers are in plainclothes, consideration should be given to carrying a firearm and police radio for communicating with other investigators. It is suggested that the investigators be armed and have a firearm in proximity, where it can be readily available. It is not suggested that the officer wear an ankle holster unless he is trained proficiently in this type of holster. If possible, the firearm should be concealed so as not to cause an issue of coercion. Handcuffs and other items such as mace or pepper spray should be concealed. An officer may opt to wear a jacket identifying him as law enforcement. There are windbreaker type jackets with POLICE or SHERIFF on the front and back.

What generally happens during a knock and talk technique is illustrated in Figure 3.1. Investigators are able to make entry to a location approximately 99% of the time. That percentage would depend on the environment and the suspect's prior contact with law enforcement. Once inside, one of four situations is going to occur.

1.  The investigators will obtain consent to search the premises for narcotics.
2.  Probable cause may be established based on what the investigators see in plain view. The officers may observe narcotics or other evidence such as paraphernalia or drugs in plain view once they are inside.
3.  There may be an exigent circumstance. In this case, the investigators must articulate the exigency of the circumstances and describe what was occurring. There may be a situation where the subject is attempting to destroy evidence such as narcotics. For example, the subject might attempt flushing narcotics down the commode.
4.  The investigators may receive a refusal to search or cooperate. An individual may say that he will not submit to a consent search or will not surrender any narcotics to the investigators, and requests them to leave. Under these circumstances, unless evidence is seen in plain view, there is no choice but to depart the premises.

A refusal by the subject puts him on notice that the police are aware of his activities and that they would be conducting further investigation. This may put the trafficker on edge, and the subject may move from the area. The knock and talk gives the perception of the police being everywhere, and the subject may be trying to figure out how law enforcement knew that he was dealing narcotics.

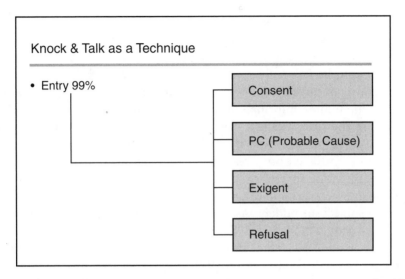

**Figure 3.1** (Courtesy of Schlim, J.R., McCabe, L.T., Mornson, L.T., and Schlim, J.G. *Drug/Narcotic Investigations* , 1997, Fremont, CA, pp. 3–11.)

If the individual cooperates and provides consent to the officers to enter the premises, there are a number of options at this point. The first thing the officers should ask is if anyone else is in the residence at that time. The subject may or may not tell the investigators whether there are other individuals on the premises, but there is an option to ask the subject for his consent to conduct a cursory examination of the residence to identify any other people for their protection. If the subject consents, it is permissible for the officer to do a walkthrough and examine areas in which a person may hide. This does not give the officers the authority to search areas in which a person cannot hide such as dresser drawers, medicine cabinets, and other like areas. The officers may examine areas such as a room, a closet, under a bed, and other areas where a person may hide.

An officer may examine the premises for people and, for example, open a closet and find narcotics, such as bales of marijuana or a marijuana-growing operation. Under these circumstances, the officer should leave the items as they were found and go back to the subject and either secure the location for a search warrant or interview the subject further under *Miranda* warnings.

Once the premises have been cleared of other individuals, you may want to ask the subject if he has any knowledge as to why you would be making contact with him. Speak calmly and not authoritatively; tell the subject of your intent and tell him the nature of the complaint. Do not become accusatory, saying something like, "You are dealing." Indicate that you are there to prove or disprove the information. Use your training and experience as an officer to guide you in the proper direction.

Investigators may be surprised to learn that the subject may actually admit to drug trafficking or drug dealing from the residence. He may first state that he has no idea why the officers would be there. At this time, the subject should be asked if he has a moment to speak with investigators to discuss some concerns regarding information that they received. The officers may provide limited information regarding the intelligence or information concerning the drug dealing. They may ask the subject if there are any narcotics in the premises and if so, if the subject would surrender them to law enforcement. There are cases where individuals will surrender a quantity of narcotics to the investigator. In other cases, the subject will deny that involvement, or possession of any narcotics.

If the subject surrenders an amount of narcotics to the officer, the officer should not stop at that point. Sometimes a drug trafficker will provide a small amount of drugs to the officer and say that is all he has. The investigator should probe further, with consent of the subject, and ask if he has any more narcotics. Sometimes a subject will provide additional amounts of the substance. Officers must make sure that if the subject does give consent to search the premises that the consent is unequivocal. Silence or a nod of the head is not enough to provide consent to search.

A subject may ask the officer if he has a search warrant, and ask if it is required to search the premises. The answer to that question should be that a search warrant is not required if the person gives consent. Do not make the mistake of telling the individual, "No, but I can get one." This mistake could be construed as a threat, and could cause the search to be inadmissible in criminal court. No threats or promises should be made to the person who owns, leases, or rents the premises.

### Case Study

In a knock and talk case in Florida, a tip complaint alleged that a person was dealing marijuana from his residence. During the encounter at his premises, the subject invited two detectives into his residence. He was asked if he had marijuana in the home, based on the tip. The subject provided several grams of marijuana to the investigators. When asked if he had additional cannabis in the residence, he stated that he "had a little more." He then showed the investigator a dresser drawer where he had several pounds of marijuana. The officer asked again if he had additional quantities of marijuana and he stated that he had just a "bit" more. The subject led investigators to another part of the residence and showed them the other marijuana, which weighed multiple pounds.

The advice is not to give up on the first thing the subject offers, but continue to ask if he may have other quantities of drugs or other evidence.

If the subject does not surrender any substance, the officer would then ask for a consent search of the premises. If the subject refuses and there is no probable cause such as narcotics in plain view, the officers must terminate the encounter and leave the premises. If the individual agrees, one of the investigators should continue to speak with the individual as the other investigator immediately begins the search. If there is specific information as to where the narcotics are kept, investigators should go to that location first. It is important for the individual who takes the information during a tip complaint or during the debriefing of an informant to attempt to pinpoint where the narcotics may be situated in the premises. For example, a tip may indicate that the marijuana is kept in the refrigerator, above the kitchen cabinet, or in the bedroom. These are the first sites that the investigator should examine.

If narcotics are found, investigators do not have to immediately confront the individual, but may continue to search. Many agencies use code words for communication between investigators under these circumstances. Code words are a safe and effective way to communicate. If narcotics are located or an arrest is to be effected, a code word or phrase should be simple and, of course, be known by the investigators before the execution of the knock and talk. Investigators who have worked together for long periods of time should always use the same phrases. During a knock and talk situation, one of the investigators may be searching in a back bedroom location while his partner is speaking to the owner of the premises. Once the contraband is found, the searching officer does not want to alert the individual that narcotics have been located. This is an opportunity to use a code word or phrase. Simple code words or phrases may be something like "Did you return the video?" or "What time are we going to lunch?" These are simple but effective phrases to alert your partner that you have found narcotics. This puts your partner in a better position, and the individual is not on alert that drugs have been located.

The drugs should be left in the same position in the area in which they were located so the substance can be photographed by evidence technicians. This provides an accurate representation as to where the substance was found and how it was packaged. Additionally, the investigators should process the packaging for latent fingerprints for further identification. Further examination is suggested based on the consent search at the premises. Once the investigator feels comfortable that the search is complete, this may be the time to interview the subject further. Based on many of the court decisions with respect to recent case law, *Miranda* warnings should be read to the subject before questioning once narcotics have been found. The individual may be escorted to the location where the narcotics have been found, or the interview process may begin before confronting the individual with the narcotics. Once the narcotics have been found and the person admits or denies ownership of the narcotics, the officers have several opportunities to further the investigation. If the subject admits to the narcotics and provides information as to the source of the drugs, investigators may take steps in attempting to identify and possibly further investigate the source.

In many jurisdictions, officers have an option of not initially charging the person criminally, based on his or her cooperation in the case. If the person does not cooperate, officers can make an arrest. The knock and talk provides variety of different investigative options. Once a subject indicates he wants to cooperate, the investigator may want to use the person to contact his source to possibly make additional deliveries, or incriminating statements may be obtained with the help of the cooperative individual. A series of controlled telephone calls or contact with the source under controlled circumstances can be options.

There are a number of other considerations during the knock and talk. One is written consent versus verbal consent. The law does not require written consent; however, it is a plus in the eyes of a court. A verbal consent is just as proper, and often more practical. If it is the policy of the prosecutor's office or individual police agency to have a written consent before a search, that should be adopted. Most police agencies today have a standard consent-to-search form which should be signed by the subject and witness officer.

Some police agencies audio- or videotape their encounters. Each state is different; however, many have a one-party consent to audiotaping, using a recorder, and videotaping of encounters. Other states require a two-party consent for audio- and videotaping. If the police agency has made a decision to use audiotaping during their encounters, it is strongly suggested that they do not use a "selective taping" technique. This puts the investigator and police agency in a precarious position. If officers record some encounters and not others, the court may question this, and the evidence may become inadmissible. The defense may question why his client was not audiotaped when subjects in other cases were. This puts the investigator in the position of having to defend himself as to why he did not audiotape a particular encounter. The defense may claim that the officer had something to hide in the case.

It is a never a good policy to provide the subject of the allegation with any names, sources, or tips information when doing a knock and talk. Many knock and talk cases are because of information provided by an anonymous individual or source.

Before conducting a knock and talk, presurveillance should be a consideration. The surveillance may be able to provide information as to how many people reside at the premises and other factors that will assist the investigator in determining when it would be most advantageous for the investigator to do the knock and talk.

Another issue to consider is withdrawal of consent. If an officer obtains consent to conduct a knock and talk and, while conducting the consensual search, the subject withdraws that consent, the officer must immediately terminate the search. If the evidence of narcotics has already been found and the subject withdraws consent, the consent search should stop and a search warrant be considered for the remainder of the premises.

## Use of a Drug Canine Team

Trained drug canine teams are essential to an interdiction group. They can be used in a knock and talk situation if the suspect consents to the use of the dog after consent is provided. The knock and talk team should not take the dog with them to the door when making contact with the suspect. This creates an intimidating and coercive environment. If a drug canine is available, it should be kept out of sight while the consent is obtained by officers. The knock and talk team may ask the suspect to consent to a trained drug dog examining the residence to expedite the search process. The officers may then ask for the canine team to enter the residence. This can be done in circumstances where there is information about hidden compartments in the residence or business. The use of the dog should be explained in detail to the suspect.

## Determination in Obtaining Consent

The knock and talk is no exception to any consensual encounter in determining several factors in obtaining consent. It is important to determine the standing of the person who is providing the consent before a search, while doing a knock and talk in a premises or business. Can the subject give consent overall, and does he have control over the area? Does he have access to the premises or certain portions of the premises? It is incumbent upon the investigator to determine the answers to all of these questions about who exercises control. There may be a visitor in the home who does not have access or control over any of the areas. There may be a tenant who rents a portion of the residence such as a bedroom. That person may be able to provide consent to the investigator over areas to which that person has access or control such as a mutual bathroom, kitchen area, or some living area. That person may not be able to give a consent, however, to another person's bedroom for which he does not have access. These are all determining factors in conducting a search of premises.

With respect to juveniles and consent, there is no real black-and-white answer. This is a gray area with respect to case law. The same factors should apply in obtaining consent and asking who has control over the area, who has access, and does the person providing the consent go into the area to be searched. There may be a situation in which the parent is present at the residence but the juvenile is not. If the parent does not have access to the area to be searched, such as a juvenile's bedroom which the parent indicates he never enters, the parent may not be able to provide consent to that particular room. Locked containers to which a parent does not have access may be an issue as well. The parent does not have the authority to provide you with consent to locked areas or containers, for example, in a juvenile's bedroom. There are situations where juveniles are providing monies to their parents for rent. In this case it should be determined whether the whole room belongs to the juvenile, and does the parent have access to areas of a particular room the juvenile is occupying. The documentation of the consent must be clear and concise. The investigative report should describe the consent to be free of intimidation and coercion and unequivocal.

When it is time to ask someone's consent to search, law enforcement officers may be reluctant to use the word "search." It is important to avoid phrases such as "Can I look around?" " Can I take a peek?" or "Can I take a quick look around?" There must be verbal clarity with a request to search. The courts do not want law enforcement to be vague. The officer must be clear about what he wants to search and should say the word "search." Consent must be defined. Some courts have taken the position that in response to a request to "take a quick look around," a reasonable person may not expect the search to go beyond a plain view search. A defense would be that a "quick look around" did not mean an actual search, and the consent search would be contested.

Consider how you knock on the door of a residence when you conduct a knock and talk. There is a distinction between a "police knock" and a casual, normal knock. The "normal" knock should be described as normal in force and duration. How the officer knocked on the door may be a factor during a court hearing. The defense may claim that the knock was intimidating and put their client in a position of being fearful and anxious.

There are other factors to consider with respect to contact with the person in their home. As a general rule, a command to a person almost automatically converts the encounter in someone's home from voluntary into a detention. Commands to a person in his home should be avoided. Some examples are phrases such as "Come over here, I want to talk with you." "Get out of bed, I want to talk with you." or "Get your hands out of your pockets." Avoid using words and phrases such as "stop," or "stay there," and avoid asking someone to step away from a particular part of the residence. Officers run a fine line when commands such as these are given. We do want to emphasize, however, that if there is an issue of safety, commands can be appropriate. Even if the search may be lost, the goal is to make the officer safe.

The investigator should avoid putting his hands on a subject; this may be construed as a detention situation, even if it is a casual hand on the shoulder while speaking to the subject. Asking someone to move from one place of the premises to another or to sit may be construed as a detention as well.

Length of time of an encounter during a knock and talk should be considered. Although there is no definition of the amount of time when an encounter becomes a detention, at some point that encounter may take too long. If the investigator takes a long time to obtain a consent search of the premises, the encounter may become too long.

The age and intelligence of the person whose premises the investigator is asking to search should be taken into consideration. For instance, if a child is left alone in the home by the parents; the child may be in a position intellectually to provide a consent search of the areas in which they have access.

## Consensual Search Inventory

When a search warrant is executed and items of evidence have been seized, law enforcement will provide the suspect with a search warrant inventory of items taken during the search. This search warrant inventory provides a detailed list of items seized as part of the execution of the search warrant. Similar to a search warrant inventory list is a consensual search inventory form. This provides the subject with a list of items seized or surrendered by the individual during a knock and talk consensual encounter.

It is suggested that police agencies use something similar to this inventory form when collecting items of evidence during a knock and talk. The consent-to-search inventory form (Figure 3.2) is a simple form that can be useful to investigators. It provides the name of the detective or agent receiving permission to conduct a consensual encounter on a particular day, describes if the detective provided written or verbal consent from the party to search the premises, and upon completion, provides a written inventory and description of any property taken. The document is signed by the investigator, notarized, and signed by the party from whom the items were seized. A copy of the consent-to-search and inventory form is provided to the subject for his or her records. This document should be made part of the case file in the investigation to accurately reflect what was seized at the time of the consent search.

## Consent to Search Inventory Form

Detective/Agent _____received permission to conduct a consensual search on the _____day of _____, 20___, and executed same on the _____ day of _____, 20____, by obtaining written/verbal consent from _____ and searching the premises herein described, and upon completing said search, I Detective _____, did deliver to _____ a written inventory of the property taken, and set forth same specifying such property in detail. A true and correct list of the articles taken in said search is set forth in the foregoing inventory.

_____

Detective/Agent

### Inventory or Property and Articles Obtained during Consensual Search

_____

_____

_____

_____

_____

I, Detective/Agent _____, the investigator by whom this search was executed, do swear or affirm that the above inventory contains a true and accurate detailed account of all property taken by me.

_____

The foregoing instrument was acknowledged

Before me this ___ day of _____, 20____,

By _____ who is personally

Known to me or who has produced

_____

_____ As identification and did

Take an oath.

Notary Public

My commission expires _____

### Figure 3.2

The consent-to-search form has many advantages. It can protect the investigator by being a good faith document, inventorying the property and providing the subject with a copy. This inventory form, which has been signed by the defendant acknowledging that certain items were taken from the premises, can be used in litigation. If the subject refuses to sign the form, the investigator should write "refused" on the form and provide a copy to the subject.

## Conclusion

The knock and talk technique can help develop cooperating individuals who are interested in assisting law enforcement to further their investigative endeavors. Cultivating people to assist in an investigation may be a result of a knock and talk. A situation in which a small amount of drugs turns into a major case may occur because of the use of a knock and talk. It is an extremely effective technique for law enforcement. Any size police agency can use this technique, whether it has several officers to several thousands of officers. The technique can be used in a variety of settings. It is always important, however, that the police conduct be noncoercive and nonauthoritative.

The knock and talk is a consensual encounter that is effective in investigation of crime, particularly narcotics. The more the officer participates in the knock and talk procedure, the more proficient he becomes. Practice does make perfect, but remember that the method is a technique of last resort.

The techniques described in this chapter provide the law enforcement officer with an opportunity to create investigative opportunities. Try it — it really works!

## Key Terms

Consent to search
Consent versus detention
Consensual search inventory
    form
Fourth Amendment
Knock and talk
Presurveillance
Search and seizure
Selective taping
Talker and scanner

Tip complaints
Tip line
Tip programs
Tip processing
Verbal consent
Wrapping 101
Written consent
*U.S. v. Bostick*
*U.S. v. Cormier*
*U.S v. Werking*

# Use of the Drug Canine in Drug Interdiction

# 4

A dog's sense of smell is superior to ours. These animals live in a completely different scent world than we do. We have used these animals to our benefit for many years. We have trained them to track criminals, find people trapped in settings such as collapsed buildings and snow avalanches, find lost children, and search for bombs and drugs.

Why are dogs so proficient in detecting odor compared to humans? The anatomy of a dog's nose reveals a number of differences from the human nose. When one inhales sharply or sniffs, swirling currents of air are created inside the nasal cavity. This helps carry odors to the olfactory cells, which detect smells. Dogs have about 150 million of these cells, compared to 5 million in humans. The analogy we often use is that the human olfactory bulb is the size of a postage stamp, while in a dog it is about 1 square foot. Dogs also have a nasal cavity volume close to 4 times that of a human, which means dogs have a larger surface area for detecting odor.

Domestic drug interdiction encompasses a wide variety of investigative opportunities with respect to counter-drug efforts. The use of a properly trained drug canine team is absolutely essential in the operation of a domestic drug interdiction group. The police drug canine, when properly trained and handled, provides law enforcement with a competitive edge in traditional narcotic enforcement and the domestic drug interdiction arena.

An abundance of case law exists with respect to the use of the narcotic canine which supports the efforts and operation of an interdiction group. Trained canine teams must remember a number of factors concerning search and seizure, and privacy issues. One key factor is whether the canine team has the legal right to be present at a scene. The question should always be asked not only of the canine team, but of investigators operating in the drug interdiction environment "Am I here lawfully?"

Positive canine alerts provide probable cause for search warrants or warrantless searches, depending on the circumstances. The canine team can be used in vehicle examinations, parcel and freight examinations, knock and talk scenarios within a dwelling, business, or hotel/motel, airport, commercial bus operations (in which the drug canine team can examine bags, luggage, interior lockers, and parcels and packages in the bus terminal), and storage unit facilities. These may be random examinations or follow-ups of tip information. The drug canine can be used at airports to examine luggage, interior lockers, and aircraft. A passive alert dog (one that sits when the odor of narcotics is detected) can be used in a variety of settings, such as examining persons, on cruise ships, ship rooms, and in luggage and freight compartments. The dog is an asset in examining hidden compartments in a residence, or finding contraband buried underground.

## Cost to Police Agency

Depending on the resources of a police agency, a canine team directly assigned to an interdiction group is the most desirable proposition. The domestic drug interdiction group can also use a dual-purpose dog (one that does track and bite work and drug detection) that is generally assigned to the patrol operations section. It has been our experience, however, that a dual-purpose dog is not as effective as a single-purpose dog (drug detection only). The dual-purpose dog is easily distracted because of its aggressive training regimen, which makes it difficult for it to stay on task when working in busy environments such as a bus or airport terminal. If the agency is serious about putting an interdiction program together, a single-purpose dog is best. The dog will pay for itself in the long run, with the seizure of drugs.

If an interdiction group is to solely handle the responsibility of the canine team, there are certain costs associated with the animal. The cost of the dog itself is a consideration. Does the police agency have a source from which to purchase a dog to be trained, or will a trained dog be purchased? The average price of a dog purchased from a vendor is $3000 to $5000. There are also associated personnel costs for care and maintenance of the dog as well as equipment, including handling supplies, towels, tape, collars, flea spray, leashes, food, canine vehicle, and alarms such as a heat sensor alarm. The agency should consider purchasing a newer vehicle for the canine team. There is a lot invested in the dog and its training. A sound vehicle in good condition should be used.

Veterinarian costs are a consideration when budgeting for a drug canine. It will typically cost at least $500 per year to maintain the dog with regular examinations, barring any medical problems the dog may have.

The cost of maintaining the canine and compensating the handler for care of the dog on a daily basis is a consideration and must be budgeted as part of the overall cost of having a canine team. Unless the dog is kept in a central kennel, the handler must be compensated for the upkeep of the animal. Typically, based on the Garcia ruling, 1 hour per day in minimum wage straight or overtime must be paid to the handler.

Training costs are added to the overall fiscal responsibilities of the police agency using the dog. Training time and the maintenance of training records are essential to the credibility of the canine team.

## Acquiring a Drug Dog

Once a decision has been made to institute a domestic drug interdiction group, the agency makes a decision to obtain a dog to be part of the interdiction group. There are varying opinions regarding the purchase of an existing trained narcotics dog as opposed to purchasing a dog and sending the canine team to receive training either locally or out of the area. There are advantages and disadvantages to buying a pretrained dog. An advantage is that time is not spent initially training the dog. One of the pitfalls to purchasing a pretrained dog is that if problems exist or are identified, it will be difficult to correct them if the handler is not aware of how the animal was trained. The handler may only attend a handler course, which is normally 2 weeks long. The handler is at a disadvantage in not knowing the theory of how the dog was trained and the nuances that go with comprehensive training.

When deciding whether to send a team to a drug training school, training time is an issue. An average timetable for a drug school is 9 weeks or more. The canine team can be in training for several months before being deployed in an actual street setting. The advantage to having the drug team train from the beginning is that the handler is sent to a structured school where he or she will become proficient, learn how to correct problems, and learn about scent and conditioning theory. The handler and the animal are together from the beginning, and any difficulties that arise can be corrected during the course of the training. If a dog is identified early to not be the caliber of animal that is required to operate as a drug dog, it can be "washed out" early and the training time and cost are reduced.

A number of available vendors throughout the United States train and sell trained drug dogs. Some are good; some are not so good. A police agency should take care in selecting a vendor and dog, whether pretrained or not. The selection of a dog is important to the success of the canine team. A priority must be that the dog possesses a drive to work in various environments and for long periods. An experienced drug dog trainer or handler must test the drive of the dog. It is not always wise to take the word of a dog vendor or trainer. A potential drug canine should have high energy and should initiate and like to play. The dog must be highly curious, inquisitive, and confident in any environment. Note whether the dog is easily distracted and whether it displays any stress in the environment in which the observations are being made. Independent evaluations of the pretrained dog and training program are suggested.

The law enforcement agency must examine dog vendor's qualifications and do a complete and thorough background check. The vendor/trainer should be asked for his qualifications and certifications. Does he belong to any national organizations such as the United States Police Canine Association (USPCA) or the National Narcotic Detector Dog Association (NNDA)? There may be an occasion in which the vendor/trainer is asked to testify in a criminal case where the dog he trained was used. The defense will certainly ask for his qualifications and certification. Are the training records of the vendor available for the police agency to examine? Questions should be asked about how the drug canine was trained and in what environments. The dog should be trained in a variety of settings and work situations such as luggage, parcels, and bags. Evaluations of prospective dogs should be done before purchase at a location with which the dog is not familiar. This will provide the evaluator with a true picture of the ability of the drug dog. Before purchasing a trained dog, a guarantee should be obtained from the vendor, and the dog should be evaluated upon arrival.

The training of the narcotics dog is important. The decision must be made as to what type of trained dog will be most successful in the environment that the group will be operating in. There are typically two types of an "alert" that a dog will present when detecting a narcotic odor. An aggressive alert dog will bite, scratch, and bark where the narcotic odor is identified. A passive alert dog will sit when he locates the narcotic odor. Depending on the environment and locations in which the canine team will be operating, a decision by the police agency should be made regarding what type of trained dog would be best suited for their purpose. As previously mentioned, the most desirable trained dog is a single-purpose dog that is trained specifically for the detection of narcotic odor.

Breed is a consideration when purchasing and training for a single-purpose function. Labradors and Golden Retrievers are often used because of their nonaggressive attributes.

The single-purpose dog is most desirable because it is less easily distracted by individuals or crowds. The dog concentrates on a single task, the detection of narcotics odor. A single-purpose dog does not track or bite, but is strictly trained to detect drugs, bombs, or people. A dual-purpose or cross-trained dog is trained to track and bite. It is the typical "street dog" and is trained to detect drugs as well. The only goal in the single-purpose dog's life is to fetch his toy or get his towel. Businesses are more receptive to allowing a nonbite-trained dog on the premises such as an airport or bus station. Another consideration is the civil liability issue, in that it would be less likely that a police agency would be liable with a single-purpose dog. A dual-purpose dog (bite trained and drug trained) may become distracted and bite an innocent bystander. Another consideration regarding a dual-purpose dog or cross-trained dog is whether the canine will be a good candidate for a drug dog. Because the dog is a "good street dog" does not mean that it will be a good drug dog. The training of a street dog is different than that of a drug dog.

Handlers are encouraged to train with other police agencies in their area. The use of different drugs and environments is especially useful. It is also a good venue for the exchange of ideas and opinions on the training and deployment of drug dogs.

## Selection of Dog Handlers

The selection of a potential drug dog handler is extremely important to the success of the canine team. The handler assumes much responsibility for the success of the team.

A supervisor and part of the domestic interdiction investigation group must consider several factors in selecting a handler for the team. The handler should be observed for the ability to praise, encourage, and motivate the animal. When selecting a handler for an interdiction unit, experience is preferred. An experienced dog handler is aware of the maintenance and conditioning of the dog as well as adaptability to the expanding areas of deployment of the canine team.

The psychological profile of a good dog handler, whether experienced or not, should reveal positive attributes. His home environment should be stable. The individual should be a self-starter. His work history should be reviewed as well as past evaluations of handling abilities. The handler should need little supervision. The primary focus of the handler should be the dog when in a work and training environment.

Administrative staff should also require policies and guidelines such as deployment criteria and areas of responsibility for the canine team. Standard operating procedures should be established for training in other areas of the canine team.

## Training and Training Records

Standards should be set for a regular training program for the canine team once they have conducted their initial training. The canine team should meet or exceed standards of proficiency as set by national organizations such as the USPCA, North American Police Work Dog Association (NAPWDA), and the NNDA. The canine team should receive constant task and non task-related training, and should show proficiency before being deployed. The team should conduct daily training in the environments in which they will be deployed. For example, if the team is going to be operating in a commercial bus terminal and within areas of commercial buses, the team should train in that type of environment. A minimum of 4 hours of weekly training should be conducted with the canine team. This required amount of training days should be documented, and the canine team should maintain training records.

Training records are extremely important, and being able to produce them is critical during use of a drug canine. Defense counsel will often request training records for the drug canine. The defense counsel may argue that canine training records are "material" to the preparation of the defense.

The handler, as part of the documentation and training process, needs a number of records. These records should be maintained in good order and be available for inspection. They should be required as part of the agency's standard operating procedure. The records should include proficiency training, search–find sheets, and training logs. Certification and qualification records should be part of the file including trainer, handler, and canine team.

Training logs for daily task- and non task-related training should be maintained by the canine team. Task-related training logs must include type and amount of drug used, number of searches, type of exercise done, location where the drug was hidden, time lapse of find, location of training environment, and whether the location of the drugs was known to the handler. There should be some sort of rating device, such as excellent, good, fair, and poor. Comments concerning the dog's actions should be included in the training logs.

Training logs should include "search–find sheets," and be completed whenever the drug canine alerts. If drugs are located, the handler must identify any masking agents that are present, type of drugs, and the weight of the narcotics. The location of the find or alert should be documented as well as the container in which it was housed, such as a parcel, luggage, or other.

The handler must be prepared to demonstrate a number of facts as they relate to the training records and logs. He should document all corrective actions taken during training of the dog. Alerts without finds should be documented. Dogs are not perfect, and the courts recognize this fact.

Case law with respect to training records of a drug canine was evident in the case *U.S. v. Florez*, 871 F. Supp. 1411 (1994). In this case, the keeping of canine records became extremely important. This case law supports record keeping. The court noted, "where records are not kept or are insufficient to establish the dog's reliability, an alert by such a dog is much like a tip from an anonymous informant." This opinion points to the importance of keeping records of dog training. It is virtually impossible for the drug canine handler to remember tasks that the dog performed on a daily basis. This would include false-positive and accurate alerts without documentation of such actions.

The interdiction supervisor should observe all training activities when possible and attend canine-related seminars with the handler to observe and learn about the role and deployment of the dog. The supervisor should be familiar with task and nontask training and have a working knowledge of the drug canine. The supervisor has the responsibility to know the dog's limitations and capabilities. The supervisor should be familiar with minimum standards and certification of his drug canine team. He should always be part of the policy and procedure process and be well versed and informed with regard to them.

In-service training should be conducted routinely and the dog provided with "positive finds" in a variety of environments. A positive find would be that of drugs that are placed in a location where the dog is typically deployed, so that finding the drugs would motivate the animal to continue to work under those conditions. "Loaded bags" (luggage containing drugs such as marijuana or cocaine, for training purposes) are placed in a variety of locations such as under a bus or in areas of an aircraft. The regular weekly training sessions should be conducted with a certified canine trainer to prevent and diagnose any problems.

## Standard Operating Procedures

A business or government entity must have standard operating procedures (SOPs) in place to ensure compliance with certain directions necessary to operate in an effective and efficient manner. A drug canine team or group must also have in place SOPs to ensure that regulations are met and proper protocol is maintained.

SOPs should be designed to maintain certain criteria for canine groups, whether drug dogs or street dogs. Procedures and policy should include but are limited to:

- How often the dog will go to a veterinarian (every 6 months or annu-ally?)
- Where the dog will stay when handler is out of town (vacation) or in court
- How dog is to be housed (cage or kennel?)
- Areas of responsibility (biting of innocent civilians, dog running in the street and getting hurt)
- Grooming of the dog
- Required training protocol
- Required standards and certification
- Recordkeeping
- Drug logs — protocol for signing out drugs (required by DEA)
- Definition of agency responsibility and handler responsibility
- How the dog is to be deployed and under what circumstances and criteria

The described policies should make for a well-run, professional canine group. Areas of responsibility and protocol must be defined. It is the responsibility of the unit supervisor to implement these policies and main-tain them.

## Use of Training Drugs

The canine team should be provided with actual drugs for training. A certified drug laboratory should perform quantitative and qualitative analysis of the training drugs for the purpose of court testimony regarding the types of drugs used in training.

Many police agencies train strictly with pseudo drugs. Pseudo drugs can be purchased from laboratories such as Sigma Labs in St. Louis, Missouri, for initial training of new drug dogs, or for other specific drug training. Pseudo drugs mimic the scent of actual drugs such as cocaine and marijuana. Although appropriate in some instances, to mimic potentially toxic drugs such as LSD, the use of only pseudo drugs can cause potential issues in criminal court. It may threaten credibility in courtroom testimony. The defense may point out that the dog has been trained and tested with a substance that a suspect was not arrested for.

It is important that the dog is exposed to a variety of different quantities of drugs. This is known as a different "scent picture" with different quantities of drugs. A scent picture, for example, of a gram of cocaine versus a kilogram of cocaine is certainly different. The theory is that if the dog can locate a smaller quantity of drugs, then it can certainly identify a much larger quantity. That is not always the case, as these scent pictures are different and can be overwhelming to the dog. It is important to train with a variety of quantities of drugs to be effective. This is where recordkeeping is important. Training drugs should be rotated on a regular basis to provide "fresh" drugs for training purposes.

Procedures should be in place for storage of training drugs. Security is the first consideration — where are the drugs to be kept, and are they secure? Another consideration is the separation of drugs so contamination does not occur. Drugs such as marijuana and cocaine should not be stored together to avoid a situation where the canine may alert on the cannabis rather than the cocaine, so true training is not accomplished.

Where do we get drugs to train with? The canine trainer has a number of options. The police agency's Property and Evidence section is a source for training drugs. Seized drugs — cocaine, crack cocaine, heroin, or marijuana — can be used for training purposes. Use of these drugs must be documented with the evidence clerk. Procedures should be in place for documentation of the release of the training drugs. Recently seized drugs in a variety of quantities should be used to train with. Documentation of quantities and how the drug was obtained should also be part of training records.

The Drug Enforcement Administration (DEA) issues licenses to possess narcotics for drug canine training. A background investigation, including criminal history, is required for a person applying for a DEA license. DEA requires that the training officer indicate his training background and where the drugs will be stored. A list of all the individuals who will have access to the drugs must be disclosed. Once a license is issued, the trainer can travel freely with the substances. Every police agency should have a DEA registration. Most states have to first go through their state agency, state police, or so on to obtain a state license before receiving a DEA license.

The DEA license is called a Researcher's License, and is free to law enforcement or government. An annual fee of $70.00 is required for other entities. The license must be renewed annually.

To apply for a license as a law enforcement agency, forms can be obtained by contacting:

U.S. Department of Justice
Drug Enforcement Administration
Central Section
P.O. Box 28083
Washington, D.C. 20038–7255

## Other Factors

Certain factors should be considered when working as a canine team. There are many misconceptions about dealing with dogs. One thing to remember is that a dog is not perfect, and that it will sometimes not find drugs. There must be some scent availability if the properly trained dog is to detect an odor of a drug. The animal is not trained specifically on the drug, but on the *odor* of the drug. There may be instances where drugs were stored at a location and then removed, and a residual odor is still in place; known as "dead scent." The dog may alert, but no drugs may be found. The dog actually did its job and located the odor of narcotics. Many fault the canine team for this type of scenario. An analogy for "dead scent" is the popcorn similarity. If someone is popping popcorn in a room and leaves that room, the odor of popcorn is still present when others walk in. The odor is in the room, but no popcorn is in the room.

On the other hand, if there is no scent available, the dog will not alert. Many times odor is not available. Drug traffickers and organizations go to a great deal of trouble to mask the odor of narcotics. They use a variety of different masking agents such as coffee, scented dryer sheets, axle grease, motor oil, peanut butter, and so on to try to prevent the animal from detecting the drug odor.

It is permissible for the handler to push on a bag, parcel, or piece of luggage to extract air. This is commonly known as "burping" or "breathing" the item. This provides the drug canine with an opportunity to detect the odor of narcotics. The officer cannot manipulate the bag, to enable him to feel the contents. This has been deemed by some courts as intrusive, and constitutes a search.

In the majority of cases, the properly trained dog will alert on the odor of narcotics. The dog has the ability of scent discrimination. It will run through all of the available masking agents, key in on the narcotic odor, and alert. The analogy many use is the "beef stew" description. When you come home from work and walk into your house and smell beef stew, you recognize it as just that. A trained narcotic canine also smells the beef stew, but can differentiate between the odors of carrots, peas, potatoes, celery, and beef. This is the difference between the ability of a properly trained dog and human ability.

Sometimes there is no scent available in a particular environment. A good example is parcel/package investigations. Drug traffickers will essentially remove the odor and the availability of the scent by extracting all of the air from the package. They may vacuum seal the substance. In this case, it is virtually impossible for the dog to alert on a particular suspected parcel. However, with time the odor will permeate through the packaging, depending on the volatility of the drug, and will become available. Sometimes drug traffickers may inadvertently contaminate a parcel, and in this case the dog will alert on the residual odor left by the person handling the package or other effects. A properly trained dog is extremely effective and should not be criticized if it sometimes misses drugs.

Current court case law is related directly to drug detection teams for the search and seizure of evidence. There is a purpose for conducting good legal searches. Bad searches can have a far-reaching negative effect on the use of a canine. The canine team must know the legal areas of deployment that dictate how the dog can be deployed in each search situation. Unfortunately, a lot of pressure is placed on handlers by co-workers during deployment. Law enforcement officers certainly want to locate drugs and make good cases. The added pressure to a canine team when told, "We know there are drugs in there" makes it difficult for them. The canine handler must be consistent and not be swayed by officers trying to convince him there are drugs in a particular location when the dog is not alerting.

## Currency Examinations

Inevitably, the drug canine will alert to currency. The quantities of currency will vary and will be in a variety of situations and environments. A parcel/package could contain a quantity of cash or the dog alerts on a piece of luggage containing money. Drug dogs are not trained to alert to the odor of money. However, if there is contamination of the currency by the drug trafficker, the dog is alerting to the odor of narcotics. This can easily happen when a trafficker handles drugs and the money or the cash is in proximity to the drugs.

Dr. Kenneth G. Furton, professor at Florida International University, Department of Chemistry, Miami, Florida, an expert in the fields of analytical chemistry and forensic chemistry, has done extensive research with respect to the theory that all U.S. currency is innocently contaminated with drugs, specifically microscopic quantities of cocaine.[1] He found that this premise is incorrect. This opinion is based on reasonable scientific certainty. His research and analysis have indicated that the odor of the controlled substance dissipates with time. A drug canine alerts on the odor of methyl benzoate, the dominant odor of cocaine. Methyl benzoate is a highly volatile substance and evaporates very quickly when handled and/or exposed to air. He believes that if a properly trained narcotics canine alerts on currency that has recently been in proximity to a significant quantity of drugs such as cocaine, it is not the result of innocent environmental contamination of

[1] From Furton, K.G., 2002, *J. Chromatographic Sci.*, 40, 147–155. With permission.

circulated U.S. currency by microscopic traces of cocaine. His studies have also shown that properly trained drug canines have consistently not alerted to large quantities of U.S. currency.

It is imperative that the handler document all currency finds and times when the dog does not alert to money as well. This could be under various conditions, such as money in a vehicle, pocket, purse, or other location where money is located and the dog does not alert. The handler can then testify that the drug canine does not always alert to money.

## Person Examinations and Passive Alert Dogs

Many agencies have used passive alert dogs (dogs that will sit when alerting to drugs) to conduct searches on people in a variety of environments. Such locations include airport, bus, and train terminals. The courts are divided on this issue. It appears that the majority of courts have ruled that a canine examination of a person, whether random or by design, is a search. Only a passive alert dog should be used to examine persons. An aggressive alert dog should never be used for this purpose.

Many courts indicate that "reasonable suspicion" is required to conduct an examination of a person for narcotic odor. There is case law relating to the examination of people in a variety of settings. It is suggested that domestic drug investigation groups contact their state or district attorney's office to research case law in a particular jurisdiction concerning this issue. If an agency is working with the U.S. Attorney's office in a particular district, the agent should contact that office to research federal case law regarding this issue.

Several cases of note that outline the issues of people examinations are divided on the practice. In *Horton v. Goose Creek Independent School District*, 690 F.2d 470, (1982), Fifth Circuit, the court indicated that a canine sniffing students was a search under the Fourth Amendment, and that canine searches of students could not be justified without reasonable suspicion. This particular environment was a school in which officers used a dog to conduct examinations of students.

In *Doe v. Renfrow*, 631 F.2d 91 (1980), Seventh Circuit, the court ruled that walking up aisles and sniffing by a narcotic detector dog did not violate students' rights. It was found that a dog sniff of students is not a search. This case is in direct opposition to *Horton v. Goose Creek*.

In *B.C. v. Plumas Unified School District*, 192 F.3d 1260 (1999), Ninth Circuit, the court agreed with the Horton case. A dog sniff of a person infringes on a reasonable expectation of privacy and constitutes a search. A random and suspicionless dog sniff search of a person is unreasonable.

There may be less of an expectation of privacy in a mass transit area, such as an airport, bus terminal, or train station. It is not recommended that a passive alert dog be used to examine persons in an area such as a street corner, full of people. Some parts of the country are more liberal on the issue of people examinations than others. It is important that the drug canine team stay current with changes in case law.

The question is frequently asked "Does the use of a canine constitute a search?" In the case *U.S. v. Place*, 462 U.S. 696 (1983), the court indicated that the use of a drug detection canine is not considered a search. The canine either proves or disproves only the presence of a narcotic odor. The use of a canine does not expose the contents of the bag to the general public. A number of cases side with the Place case, which indicates that the use of a canine is not a search.

Another factor that should be noted is the delay in the use of the canine, such as if the canine is summoned from a distant location. Depending on the particular circumstances in which the canine team is operating, during domestic drug investigations the delay and the deployment of the dog should be considered a factor. The courts are divided as far as the actual time of delay — anywhere from 30 to 80 minutes is not considered unreasonable.

## Courtroom Testimony

A canine handler should also be instructed in the correct and proper testimony related to his or her duties in that capacity. The handler should be prepared to answer questions from the prosecution and the defense team with respect to the drug dog. The prosecution wants to be ready to explain to a jury how your dog works, and discuss the reliability of the canine. The defense wants to discredit the dog and make it appear unreliable. Each has a different purpose. The handler wants to do the best he or she can to depict the dog's reliability and show that all records and training logs are in proper order.

The canine team may be challenged by the defense concerning the use and training of the drug canine. The handler must be prepared to answer all related questions about the dog. The handler should be prepared to describe how records and training logs are kept. Questions concerning how the drug canine finds drugs and how it alerts to the odor of narcotics. Does it sit or scratch? The defense attorney will ask if the dog has ever made a mistake, and if it has ever missed drugs. The handler must be honest and testify to anything that has occurred with the canine. There will be questions, such as "Has the dog ever alerted to anything other than drugs?" or "Has the canine ever false alerted?" These are all legitimate questions that may be part of testimony in a criminal trial.

# Conclusion

One of the greatest assets to domestic drug investigation groups is the drug canine team. This invaluable tool provides the ultimate instrument coupled with a good investigative effort in interdiction operations.

# Case Law

### U.S. v. Meyer and Skelcher (1976)

The defendants were convicted in the District Court (Puerto Rico). Held: That affidavit which indicated that dog had reacted positively to scent of narcotics in defendant's room aboard ship and which indicated that the dog was trained was sufficient to show reliability of the dog; and that affidavits established probable cause for search of defendant's hotel room.

### U.S. v. Spetz, 721 F.2d 1456 (1983)

A validly conducted dog sniff can supply the probable cause for issuing a search warrant only if sufficient reliability is established by the application for the warrant. In this case the affidavit contained mistaken information pertaining to the reliability of the two dogs who had alerted. (The percentage of accuracy was represented as higher.) The Court found the reliability misstatements to be immaterial because the alert of each dog corroborated the other. Also the record developed that the misstatements were not made in deliberate or reckless regard for the truth.

### U.S. v. Dicesare, 765 F.2d 890 (1985) 9th Cir.

In a motion to suppress evidence, the defense tried to get access to the U.S. Customs' Service Canine Training Manual in order to attack the agent's reasonableness in relying on the responses of his dog. Federal regulations prohibit disclose to the extent the manual would disclose investigative techniques. The Court provided some sections of the manual and not others after an in-camera review. On appeal the Court determined that the most critical information (the actual training records of the dogs) had been provided as well as 2 of 5 chapters of the manual and, therefore, if there was any error, it was harmless.

### U.S. v. Campbell, 920 F.2d 793 (1991) 11th Cir.

First dog failed to alert to truck; second dog brought in, picked up scent of marijuana near rear bumper. Officers removed bumper, discovered false bottom in bed of pickup hiding marijuana. Note: Court did not question dog's reliability.

### U.S. v. Nurse, 916 F.2d 20 (1990) D.C. Cir.

Handler testified first dog "showed some interest" in the suspect's tote bag, but "he wouldn't declare alert, because dog wasn't working properly." Second dog alerted. Court commented that sniff "appears to have been conducted diligently, notwithstanding the first dog's failure to perform properly."

### U.S. v. Battista, 876 F.2d 201 (1989) D.C. Cir.

Defendant challenged qualification, but not use, of dog on train. Court did not consider dog's training at all, because it was reasonable for officer, having asked DEA agent to provide dog, to rely on dog to furnish reasonable suspicion (not probable cause) without checking dog's background.

### U.S. v. Tartaglia, 864 F.2d 201 (1989) D.C. Cir.

Dog had 52 successes, 2 alerts where a "measurable deposit" of contraband not found, handler had 4 months training with dog; sufficiently reliable.

### U.S. v. Vermouth, 9th Cir. (1985) (unpublished), cert, denied, 475 U.S. 1045 (1986)

Dogs' reliability in windy conditions, susceptibility to fatigue, alleged reliability rate of 38 to 68% urged as grounds to exclude affidavit based on dogs' alert; counter affidavit satisfied court dogs were reliable; trial court's decision not to order field test of dogs was upheld.

### U.S. v. Williams, 726 F.2d 661 (1984) 10th Cir.

Detection dog graduated first in all categories at U.S. Customs School, alerted to two pieces of luggage, contraband found in only one of them.

### U.S. v. Robinson, 707 F.2d 811 (1983) 4th Cir.

Dog alerted to package containing drugs dog not trained on; alert still good for probable cause because dog trained to alert to packages handled by persons handling marijuana, cocaine, or heroin.

### State v. Latham, Supreme Court of Nevada (1981)

Defendant was convicted in Washoe County of possession of controlled substance, and he appealed. The Supreme Court of Nevada held that issuance of search warrant based upon canine investigation which indicated defendant's van might contain drugs was proper.

### U.S. v. Sentovich, 677, F.2d 834 (1982) 11th Cir.

Proof of dog's training sufficient to show reliability.

### U.S. v. Watson, 551 F. Supp. 1123 (1982) C.C.

"The technique is now sufficiently well established to make a formal recitation of police dogs curriculum vitae unnecessary in the content of ordinary warrant applications."

### Washington v. Gross, 789 P.2d 317 (1990) Wash. App.

Dog's reliability may be premised on statement that dog is trained or certified, without a showing of dog's track record, citing Watson. Here, telephonic warrant transcript stated "dog trained in narcotics detection, certified by two state organizations, utilized on other occasions." qualified in local and federal courts as an "expert narcotics dog." "This is more than sufficient," Court ruled.

### Wright v. Alaska, 795 P.2d 812 (1990) Alaska App.

Defendant complained that officer applying for search warrant based on dog's alert did not tell issuing magistrate that defendant disputed dog's alert. Court held this omission did not affect warrant as handler had observed the dog respond "literally hundreds of times" and defendant had "obvious motive" to deny alert.

Conservative recommendation for supporting search warrant based on alert:

    a. Exact training dog has received
    b. Standards or criteria employed in selecting dogs for training
    c. Standards dog required to meet to successfully complete training
    d. "Track record" up until search, including number of "false alerts" or
       mistakes

## Key Terms

| | |
|---|---|
| Aggressive alert | Cross-trained dog |
| "Burping" or "breathing" | Daily task records |
| Canine deployment | DEA license |
| Canine drives | Dead scent |
| Canine examinations | Dog certification |
| Constant task | Dog vendor |

Dual purpose dog
Drug rotation
Handling supplies
Heat sensor alarm
Loaded bags
Masking agents
Minimum standards
NATWDA
NNDA
Non-task related training
Olfactory bulb
Passive alert
Positive find
Pretrained canines

Quantitative and qualitative
    analysis
Reasonable suspicion
Researcher's license
Scent discrimination
Scent picture
Search find sheets
Standard operating procedures
    (SOP)
Training logs
Training records
USPCA
"Wash out"

# Hotel/Motel Interdiction 5

Hotels and motels — we have all stayed in them for business, pleasure, or while just passing through a city or town. These are legitimate purposes for utilizing the services of a hotel or motel. Hotels and motels are also places of opportunity for a variety of illicit activities, including narcotics trafficking. In this chapter we outline, in detail, how to initiate a hotel/motel interdiction program utilizing a network of sources, how to form partnerships with the hotel/motel community, how to identify indicators of possible criminal activity, and we describe investigative methods once the activity is identified. This is a unique and fascinating program in that it pulls away from traditional drug enforcement.

## What is Hotel/Motel Interdiction?

Hotel/motel interdiction programs have been in existence since the mid-1980s. It is believed that the Los Angeles Police Department, California, established the first such program in 1985. There are now a number of these programs in existence throughout the United States. This type of program is generally attached to an interdiction group, such as airport, train, and bus. Domestic interdiction counterdrug efforts have proven to be extremely successful. These efforts are sometimes characterized as an aggressive way to combat drug trafficking, and although that may be true, we think it is another innovative way to address the drug problem in our communities.

The purpose of this program is to identify hotel guests who are utilizing the establishment to conduct illegal activities, such as narcotics trafficking. Fundamentally, it is a fairly simple task that consists of the separation of legitimate guests from those who are utilizing hotels or motels for criminal activity. We are searching for anomalies; behavior that is different from that of other guests. We do that based on law enforcement training and experience.

91

We train hotel staff to identify certain types of behavior and to contact us when they observe this behavior. Certain patterns of behavior will indicate whether a guest may be involved in criminal activity. We refer to this as not displaying normal guest pattern activity. Human behavior while participating in criminal activity stands out, and a trained law enforcement officer knows what to look for. The law enforcement officer's experience provides him with a frame of reference and a foundation. An innocent individual who rents a room will generally display normal conduct, and does not draw attention based on his or her behavior. An individual who may be involved in criminal activity displays certain characteristics or indicators of behavior, which we will examine and explore in this chapter,

Once the behavior is identified, investigators initiate an inquiry and may commence an investigation to determine what type of criminal activity the person(s) may be involved in. Critics of this type of program argue that a hotel guest has an "expectation of privacy" regarding personal information he or she has provided to the hotel, and that is certainly true in some circumstances. All the rights and privileges of law are afforded to a hotel guest when he or she rents a room. However, law enforcement has the obligation to examine, explore, and investigate possible criminal activity at a hotel or motel when it comes to their attention. In this program, law enforcement networks with hotel staff, and staff has been trained to contact law enforcement when suspicious conduct is observed. Hotels have an obligation as a community business partner to make law enforcement aware of possible criminal activity. The police are not interested in legitimate guests who are utilizing a facility for legitimate purposes.

## Benefits to the Hotel/Motel Community

The hotel/motel industry is a multibillion dollar a year business. The *American Hotel & Lodging Association: 2001 Lodging Industry Profile*, which included the year 2000 statistical figures of the lodging industry, indicated $108.5 billion dollars in sales were made. As of the year 2000 there were 53,500 properties, 4.1 million rooms, and an average occupancy rate of 63.7%. The year 2000 surpassed 1999 as the most profitable year in the lodging industry, grossing $24.0 billion in pretax profits. As we can see, the hotel/motel community is big business, and millions of people utilize their services for a variety of reasons, most of which are legitimate. However, there is an element of society who uses hotels and motels for illicit purposes, such as prostitution, drug trafficking, and other criminal activity. When we ask a business to volunteer for this program, we must be careful not to disrupt their business, and we must be professional at all times to avoid disturbing legitimate guests.

The benefits to the hotel/motel community when implementing this type of program are obvious. The liaison with law enforcement on a continuous basis is an exceptional benefit to a business. Their participation will include access to the hotel/motel interdiction group 24 hours a day, 7 days a week to report suspicious activity. In addition, the group will provide speaking engagements by officers at hotel/motel meetings with staff concerning other related awareness issues, such a drug abuse, credit card fraud, theft, robbery, and other criminal activities.

## How Do We Get Started?

Selling this type of program to your administrators and supervisors is key to the success of the program. This type of investigative technique requires commitment by the agency, whether federal, state, or local. The agency must embrace the interdiction philosophy, which is not traditional narcotic enforcement. It is a controversial but extremely effective method of narcotic enforcement. Time to initiate, retain, and maintain an interdiction program is required, and commitment is the key to its success. We want to preface all this by noting that we don't want to give the reader the impression that hotel/motel investigations of this type are easy. These cases certainly are not simple cases to make, and can be extremely challenging. The difficulty is that the investigator does not always have the benefit of having a traditional informant or undercover officer on the inside. He simply has information from a hotel source, such as the front desk clerk, about a suspicious guest or guests. What is frustrating for the hotel squad members is that often they are looking in from the outside and trying to determine what is really going on. This is where training and experience come into play; where the investigator deploys a variety of investigative methodologies to solve the puzzle. On many occasions law enforcement is right on track; however, many cases are unpredictable and hotel squad members sometimes make contact with suspicious guests prematurely. It may be a case where a drug transaction has not yet taken place, or the parties are simply in negotiation and narcotics have not been exchanged. Challenging, to say the least; frustrating and demanding at most.

As with all interdiction programs, supervisors and investigators should inform the U.S. Attorney's Office or District Attorney's Office of the agency's intention of starting such a program. Ultimately, the prosecutors will litigate cases that will be made as a result of the program. It is of great importance to have the prosecutor on board, so that he may be prepared to go to court on this type of case. The U.S Attorney's Office or the State or District Attorney's Office should research case law; federal and state, to provide law enforcement with information relating to such cases in their particular jurisdiction. Although prosecutors may be prosecuting traditional drug cases, such as undercover drug buys, search warrants, trafficking, and conspiracy cases, interdiction cases are a completely different animal. Bring relative case law to the prosecutor's attention. It is suggested that investigators research case law related to hotel/motel investigations and interdiction in general. The Internet is a good source of information. Various legal web sites such as www.Lawcrawler.com and www.thecre.com/fedlaw/default.htm are good resources.

Once the prosecutor is aware of your intentions, the supervisor should select a group of investigators who are interested in working these types of cases. A hotel/motel interdiction team is generally worked from the police agency's narcotics division. Although other segments of the agency, such as the patrol or special operations groups (street crimes unit) can work a hotel/motel interdiction program with success, a dedicated group from the narcotics division is most successful. An investigator should possess certain traits important for an interdiction officer such as flexibility, creativeness, assertiveness, and patience. He should be a self-starter with good interview skills, good surveillance techniques, and knowledge of search and seizure.

How many investigators should be part of this hotel/motel group? That would depend on how many members of the agency are working other active interdiction programs and how many officers supervision is willing to dedicate to working hotels. Experience has shown that it takes several people to effectively work such a program. The number of people available will dictate how many hotels are put on-line. The agency must evaluate its resources and make that decision. If, for example, three to five hotels are utilized in the program, at least three investigators should be assigned to initiate and maintain the program in a hotel. Other support personnel will be needed to assist in hotel investigations initiated during the course of program, for surveillance, for example.

We suggest that this program be implemented through partnerships with the business community. These partnerships or business watch programs are critical to the success of interdiction programs, especially hotel/motel investigations. They are all voluntary in nature. We cannot force hotel and motel owners and managers to participate in the program. The premise of the program is similar to that of the Community Policing Concept in that we are working with local businesses, specifically hotels and motels, to solve our problems together as a community. We must remember, however, that businesses are created and sustained by money, and we do not want to disrupt the normal business flow.

You can research nearby jurisdictions within the county or state to inquire if they have a hotel program in which they are currently engaged. Why reinvent the wheel, when other agencies can provide information and guidance to start a hotel/motel program. There a number of programs nationally that have proven to be extremely successful. Several federal agencies participate in hotel investigation in conjunction with other interdiction programs, such as airport, bus, and train. That is how we started our own programs in Florida and New Mexico. Police agencies may want to collaborate and initiate a regional group with several agencies participating in such a program. This is an effective method for smaller jurisdictions. Most agencies are happy to provide an agency that is starting interdiction efforts with information such as how to start, what to look for in a particular program, common pitfalls, and what documents to utilize. Most will send examples of "commitment letters" to provide to hotel/motel managers and owners. These letters are professional documents given to hotel/motel managers and owners outlining an agency's intent in creating a hotel/motel program with their assistance. Ask the other agency for a list of possible criminal indicators that they may be using. This will assist in providing ideas for the type of behavior they are concentrating on.

## Selecting Hotels to Implement the Program

Once the decision is made to implement this type of program, the agency must look at its jurisdiction and the layout of its city or county. Identify how many hotels and motels are in the jurisdiction. Many ask the difference between a hotel and motel. According to the American Hotel and Lodging Association, there really is none. However, the term "motel" is derived from the term "motor hotel," which originally meant that the hotel provided parking. The difference between the two is that a hotel often provides more "service" and has more amenities than a motel.

The police agency must look at what is manageable by examining its resources and area. It has been proven time and time again when implementing interdiction programs that if you bite off more than you can chew, the program will generally not be as successful. Hotel/motel programs are much more fruitful if investigators choose a certain few hotels and concentrate their efforts on them. As the program progresses, the investigator will find that some hotels are more productive than others, and the number will be narrowed down, which will make the program easier to manage.

For the purpose of this chapter we will refer to the establishments as hotels, which include a motel setting. Hotels are generally categorized into three types: large, five-star; medium, mid-sized; and small, mom-and-pop. The differences are of course evident by size alone. A large five-star hotel may have several hundred rooms with high room rates. Examples include the Hilton, Marriott, Hyatt, and Sheraton chain hotels. Mid-sized hotels are moderately priced and are the most popular with travelers. Examples are Holiday Inn, Ramada, Super 8, Hampton Inn, and Motel 6 chains. A mom-and-pop style motel is generally smaller, owner operated, and inexpensive. The question often arises as to which type of hotel generally has the most successful hotel/motel interdiction programs. It has been our experience and that of many other programs nationally that the mid-sized hotel is usually the most successful, once a program has been initiated. There are several reasons for this; a medium-sized hotel is not as busy as a large hotel, and the staff is more likely to identify unusual guest behavior. Other reasons are the locations of many mid-range hotels, such as near busy interstates or thoroughfares, and close to transportation centers such as airports, and train and bus stations. This does not necessarily mean that drug traffickers and other criminals do not stay in large or small hotels. However, generally in large hotels it is difficult to keep track of activity by trained staff, and experience has shown that small mom-and-pop motels are not usually very successful in participating in interdiction programs. Many owner operators live on premises and may indicate to the investigator that they will assist, but then rarely cooperate or call.

Once the hotels have been identified, the selection process commences. What hotels are probably more suited for this program? Identify hotels that are geographically significant, such as near or off main thoroughfares, interstates, and highways. Good choices are hotels near transportation centers. Drug traffickers will often stop at a hotel that is near a highway or airport because they generally want easy access and do not want to be stuck deep in a city or a rural area. However, they can surprise us by being in a hotel where we might not think they would rent a room. This plays heavily into what the drug trafficker is doing at the time.

There are many factors involved into where the drug dealer rents a room. Psychological factors play a role. Drug dealers are often creatures of habit and feel comfortable in staying in the same hotel and room. Many dealers have told us that they felt safe in a particular brand of hotel where they were familiar with the layout. Other drug dealers may feel that a particular hotel is safe because they have never been compromised there. Other factors include the type of activity the dealer is engaging in at the time. For example, he may only be negotiating a transaction with no actual exchange of drugs at that time. A drug trafficker may not pick a particular hotel for certain, but we have found the above often occurs. The police agency must work with what it has in its jurisdiction and try to narrow down its selection of hotels.

## Contacting Hotel Management

Once hotels have been selected, the management should be contacted to inform them of the agency's intent to initiate a program at their hotel with their cooperation. A supervisor or designee should contact a general manager, manager, or owner via telephone to set up a face-to-face meeting to explain the program. The telephone conversation should be brief, indicating that the police agency is starting a new program with the cooperation of the hotel/motel community, and that the agency would like to set up an appointment to explain the program at the manager's convenience. The selling of the program is much more successful when the officer has personal contact with management to explain it. The vast majority of hotel management will invite the investigator for a meeting to learn what the program is about. They may have heard about such a program or have participated in one when they worked at other hotels in other areas.

Many agencies have authored a letter of commitment (Figure 5.1) to provide to hotel management explaining the program. This is a professional statement indicating the police agency's intent and giving an explanation of the program. The letter of commitment should be on the police agency's letterhead, as illustrated in the sample. It essentially indicates that the police agency is seeking the hotel/motel business community's assistance in establishing a narcotics interdiction program. It indicates that criminal types often spend time in hotels and that the hotel/motel interdiction program enlists their cooperation. The aim of the hotel/motel interdiction program is to detect and apprehend individuals through the hotel/motel community and their staff. The letter explains that there are a variety of indicators that will assist in detection of potential criminal activity occurring on the hotel premises. It is suggested that the notification should be made to law enforcement in the interest of security and welfare of their guests. In providing information, hotel staff are not acting as police agents, but merely as concerned citizens.

Additionally, the letter of commitment may include a separate list of indicators to assist hotel staff in the detection of potential criminal activity that may be occurring in and around the hotel. The letter of commitment provides information on how to contact the investigators that will be assigned to this program.

The letter of commitment should be prepared prior to meeting with hotel management. Once all the information is organized, the investigator can set an appointment for the meeting. Generally, it will take place at the hotel in which the program is to be initiated.

The law enforcement agency has now made a decision to initiate this type of program and must sell the program with 100% commitment. The old adage "out of sight, out of mind" certainly applies here. If the agency starts a program and does not follow through, hotel staff will not call to report suspicious information.

**Use of Agency Letterhead**

The **Agency Name** is seeking your assistance in establishing a Narcotics Interdiction Program designed to have a direct impact on the hotel/motel business community.

We are currently living in a very mobile society, where people are constantly traveling from one place to another for business and pleasure. The traveling public is the foundation of the hotel/motel business.

Unfortunately, as the general public has become more mobile, so has the criminal element within our society. These people find an element of safety by leading a transient lifestyle. By constantly moving from place to place, it is difficult for law enforcement to detect and apprehend them. The majority of these people are professional criminals who derive most of all of their income through criminal activity. These activities include narcotics trafficking, armed robbery, credit card fraud, flimflam operations, etc. Many will commit any crime of opportunity.

These criminal types often spend time in hotels and motels during their travels. It is the intention of the Hotel/Motel Narcotics Interdiction Program to make you aware of the problem we face and to enlist the cooperation of our hotel and motel community in **City or County Name**. It is the aim of the Hotel/Motel Narcotics Interdiction Program to detect and apprehend these subjects through the help of the hotel/motel community. These people are bad for business and detrimental to the general community.

There are indicators, which will assist you in the detection of potential criminal activity occurring in and around your business.

Notification should be made to law enforcement in the interest of security and with the welfare of your guests in mind. In providing information, you are not acting as a police agent, but a concerned citizen.

Guests who exhibit one or more of the activities listed may or may not be engaged in criminal activity. The **Agency Name** requests that the only action you take is to observe and report those things seen during the course of your normal duties. It is the responsibility of trained law enforcement officers to evaluate your information and take appropriate action.

The investigator presenting this letter can offer a more comprehensive explanation of the Hotel/Motel Narcotics Interdiction Program.

Your assistance in this matter is greatly appreciated and is assured that any information you provided will be handled in a confidential manner.


Sincerely,

**(Signed by Agency or Division Head)**


## Figure 5.1

Once you have made a commitment to the ownership and/or management of the hotel and provided them with the information and training, follow-through is important. If you do not respond to calls or information, it has been our experience that the staff will not contact you on a regular basis, if at all.

When contact is made with hotel management or ownership, investigators should introduce themselves and provide information concerning the program. Such information should include the explanation that participation in the program is strictly voluntary on the part of the hotel. Explain that this program is a business-watch type program, in which law enforcement and the hotel community will work together to identify illicit activity in and around the hotel premises. Tell them that you would like their assistance by training their staff on certain indicators or behavior, which will better enable them to detect potential criminal activity. We would like them to be our "eyes and ears," and if suspicious activity is identified, to contact law enforcement to take the appropriate action. Emphasize that you do not want hotel employees to take any enforcement action regarding any activity.

We stress to hotel management and ownership that we would like them to only notify us to report suspected criminal activity. The investigator should stress that the hotel staff is not acting as an agent of the police, but rather as a concerned citizen through the notification process to us.

If management agrees to participate in the program, the next step would be to schedule a training session with hotel staff. Generally, hotels have either weekly or bi-weekly staff meetings in which this training session can be conducted. Management can identify a date for the training either at their meetings or another specified date and time. At this point, you should present the letter of commitment and list of indicators to the manager. The benefit to the hotel staff should be outlined to the manager, with an explanation of the program and contact with investigators on a 24-hour basis. Contact numbers such as office telephone numbers and pager numbers should be provided during the initial meeting. Investigators should advise management that the program is designed for hotel staff to feel comfortable with investigators, who will routinely have contact with staff. This allows the staff to feel free to provide valued information and intelligence on suspicious guests.

Another benefit to the hotel is that the investigators can provide speaking engagements at hotel staff meetings for employees concerning drug-related issues and robbery awareness information. Once the training session has been scheduled, the officers should request specific hotel employees to be present for the training. Historically, staff such as front desk personnel, executive housekeepers, and security personnel are the most suitable and are in a position to provide information to law enforcement regarding suspicious guests. Of the above staff positions, generally the front desk personnel are the "bread and butter" employees who can provide you with the most intelligence regarding guests, because front desk people have the most contact with guests who are checking in. Much of the suspicious activity that we will be outlining occurs while a guest checks into the hotel.

The executive housekeeper is the "head" housekeeper for the hotel. Generally, the executive housekeeper enters all of the rooms during the cleaning process. She has access to all of the housekeepers under her supervision. We sometimes suggest that investigators do not train regular housekeeping staff because of their transient nature. However, a housekeeper may be identified once the program has been implemented, who has an interest in participating and will be successful in providing information. In addition, security personnel, individuals who are in and around the hotel premises, may be of benefit to the investigator, as they may observe certain behavior and conduct while conducting their routine security operations.

Be prepared to answer questions regarding any liability concerns that the management may have if they participate in this type of a program. This frequently arises during the initial contact with management. We have found in our experience that many of the questions asked by management concern their staff and how they are going to participate. Remember that this program is strictly voluntary and that hotel management can make a decision not to participate. Hotels are in the business of making money, and we do not want to disrupt the normal course of business of the establishment. That information should be reflected during the initial meeting with the management or ownership. The management may want to know if the hotel is liable in any fashion for providing information to law enforcement regarding suspicious guests. We advocate that you respond honestly regarding their participation in this type of a program. Management should be advised that certainly, they could be sued for just about anything. We cannot guarantee that the hotel will not be sued for information given during participation in this type of a program, and, we cannot predict what an individual or individuals will do once the program is implemented and possible arrests are made as a result of the information that was provided by hotel staff.

Some additional frequently asked questions by management are how their staff will participate in a program with regard to witness issues such as courtroom testimony. We respond honestly that employees could be subpoenaed to participate in a deposition or trial by either the prosecution or defense team associated with a case. We explain that we conduct investigations independent from hotel/motel sources, and that the staff will not be used as witnesses unless absolutely necessary. An independent case is when an employee staff member of the hotel provides information about a guest and we independently confirm that information and make a case based on our own observations, which may include the behavior and conduct of the suspicious guest.

Hotel management will be concerned about the safety of their staff if the suspect(s) returns to the hotel to cause any type of harm to their employees. This is a legitimate concern; however, the investigators should provide management with honest dialogue in that they cannot predict whether an individual will return and cause harm to their staff. Based on our experience in working a hotel program and speaking with other law enforcement agencies around the country, it appears that this is a rare occurrence.

Management may ask about damage to hotel property — if there are going to be doors forced open or other damage. In many cases investigators take enforcement action, such as arrests and detainments, off of hotel property. Contact on a consensual basis is taken off the premises if possible. Sometimes that is not possible. For example, if an exchange is made on hotel property, officers need to take immediate appropriate action. Hotel management should be advised that law enforcement will do everything possible not to cause any damage to hotel property. There may be instances where search warrants need to be conducted on hotel property as part of the investigative effort, when enforcement action cannot take place away from the property. If dynamic entries need to be made into hotel rooms, certainly a door or other property may be damaged. Hotel management should be told that any damage to hotel property will be dealt with appropriately, and that the agency and its risk management section will compensate the hotel.

One of the most frequently asked questions by management is about a guest's "expectation of privacy." The answer is that a guest is afforded all rights and privileges that a person would have in his home. Nothing changes with respect to search and seizure and privacy in a rented room. The question may be asked whether the hotel staff can provide the police with guest registration information such as guest names, addresses, telephone numbers, and vehicle and auto tag numbers. Law enforcement should contact their state or district attorney to locate any possible case law related to this.

Much of what law enforcement does is based on case law, related to a specific area of investigation. With respect to the ability to examine the registration of a guest at a hotel, the case *U.S. v. Cormier*, 220 F.3d 1103, (9th Circuit, 2000) addresses the expectation of privacy issue as it relates to hotel registration information. In the Cormier case, defense counsel argued that the records are kept by law for business regulation purposes and not for police investigatory purposes. The court held that even if that were true, Cormier still had not alleged a Fourth Amendment violation in which he had no expectation to privacy in the records. The court indicated that unlike bank records that contain highly sensitive and personal information, motel records merely have name and address. The court reaffirmed its view that a person does not have a privacy interest in information revealed to a third party, even for a limited purpose, on the assumption that they will not betray that confidence or that the information would not be revealed to others. The key factor in the Cormier case is that a person does not possess a reasonable expectation of privacy in an item for which he has no possession or ownership interest.

The rule of thumb however, is that a hotel guest has a reasonable expectation of privacy in a room no different from that which he enjoys in his own home. The Cormier case is a good example of an explanation regarding hotel registration as it relates to the expectation of privacy issue. So what do we tell the hotel manager when he asks "Can we provide you with information about our guests?" and "How far do we go?" The officers should be prepared to answer that question; as outlined in the Cormier case, stating that there appears to be no expectation of privacy when one provides the information to a third party. So essentially, law enforcement can examine registrations or folio information in a hotel outlined in this particular piece of case law. Law enforcement should always respond to the concerns of hotel management honestly and to the best of their ability.

Once investigators have answered the questions of management to their satisfaction and explained the program in detail, a date to train management and staff of the hotel should be scheduled. As stated previously, management is usually asked to attend the training as well as a variety of staff from the hotel including the front desk personnel, executive housekeepers, and security employees. Once the session is scheduled, law enforcement officers should prepare to conduct a thorough and complete training for staff.

## Training of Hotel Management and Staff

Most hotels should be able to provide space to conduct training of their staff. Law enforcement should not utilize police jargon, which hotel staff may not understand. The information provided and method of contacting investigators should be as simple as possible.

At the training session, introduce yourself to the staff and provide an overview of the program. Investigators should mention that the hotel/motel program is a national program in which hotels have participated for a number of years. Before beginning the training, an attendance sheet should be filled out by the participants. This provides the law enforcement agency with a record of individuals who attended the training.

We have found during the training process that staff has observed certain behavior of guests that they thought was suspicious. Once the staff is trained to analyze guest behavior, they have an outlet to contact law enforcement to provide the information. We stress to hotel staff that we only want them to be our "eyes and ears", and that they should not take any action, but rather report information to the law enforcement officer. Once it is reported, law enforcement will take the appropriate steps to verify the information and investigate the conduct. Provide an opportunity for the staff to discuss their observations of actions and behavior of guests.

It is suggested that a "show-and-tell" portion be incorporated in the training program to provide management and staff with information through photographs, paraphernalia, and possibly a video that explains the program. Photographs have been very helpful in showing what narcotics look like or how they are packaged or secreted. A number of police agencies in the United

States have prepared short 3- to 5-minute videos featuring the hotel/motel program, explaining what the program is designed to do and breaking down the indicators that outline the conduct of the guest who may be involved in criminal activity. A video can provide the hotel management and staff with a visual of what the program is attempting to accomplish.

Once the program is explained, investigators should then explain each indicator and break down its significance. This explanation of indicators is done verbally, and if a video is available, it is presented in that fashion. Investigators may also provide a list of the indicators of possible criminal activity to each staff member. The staff should be provided with information on how to contact law enforcement once they are trained and operating in their particular capacities. Along with the indicators, detectives provide names and telephone numbers of the investigators who are going to be participating in this program.

A sticker for the internal telephones of the hotel for areas such as behind the front desk is helpful. This sticker generally is bright green, blue, or yellow, and will be placed on telephone receiver. The sticker should have the police agency's name with a star or badge, with a digital pager number and directions on its use (Figure 5.2). This type of sticker has proven to be extremely successful in that it is a constant reminder to hotel staff about the program, especially front desk personnel, every time they use the telephone. The telephone number can be to a digital pager that the supervisor or investigator carries at all times.

Investigators should respond to the concerns of hotel staff in a positive and honest fashion. Housekeeping staff will ask many questions as to the extent they can access in the normal course of their duties. Staff should not be encouraged to go beyond the scope of their particular duties. For example, a housekeeper should not be encouraged to conduct searches for law enforcement while she has access to a room, and front desk personnel should not be encouraged to listen in on telephone conversations between guests and outside parties. Sometimes overzealous staff and management want to provide information, but overstep their bounds. It should be made clear that it is not appropriate for staff to provide information based on activities that were not discovered as part of their normal course of duties. However, if the staff should overhear a conversation, they can certainly report the information. Once management or staff become involved in areas that are not part of their duties, it should be explained that they will become agents of the police and would have to testify in the government's or state's behalf. Their assistance is critical in this type of a program, and we would like them to observe and report the conduct they observe. Once management staff has been trained in the mission of the program, the difficult task of implementing the hotel/motel interdiction process begins.

# STICKER FOR PHONE

Figure 5.2

## Implementing the Program

The mission of the hotel/motel interdiction program is to identify drug traffickers and other criminals who are using the establishment to conduct their illicit activities. Partnerships established with the hotel community enables law enforcement to identify and, when appropriate, investigate any guests who exhibit certain suspicious behavior. Establishing a continuous liaison with managers, front desk personnel, security, maintenance, and housekeeping provides law enforcement with excellent sources of information within the hotel/motel community in their jurisdiction. We look at these hotel employees as sources of information — they are not your traditional informants. A traditional informant in drug law enforcement is an individual who provides information and often actively participates in drug investigations up to and including the purchase of narcotics for law enforcement under controlled circumstances. There are several suggestions regarding how law enforcement can utilize their sources in police reports or other documentation. Some categories of cooperating individuals are: confidential informants or cooperating individuals (C.I.), investigative sources (I.S.), confidential sources (C.S.), and anonymous sources (A.S.). This is how many agencies refer to their sources of information, and any one of these can be used in preparing documents such as search warrants, investigative reports, and other court documents. When the hotel/motel interdiction group receives information via a source about suspicious activity in a particular hotel, the investigator should refer to the hotel source as one of these categories, preferably an investigative source.

During training of hotel staff, investigators should express to management and staff that whenever possible, investigations will be conducted independent of hotel sources. An independent case or investigation would mean that investigators would confirm the information that is received by the hotel source but will not act solely on that information. This avoids the need for staff to be utilized as witnesses unless absolutely necessary, thus minimizing their exposure. Generally, the hotel group does not advertise the interdiction program to the media for a number of reasons, one of which is that law enforcement does not want to provide information that drug traffickers may have access to. If the media does ask about the program, the law enforcement agency should verify that the program does exist.

Many hotel groups have established zones, specific hotels assigned to specific investigators. This is designed so the hotel staff will have a relationship with the same investigator and will feel comfortable about providing valued information on suspicious guests. Hotel staff sees the same individual, and this liaison creates a trust between staff and law enforcement. Once zones and hotels have been assigned to particular investigators, it is imperative that the officer makes frequent face-to-face contact with hotel staff while attempting to obtain information regarding any suspicious activity. Access to registrations should be given to law enforcement with management's consent. This should be agreed upon before initiating the program. Responses to calls for suspicious activity should be made, especially at the start of the program, at just about any level. The information should be evaluated as it occurs. An investigator should respond or be a facilitator to any action that needs to be taken regarding information provided by the hotel staff.

On many occasions we have initially responded to a report of something minor such as stolen towels or other items taken from a room. Frequently, hotel groups will get calls about loud parties or loud guests. If the investigators do not respond quickly, the staff will be reluctant to call back. Provide feedback as allowed by the law to hotel employees on suspicious guests or activity. If the staff would like to know how things turned out, you may want to go back and tell them that a particular piece of information worked out and that an arrest was made and drugs were seized. If there is a situation where no drugs were seized or no arrest was made and the behavior was suspicious, you may still go to the employee and tell him what occurred. Without feedback to staff members and without responding to staff information promptly, the calls will diminish and so will the program. If you become complacent and not go into the hotels to make face-to-face contact with staff, there is no question that the program begins to break down and the information diminishes. The old adage "out of sight, out of mind" certainly applies here.

The amount of personnel needed initially to establish this type of a program depends on the police agency resources. This would depend on the quantity of hotels that are put on-line and how many investigators can be dedicated to the hotel squad. There is no question that there is a burnout factor if there are fewer investigators involved in the program. While initiating the program, the agency should have a commitment of various operational components including support from patrol division and other investigative operation divisions including a drug canine team.

The drug canine team is a significant component of any interdiction program and is critical to the investigative success of hotel interdiction. The most successful way to use a drug canine and handler is to have them assigned to the narcotics group and be dedicated solely to the group, as discussed in Chapter 4. Based on our experience, a single-purpose properly trained dog, rather than a dual-trained dog, is much more successful. A single-purpose dog, whether an aggressive alert or passive alert dog, that is solely trained for drug detection is an enormous resource. Generally, if the hotel group is assigned to a narcotics division, this is the way to go. If the agency is implementing a hotel program from the patrol operations division or other special investigative group, a dog typically used is the dual-purpose dog that works patrol functions such as tracking and also has training in narcotics detection. Either way, it is important that the trainer be part of a good training regimen for his or her dog.

Some agencies provide monetary payment or rewards for reliable information from a hotel source. If the agency policy and hotel management policy permit such payments, it is certainly something that should be explored. Investigators should look for signs of abuse as with any informant in the drug enforcement arena. An informant may take advantage of the situation and provide erroneous information. However, if a hotel source provides you with valuable information and good solid cases are developed, it is certainly an option for the law enforcement agency to provide some sort of reward or payment.

The payment process for hotel/motel personnel should be the same as with any traditional informant with receipt verification and witness verification by another officer. The purpose and justification for the payment should be documented in the police agency's documentation file.

Many investigators ask who the most reliable hotel source is once a program is established, as previously discussed. The front desk person or night auditor is probably the most valuable asset or source of information for a hotel squad. They are known as "bread and butter" employees in this type of a program. The reasons are many: the front desk employee is the person who makes contact with the guest at check-in. He will notice much of the guest's behavior from the initial check-in to the activities of the guest after entering the room. The front desk person is generally the one who monitors the telephone activity and if incoming calls that appear to be suspicious are being made to a specific room, the front desk person will be able to monitor that activity. The front desk person or night auditor will be able to describe nervous behavior that a guest may display. In hotels and many motels, there are three shifts that front desk personnel occupy: the day shift, evening shift, and the night auditor. Hotel staff other than front desk, such as the executive housekeeper and staff housekeepers will also be able to provide information. They work in other environments and could provide insight into other suspicious behavior.

## Investigative Methodologies

A hotel room should generally be treated the same as a private residence; the guest enjoys the same expectation of privacy as in his or her home. The hotel room should be considered a private dwelling if the guest has paid or arranged to pay for the room and has not been asked to leave by hotel staff or management. A guest maintains the same privacy rights until it is clear that he has abandoned the room. If the guest has personal items in the room, it should be presumed that the individual intends to return; thus he maintains the same privacy rights.

We have categorized hotel investigations into two separate models. These categories are cold versus tip investigations. A cold investigation is a proactive self-initiating investigation in which the investigator examines various information to determine if there is a guest in the hotel who is displaying certain conduct or other factors indicative of criminal behavior. A tip investigation is generally an investigation initiated by a tip from a hotel staff member, such as a front desk person or executive housekeeper.

In a cold investigation, the officer makes contact with the front desk person and asks to examine the guest list, which is generally a computerized list of all guests occupying rooms in that hotel. Most hotels use computers to store and track guest information. Generally, a computer guest list will provide the guest's name, the room that he is occupying, the purpose for which he is staying at the hotel, and whether he is in or out. Despite providing limited information, the list should be scrutinized for names that the investigator may recognize as drug traffickers from their area or nearby areas. The computer-generated list will indicate if the person is there on business or pleasure. What we have found on many occasions is that the suspicious guest will indicate that he is there for pleasure, or may indicate a fictitious business name that often will stand out, such as a very generic or strange name for a business. Once the officer examines the computer guest list, he should then examine the actual hotel registration card the guest filled out.

The registration cards are either kept in alphabetical order or by room number in a container called a "bucket." This examination of the registration cards is called "running the bucket." Investigators are looking for names that they recognize from the computer-generated list. We have all seen and filled out hotel registrations and know the information that is asked: name, address, telephone number, business name, and vehicle information such as type, color, and tag number. The investigator should look for subtle things that may stand out when he examines the registration. Things to be look out for are common names such as Smith and Jones. That is not to say that an individual by the name of Smith or Jones is engaged in criminal activity; however, further investigation is recommended. Look for anomalies that may appear on the registration form such as addresses that may not exist or numbers such as house numbers that may have been inverted, telephone numbers that are fictitious or have inverted numbers. We have found that for good reason, drug traffickers, couriers, and other criminal types manipulate information in attempt to conceal their identity. They do not want to be found in a hotel if they are conducting criminal activities.

Other details to examine are whether the guest is a local or out-of-town guest. Investigators should also look for areas that are known sources for drugs from a particular city or state. Most hotels provide detailed telephone billing from rooms from which calls have been made. Hotels may provide free local calls. Others charge for local calls, and the number will appear on the telephone log. Investigators can examine the telephone calls and if a database is available, information regarding telephone numbers can be provided. The guest may be calling source cities or states from the motel room in addition to local traffickers. Once the subscribed information has been identified and the subject called has intelligence for narcotics or criminal activity, the investigator may pursue the information further. Law enforcement should obtain subpoenas for nonpublished numbers. In addition, subpoenas should be utilized for information that may be used in police reports where legal documents such as telephone subscriber information is requested.

While investigators are researching registered guest information, a narcotics canine team can conduct random parking lot examinations to examine vehicles in the hotel lot for the odor of narcotics. Remember that investigators must have management's consent before initiating these cold investigations and being on property. It is a good practice to contact management or a staff member who has been through the training process to inform them that investigators are on hotel property. This could become a court issue later where management or staff is asked by the defense if investigators had consent to come on property to conduct random type inquiries.

Time of day is a factor in deploying a narcotics canine. Temperature and other environmental factors play a role in the success of the canine, so discuss these with your canine officer. If the dog is deployed in a random fashion and alerts to the odor of narcotics, there are several available options for the investigator. One is to wait out the owner or driver, make contact with him when he approaches the vehicle and ask for a consensual search of the vehicle. If the individual refuses, then a search warrant is drafted. Before the individual comes out to the vehicle, the investigator must do his homework. Prior to an individual being approached, it is important that indices inquiries be made regarding the owner of the vehicle. A room should be identified if possible to determine the driver and other individuals who may be present. The vehicle could be a rental vehicle or it could be registered to someone not staying in the hotel. If this information is not provided during registration, it is difficult to identify who is related to the vehicle. However, if a subject is identified, the appropriate investigative steps should be taken. A background criminal history inquiry should be made with a check on arrest warrants. Any intelligence concerning the individual regarding narcotics trafficking or other criminal activities is important. A driver's license check should be done in addition to information regarding any violent behavior information that the individual may have displayed in the past. Surveillance of the car and hotel room should be carried out to observe the activities of the suspect. Many cases have been made by conducting random examinations of vehicles in hotel parking lots.

### Case Study

In Albuquerque, New Mexico, in a random examination of a hotel parking lot, the narcotics detection dog alerted for the odor of narcotics on a Ryder truck. Investigators were conducting cold operations in the hotel and identified the driver, who had rented a room at the local hotel. A surveillance was initiated, at which time the subject was seen approaching the vehicle. He was encountered and refused a consent search, which was provided as an option to him. The investigators told him that a narcotics detection dog had alerted for the odor of narcotics from the Ryder truck. Since the subject refused the option of a consent search, a search warrant was drafted and executed. A quantity of 1500 pounds of marijuana was discovered during the execution of the search warrant. The marijuana was destined for the eastern seaboard of the United States.

While a canine is conducting examinations in the parking lot, investigators should drive through or walk the parking lot of the hotel. This is known as "running the lot." The purpose for doing this is to see if investigators recognize any of the vehicles in the parking lot as belonging to possible local dealers. In addition, officers should look for vehicles from drug source states or cities. However, just because a vehicle is from a source state or city does not mean that the owner or driver is involved in narcotic or criminal activity. An inquiry regarding the driver and his behavior should be conducted to determine if he is possibly involved in narcotics trafficking. Once a vehicle has been found to have a vehicle tag from a source state, such as Texas or Florida, the inquiry begins. At that point, hotel squad members would conduct an indices inquiry on a potential guest. Surveillance may be initiated if it is determined that the guest or other individuals with him are displaying certain characteristics or behavior with respect to criminal activity. Another option, once it has been determined either via surveillance or background that an individual may be involved in criminal activity, is to collect the garbage/trash from the room in which the individual was staying for any evidence that may have been discarded by the guest. There is case law regarding the collection of abandoned garbage or trash from residences or hotel rooms. Individuals often may leave evidence behind such as drugs, paraphernalia, and notations such as drug weights or money notations. We have seen where the drug dealers have notations on discarded pieces of paper which include such abbreviations as "oz.," "lb.", "$1/_8$," and so on. Abandoned garbage can be collected in a variety of ways, such as when housekeeping staff, during their normal course of duty, obtains the garbage from the room, which later would be discarded: this can be collected for examination. We always say that "garbage tells a story."

There are numerous notations that can be identified to represent drug notes. The investigator may testify to this in criminal trial. It would be based on the officer's training and experience, where he or she has seen this type of notation during prior drug investigations. Substances such as refuse from marijuana that has been manicured, roaches (small cigarettes of marijuana) and remnants of cocaine trafficking, such as small amounts of powder or tape from packaging, have been discarded in the trash. Any evidence that has been discarded can be used to establish probable cause to secure a search warrant. Once this has been determined, surveillance may be an option to observe activities of the suspicious guest. There are a number of investigative options in these cases, such as whether to conduct appropriate consensual encounters or detainment if appropriate, and the findings that there is reasonable suspicion or probable cause.

The majority of cases made in a hotel interdiction program are self-initiated cold cases in which the investigator finds the activity. As in many interdiction cases, self-initiated cases done by "shaking the bush" are often successful. The more investigators are out in the field contacting sources of information and actively seeking out the behavior, the more successful the hotel program will be.

The other type of investigation in hotel interdiction is tip information, in which the investigator receives information about suspicious guests from a trained hotel staff member. This is where the hotel training pays off for a hotel squad. You train hotel employees to look for certain conduct of the guests, and once this conduct or portions of it is identified, the staff member contacts law enforcement to make them aware of the activity.

Once all of the training and contact numbers have been provided to hotel staff, a hotel squad member will typically receive a page on their pager from a hotel source. At this point, the investigator debriefs the hotel employee of the guest activity and what appears to be suspicious. Let the hotel staff person provide the specific behavior and explain why he or she thinks that it appears suspicious. Collect all the data possible regarding the guest's name, address, vehicle description, tag number, and room number. If possible, the investigator should travel to the hotel to obtain the information personally and to verify the information. As with all investigations, the investigator must conduct a background inquiry of the guest and others who may have been identified with them.

To verify the information and to conduct an independent investigation from the hotel source, surveillance is the key to confirming the information through observation. Surveillance can provide the investigator with sufficient reasonable suspicion, or consensual encounter may be an option if it does not rise to the level of reasonable suspicion. Reasonable suspicion is a less demanding standard than probable cause. The investigator may conduct a brief investigatory stop.

Approaches of suspicious guests should be taken away from the hotel premises whenever possible. This includes arrests, consensual encounters, and detainment of individuals. Certainly, there are circumstances where activity is happening quickly and there is no choice but to make an approach on hotel property. The reason for making the approach away from the hotel premises is it takes the onus or burden off of the hotel and any police activity that may be occurring that other guests would see. Hotel managers may become upset that the police activity is on the premises. The majority of guests in hotels are legitimate business people or families. The hotel squad should not become so involved in the moment that this is forgotten. Additionally, investigators must

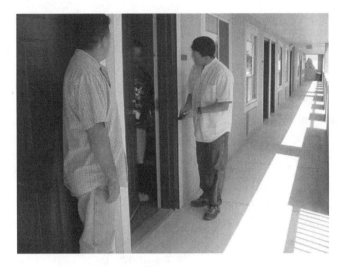

**Figure 5.3**

**Figure 5.4**

respect the fact that hotels are businesses that provide a service. Any interruption in the daily activities of a hotel should be avoided whenever possible.

Once a guest has been identified based on a tip, locating a vehicle should be next. A vehicle examination by the narcotic canine team should be done as soon as or if practical. This gives investigators an opportunity to examine the vehicle by the canine for narcotic odor. If an opportunity exists, abandoned trash or garbage from the room should be collected. If investigators want to make an approach based on the activities observed, they should attempt to make the approach as low-key as possible (Figures 5.3 through 5.5).

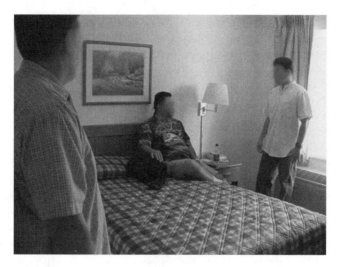

**Figure 5.5**

We obviously cannot cover every potential scenario that a hotel squad may encounter. The investigators must rely on their observations and experience. These cases are not always easy to make, as we have mentioned earlier in this chapter. The difficulty for the investigator is that he is not in a position to benefit from having inside sources to provide him with information. This makes conducting these investigations challenging and sometimes frustrating. Sometimes approaches are premature. The saying "timing is everything" certainly applies. We can only do the best we can in making investigative decisions, and many factors play into what occurs. These investigations can last from just a few minutes to several days. Supervisors should be aware that these operations could go on for several days with extensive surveillance, which makes them extremely demanding. Many times, we have found that we must "cut our losses" and make an approach either by making contact with the suspicious guest or conducting a consensual encounter such as a knock and talk situation. Unfortunately, when it comes to drug investigations, drug dealers are on a totally different time schedule.

### Case Study

In a case in Florida as part of our hotel program, several investigators were checking their hotels for any activity. They entered a hotel in which staff was trained and had been on-line for a short time. Investigators were assigned to the hotel as part of their zone area and were conducting cold investigative operations in the hotels. They examined the hotel guest list and learned that a local subject was staying there. The subject was a significant narcotic violator in the area and generally dealt with multi-kilogram levels of cocaine, according to intelligence sources. There had been several investigations in which the guest was implicated in narcotic trafficking organizations. The hotel squad members learned that the subject had been at the hotel for at least $1^1/_2$ days. An examination of the registration card revealed that the guest address was incorrect and that he had inverted two numbers on the house number, but the street name was correct. According to hotel staff, there was much telephone activity incoming and outgoing from the subject's room. Once the phone numbers were obtained, a database revealed that many of them were to other hotels in the area and to other drug dealers' homes and pager numbers. Surveillance was initiated at that location. Investigators observed a variety of activities from the room that were not normal guest behavior including individuals arriving at the location, staying for a short time, and then exiting the room. The suspect guest was observed to be frequently pulling the drapes back and peeking out into the parking lot of the hotel. He frequently walked outside of the room and looked around the parking lot suspiciously. It was learned from hotel staff that when the subject checked in, he wanted a particular room at the rear of the hotel. Additional surveillance was initiated at hotels that were identified from the telephone activity. Other individuals were identified as drug traffickers from the local area and from other parts of Florida.

The guest frequently had food delivered to the room and stayed in the room for long periods without leaving. Surveillance teams frequently observed pizza delivery vehicles arriving and delivering food to the room. At one point during the surveillance, the team observed a subject exiting the hotel with a duffle bag. The subject was followed to another nearby hotel where he entered an elevator. Two investigators conducting surveillance entered the elevator with him as another subject entered behind them. The initial subject handed the other subject the duffle bag in a very subtle fashion and did not say anything to him. The elevator doors opened and the two subjects exited, one with the duffle bag. The investigators thought that this appeared suspicious, and based on all of the prior observations during the course of the surveillance, the investigators approached each of the individuals. The subject with the duffle bag provided the officer with a consent search of the duffle bag. The search revealed 7 kg of cocaine in the duffle bag.

The individuals cooperated with the investigators in the case. Officers traveled to the initial hotel, and an additional $1^1/_2$ kg of cocaine was seized. As the investigation progressed, the main target who was staying as a guest in the hotel had been provided with 10 kg of cocaine from a 500-kg load that entered through Gulf Coast area of Florida. The main suspect and his associates were off-loaders for an organization. Their job was to unload a shipment of cocaine from a vessel, and they received 10 kg of cocaine as payment. The suspect was distributing the cocaine from the hotel room to a variety of buyers. As a result of the hotel operation, numerous individuals were indicted concerning the vessel off-load of cocaine. The cocaine from the seizure in the hotel operation was used at the trial to convict a number of suspects.

The surveillance lasted approximately 48 hours. Good surveillance techniques were used and the investigators took an opportunity in making an approach, which paid off. Essentially, what occurred was investigators were proactive and initiated a cold case by checking a hotel in their zone. All it took was recognizing a name, and the investigation progressed from there. This is an example of what this type of a program can mean to a law enforcement agency that implements and stays committed to the program.

Many times we are asked to describe the type of drug dealers that may utilize hotels. We categorize types of traffickers in four groups. There is the *local drug dealer, courier, significant violator,* and *other crime* (such as robbery, burglary, and prostitution activity). A local drug dealer is the one who lives locally and takes the opportunity to deal drugs from a hotel room rather than on the street or in his or her home. The *local dealer* will generally rent a room anywhere from a few hours to several days. He will usually have many incoming telephone calls. Many times the dealers will page individuals to advise them that they have drugs available and they will enter, after the telephone number, the number of the room they are staying in. Other times, they may use a code on the pager to alert the person who is calling them. A local dealer will have foot traffic or vehicle traffic coming into the hotel, and subjects may stay for short periods. This is indicative of drug dealing. The local dealer may also set up "shop", cooking or making either crack cocaine or methamphetamine.

The *courier* may not display any particular behavior and will usually stay for a short period — often just overnight — and check out. The courier will not have much incoming telephone activity because generally he is traveling from point A to point B and does not know anyone in the area. He may contact his associates to advise them of his location, so there may be some telephone activity coming from the room as a result. The courier may ask for special room conditions such as a room in a specific part of the hotel, and possibly may back his vehicle into a parking space. Drugs are frequently left in the vehicle, secreted in various parts of the car. There are other times when couriers are seen to take items into the hotel room, such as duffle bags.

The *significant violator* is a significant drug trafficker who may be either a local or out-of-town individual conducting drug transactions or negotiations at a hotel. He may be dealing narcotics out of the room or simply preparing narcotics in the room and not selling from there. These individuals rent a room rather than being in their residence once they obtain the drugs. They may come in from other parts of the state or country to negotiate or to deliver money for drugs. There may be a transaction at the hotel itself or at another location. This is where surveillance plays a role in being able to identify the activity of these violators. These individuals may also have contact with other hotels in the surrounding area and may change rooms or hotels frequently.

*Other crimes* refer to other types of criminal activity that may be committed while individuals are staying at a hotel. These crimes may include robbery, burglary, theft, and fraud. Individuals who may have committed a homicide in the local area or other jurisdictions may flee and stay at hotels. Individuals who are committing other crime exhibit much of the same behavior. Many fugitives from other jurisdictions flee the area and stay at hotels and motels. Investigators will see or be called to a hotel concerning behavior which may indicate prostitution activity.

The question of when to conduct hotel operations is frequently asked. What is the best time of day? Would it be during the day, evening, or midnight shifts? Hotel squads have had success in working a variety of hours. Drug activity in hotels cannot be easily pinpointed. Activity may occur any time of the day or night. This is why the hotel program is a 24-hour, 7-day-a-week operation. Law enforcement cannot be everywhere all of the time. Hours can be rotated to complement certain activities. Depending on the activity, surveillance operations may continue for several days. Flexibility is the key to this type of a program.

## Indicators of Possible Criminal Activity

The success of a hotel program relies on the training of hotel staff and the assertiveness of law enforcement in identifying guests who may be using hotels to conduct various illicit activities. Indicators of possible criminal activity are based on the behavior and conduct of the guest. Certain behavior is not consistent with normal guest patterns. One or a few indicators are not necessarily indicative of criminal activity; other observations are necessary to determine whether an individual is engaged in criminal activity such as drug trafficking. An indicator is simply a means by which law enforcement communicates its collective expertise of the significance of certain characteristics that a lay person may not recognize. This is the purpose of hotel staff training: to be able to provide tools and the knowledge to identify certain characteristics so staff can then contact law enforcement to further investigate the activity.

There are a number of indicators of possible criminal activity which have been developed by law enforcement officers throughout the United States, that attempt to pinpoint what a guest engaged in criminal activity may display while utilizing the services of a hotel. During the process of training hotel staff, management and staff such as front desk personnel and executive housekeepers should be provided a list of indicators to assist them in recognizing the behavior. A cover letter and list of indicators are provided during the training (Figures 5.6 and 5.7). The cover letter attached to the indicators may be marked "confidential." It should indicate that the attached list of indicators has been prepared to assist hotel employees in the detection of potential criminal activity that may occur in or around their establishment. It should also indicate that by providing information, they are not acting as agents of the police, but as concerned citizens, and that notification should be made by either calling the digital pager number or one of the telephone numbers that has been provided for investigators. Notification should be made in the interest of security, and with the welfare of the staff and guests in mind.

At the end of the indicator list, information should be provided to staff indicating that guests who engage in the listed activities may or may not be involved in narcotic or other illicit activity. They are asked to observe and report the information and take no action. The information will be evaluated by law enforcement and the appropriate enforcement action may be taken,

---

**Confidential**

The attached list of indicators has been prepared to assist Hotel and Motel employees in the direction of potential criminal activity that may occur in or around your establishment.

In providing information, you are not acting as an agent of the **Police Agency Name**, but as a concerned citizen.

Notification should be made to one of the law enforcement personnel listed below in the interest of security and with the welfare of you and the guests in mind.

Your assistance in these endeavors will be greatly appreciated.

To report suspected criminal activity, call **Pager Number**, which is a digital pager. Your call will be returned immediately.

Hotel – Motel Narcotics Interdiction Unit

**List Detectives Here:**
      **Names:**
      **Office Phone**
      **Pager Number**

In the event you are unable to contact the above listed personnel, please contact the following:

**List Supervisor Name, Office Phone,**
**And Pager Number**

**Figure 5.6**

or no action may be taken at all. There is certainly an element of risk by providing this type of information to staff, as these indicators may end up in the hands of criminal types. However, law enforcement's position should

### Indicators of Possible Criminal Activity

1. Guest visitors from cities/states, which are a port of entry for narcotics, such as Miami and New York and the states of Texas and Florida. Source cities and states.

2. Local or out of town guests who frequent the establishment and have a consistent pattern of suspicious activity.

3. Guests checking in without reservations, extending stay on day-today basis, or may check out prematurely.

4. Fictitious information given by guest upon registration or guest may be evasive as to length of stay utilizing fictitious names and identification upon registering.

5. Guests checking in for other individuals without the knowledge of the hotel/motel, exhibiting indicators described.

6. Guests having little or no luggage upon checking in (arrive empty-handed), they may purchase luggage, clothing, souvenirs, or briefcases. Leaving with parcels or packages.

7. Auto license numbers furnished at time of registration not coinciding with plates displayed on the vehicle.

8. Guests and their visitors who park vehicle some distance away and walk to rooms even when spaces are available.

9. Guests displaying large amounts of U.S. currency and paying cash for their lodging, meals, and expenses.

10. Guests paying for rooms on a day-to-day basis in cash.

11. Several guests checking into different rooms, different floors, later joining in one room. Excessive calls between rooms. Switching rooms, possibly on a day-to-day basis.

12. Guests having numerous incoming and outgoing telephone calls, including calls to source areas such as Florida, Texas, California others.

13. Guests who frequently utilize pay phones instead of phone in room. Guests may request large quantities of quarters for telephone calls.

14. Guests who exhibit unusual behavior, such as staying in room and does not go out for long periods of time. Guest has food brought to his room at all times.

15. Guests who refuse maid service or stay in room while maid cleans extensive use of "DO NOT DISTURB" sign.

16. Guests who display nervous tendencies and re observed to conduct suspicious activities in and around hotel/motel property.

17. Guest frequently having late visitors, usually but not always of similar appearance, whom will frequently obtain a room and maintain phone communications with the original guests.

### Figure 5.7a

18.     Foot traffic, which is later or unusual, not consistent with normal guest patterns, with frequent visitors who stay for a brief period of time.

19.     Narcotics or narcotic paraphernalia observed in rooms.

20.     Plastic bags, scales, rubber bands, money wrappers, empty luggage, large sums of U.S. currency observed in guest's room.

21.     Possesses large quantities of unusual shaped packages.
a. Bundles wrapped in tape, usually multiple layers of tape, tan or Grey in color, at times shiny in nature.
b. Parcels roughly the shape and size of a football or shoebox, possibly bearing strange markings.
c. Discarded tape in garbage cans.

22.     Guests' receiving packages or parcels from major parcel services at the hotel/motel.

23.     Presence of sophisticated electronic communications equipment in rooms.

24.     Any firearms or evidence of firearms such as loose cartridges, ammunition or empty holsters observed in rooms by hotel personnel.

25.     Female guests who exhibit indicators should not be overlooked. Females are used as couriers and guard drugs until dealers arrive.

26.     Any person or persons who attract your suspicions for any other reason than those set forth. Again, guests who engage in the above listed activities may or may not be involved in narcotic or other illicit activity. The **Police Agency Name** requests that you take no action other than to observe and report information. Law enforcement officers will evaluate your information and take appropriate enforcement action. Your assistance in reducing organized narcotic trafficking and other crime in **City or County Name** is greatly appreciated.

**Figure 5.7b**

be that they have nothing to hide. By the very nature of drug trafficking, individuals who are engaged in this activity put themselves in a position where they behave in a certain predictable fashion.

As we go through each indicator, it is not difficult to see why people involved in drug trafficking or other illicit activities act in certain ways. The indicators may vary in different jurisdictions, which directly relates to the narcotic activity in that area. Certain behavior is consistent throughout and does not change. Once the police agency starts this program, they will see other patterns of activity which guests display. Each indicator should be evaluated for what it is. As we have said, one or even several of these characteristics are not necessarily indicative of criminal activity. The investigators must take the totality of all of the circumstances and make a decision. There may be a logical explanation for the activity, and it may not be criminal at all.

The following are some of the indicators which have been found to be part of criminal conduct.

Guests and visitors from cities or states that are source areas or points of entry for narcotics may cause suspicion. Examples of states are Texas, Florida, and some of the southwest border states. Some cities include Miami and Los Angeles. This is not to suggest that an individual from a particular city or state that is known for drug trafficking is involved in narcotics activity while staying in a hotel. It is simply one indicator that should be evaluated further. We know these are locations that are sources for illicit narcotics.

Is a local or out-of-town guest who frequently uses the hotel and has a consistent pattern of suspicious activity present? Drug traffickers are often creatures of habit. Hotel squad members may see the same individuals, whether from their local jurisdiction or from another source area, arriving at a hotel and displaying suspicious characteristics that may be indicative of drug activity. An example would be a front desk person telling the investigator that a particular individual arrives at the hotel every 2 weeks and during his stay there is suspicious activity at the room, such as many people coming and going from the room and staying for short periods of time, or the guest asking for a specific room. Another indicator would be a guest checking in without reservation, extending his stay on a day-to-day basis, or checking out prematurely. Certainly there are legitimate reasons an individual may check into a hotel without a reservation. A person who is traveling may become tired and pull into a hotel without a reservation and ask for a room. Typically, however, a drug trafficker will not call several weeks ahead to make a reservation for a particular date. This is because of the nature of the drug business. A source of supply does not always know when he will be obtaining the drugs, and so cannot give a buyer an exact date. This may be drug dealers checking in without reservations.

Law enforcement does know, based on training and experience, that a source of supply may call a buyer and say that the drugs are in and that the buyer needs to get there as soon as possible. This may be a local or out-of-town buyer. The reason an individual may extend their stay on a day-to-day basis is that once he arrives to obtain the drugs there may be a delay, which is not uncommon in the drug trade. So, what an investigator may see is an individual who comes into a hotel without a reservation and asks to stay one night. He then extends his stay on a day-to-day basis while waiting for the deal to come through. He may call the front desk person or walk to the front desk asking to stay another night. He would then pay for the room. He may do this several times in a span of several days. Generally, what is occurring is that the drugs have been promised on a particular day and have not been delivered, so the guest is extending his stay daily in order to accommodate the circumstances in obtaining the drugs. The guest may suddenly check out prematurely. This may be indicative of the narcotics being delivered or, in some situations, negotiations have broken down and no drugs are delivered. Investigators may see this during their surveillance where the subject is extending day to day — there is some activity as people arrive at and leave the hotel. There may be an opportunity once the suspect departs the hotel for law enforcement to make contact. These individuals usually do not go to the front desk and check out. Once contact is made, there may be no drugs found. The individual may have a large amount of currency in his possession. This may indicate that the drug deal did not materialize and that the individual is leaving the area with his money.

A guest may provide fictitious information upon registration using a false name, alias, or fictitious identification, or he may be evasive as to his length of stay. Suggest to hotel management that they request some form of identification from a guest who pays cash. A hotel will not ask for identification if the person pays with a credit card. Very seldom do drug traffickers use credit cards to pay for the rooms; however, it is not out of the question. Sometimes drug traffickers or organizations use credit cards to keep a record of expenses. It is a good idea to ask for identification from cash-paying customers in case there is some kind of damage or theft to the hotel premises. It also assists law enforcement in identifying individuals. Investigators and hotel staff should be aware of guests checking in for other individuals without the knowledge of the hotel. There may be a legitimate reason for a guest checking in for someone else; however, it is a common practice of drug dealers. A young female or other adult may check into the hotel, and the true guests are never identified. The guests that check in may never be seen again by hotel staff other than during the check-in process. The reason behind checking in for someone else typically is that the drug trafficker, who may have a criminal history or other information he does not want to be known, wants to keep his anonymity. Historically, drug traffickers like to use individuals who do not have criminal histories to transport or hold drugs for them.

Hotel guests may check in with little or no luggage. They may purchase luggage, clothing, or other items during their stay. Arriving at the hotel with little or no luggage may be an indication that an individual's stay will be very short. There are many instances where drug traffickers purposely do not arrive with any type of luggage such as duffle bags or suitcases because they do not have information on how the drugs are packaged. For instance, if the buyer is purchasing marijuana, he may not know if the drugs purchased or received are packaged in kilograms or bales weighing anywhere from 10 to 20 to 30 pounds, or more. If investigators have an opportunity to do surveillance, they may see these individuals traveling to a mall or luggage store and purchasing new luggage to transfer the narcotics for transportation. New luggage is a strong indicator that the person may be transporting narcotics. Investigators may see that guests are traveling to nearby stores to purchase clothing such as underwear and t-shirts. These individuals may stay at a hotel on a day-to-day basis. They may arrive and not anticipate staying at the hotel for long periods, due to the delay in the delivery of the narcotics. Many individuals run out of clothes and need to purchase them while they are staying at the location.

Many drug traffickers and drug organizations use commercial parcel package services such as Federal Express, United Parcel Service, and the U.S. Postal Service. Many drug traffickers use hotels in conjunction with receiving parcels at the particular hotel that they are using. Traffickers send narcotics through commercial parcel systems to themselves to another location, such as a hotel, and disseminate the drugs in the area.

## Case Study

An example of parcel activity in a hotel was revealed during a Florida case in which an individual contacted a hotel to make reservations the night before arrival. The individual indicated on the telephone to reservation personnel that he would like a room for the next night. Reservations indicated that a room was available. The person asked if hotel staff would accept several parcels in his behalf and he would retrieve them when he arrived the following day. This particular request was not suspicious in that many business people who travel request that parcels be accepted for them by hotels.

This particular hotel was part of the police agency hotel/motel program. Investigators assigned to the hotel arrived to make contact with staff to see if any suspicious activity was occurring at the location. While at the hotel they noticed two cardboard boxes approximately $3' \times 3'$ in size, each weighing approximately 50 pounds. The boxes were addressed to the hotel and were sent from Texas, a source state for marijuana. The staff was asked to whom the parcels belonged. The hotel staff provided the information regarding the subject who asked that the parcels be accepted for him and that he would be checking in on that day. The investigators asked their narcotics canine team to have the narcotics canine examine the parcels for the odor of narcotics. The dog subsequently alerted to the odor of narcotics to those packages.

The person arrived at the location while investigators were present and stated that he had changed his mind and he did not want the room, but asked if his packages had been delivered. The front desk personnel acknowledged that the parcels had been delivered. The suspect was given the boxes and departed the area. A surveillance team followed the subject and he was later stopped leaving the hotel. The subject provided consent for officers to open the packages, which revealed 50 pounds of marijuana in each box, totaling 100 pounds. The subject cooperated, providing officers with information concerning the marijuana. He indicated that he sent the parcels to himself from Texas. He stayed across the street from that hotel and asked for a room facing the road where he could monitor the receiving hotel across the street. He observed the parcel company arrive and drop off the two boxes, which he recognized. He waited for a short time, then walked into the hotel and stated that he had changed his mind and would take the parcels they had accepted for him. This had gone on for several months, and the person admitted that several hundred pounds of marijuana had been sent to that area using the same method. The marijuana was sold to various buyers in the area.

This type of scenario occurs frequently, and hotel staff should be provided with information about parcels that appear suspicious arriving at the location. Investigators from hotel squads should ask hotel staff if any parcels have been delivered to the hotel and, if the opportunity presents itself, the drug canine team can examine the parcels for narcotic odor.

When investigators are reviewing hotel registrations, they should check for auto tag license numbers furnished by the guests. Many times, the guest does not fill that in; however, there are times when the person will provide a fictitious license number which does not match the vehicle that he is operating. This does not necessarily mean that the person is engaged in narcotic activity, but may be significant in combination with other factors.

Some guests and their visitors may park some distance away and walk to their rooms even though closer spaces are available. Most people want to find a space available that is closest to their room. Investigators may learn that the guest parked on the other side of the parking lot away from the room and backed his vehicle in so that the license plate cannot be seen. Many times during surveillance, investigators will observe a guest exit his vehicle, look around nervously, and walk some distance to enter his room.

The drug business is a cash business. If a guest displays large amounts of currency and pays for his lodging in cash, including meals and other hotel expenses, this may be an indicator along with other factors that the subject may be involved in some type of criminal activity. Some individuals will provide the front desk personnel with "up front" money while staying at the location. This generally coincides with someone paying day-to-day and providing several hundred dollars at a time to the front desk clerk for expenses such as additional room days, movie rentals, room service, and other amenities. There may be several guests checking into different rooms, different floors, and later joining in one of the rooms. There may be excessive calls between the rooms and switching of rooms, possibly on a day-to-day basis. There may be significant reasons why guests would be checking into different rooms on different floors and later joining in a particular room. The reason may be that they want separation from each other and they do not want to be identified. A source of drugs may be in one room and a go-between or broker, who would be selling the drugs to a buyer, in another room. Once a purchase is made, the source and broker may join in one room. There may be a situation where there are drugs or money being shown to a prospective buyer or seller in one room, and other individuals who are part of the transaction but do not want to be identified are in different rooms. There may be telephone calls between the rooms or calls to other hotels in the area. Not only do they check into different rooms, but they may also have checked into different hotels to be totally separate from each other.

Guests may switch rooms, sometimes on a day-to-day basis. Switching of rooms may be indicative of the dealer having concerns about being robbed by other drug dealers. Many times, hotel rooms are used to display a quantity of narcotics that is to be purchased or money that is to be utilized to purchase narcotics. For fear of being "ripped off," the guest may contact the front desk and ask to switch his room for the night. This may go on for several days. Typically the guest will ask to switch rooms with excuses such as the remote control on the television not working, or that he does not like the view from the room. Other strange or suspicious excuses may be given as to why the guest wants to switch rooms constantly.

Guests who have numerous incoming or outgoing telephone calls to source areas are another indicator. With the use of a database, if available, those numbers may be identified to other drug sources or traffickers. A guest may be observed to frequently use the pay telephone instead of the telephone in their room. They may use prepaid telephone cards to make these calls. An individual may be constantly on his cellular telephone either outside of the room or on hotel property; this includes a guest sitting in his vehicle talking on the cellular telephone.

Other unusual activities may be observed, including guests who stay in their hotel room for long periods and have food brought to their rooms either by room service or outside food sources such as pizza delivery and others. A person who exhibits suspicious behavior and stays in his room for a long time may have drugs or currency in the room and not want to leave the items unattended. Sometimes individuals will stay in a room for several days at a time. When these individuals are later contacted by law enforcement, a question that should be asked is why they were staying in the room for long periods. Investigators should try to obtain any information that could possibly be used later and was contradictory to what the guest has said or what was observed by officers.

Many drug traffickers refuse maid service, stay in the room while the maid cleans, or use the "Do Not Disturb" sign extensively (Figure 5.8). These individuals will not allow the maid to come into the room and many times will ask the maid just for towels to replace the ones that have been used. Once the housekeeper enters the room, they may sit in the room while the housekeeper cleans and watch them very intently. This may mean that there are drugs in the room and the guest wants to ensure that the housekeeper does not come in contact with the drugs.

Once the housekeeper does enter the room, she may observe, whether or not the guest is in the room, that narcotics activity is occurring. She may

**Figure 5.8**

see narcotics or narcotic paraphernalia while in the process of conducting her routine duties. She may see plastic bags, empty luggage, or large sums of currency. Housekeepers and other hotel staff have certain authority to enter a hotel room while it is occupied. This is known as implied consent, entering a room for a specific purpose, such as to clean it or fix a problem. There is an expectation from the guest that staff will enter the room for such activities. Law enforcement must have express consent from the occupant to enter an occupied room. A manager or housekeeper cannot invite police into the room after they discover contraband. A search warrant must be obtained. Additionally, a guest maintains privacy rights until it is clear that he has abandoned the room. If the investigator observes the presence of personal effects, such as clothing or luggage, it raises the presumption that the person intends to return. Consequently, it is not recommended that a search be conducted based only on those circumstances. Either a search warrant must be obtained or a reasonable time should be allotted to have a true abandonment of the room.

Another red flag is a guest who displays nervous tendencies and is observed to conduct suspicious activities in and around the hotel property. This could mean a variety of different things, including meeting people in the parking lot, where there may be some type of an exchange made. There may be other individuals frequently coming to the room to stay for short periods. The foot traffic, which is usually late or unusual, is not consistent with what a normal guest would exhibit. A housekeeper may also see bundles of items wrapped in tape in a variety of different colors. Parcels and tape may be discarded in the trash or garbage. This could be an instance where the narcotics were removed from the original packaging to be broken down, and the tape may have been discarded.

There may be the presence of sophisticated electronic equipment in the room as observed by the housekeeper such as police scanners, walkie-talkies, or portable global positioning satellite (GPS). The guest may be involved in drug trafficking, burglary, theft, robbery, and other types of criminal activity.

Several cases have been made in a hotel/motel program where electronic equipment or communications are present in the room as observed by a housekeeper. These individuals would be in the room all during the daytime hours and would be observed to be out during the evening hours. The individuals were commercial burglars who by night would burglarize electronic stores and take televisions, stereos, computers, and other electronic equipment. They would communicate by walkie-talkie and use police scanners to hear the local police agency activities. The equipment was placed in a rental truck and transported to other locations. These individuals would go from jurisdiction to jurisdiction, hotel to hotel, and commit commercial sophisticated burglaries during the night. They exhibited much of the same behavior that drug traffickers would display, in that they would ask for a specific room and have telephone contact with known criminals.

Any evidence of firearms or loose cartridges, ammunition, or empty holsters observed in a room by hotel personnel may arouse their suspicion. Many states have concealed firearms permits available; however, with other suspicious behavior, individuals with firearms should be scrutinized carefully. Individuals who "hotel hop" typically go from hotel to hotel in the area. They generally stay for one to several days and then move to another hotel in the area. These people may be avoiding law enforcement, avoiding other associates, or just move their operations because they feel uncomfortable being in once place for a long period.

Over the past several years, clandestine laboratory operations such as methamphetamine labs have been operating out of hotel rooms in various parts of the country. The indicators are essentially the same with a few exceptions with regard to clandestine lab operations. Many of the guests ask for special conditions for the room; for instance, near a side exit or in a particular part of the hotel. These individuals are looking for easy access. An individual may be observed to empty his own trash into a dumpster or take the trash in his vehicle off the hotel property and dump it in a remote dumpster. One might wonder why anyone would take his own trash and dump it some distance away. This is not a normal hotel guest activity. These guests are aware that law enforcement has the ability to examine trash that has been abandoned and utilize the information or narcotics gleaned from that examination against the individual, whether it is at a residence or hotel.

Clandestine laboratory operations often have unusual odors or sounds emitting from the hotel room. These include but are not limited to ether smells, ammonia, or other chemical smells. The windows of the hotel room may be open regardless of the weather. A small fan may be used to ventilate the room. These guests may be forced to smoke in the hallway or the parking lot of the hotel to avoid an explosion or fire within the room. Many of these chemicals are very volatile and could cause serious damage. Sounds of small vacuum pumps or other equipment may be heard coming from the room. If a housekeeper happens to enter the room and observes a variety of hardware, which is typically set up in a shower area of the bathroom, this may be a lab operation. Some of these items include glass containers, unusual household product containers, empty cold medicine boxes, plastic tubing, and hot plates. These may be used to manufacture methamphetamine and other products.

Methamphetamine usually produces paranoia, which may lead to strange behavior. The guest may report that other guests are watching them. These people may be awake for days at a time and stay in their rooms for long periods.

Once a laboratory operation is identified, it is suggested that law enforcement officers who have extensive training in dismantling of laboratory operations be contacted. Members who are part of a hotel program, or a uniform officer, should leave the room exactly as it is. It is estimated that 20% of laboratory operations found in the United States have resulted in some fire or explosion. Investigators should not touch anything, including light switches. The recommended minimum safe perimeter surrounding a clandestine laboratory is 1000 feet.

The indicators that have been outlined here are merely guidelines for investigators who will be part of a hotel interdiction program. If these characteristics are exhibited by a hotel guest, a thorough investigation should be conducted to confirm the conduct. Certainly we cannot predict all of the conduct a drug trafficker would display while renting a hotel room, but human behavior does not lie. Trends may change, but human behavior does not. (See Figures 5.9 and 5.10).

## Areas of Concealment

During hotel investigations, investigators will be in hotel rooms during a variety of circumstances (Figure 5.11). It is important to know some of the concealment areas in a hotel room in which traffickers hide drugs. They are innovative in their concealment methods. The following have been identified as concealment locations within a hotel room:

**Figure 5.9**

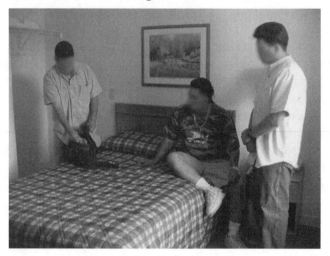

**Figure 5.10**

- Commode tank and bowl
- Bathroom ceiling fan
- Items taped under sink
- Tissue dispensers and toilet paper dispensers
- False ceiling areas
- Air conditioner and heater units (Figure 5.12)
- Slits in mattresses
- Under and between mattress and box spring
- Under dresser drawers (Figures 5.13 and 5.14)

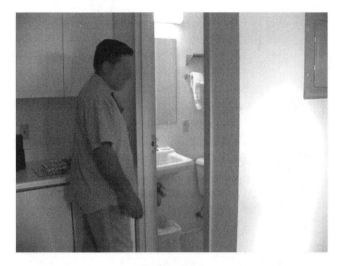

**Figure 5.11**

**Figure 5.12**

- Wall fixtures
- Electrical outlet plates and smoke detectors (Figures 5.15 and 5.16)

Traffickers may hide things in other items in the room that they have brought with them, such as luggage, bags, and radios. Anything that may be a concealment area should be examined.

**Figure 5.13**

**Figure 5.14**

## Investigative Techniques

The documentation as it relates to hotel/motel interdiction should be detailed and concise. Investigative reporting by law enforcement as it relates to hotel/motel cases should include a variety of information, including personal observations made by officers through their surveillance, management consent, and other investigative techniques used during these operations. Once these cases are litigated, this information becomes crucial.

**Figure 5.15**

**Figure 5.16**

The use of electronic equipment to support the officer's personal observations during surveillance is very useful. This includes video surveillance in a variety of areas of the hotel such as interior hallways near a suspicious guest's room and parking lot video surveillance. All expectations of privacy must be respected with regard to electronic surveillance.

Other investigative techniques include what are known as "flush outs" or "draw outs." This is a situation where law enforcement wants to draw a guest out of a room. They may make a telephone call to the hotel room and say something that would draw the person out and give the officer an opportunity to make contact. Investigators should then be prepared to either contact the individual or observe his behavior further.

With respect to the expectation of privacy issues, law enforcement cannot monitor conversation or use any enhancement devices to monitor conversations, for instance from room to room. However, if the individuals were talking loud enough so that parties next door could hear them clearly without the use of enhancement devices, this would be permissible. Many cases have been made by law enforcement overhearing conversations when they are in a legitimate position to do so.

Hotel squads should also be cognizant of any vehicles that are left in the parking lot for long periods of time. Rental trucks are very popular in the transportation of narcotics. An examination by a drug canine team may be conducted on a vehicle that has been in the parking lot for an unusually long time, for the purpose of attempting to detect an odor of narcotics.

## Conclusion

Implementation of a hotel interdiction program is an effective law enforcement tool in narcotic and other related criminal investigations. Using the hotel/motel community to aid in identifying various criminal elements through the use of training hotel staff is an enormous benefit to law enforcement. This includes the identifying of sources of supply, drug couriers and drug traffickers gaining valuable intelligence and cultivating sources of information from the hotel/motel community. These partnerships have proven to be invaluable in the fight against drug trafficking.

## Case Law

### U.S. v. Roby, 122 F.3d 1120 (1997) 8th Cir.

A warrantless canine sniff conducted in the corridor outside of the defendant's hotel room was reasonable. Just as evidence in plain view of officers may be searched without warrant, evidence in plain smell may be detected without warrant. Trained dog's detection of odor in a common corridor does not contravene the Fourth Amendment. Officers can secure defendant's motel room while waiting for search warrant to issue, after a positive canine alert from corridor outside a room.

### U.S. v. Burns, 624 F.2d 95 (1986) 10th Cir.

Arresting officer's use of a drug detection police dog prior to procurement of a search warrant was not a search. Mere sniffing of locked briefcase in motel room by drug dog was not a search.

### U.S. v. Rivera, 825 F.2d 152 (1987) 7th Cir.

Subjecting luggage, which has been seized from hotel room under plain view exception to warrant requirement on theory that it contained contraband, to a narcotic detector dog was not a search.

### *U.S. v. Esquilin*, 208 F.3d 315 (2000) 1st Cir.

Dog's sniffing behavior in motel room while held on a leash by officer was not a search. The defendant had invited the officers into his room. Important factor in determining whether dog's sniffing behavior constitutes a search is not whether the sniff occurs in a public place but whether the observing officer or the sniffing canine are legally present at their vantage when their respective senses are aroused by obviously incriminating evidence.

## Key Terms

Aggressive alert dog

Anonymity

Anonymous source (AS)

"Bread-and-butter" employees

Bucket

Business regulation purposes

Characteristics of behavior

Clandestine lab

Cold versus tip investigation

Commercial parcel services

Community policing concept

Computer-generated guest list

Confidential source (CS)

Consensual encounter

Cooperating individual (CI)

Drug courier

Dual-purpose dog

Electronic equipment

Executive housekeeper

Expectation of privacy

"Eyes and ears" concept

Five-star hotels

"Flush outs" and "draw outs"

Front desk personnel

"Garbage tells a story"

Guest registration

Hotel hopping

Hotel pager

Hotel property

Housekeeper

Independent case

Indicators of criminal activity

Interdiction sticker

Investigative source (IS)

Investigatory purposes

Knock and talk

Letter of commitment

Local dealer

Management consent

Medium mid-size hotels

Minimizing exposure of staff

"Mom and Pop" Hotels

Notations

Normal guest pattern activity

On-line hotels

Out of sight, out of mind

Paraphernalia

Passive alert dog

Pattern of suspicious activity

Probable cause

Reasonable suspicion

Registration card

Rewards and payments

"Running the lot"

Security personnel

"Shaking the bush"

"Show and tell"

Significant violator

Single-purpose dog

Source cities and states

Sources of information

Subpoenas

Third party                                    *U.S. v. Cormier*
Training and experience                        Video training
Use of "Do not Disturb" sign

# Airport Investigations

# 6

On Monday evening, September 10, 2001, I had just flown into Salt Lake City Airport from Montana, where I had conducted a 1-day class on consensual encounter techniques. As usual, I checked the flight monitor to make sure my flight was on time. Never leaving the job at home, I began to look around the terminal at the passengers also waiting for flights. I picked a spot near the escalator and the gift shop; from here I had a good surveillance point. I began to watch the waiting passengers, first those seated — was anyone looking around nervously? I paused to look at a young couple, and I watched them as they whispered to each other and looked up occasionally at the waiting passengers in their vicinity. They appeared young — in their 20s — and were casually dressed. I could see that they had one carry-on bag, and she had a purse. The bag appeared to be new and it was positioned on the floor between them. I noticed that he had his left hand on the handle and he was slightly bent forward so he could have a grasp on the bag. She was seated to the left of him. I looked at him and he appeared uncomfortable in the position he was sitting. Again they would whisper to each other and then they would stop talking and they would each look around the terminal area, watching passengers walk past them and looking at the passengers seated in the area around them. The female looked up at me and noticed I was looking at her. She immediately looked away and bent forward to whisper into her companion's ear. He sat up but did not look in my direction; he then raised his arms up as if he was stretching and he had to let go of the carry-on bag. As he let go of the bag, I observed him swing his right leg over the bag and move it directly in front of him. As he stretched his arms upward he slowly glanced in my direction attempting to not look at me, but we did make eye contact.

Now here I am, waiting for my long-awaited flight home. I don't have any type of jurisdiction, and I look around to see if I might be able to spot a possible interdiction officer. My heart was beginning to beat faster as it usually did whenever I observed behavior such as this. Were they just nervous about flying, were they involved in some type of domestic dispute, or were they carrying some type of drug or possibly currency or involved in some other type of criminal activity? My increased heartbeat directed me to continue to observe the couple's behavior.

He finished his stretch and as he placed his hands back down I saw him reach for the carry-on bag that was on the floor. He didn't pick up the bag but just grasped the handle again as he had done earlier. Now I began to think to myself that I should call for the local police or see if the interdiction detail at the airport was still working. Again they bent their heads toward each other and continued to talk in a low tone. The female looked up and turned her head toward me and again we made eye contact, and she again immediately looked away. I thought to myself, "Do I look that much like a cop? Yes, I do." I wasn't carrying my fanny pack where I usually had my firearm concealed, along with my cuffs, business cards, and set of luggage keys.

I decided to move, and walked about 15 feet over to the public telephones and stood next to one of them. The female again nonchalantly looked over to the area where I had been standing. She looked around the area and I was wondering if she was looking for me. Where I was standing she couldn't see me. Now my heart began to beat just a little harder. This was conduct and behavior that I had seen in the past, and that behavior resulted in me walking up to people, asking for and receiving permission to speak to them, engaging them in conversation, and eventually seizing dope and arresting them. But I couldn't do that here.

I continued to surveil the couple, and I watched him reach down with his left hand and unzip the carry-on bag. I then observed him as he looked around again and she did the same; they still could not see me where I was standing. He then reached into the carry-on bag with his left hand and removed what appeared to be a bottle contained inside of a paper bag. I watched him as he twisted the lid off of the bottle and handed it to his female companion; what a gentleman. They each drank from the beer bottle.

The couple displayed this type of conduct and behavior because they thought they were doing something illegal. My connecting flight arrived and I boarded and took off for home.

The following morning I, as well as all of America, was shocked and devastated as international terrorists hit our country. The terrorists commandeered four airplanes that were flown into strategic points, the World Trade Center, the Pentagon, and a botched crash landing that was diverted by the planes passengers to avoid more massive destruction and carnage.

Here I was the night before watching a young couple's unusual conduct and behavior thinking they might be drug or currency curriers, and never in my wildest dream would I have ever thought that it could be terrorist activity. But it is all about conduct and behavior of those persons involved in criminal activity, whether that activity is drug trafficking or terrorism.

Before September 11, 2001, we lived in a comfortable and mobile society that enjoyed the comforts of traveling not only domestically but also internationally, without too much disruption or inconvenience. The events of September 11, 2001 greatly changed the way in which Americans and the world enjoyed the comfort, convenience, and speed of air travel.

Despite the tragedies and loss of life on September 11, air travel is by far still the most convenient, comfortable, and quickest method of traveling, not only for the legitimate passenger but also for the criminal element.

This chapter will focus on air travel and the methods in which drug couriers and persons involved in criminal activity have used the airline industry to facilitate their illegal activities. Whether the criminal traveler is related to narcotic or currency trafficking, terrorism, or other types of criminal activity, the properly trained law enforcement officer will be able to identify and react to the traveler in an appropriate manner, safely and legally.

Because we have been involved in working drug interdiction for a number of years, we know that there are certain characteristics or indicators that are consistent with drug trafficking in an airport arena. Although some of these characteristics or indicators are also consistent with drug trafficking in other modes of transportation, certain indicators are particular to the airport setting.

Airport investigations and the case law concerning them were the basis for what we know as consensual encounters, which was discussed in Chapter 1. All airport cases involved the early use of the consensual encounter, and the case law that stemmed from these cases set the standard in how the court determined what a consensual encounter was.

This chapter will cover working in an airport setting and the "airport family," utilization of employees as our eyes and ears, establishing an airport office or detail, the use of airline passenger name records (PNRs) and whether we can have access to them, conducting consensual encounters in the airport setting, and a look at the case law concerning airport investigations.

Working in an airport setting is like working in a self-contained city. There are many things that go on in an airport and the employees working there that can be compared to some small towns. We must be able to work in that setting and be able to blend into the environment and also be able to entrust and educate the employees of the airport. We cannot be at the airport 24 hours a day; therefore, we must rely on individuals within the airport family to assist us.

Establishing an airport group is one of the most important factors in having a successful detail that will have a positive impact on your community and be able to intercept the drugs and currency that are transported through your airport on a daily basis. The personnel involved in the detail must be able to work well with others, especially those not in law enforcement.

In our law enforcement careers and as professionals we must be familiar with the rights guaranteed to all persons, including the police. We must be very familiar with the Fourth Amendment to the U.S. Constitution, which guarantees:

> The right of the people to be secure in their persons, houses, papers, and effects against unreasonable searches and seizures shall not be violated, and no warrants shall issue, but upon probable cause, supported by oath or affirmation, and particularly describing the place to be searched and the person or things to be seized.

The criteria for selecting the personnel will be as follows: your detail should be made up of people who are familiar with Fourth Amendment search and seizure, are able to talk with people, have good presence and professionalism, are sensitive to the goals of the airline industry, are creative, and have good surveillance skills and patience. Training is an important aspect in working an airport detail. There are several agencies around the country that provide training in airport interdiction. One such organization is the Drug Enforcement Administration (DEA) and Operation Jetway, which conducts training in airport interdiction. The Multijurisdictional Counterdrug Task Force Training Program, based at St. Petersburg College in St. Petersburg, Florida, also provides training in airport interdiction. The International Narcotics Interdiction Association (INIA) provides training in airport interdiction and hosts an annual conference for all it members, both national and international.

It is essential to be properly trained and to be aware of the most recent opinions in State and in Federal court. Whichever direction you will take to prosecute your cases, you must be familiar with all recent court decisions.

In initiating an airport program, we must first have 100% commitment from our administration and supervisors. It is very important that they understand the "rollercoaster ride" that interdiction programs will experience. Even though we are out there every day attempting to identify drug or money couriers and intercept those items, we do not always return to the office with bad guys and contraband; that doesn't mean we were not looking and talking with potential targets. Administration must give full cooperation and backing to the detail. This type of program is one that once started should not be allowed to dissolve because of the lack of statistics, although we know that is how the program will be rated. It takes time for an airport group to become established.

There are jurisdictional considerations to keep in mind, and it is also important to have the support and backing of your state and federal prosecutors. Establish a liaison with those who will be prosecuting your cases. It is important to research the case law in the jurisdiction where you will present your cases. As you have already seen in this book, there is an abundance of federal case law concerning all methods of drug interdiction. Meet with your prosecutors and explain your program to them. Provide them with detail concerning your unit and the areas of interdiction that will be initiated and worked. Make sure that they keep you abreast of all recent case law and any new opinions in state or federal court.

As in any environment where law enforcement is introduced, we are a "welcome/unwelcome" sight. Many people will not want to become involved, or will feel that this type of activity is strictly a law enforcement problem, but it is a community problem that effects everyone either directly or indirectly. Drug trafficking affects all of us, and all of us must become involved, if only to be an extra set of eyes and ears.

In this environment we must rely on employees of the airline industry to assist in identifying potential individuals involved in criminal activity. These employees will not know if these individuals are involved in criminal activity, but we will educate them on some of the characteristics or indicators that people involved in criminal activity, especially drug or money trafficking, will display.

You will want to address several groups of people within the airport community and make yourselves known to them, including airport police, airline employees, security personnel, or security screeners.

## Airport Police

The airport police will be one of the first groups you will want to contact to initiate your airport program. The airport police and administration can greatly enhance your opportunities to become a successful airport detail. Having their cooperation and vice-versa is important. You must work together, because in essence you all are performing the same job, protecting the safety of the public. The airport police have a specific mission at the airport, but you can work in a partnership with them. In many airports, the airport police have assigned officers to the drug interdiction detail, making the detail a more complete and cohesive unit within the airport community. This not only gives the airport detail more manpower, but the airport police officer can be a buffer between the airport detail and the airport administration as well. The airport police officer assigned to your detail can keep the lines of communication open between the airport detail and the uniformed officers at the airport.

All the airlines in an airport have monthly or bi-monthly administrative meetings. It is in your best interest for success of the detail to contact all managers in your airport. Once contact has been made, request a meeting with them. Do not discuss your program over the telephone, but meet with them face to face. The majority of commercial airports have drug interdiction details, so many managers are aware that there are airport programs. Once your meeting has been set, make sure you have your topic prepared.

Research your area and the surrounding states concerning other airport details. Research which other airports feed into your airport, and ascertain if those airports have details. Consider where your city is in relation to the drug network. Is your city a distribution point or a source location? Let the airport managers know that airport details have been in existence since the early to mid-1970s, and that these airport details began as a way to stem the flow of narcotics in and out of the United States.

Be prepared for many questions from these managers during your meeting. It is a good idea to speak to other supervisors from airport details, and especially any details that were just created. Ask them what type of questions were asked and what the concerns of the airlines were. Some questions you should prepare for are:

1.  *What are the liability issues should our airline become involved in the airport detail?* The airline's major concern is lawsuits filed against their airline as a result of their cooperation in the program. Answer truthfully that anyone and any company can be sued at any time for anything. We cannot tell them that there will never be a circumstance where they could be sued.

2.  *How will our employees assist the airport detail?* We must stress that we want the airline's employees to act only as "eyes and ears." We do not want them doing anything that goes against their policy. We do not want the employees to become over-inquisitive with the passengers. We want the employees to behave the same way they behave with all passengers. We do not want the employee to take any enforcement action, but only to report their observations and concerns to us. All airline employees have been instructed on the "terrorist profile." When we meet with the managers and employees and explain our program, they will find that many of the characteristics and indicators that law enforcement uses to identify a potential narcotic violator are similar to those of their terrorist profile. Because as law enforcement officers we are professionals and that is how we will relate to them in notifying us, they should contact us and let us determine if, in fact, the passenger is involved in criminal activity. We want to utilize their information, but we want to distance that employee as far from our investigation

as possible, and we will conduct or our independent investigation on any information that we get from them.

3. *Will our employees have to testify in court?* We must inform the airlines that this is always a possibility, but we will do all we can to keep their employees out of court. We do not want to have to subpoena an employee to testify for us. We do not want to bring any of our "eyes and ears" forward on our behalf. That is why we conduct our own independent investigations from the information provided to us by the airline employee. If an employee calls with information concerning a passenger and asks whether they should question a passenger further or search a passenger's luggage, you would want to relay to them not to ask any more questions than they would of a regular passenger. Airlines also have their own policies concerning searching luggage, and their employees should adhere to their airline's policy. You do not want an employee searching a piece of luggage because he thought there might be drugs or money in the luggage, and then contacting you when they find it. That would make it difficult to keep the employee out of your investigation due to his discovery. Tell employees to rely on their airline's policy and do not search any article or piece of luggage on our behalf. If it is a suspicious piece of luggage that they think might contain drugs or money, they should allow us to have it examined by a trained narcotic detection canine and let us make that determination. No enforcement action whatsoever should be taken on our behalf.

These are some of the questions to anticipate from airline administration. All questions should be answered truthfully.

Once you have had a chance to explain your program to management, make sure there is ample time for questions. Allow some discussion on their part regarding their employees' participation and how will it affect them. Let them know that you are there one hundred percent.

Some interdiction details provide the cooperating airline companies with a letter of commitment. This letter also describes to the airline company the effect the role, mission, and participation the airport detail will have on the airline company and airport community. The letter of commitment also lists the members of the interdiction detail and the office telephone number as well as a duty telephone number so that detectives or agents can be contacted after hours.

If you provide a 24-hour on-call telephone number to the airlines, then you must be able to answer that telephone 24 hours a day. Many airport details have developed an on-call list with all the agents or detectives assigned to the detail. Regardless of the time of day or night, you must respond to the call. It is important to return calls as soon as possible. If you receive information from an airline employee and you are unable to react quickly enough before the flight leaves, calling ahead to the destination city might suffice. But remember, you must respond to all calls and inquiries in a timely manner, because if you do not, the employees might not call back the next time.

After you have met with managers and established a working relationship with an airline, it is up to you to continue the liaison with all employees. Carrying business cards is essential. You want to make as many contacts with employees as possible; you want to get to know all of the them so when they see you in the terminal, they know you by first name, and hopefully you know them by first name as well. Passing out your business card to all the employees of an airline you are working with is important; remember they all can be your "eyes and ears." From the baggage handler to the shift supervisor, from the ticket agent to the ramp agent, these people are all potential sources of information for you. We want to educate these employees on the characteristics displayed by drug and money couriers. We will explore these later on in this chapter.

Now that you have made yourself and your team known to all airline employees, it is time to make yourself known to the security screeners at your airport. The screeners will eventually be taken over by the federal government, but it is still important that the managers and security screeners know who you are as well as all of those in your unit. There has been a large turnover with security screeners in the past because they were only paid minimum wage, but that could change with the federal government taking over this process. They also can be excellent sources for you, although you must be careful that these security screeners do not focus on what we are looking for, but focus on their job at hand.

It is important to request office space at the airport. This allows for quicker response time. Some details are located in proximity to the airport. Having an office within the airport will be a greater asset to your detail. With an office inside the airport, it is easier to respond each day to your airport instead of reporting off-site or to a different office location. Many of us know that once we report to our prospective offices, if in an off-site location, it is harder to get out to the airport. Make the fact that you are physically located at the airport known to all you come in contact with — airport police, airline employees, security screeners, and other personnel.

Now you are open for business and should get out and explore your airport. It will take you some time to become familiar with the ins and outs of working in an airport community and to become familiar with the peculiarities associated with it. It's all about "face time," and letting everyone at the airport know that you are there to assist them and intercept the illegal narcotics and currency that are flowing through our airports. The more the airport community sees you, the more likely they are going to make you a part of their community.

Where is your airport in relation to how drugs come in and out of the country — is your city a source location, distribution point, or both? Researching the airlines and frequency of flights is also important. Which airlines and which flights will be most productive for you? This will not always be the same. You will have to spend time on the concourse familiarizing yourself with the frequency of flights and scheduled times; you want to "work smart, not hard."

Once you have established your airport detail and have made yourself known, you must begin the process of educating the "eyes and ears" of the airport. They may ask, "What are you looking for," or "What do these people look like?" There are no hard rules when it comes to the drug world, and we must educate the airport community of this fact; you must not proceed into this community with blinders on.

## Educating Your "Eyes and Ears"

We know that we will not be able to man our airport 24/7; this is impossible, and even with a large airport group you would still not be able to cover every airline and every flight. Therefore, we must rely on the airport community to assist us. How will we accomplish this?

There are several ways that this is going to occur. First of all, we know that the different airlines conduct meetings of the administration as well as their regular employees, the people you will most likely come in contact with — ticket agents, baggage handlers, ramp agents, and first-line supervisors. Request permission from management to attend some of these meetings and conduct some question-and-answer sessions. We want to stress to airline employees that we are not interested in the legitimate, law-abiding passenger; we are seeking out that passenger who is involved in criminal activity — the drug or currency courier.

Another useful method is getting to know all employees and, when possible, spending some one-on-one time with them. Some airline employees will be more inquisitive than others; some will want nothing to do with your program, and that is fine, too. Those not interested in keeping criminal activity from their airlines or keeping the aircraft safe for the legitimate passenger will be treated with the same respect and cordiality that you should show to all employees. We cannot force the airport community to cooperate with us, but you will find that the majority is behind us. Those who are not, again, will be treated with the same respect as those who are. The employees who do want to assist us in keeping their airport free of drug and money couriers and general criminal activity are the ones we will focus our attention on.

If you are allowed to present your information in a meeting type setting, make sure you have plenty of time to explain your mission at the airport, your goals, and to be able to educate employees on the characteristics or indicators that will alert them to unusual or even suspicious passenger conduct.

Each airline will have its own version of a passenger name record (PNR), which is a record of the reservation or ticket purchase, even if the person walked up to the counter and purchased a ticket without a reservation. The PNR is a record of any activity a passenger may have initiated, whether he purchased the ticket himself or not. The PNR is a valuable tool to assist in narrowing down the persons most likely involved in criminal activity. Because drug and money couriers and people involved in other types of criminal activity cannot plan in advance when dope will be available or money ready for transport, they must travel in a certain method. The PNR will identify these people. The authors stress that you focus on conduct and behavior, and not on names and nationalities.

Seek out the assistance of airline employees to help you to understand their particular airline PNR. Ask the employees to explain their system and help you to read their PNR system. In turn, you will be educating them on the characteristics of the courier. The employees will understand when you ask them a question concerning a particular passenger and their method of travel, not their name, race, age, or national origin. Let them know that the focus is on conduct and behavior. The airline employees will educate you on their particular airline, their flight schedules, and frequency of flights.

## Equipment and Material Needed

If you are fortunate enough to have office space at the airport, make sure it is set up to accommodate you and your partners. Make sure all the necessary forms and documents are in place, such as:

- Airport security passes or badges
- Airline schedules
- Telephone numbers for direct access to ticket counters or gate areas
- Computers or laptops
- Evidence bags and seals
- Fingerprinting equipment
- Cameras, video, Polaroid, or digital
- Luggage keys (most name brand luggage such as American Tourister and Samsonite have keys similar to those of off brands)
- Handcuffs and leg irons

You will be asked, "What do these people look like?" "What does a drug courier look like," or "What does a money courier look like"" The answer is that it's not what they look like, it's what they do; their conduct and behavior.

## Characteristics or Indicators

Make sure the ticket agent understands that if he has any overall suspicion about a passenger, he should notify you, and then you will conduct your own investigation to verify if, in fact, the passenger is involved in some kind of criminal activity. The methods that couriers utilize will change, and not only must you keep up with those changes, but you must also keep your "eyes and ears" informed of them. Here are some of the characteristics that airline personnel should look out for.

### Last-Minute Reservations

This can be day of departure or 1 or 2 days before departure from the origination city. Because of how the drug world operates, the distribution networks have many obstacles to overcome in preparing and transporting a load of dope. There is no set time frame when dope is due to arrive; it could be early because some of those obstacles were already taken care of, it could be on time (which is very rare), and, in most instances, the load is late. Therefore, the time the load arrives is the time couriers will be summoned by the distribution networks. They have to travel immediately to meet the demands and continue the transportation of the load. The reservation will almost always be one-way. Even though the courier knows he is going to return, he does not want to give advance notice to law enforcement about a return trip. Also, he could return via a different mode of transportation. So, we want to educate those in a position to observe this type of activity, ticket agents especially, to watch for it. Regardless of whether couriers are transporting drugs or money, they will usually travel in this manner, making last minute reservations.

### Purchasing Ticket Shortly before Flight Leaves

With the terrorist incidents of September 11, 2001, it is more difficult for couriers to show up 1/2 hour before a scheduled flight and try to get on it. However, a ticket agent might see a passenger show up as close to the required time as possible to purchase his ticket and get through security. This also keeps the courier from staying in the airport terminal for too long. Explain to the ticket agents that the individual might seemed rushed or nervous at the ticket counter. He may continuously look over his shoulder or scan other passengers as he waits in the ticket line. The individual might not know his reservation information, because the drug source may have made the travel arrangements and not given the courier all the pertinent information. Inform ticket agents that several couriers could be traveling together on the same reservation but showing up at different times to purchase their tickets, or the couriers could be staggered through the waiting line so that they do not appear to be together. However, their reservation would indicate whether several passengers were listed on the same reservation.

## Purchasing Tickets with Cash

This is a widely used tactic by drug and money couriers and people involved in criminal activity. Let the ticket agents know that these people will almost always pay in cash, usually in small denominations such as fives, tens, and twenties; street drug money. The ticket agents might see large sums of money, or on some occasions the couriers might just have the exact amount of money, because the source made the travel arrangements and knew exactly how much the ticket would cost. Credit cards are not usually used, because the drug business is a cash business.

## False Identification

Persons involved in criminal activity can obtain false identification through illegal means and use it for travel purposes. Explain to the ticket agents that the passenger might not be familiar with the documents he is using, or will appear nervous when asked to produce identification.

## Little or No Luggage, or Inappropriate Amount of Luggage for Length of Stay

The drug courier, if summoned to pick up and move a load, will not be traveling with an empty piece of luggage. He may have a small bag with personal items, or no luggage at all, especially if he is expecting to pick up the load and leave. If the courier has just picked up a load, the luggage will usually be new, because when he arrived he picked up the load of dope and then went out to buy a suitcase to fit the dope. In some instances a courier will pick up the dope in a suitcase, and, again, the suitcase will almost always be new. The same is true with currency couriers, although the currency will remain close to the courier and he may opt to carry the luggage on rather than check it as a drug courier might if he is carrying a sizeable amount of drugs.

## Passengers Hiding the Fact that They are Traveling Together

The ticket agent might observe several passengers meeting and talking together and then splitting up when they are in line to purchase their tickets, attempting to distance themselves from one another. Multiple couriers have been utilized in the past to transport larger loads of drugs.

## Luggage Indicators

If the passenger is checking in luggage, is the luggage new with the name brand tag still attached to the handle? Is there still a protective plastic covering over the handles of the luggage? Does the passenger not fill in the luggage nametag until the ticket agent asks him to do so? Inform the ticket agents and baggage handlers to watch for any unusual odor emanating from a suitcase. Are there odors such as fabric dryer sheets, baby oil, coffee, grease, or heavy perfume? Is the passenger protective of the suitcase or does he try to help the ticket agent load the luggage onto the conveyor belt? Is the luggage heavy and the passenger readily agrees to pay an extra charge for overweight luggage?

## Frequent Flyer Couriers

Many couriers are quite good at their jobs and opt for the benefits of the frequent flyer programs offered by most airlines. The courier has become so adept at the job of transporting dope or money and has become so comfortable that he will apply for the frequent flyer programs. You can access information via subpoena to determine the frequency of flying and destinations of the courier, which will let you know where he is picking up the dope or where he is taking it to. Source locations can be determined as well as distribution points.

## Call-Back Telephone Numbers

These are usually requested by the reservationist so that the number can be logged on the PNR. Call-back telephone numbers are used by the airline to notify passengers of possible delays or cancellations. The call-back number that a passenger gives is another factor that can assist in identifying a potential courier. In many instances the telephone number provided by the courier or source is fictitious. They do not want to be identified or have a trail lead back to them. Check with the ticket agent to see if the passenger had difficulty in providing a call-back telephone number or if he was evasive about it. The call-back telephone number can be called by you to verify whether in fact the passenger does reside at a certain address or if anyone at that location knows him. In many cases the call-back telephone number is fictitious or the answering party might inform you that the person just stepped out and will be returning shortly.

## Surveillance and Encounter Locations

There are many areas within the airport terminal where surveillance can be conducted to identify potential drug or currency couriers. We will look at these areas and explore the different situations and activities you will observe in these areas.

The most common areas for working in an airport setting will be the curb area for departing flights, ticket counter, gate areas, and restaurant and lounge locations.

### The Curb Area

The curb or passenger drop-off area in front of the departing flight and ticket counters are prime areas for identifying potential drug or money couriers. Every airport and airport terminal is different. Whether you are looking for drug or money couriers, the activity you observe at the curb will be similar.

Think of the last time you dropped off a loved one, friend, or business associate at the airport. What did you do when you exited the car and helped retrieve the luggage from the back seat or trunk? If it was a loved one or friend, you may have placed the luggage on the curb and exchanged some pleasantries, and you may have given them a big hug and a kiss; and people in proximity to you could probably overhear your conversation and observe your behavior. You may have cried as you hugged them and said goodbye. If it was a business associate, you may have helped them with their luggage. There may have been a hearty handshake and some small business discussion before that person entered the terminal. You probably waved goodbye.

Reflecting back on your own personal experiences concerning dropping people off at the airport is a good reference point for what you are about to observe at the curb as you watch hundreds of people being dropped at your airport. As you become familiar with the flight schedules, you will become familiar with the busy times at your airport.

As you stand out in front of the curb of the departing flight area and watch passengers being dropped off, your personal experiences will come into play. You will see over and over again the same type of activity. People hugging, exchanging pleasantries, hearty hand shakes between business associates, and, on occasion, maybe someone did not have a good trip and you will overhear a heated exchange or an argument between loved ones. You will need to spend some time on the curb to observe this activity; this will also strengthen your credibility when you get into court. Patience and paying attention to small details is what it will take to be successful at this type of surveillance.

Couriers that are dropped off with their loads of dope or money will be without these activities. You will not see an exchange of pleasantries; you will probably not see any exchange of words at all. The person dropping off the courier will be in hurry to get rid of him. You might not even see the driver shift gears into park, but just idle, waiting for the courier to exit the car and retrieve his luggage. The driver might not even look at the passenger as he exits; he will undoubtedly be looking for law enforcement. As soon as the passenger has exited the car with his luggage, the vehicle will leave immediately.

If the passenger or courier has multiple pieces of luggage, you will probably not see the driver assist the passenger in retrieving luggage from the car. If the luggage is in the back seat, again the passenger or courier will take the luggage out himself without any help from the driver. If the luggage is in the trunk, that will be the only time you may see the driver exit the vehicle — long enough to open the trunk — and in some cases the driver will get back into the front seat immediately without helping the passenger take the luggage from the trunk.

You might observe a courier being dropped off with no luggage; he will have the drugs or money secreted on his person. This is becoming very common not only in airport travel but in other modes of transportation. Watch for any unusual bulges on the body.

When the passenger or courier has exited the car and, if they have luggage with them, once the luggage has been retrieved from the car, you might observe the courier conduct some countersurveillance before proceeding into the terminal. The countersurveillance techniques might be subtle; a quick glance around the area for any uniformed law enforcement presence, and he will undoubtedly be looking for you as you conduct surveillance of him.

Many times couriers will check their luggage in at the curb. Be aware of this and try to establish a position where you can see passengers going to the curbside luggage check-in.

Once you have seen any unusual activity, your surveillance of the passenger or courier will continue from here. If the courier has checked luggage at the curb, make sure that at least one detective or agent checks with the luggage handler after the passenger or courier has left the area and entered the terminal. The agent checking with the baggage handler should try to obtain information on the luggage, such as newness, weight, luggage identification tags, and of course destination and flight information from the luggage claim tag. Attempt to obtain as much information as possible from your "eyes and ears" concerning any conversation the passenger might have had with the baggage handler. Were any specific instructions given concerning the checked in luggage? Were any tips given, large or small? What type of behavior did the passenger display; was there any nervousness or apprehension?

As one agent or detective establishes as much information about the passenger and luggage as possible, one or two more agents should maintain surveillance on the passenger as he enters the terminal. Patience again will prevail in observing the passenger's conduct and behavior. If you cannot remember everything you observe or hear, have your note pad handy so you can write down details.

If you work in a source location, you will most likely be looking for dope going out. Being able to have your canine examine the luggage that was just checked in out of sight of the general public will be most favorable. You have to be discreet with this issue. The examination of luggage by the canine should be done immediately due to time constraints. If the canine alerts to the luggage, then this information will be relayed to the agents or detectives conducting surveillance of the passenger. The luggage should not be left alone until this has been determined. Of course, if there is no canine alert, then a decision must be made as to whether the passenger is going to be encountered anyway. Again, you need to focus on the conduct and behavior of the passenger; just because a canine does not alert to a piece of luggage does not mean there are no drugs in the suitcase, or money could be inside rather than drugs. With the insurgence of designer drugs on the market, canines may not be trained to detect these substances.

Just because you observe one passenger with unusual behavior check luggage in and you and your partners are concentrating on him, does not mean that additional couriers working for the same source were not being let off afterward, so you still need to be aware of other people in the area and not put all of your focus on a single suspect.

The authors on occasion have experienced money instead of dope coming out of source locations, or money and dope in the same situation. A courier may travel to a city to pick up drugs and the drugs were not in or he could not locate the source, so now he has to return to his home city. Or the courier may pick up only a portion of the dope, and not all the money he came with was used.

Whether or not the canine has alerted to the luggage needs to be relayed to the detectives or agents conducting surveillance of the passenger. The agents will then make the decision whether or not to encounter the passenger. If the detectives do decide to encounter the passenger, a consensual encounter will be conducted. In this encounter remember that you do not have to tell the passenger anything that you know, what you observed, or that you saw him check luggage in. Ask the passenger "do you have any luggage?" The passenger can choose to abandon the luggage if he wants. You don't have to argue with him that you saw him checking in luggage. You might want to be explicit and ask him if he has any checked-in luggage; again, he can still abandon his checked-in luggage. Remember, they don't know what you know.

The canine handler should remain with the luggage at this time, especially if the canine has alerted to the luggage. Even if the canine did not alert to the luggage and the detectives or agents are going to conduct a consensual encounter, the canine handler should remain with the luggage.

Once the encounter has been conducted and permission to search has been requested and granted, does the detective or agent who requested the permission have to be the one to search the luggage? No, the requesting detective or agent can relay the information to the canine handler standing by with the luggage. If the passenger wants to be present during the search of the luggage, should the officer allow him to witness this? Yes. Again, we must remember the time constraints once the encounter has been conducted. If the passenger denies consent to search, then you can rely on your probable cause of the dog alert.

## Ticket Counters

This is another great location to conduct surveillance of potential drug and money couriers. If you are working the curb, you will probably go back and forth from the curb to the ticket counter. Establishing a liaison with all ticket agents is very important.

As you conduct surveillance of the ticket counters, you have more of a chance to observe nervous conduct and behavior. Now the courier is wait-ing in line to be serviced. You will see nervous behavior in line. He will continuously be watching approaching passengers that enter the line. You will observe the courier keeping a close eye on his luggage, whether it is a piece of carry-on luggage or luggage to be checked in. You might observe him conversing with other passengers (couriers) also standing in line. This will allow you to identify additional couriers. Observe conduct and behav-ior as he stands in line; again, if you cannot remember everything you see, write it down.

Once the person has approached a ticket agent and the check-in process has been completed, allow the passenger time to leave the area of the ticket counter and proceed to his flight. One detective or agent should remain at the ticket counter to talk with the ticket agent while one or more partners continue surveillance of the courier.

The agent talking to the ticket agent should obtain as much information from the ticket agent as possible.

- When was the reservation made; day and time?
- What flight is the passenger on and what time is it due to depart?
- How did he or she purchase the ticket; what was method of payment?
- Was any luggage checked in (if you missed this activity)?
- Were there additional passengers on the reservation?
- Was the passenger nervous?
- Did the passenger ask any questions concerning the flight?

- Was the passenger hesitant in answering the security questions?
- Was there any type of language barrier?

Arm yourself with as many answers to questions that you or your partner are going to ask the passenger during the conversation. The decision to approach and contact the passenger will be determined by what you have learned from travel arrangements.

Once you have obtained the necessary information to assist in contacting the passenger or courier, this information should be relayed to the detectives or agents still maintaining surveillance of the passenger, if possible.

## Passenger Waiting Areas

These areas near the jetway are other good locations for conducting surveillance. In these areas, you will observe passengers waiting to depart on flights and you will also be observing passengers arriving in your city. Watching the passengers in the waiting area will also give you a chance to become familiar with what passengers do as they wait; rely on your own experiences. Some people are apprehensive about flying, especially since the activities of September 11, 2001, although in our experience, legitimate passengers who are contacted in the terminal area are usually relieved to see law enforcement.

As you watch passengers stand in line for boarding, you will see nervous behavior and conduct of a potential drug or currency courier similar to what you would have seen at the ticket counter. As the courier stands in line, he or she will begin to conduct countersurveillance, watching other passengers as they enter or leave the line. The courier will also conduct himself in the same manner if he is carrying the drugs or currency in a carry-on bag. If the courier has drugs or money secreted on his body, you might observe him adjusting the load or continuously looking at where the load is secreted. You might even see unusual bulges on his person. Encounters can be conducted as the courier waits in line to board.

From the boarding area you can also watch as passengers exit from the jetway of arriving flights. Surveillance of this activity is also important. As you rely on your personal experiences, remember what you did when you landed and as you exited from the jetway and entered into the terminal. As you watch passengers exiting from the jetway area, you will observe the same type activity from legitimate passengers. Become familiar with normal habits of people as they exit from the jetway and proceed through the airport terminal. With the new restrictions allowing only ticketed passengers to have access beyond the screening areas, you will not have a lot of people waiting in this area for arriving passengers. It is important to watch the behavior of arriving passengers as they enter the terminal area. Remember they have made it out of the destination city, whether that city was a source location or a distribution point. Their nervousness might be visible upon their arrival at their destination point. Now they have to worry again about encountering law enforcement, even if your city is only a connecting city to their final destination.

Some of the activity you will observe from persons involved in criminal activity, especially a drug or money courier, should be described in your report. You are conducting surveillance of the criminal, and the criminal is conducting countersurveillance of you. In the past, emphasis was placed on where a passenger was seated to help determine if the passenger was a potential courier. Some interdiction officers would look for the first passengers off the flight, some would look for the last. Most larger airlines, except for Southwest Airlines, have first-class seating, so the first passengers off those airlines would normally be first-class passengers. If the courier has made his reservations in accordance with normal courier activity, his seat selection might be limited to one of the last seats left on the flight. If the courier had no reservation and bought his ticket shortly before departure time, the ticket agent might put the courier at the back of the plane, unless the courier requests certain seating. With Southwest Airlines, there is no assigned seating and it is first come, first serve. If the courier shows up with minimal amount of time to purchase his ticket or check in luggage, he will be boarding with some of the last groups to board the flight. Again, the seating at the front of the plane will begin to fill up, thus the courier might have to sit in the back of the plane and therefore will be deplaning last.

## Countersurveillance Activity

Following are some scenarios that you might encounter during surveillance/countersurveillance:

> The courier walks slowly out of the jetway area into the airport terminal, scanning all persons waiting in the passenger waiting area.
> He will watch all persons intently to see if anyone is watching him.
> He might walk in a circuitous manner, not taking a direct route to the bathroom, to his connecting flight gate, or to check the flight display board, again checking to see who might be watching them or following him.
> The courier walks into the bathroom and enters a stall, but you do not see or hear any activity consistent with someone relieving himself; instead you hear unusual movement or noise, tape being removed, the rustling of cellophane or plastic wrap, or elastic bandages falling to the floor. You can tell that the person is still standing and he is

removing his bottom clothing articles; you can see them bunched up around his ankles.

If a suspect enters a stall in the bathroom and remains there without using the facility, this could be a stalling technique, especially if he observed you watching him.

As a courier walks toward the exit after deplaning, he might walk in and out of several bathrooms, watching to see who might be following him.

The courier may discard any ticketing documents immediately upon arrival. He may remove luggage claim tags from ticket folders and keep them separate.

The courier will immediately take a seat in the passenger waiting area to scan the people in the terminal area.

If the courier has only carry-on luggage, he might be clutching the bag tightly while exiting the jetway area; pay attention in the manner in which the suspect is carrying the bag — is the bag heavy or is it very light? If the luggage is a soft-sided bag, can you see the imprint of bundles or bricks?

If the courier has no luggage at all or no items or documents in his hand, is the load secreted on his body? What type of clothing is the courier wearing; is it conducive to the time of year and temperature in your area?

Is the courier's clothing brand new? Sources will often attempt to dress up the courier, or if the courier is a gang member, the courier will wear clothing to blend into the crowd but the gang clothing will be packed inside a suitcase.

Is the clothing overly big? (With today's fashions that might not be out of place.) With baggy clothing, many couriers will wear spandex type shorts or tops to keep the load of drugs or money firmly secured to his or her body.

Is the courier continuously adjusting his or her clothing (the "body carrier")?

As the courier walks through the terminal, can you see the outline of a brick or bundle on his body?

Is the courier having problems walking? Many couriers will secret their load in shoes or boots, or in the socks.

What type of items is the courier carrying, and are they in keeping with the courier's overall appearance or style? Do not overlook obvious items, such as those listed below. These are just a few items you might observe someone carrying, but you should always look at obvious items as possible concealment areas:

> Diaper bag (with no baby)
> Store bags

Stuffed animals

Food containers

Unopened food bags or boxes; bags of chips or Pringles, boxes of cookies or candy

Drink containers, unopened cans and bottles, bottles of water; PCP is often transported this way. PCP is a liquid and can vary from clear to a yellowish color, so it may be packed in a container whose liquid resembles the color of PCP; apple juice, beer, wine, Listerine, etc. Examine the lids carefully; couriers will often use silicone, putty, some other type of sealant, or black tape to keep the odor of the PCP from escaping the bottle. The odor of PCP is very strong and toxic.

Gift-wrapped presents

Bouquets of flowers

Magazines, books, and newspapers

Sporting articles such as baseball bats, basketballs, soccer balls, baseballs, helmets, gloves, skis, etc.

If there are multiple couriers, they will not walk off of the airplane together. They will stay separate, but you will see occasional glances between them. After a time they might meet and talk or they may remain separate during the entire time after they have exited the aircraft.

A courier might proceed directly to a lounge or bar area to have a drink to calm his nerves. He may go into a restaurant or gift shop and look around the gift shop, all the time watching for persons following him.

Immediately upon entering the terminal area, the courier may be on a cellular telephone advising a source or purchaser that he has arrived and is ready to be picked up. If the courier does not have a cellular telephone, he will proceed directly to a public telephone to place a page or call to notify his contacts that he has arrived. Standing in an adjacent telephone next to someone to overhear the conversation is legal.

Couriers will come in every imaginable fashion and number, couriers traveling as friends, husband and wife, boyfriend and girlfriend, mother and daughter, families, families with small children. Do not overlook the small children and the elderly.

If you observe a courier who is waiting for a connecting flight, you will have to make the decision to make the approach at this time or to call ahead to his final destination city. If he is going to a city that has no airport detail or you are unable to contact a group that handles the airport there, then the decision will be easier as to whether to approach.

If the passenger exits the secure area and appears to be headed toward the exit and not to the luggage carousel, then a consensual encounter will be imminent. At this point timing is crucial, especially if he walks out of the terminal and a vehicle is waiting for him. Do we contact him inside of the terminal for safety reasons or outside of the terminal? Once you have stepped outside of the airport terminal, the danger increases because other persons may be waiting to pick up the courier, or the courier may run from you or try to fight with you. Watch for the courier meeting up with other passengers not only from his flight, but from other flights that have arrived. Multiple couriers could arrive by different airlines. Surveillance is a key component in working airport interdiction.

## Approach and Encounter

Once you have selected a potential target to approach and engage in conversation, the same rules apply as to any consensual encounter (refer to Chapter 1). Keep in mind all the information you already have about the passenger before you even approach, knowing the answers to your questions.

Since September 11, 2001, activity at airports has changed, although some airport groups are still busy with drug and money couriers attempting to evade the security measures. It is much harder for couriers to adhere to their usual methods of travel without drawing attention to themselves. Although the airlines' major concern is passenger safety, the conduct and behavior of a terrorist and a drug courier are similar.

## Related Airport Case Law

### First Circuit

*United States v. De Los Santos Ferrer*, 999 F.2d 7, cert. denied, 114 St. Ct. 562 (1993) 1st Cir.
*United States v. Colon-Pagan*, 1 F.3d 80 (1993) 1st Cir.
*United States v. Nunez*, 19 F.3d 179 (1994) 1st Cir.

### Third Circuit

*United States v. Coggins*, 986 F.2d 651 (1993) 3rd Cir.
*United Sates v. Frost*, 999 F.2d 737 (1993) cert. denied, 114 S. Ct. 573, 3rd Cir.

## Fourth Circuit

*United States v. Williams*, 41 F.3d 192 (1994) cert. denied, 131 L.Ed. 2d 321 (1995), 4th Cir.

## Fifth Circuit

*United States v. Daniel*, 982 F.2d 146 (1993) 5th Cir.

*United States v. Butler*, 988 F.2d 537 (1993) cert. denied, 114 S. Ct. 413 (1993), 5th Cir.

*United States v. Mendez*, 27 F.3d 126 (1994) 5th Cir.

*United States v. Harlan*, 35 F.3d 176 (1994) 5th Cir.

## Sixth Circuit

*United States v. Ogbuh*, 982 F.2d 1000 (1993) 6th Cir.

*United States v. $53,082.00 in U.S. Currency*, 985 F. 2d 245 (1993) 6th Cir.

*United States v. Repress*, 9 F.3d 483 (1993) 6th Cir.

*United States v. Baro* 15 F.3d 563, (1994) cert. denied, 115 S. Ct. 285, 6th Cir. †

## Key Terms

Airport family
Airport screeners
Baggage handler
Characteristics
Consensual encounter techniques
"Eyes and ears"
Fourth Amendment
Gate or ramp agent
Indicators

Jetway
Jurisdiction
Letter of commitment
Mobile society
Passenger name record (PNR)
Shift supervisor
Terrorist profile
Ticket agent
Work smart, not hard

# Storage Unit Investigations

7

Storage facilities, commonly referred to as mini-storage units, are popular throughout the United States. They can be found in urban and rural settings and are in demand in both environments. There are a variety of types, including outdoor and indoor climate control facilities. There is also a new service known as Portable On-Demand storage (PODS). This innovative approach to storage brings the mobile storage unit directly to a particular location, business or residence, lets the customer pack it, and then picks the unit up and transports it to another location or a storage facility. PODS was established in St. Petersburg, Florida in 1998 and the service is available in various parts of the country. Indoor climate-controlled storage facilities are popular for businesses and personal document storage. Outdoor mini-storage facilities are used for storage of vehicles, boats, furniture, lawn equipment, or anything else that can be stored out of doors. There are also large storage facilities located within industrial complexes that are available for business and personal use. Many businesses such as lawn maintenance, boat building, sign making, and vehicle maintenance work out of large storage facilities. Individuals also rent these large storage units to use for restoration of vehicles and boats, etc.

Storage facilities have a variety of amenities such as security systems, mailboxes, and shipping and receiving of postal items. Some facilities can receive parcels via Federal Express and United Parcel Service for their customers. They have mailboxes available and sell moving supplies, such as boxes, tape, and other shipping supplies. What a perfect environment for a drug trafficker. A one-stop place for all of the drug dealer's needs — storing drugs, and receiving and shipping the drugs. This does not mean that storage facilities cater to the drug element; but the services that they offer to legitimate customers happen to be convenient for drug traffickers as well.

Storage units come in all sizes and price ranges. Sizes range from 3' × 3' to 16,000 cubic feet. The price range may be from $25 up to $3000 per month with options for electricity and climate-control units. Climate-control units can be set at 60° year round. State-of-the-art security systems are also available in some facilities. Some of the larger franchise facilities offer interior and exterior video surveillance, motion detectors, listening devices, controlled entry sign-in and sign-out logs, and resident on-site managers.

Storage facilities are popular with drug traffickers for several reasons. They can store their narcotics in a relatively safe off-site environment. Dealers feel secure because the drugs are not in their residences or other locations they do not feel are safe. Many drug dealers store their illegal gains (currency) and use storage facilities to take delivery of narcotics either via a commercial parcel service or other means. Eliminating risk from forfeiture of their residence and real property is another compelling reason for the popularity of storage facilities. In many states, the government may initiate forfeiture proceedings against the individual with respect to real property. If the government can prove that there is a drug nexus and that drug or other illicit proceeds paid for the property, the properties are subject to civil forfeiture. Removing the drugs from one's home and storing them in a storage unit reduces this risk for the drug trafficker.

Storage facilities are generally open 7 days a week, 24 hours a day, and include easy access to a unit. Numerous storage facilities, some with hundreds of units, provide an environment conducive to the drug trafficker and his covert method of operation. A drug trafficker may be one of hundreds of tenants in a facility, and may be in the middle of several buildings.

In this chapter we will explore how to initiate a storage facility interdiction program, how to use a network of sources by partnering with the storage unit community, how to identify behavior of drug traffickers who are using storage facilities, and we will describe investigative methods to use once the behavior is identified. As with all interdiction programs, this is a unique investigative avenue and another opportunity for narcotic investigations. Typically, a storage facility program is worked in conjunction with an interdiction group.

## What is Storage Facility Interdiction?

Storage facility interdiction programs have been in existence for a number of years. This type of program, as with many of the interdiction programs, is typically attached to interdiction groups that work hotel/motel, airport, bus, and train. The purpose of this program is to identify individuals who are using storage unit facilities to conduct illicit activities; namely, narcotics trafficking. The mission of a storage facility program is to identify drug traffickers with use of information developed by investigators through a unique training program. Staff is trained in identifying individuals who may be renting storage units to store and distribute illicit drugs.

We are searching for anomalies, behavior that is different from that of individuals who rent storage facilities for legitimate purposes. The identification of behavior of individuals who are using these facilities to conduct their drug trafficking is based on law enforcement's training and experience. The facility staff is trained to identify certain conduct and asked to contact law enforcement if the behavior is observed. The pattern of behavior of the renter will dictate whether he or she is possibly involved in a criminal activity. As with all interdiction investigations, all rights and privileges of the law with respect to the expectation of privacy are afforded to the renter when he or she rents a facility. This program affords law enforcement an opportunity to build partnerships and network with storage facility management and staff. The establishment of reliable narcotic intelligence sources utilizing storage unit employees such as facility managers, staff, other reliable tenants, and security personnel is a proven benefit to the investigation to drug violations in this environment.

## How Do We Get Started?

As with all interdiction programs, commitment to the program is the key to its success. Supervisors and investigators should make contact with the United States Attorney, and State or District Attorney's office to make them aware of the intention of the agency participating and initiating a storage facility program. The prosecutor's office should research case law, federal and state, to provide law enforcement information related to such cases in their particular jurisdiction or their part of the country. Once the prosecutor is aware of the agency's intentions, the supervisor should select a group of investigators who are interested in working these types of cases. The storage unit facility program can be part of an interdiction team, which is generally part of the police agency's narcotics bureau or division. Special operations groups such as street crime units and patrol groups may want to dedicate resources to this type of a program.

It is imperative that a trained narcotics canine team be part of this program. It is extremely difficult to make cases without such a resource. The agency should implement this program through partnerships with the business community. These partnerships, or business-watch programs, are critical to the success of the storage facility program. Researching nearby jurisdictions within the county or state to inquire if they have storage facility programs is recommended. Information regarding current trends on drug traffickers' methods of operation will assist in starting the program.

## Implementation of the Program

Storage unit facilities within the police agency jurisdiction need to be selected to implement the program. In choosing a facility, the agency must look at its resources before committing to a program. Although it is not as demanding as a hotel/motel program, investigators should keep in mind that if a call is made by storage facility staff to report suspicious activity, a response should be made rapidly.

Storage unit facilities are located in many different settings. They can be in the middle of large urban settings or rural environments. They are available in a number of sizes, from several hundred units to just a few. The advantage of a particular type of location depends on the trafficker and his needs. A drug trafficker typically will select a facility that is close to where he lives. As previously mentioned, there are also indoor climate-controlled facilities, and there are many facilities where owner/operators or managers live on the premises.

Once the storage facilities have been selected, the owner or management should be contacted to provide them with information concerning the storage facility program and to solicit their cooperation. Contact can be initiated by telephone to set up a face-to-face appointment to explain the program. Investigators can also stop by the facility and make contact with the management that way. An appointment should be set at the manager's convenience to provide him with detailed information concerning the program. We suggest that the police agency offer a "letter of commitment" (Figure 7.1a) as with all interdiction programs, to provide to storage facility management an explanation of the program. It is a professional statement indicating the agency's intent and explanation of the program. The letter of commitment should be on an agency letterhead. The letter indicates that the police agency is seeking the assistance of the storage unit facility in establishing a program. It explains that some individuals utilize storage facilities to facilitate their drug trade.

There are indicators that will assist the storage facility staff in the detection of potential criminal activity. A list of indicators with an explanation and names and contact numbers should accompany the letter of commitment (Figure 7.1b). Investigators request that notification should be made to law enforcement and that the staff are not acting as agents of the police but as concerned citizens. The source facility staff is then provided with a list of possible potential behavioral characteristics which may be indicative that people are utilizing storage unit facilities to store narcotics.

An appointment is subsequently set with the management of the facility and employees who will participate in a training session. At this session, investigators will explain the program and what the expectations are. Generally,

### Use of Agency Letterhead

The ___(Insert Agency Name)___ is seeking your assistance in establishing a Narcotics Interdiction Program designed to have a direct impact on the storage facilities within ___(City or County Name)___.

We are currently living in a society where drug traffickers are constantly utilizing various methods of storing and distributing narcotics for their illicit activities. Storage unit facilities are becoming widely used to store these illegal narcotics.

Unfortunately, as the general public has become more sophisticated, so has the criminal element within our society. These people have found an alternative method of storing narcotics or other illicit items utilizing the storage unit facility systems. By constantly using these methods, it is more difficult for law enforcement to detect and apprehend them. The majority of these individuals are professional criminals who derive most or all of their income through criminal activity. These activities include narcotics trafficking, stolen property crime, transportation of weapons, robbery, etc. These individuals will commit any crime of opportunity.

These criminal types directly utilize the storage unit facilities while conducting their illicit activities. It is the intention of the Narcotics Interdiction Program to make you aware of the problem we face and enlist the cooperation of our storage facilities in __(City or County)__. It is the aim of the Narcotics Interdiction Program to detect and apprehend these individuals through the assistance of the storage unit facilities. These people are bad for business and detrimental to the general community.

There are indicators, which will assist you in the detection of potential criminal activity with individuals utilizing your storage unit facility.

Notification should be made to law enforcement in the interest of security and with the welfare of your employees and customers in mind. In providing information you are not acting as a police agent, but as a concerned citizen and business operator.

Customers who exhibit one or more off these activities listed may or may not be engaged in criminal activity. The __(Police Agency Name) requests__ that the only action you take is to observe and report those things seen during the course of your normal duties. It is the responsibility of trained law enforcement officers to evaluate your information and take appropriate action.

The investigator presenting this letter can offer a more comprehensive explanation of the Narcotics Interdiction Program.

Your assistance in this matter is greatly appreciated, and be assured that any information you provide will be handled in a confidential manner.

Sincerely,

**(Signed by Agency or Division Head)**

## Figure 7.1a

once contacted, the storage facility will agree to participate in this type of program. Some of the larger franchise type storage facilities will need to contact their legal affairs office to see if they can participate in such a program. Once investigators receive a commitment from the storage facility, a training session is scheduled. The training session can be done at the facility, and typically lasts 30 to 45 minutes. Questions should be solicited from management and staff regarding concerns or legal issues. Case law exists to support examinations by

**Confidential**

The attached list of indicators has been prepared to assist Storage Facility staff in the detection of potential criminal activity that may occur in or around your establishment.

In providing information, you are not acting as an agent of the **(Police Agency)**, but as a concerned citizen, Notification should be made to one of the law enforcement personnel listed below in the interest of security and with the welfare of you and customers in mind.

Your assistance in these endeavors is greatly appreciated.

To report suspicious criminal activity, call **(Pager or Telephone Number)**, and your call will be returned immediately.

Narcotics Interdiction Unit:

**List of Investigators here:**

**Names**
**Office Telephone**
**Pager Number**

Indicators listed on next page.

## Figure 7.1b

canine teams and other inquires by law enforcement, as long as consent is provided by ownership or management for law enforcement be on the property. Rewards or funds can also be available as part of the storage facility program. Monies can be offered for information, if departmental procedure allows for such a policy.

At the training session, investigators will provide a list of indicators or characteristics which a renter may display when using a storage facility for drug trafficking. Many agencies have prepared a short video illustrating the program that highlights many of its aspects. It should be expressed during the training process that investigators appreciate the cooperation of the storage facility owners, managers, and staff in participating in a voluntary program such as the storage facility investigations program.

Investigators should explain that they are aware that the facility is a business and that every effort will be made to not disrupt the normal course of business. Law enforcement is strictly interested in access, and wants staff to participate as the "eyes and ears" of law enforcement, and provide information regarding possible drug activity occurring in and around the premises. Staff will have 24-hour access to law enforcement if suspicious conduct is observed. The consideration of access to the facility is required for investigators to conduct operations on the premises. It should be explained that that particular storage facility is not specifically targeted as a location for which drug traffickers may store or do business from, but that all storage facilities have the potential for this type of activity. Each indicator should be explained in detail to staff, and they should then be given an opportunity ask questions.

As we have stated previously, an indicator is simply activity or behavior in which law enforcement takes its collective experience and explains its significance as it relates to criminal conduct. Certain conduct of individuals who are using storage unit facilities and are actively engaged in narcotics trafficking can be identified with training. Based on years of experience and investigation, law enforcement has identified a number of activities and conduct that traffickers display. Listed below are many of the characteristics displayed by these individuals. One or even several indicators do not mean that a renter is involved in criminal activity. A comprehensive investigation should be conducted to verify the information and conduct. Again, we must remember that we are separating legitimate renters of a storage facility from those individuals who are actively engaged in narcotics trafficking. Storage facility staffs deal with hundreds of people, depending on the size of their facility, and are well aware of how legitimate customers generally act. The following indicators will provide staff with guidance as to what to be aware of:

- Renter displays nervous tendencies
- Renter asks many questions about hours of operation, guard on duty, surveillance equipment
- Renter information is fictitious
- Vehicle traffic all hours of the day and night, or a pattern of usage every 2–3 weeks or more
- Windows, if any, covered with blankets or foil
- Large wrapped packages/boxes observed being placed in unit on a regular basis
- Numerous locks on door of unit
- Renter rarely shows up at facility, has someone else pay rent, but is frequently seen on property
- High electric bills
- Parcel deliveries to unit via USPS, Federal Express, or UPS
- Payment for unit sent from source area (city or state) such as Texas or Florida
- Advance rental payment, months/year at a time
- No means of business, when items are delivered or stored
- Unusual break-ins (burglaries) without anything claimed to have been taken, "dopers looking for dope"

- Freezers or coolers seen being placed in storage unit
- Multiple rentals in different names
- Strong odor emitting from unit (chemical or other)
- Overall suspicious behavior

An individual who wants to rent a storage facility for illicit purposes will often display nervous behavior when asking about the unit. A person may come in and ask if storage units are available. He may initially call by telephone to see if facilities are available and ask for prices on different unit sizes. Once the person comes in, he may want to actually look at the storage unit and the interior to get an idea of the layout. Coupled with that, the individual may ask for a certain storage unit in a specific part of the premises. This could be, but is not limited to, the storage facility facing away from the main road or access. The individual may ask for a storage facility that is away from heavily rented buildings.

As law enforcement, we must look at the totality of all of the circumstances and be mindful that just because an individual asks for criteria that has just been described does not necessarily mean that he is engaged in criminal activity. The investigator must look at all of the circumstances surrounding the renting of the unit.

The renter may ask many questions regarding details of the facility such as hours of operation or if there is a security guard on duty. Individuals may ask for multiple storage units within the complex and rent two or more units some distance from each other. Some drug traffickers receive and store their drugs in one storage unit and do business out of another, so there is a separation between the drugs, money, and the actual activities. We have found that in most instances, a storage facility is used for storing narcotics or money. In many cases, the customers do not know that the source has a storage facility where the drugs are kept.

The drug trafficker does not want to provide his customers with a location where the drugs are stored for fear that the drugs may be stolen. Storage unit staff may see an individual walk up to the facility and there is no vehicle in sight. The individual may be dropped off, then picked up after he has completed an application. The renter may park his vehicle around the corner, walk up, and then walk back to his vehicle, because he does not want to have his vehicle identified in the future. The staff may later learn that an individual rented a storage unit for someone else and that the actual user does not rent the facility unit. Information that is provided on the application is often fictitious or incomplete. Storage unit facilities should be encouraged to ask for some form of identification before renting a unit. Not only does this assist law enforcement, but provides information in case there is damage, fire, or other activity at the storage unit facility.

Management and staff should be aware that vehicle traffic might be prevalent at all hours of the day or night, and they may notice a specific pattern of usage. The individual may come daily, or there may be a lapse in time where there is activity on a weekly to bi-weekly basis or more. This could be an indication that the storage unit is used to store narcotics when the drugs are delivered, and there may be lapses of time between deliveries. Once the drugs are delivered, there will be much more activity.

If there is a strong odor emitting from the facility, this may be an indicator that masking agents are being used to mask the odor of narcotics. Some common masking agents are paint thinners, cedar chips, bleach, mothballs, ammonia, coffee, detergents, and anything else with a strong smell. Typically, these substances are lined up in the interior of the storage facility at the lower door level. Some narcotics traffickers believe that these masking agents will deter the narcotic canine. There may be some instances where that will occur; however, if the odor of a narcotic is available, a trained narcotics canine should be able to detect the odor regardless of masking agents. Investigators can use information concerning the use of masking agents as part of their probable cause for an affidavit for a search warrant, along with other factors such as a canine alert for the odor of narcotics. If an investigator smells an unusual odor emanating from the storage unit such as the ones described, it is part of the officer's training and experience that these items are used as masking agents. This can also be utilized as part of probable cause.

There may be a situation where the renter rarely shows up at the facility and has someone else who is frequently seen at the facility pay the rent for the unit. High power or electric bills at the storage unit may be indicative of a clandestine laboratory or marijuana growing operation. Information can be received from a source that a clandestine operation may be operating out of a storage facility. Investigators have the ability to subpoena power bills and chart the history of power from that particular unit. Not all storage facilities have a power source.

Narcotic traffickers may have parcels or packages delivered to the storage unit either via United Parcel Service, Federal Express, USPS, or some other commercial parcel system. Traffickers may attempt to legitimize the parcel by addressing it to a "suite." The suite would be the actual storage unit. Sending marijuana, cocaine, or other illicit substances is a popular method of transporting narcotics. Many traffickers travel to a source state and send the narcotics to themselves at a storage unit address.

Many storage unit facilities have mailboxes that can be rented by its customers. Investigators should inquire of staff if there are any unusual parcels or packages being delivered that are addressed to a mailbox at the facility or mail arriving infrequently with a pattern.

Some renters may indicate that they want to use a storage unit to conduct some sort of business. There are a number of legitimate businesses as previously described that can be run from a storage facility. The renter may indicate this to staff when the unit is originally rented. There may be items such as boxes, packages, and so on delivered and stored at the location. However, there may not be any means of a business. Drug traffickers may describe some sort of business to legitimize any illicit operation that they are conducting from storage unit facilities.

There may be unusual break-ins or burglaries without the renter reporting anything taken. These burglaries may occur when other drug dealers break in to steal narcotics. Several storage units within the facility may be burglarized if the thieves are not sure which unit the narcotics are stored in. They may try several units in an attempt to locate the one with the drugs. Storage units typically do not have windows; however, if they do, the windows may be covered with blankets, foil, or other material. Drug traffickers do not want anyone to see inside the unit. There may be several locks on the unit door instead of the traditional one lock.

Management may indicate to the investigators that a renter made an advance payment when renting the storage unit, several months or a year in advance. Many individuals who use storage units do not want to be bothered by making monthly payments and make advance payments, so they are not seen as often. Investigators may learn that payments are coming from a source city or state such as Texas, California, or Florida. A local renter may initially walk in and rent a unit but payments for that unit may be made via money order or cashier's check from a source area. The source of the drugs may not want that location to be identified, so a local associate will rent the unit and make the payments.

Some renters may rent multiple units in different names within a storage unit complex. They may request units on opposite ends of the facility, either in one name or in different names, so drugs are kept in one facility and other activity may be occurring at the other. Large freezers or coolers may be placed in the storage unit. Although there may not be any power in the unit, large standup freezers are a popular method of storing drugs. This makes it difficult for trained narcotic canines to locate narcotic odor. The freezers or coolers may not be totally air-tight, but they do keep the odor of narcotics tightly sealed. Management and staff should be aware that any overall suspicion about the renter should be brought to the attention of the investigator. Investigators will evaluate the behavior of the individual.

## Storage Facility Investigations

Once management and staff have been approached and agree to cooperate in this program, investigators conduct their training. When this is complete, investigators have a variety of options in examining and identifying individuals who rent a storage unit and are operating and storing narcotics from the unit. There are two methods in conducting storage facility investigations. The first, of course, is the call from management or employee of the storage facility to provide a tip regarding a possible suspicious renter. Information generally comes from personal observation of the renter either during the renting process or while staff observes something suspicious around a particular storage unit. Once trained, staff will be able to identify renters who display the conduct that has been described to them by investigators.

### Case Study

Investigators in Central Florida solicited the cooperation of a local storage facility. The staff agreed to participate in the program, and training was scheduled for management and staff. When the training was complete, management indicated that there was an individual currently renting a storage unit who was displaying many of the characteristics described by investigators during training. The subject was identified by investigators as a major narcotic trafficker in the area. He was involved in the distribution of multiple kilograms of cocaine in the Central Florida region. Investigators made a decision to use electronic video surveillance from a fixed point from within the storage facility complex to gather intelligence regarding the subject's activities. During electronic and mobile surveillance, investigators learned that several individuals arrived at various times and backed their vehicles into the storage unit. There was a pattern of this activity over time. There was a lookout, a person in front of the storage unit while the car was in the unit. The suspect and the other individuals were engaged in what was later learned to be the delivery of multiple kilograms of cocaine from South Florida. The source of the drugs had secreted the cocaine in various compartments of their vehicle such as door panels and areas of the vehicle's trunk. Multiple kilograms of cocaine were extracted from the car to be stored in the storage unit. Continuous surveillance revealed the suspect who rented the unit arrive at the storage facility, enter, and walk out with the cocaine, putting it in his vehicle and subsequently distributing the substance. This subject was subsequently arrested and convicted.

Investigators learned that the individual was obtaining multiple kilograms of cocaine several times a month, and the method of operation was the same each time. Storage facility staff was trained to observe the behavior that a person may display while involved in drug trafficking. They then put together a pattern of activity that they thought was suspicious; staff then told investigators that a person fitting those characteristics was currently occupying a unit. The renter had been there for several months. The couriers would travel from South Florida to deliver the cocaine. The storage unit staff had observed the same vehicle back into the storage facility on multiple occasions. While the vehicle was inside, they described a person as a "look out" who was looking around suspiciously while other people were inside the storage unit. Without the initiation of this type of a program, this activity probably would have gone undetected by law enforcement.

Once the management or staff contacts law enforcement to provide information relating to suspicious conduct and behavior, the investigators have a variety of investigative options concerning the information. Investigators should evaluate the information to verify who the renter is. They should meet and debrief the storage facility management and obtain details of the behavior and information concerning the suspicious renter. Officers may or may not identify the subject as a trafficker. There may or may not be intelligence information regarding the renter. The trafficker may have had someone else, who has no intelligence information or drug history, rent the unit.

Surveillance may be established at the facility in an attempt to identify any other individuals who may be involved. This could be electronic video surveillance or active mobile surveillance. A narcotic canine team can then be deployed in and around the unit in question. When the canine team is contacted, it is best that the handler is not told which unit is being looked at. Let the handler conduct examinations in the vicinity. This eliminates any bias that may occur by the handler. A well-trained narcotics canine handler does not want to know which unit is in question.

If the narcotic dog alerts the odor of narcotics from the suspect unit, there are several investigative options. One, a search warrant can be drafted and submitted to a magistrate or judge based on the probable cause of the trained narcotics dog and other documentation and information as it relates to the investigation. The renter may have a history of narcotics trafficking. That, coupled with any observations made during surveillance, can be used as part of the probable cause to obtain a search warrant. The renter may show up at the location while surveillance is occurring and investigators may opt to obtain a consent search from him at that time. This is an option if the facts warrant it. A narcotic canine may not alert to the suspect unit; however, other investigative facts may point to suspicious activity. A consent search is another avenue of investigation. Consent is one of the exceptions to a search warrant. It is suggested that law enforcement obtain a written consent explaining all personal rights signed by the renter.

Investigators may want to conduct "cold" inquiries at storage unit facilities once the program has been initiated. Cold operations are self-initiated proactive investigations. In these instances, a trained narcotic canine team is a must in conducting random examinations of storage units within the complex. Typically, cold operations involve investigators examining a computer-generated renter list. Most storage facilities have computers available that track renter information. Officers can examine renter applications in this way. They may recognize a known drug trafficker or associates who are renting a unit. Other things to look for are incomplete or fictitious renter information. Attention should be paid to items such as addresses, telephone numbers, or names that appear out of character, or common names such as John Smith. If a subject is identified, the investigator must learn everything about the renter including criminal history and intelligence information; background inquiries should be conducted. The narcotics canine team can be deployed on the premises to conduct an examination of units near the suspicious unit. If the canine team alerts on the unit for narcotic odor, a search warrant is an option, as previously described.

If no individuals are identified or recognized, the investigators may have the narcotic canine team deploy the dog in a random examination fashion for the purpose of identifying any narcotic odor that may be emanating from a storage unit. If the narcotics canine alerts to the odor of narcotics from a particular unit, the unit must be identified and a background check conducted on the renter. As with any information, search warrants may be applied for, surveillances conducted, and any other investigative work should be done. Surveillance is an important component to the investigation of any suspicious storage unit for the purpose of gathering intelligence, identifying suspicious activity, and confirming information from staff and identifying renters and associates.

It is important that the canine team and the investigators learn as much about the structure of the storage facility as possible. This is important to pinpoint the odor of the narcotics. Depending on the structure and the way it is designed, some buildings may have common ventilation. It is important to be familiar with the type of interior, the roof area, and how each of the units is sealed between each other.

Once a decision is made to do a search warrant on a storage unit, it is important to use the least amount of forced entry to avoid damage to the unit. If padlocks are on the unit, the investigator may want to use the option of picking the lock with services of a locksmith or investigator who is trained in lock picking. The unit lock should be returned as it was originally found, if possible. The other option is to cut the lock and replace it with another. If contraband is located, this should be verified by using a presumptive examination to identify the substance. The contraband can be removed totally, or portions may be left inside with constant surveillance. Under a controlled environment, the storage unit should then be closed, using the same lock, if possible. The investigators would then conduct surveillance on the area and wait for the suspect to arrive. When the renter or an associate arrives at the location, he or she can be allowed to enter the unit. The suspect will then be approached and the investigation will proceed.

The individual should be asked if he is the renter of the unit and if he is aware of the contents of the unit. If the person who arrives is not the renter, he should be asked why he is at the premises and why he has access to the unit. If he indicates that he is not aware of the contents, or describes everything other than the contraband, attempt to pin him down as to why he is at that location at that particular time. Let the individual "lock" himself into a story. The information from the interview can be used later, if and when the case is litigated. Investigators may want to provide a *Miranda* warning to the individual prior to any questioning regarding the investigation. Depending on the individual's role in the situation, the subject may want to assist law enforcement in providing information as to who may be involved, such as co-conspirators and sources of supply. Investigators should verify all of the information that an individual provides, if possible.

During the investigation, if there is a keypad entry mechanism utilized on the premises to gain access, each renter should have an ID or a personal identification number (PIN). Management and staff should be able to provide investigators with a computer profile showing how many times the PIN number was utilized to gain access to the location. This provides a historical pattern of the PIN number being used to gain access. This information can be used during the investigation.

Once contraband has been located within the storage unit, the narcotics should be photographed, and latent fingerprint processing should be conducted by the forensic science unit of the law enforcement agency. It is important to provide an accurate representation of how the items were stored, and to attempt to obtain fingerprints within the unit for identification purposes.

Investigators may find that a narcotics canine alerts to a particular storage unit and a consent or search warrant is secured, but no narcotics are found. This may occur in situations where narcotics were stored in the unit at one time, typically recently. There may be a situation where the narcotics were removed but the odor remains. Investigators must remember that the trained narcotics dog is alerting to the odor. It cannot distinguish between the quantity of actual substance and the odor. In cases where odor may be trapped in some type of compartment such as a freezer or safe, the dog may alert to it, especially in the instance of larger quantities of marijuana. In a case we encountered during a random canine examination of a storage facility, the dog alerted to a unit that contained only residue of marijuana. A search warrant was secured and the unit was opened. A safe was discovered in the unit, with its door slightly open. The safe contained trace quantities of cannabis. It was discovered that the renter had previously removed several pounds of marijuana before our arrival. The odor was still present in the unit.

Other information may lead to a storage unit facility. Individuals use storage units not only for narcotics storing, but for other criminal activity, such as stolen property from a robbery, theft, or burglary. Storage unit facilities can be used to store stolen vehicles. Robbery suspects may keep their vehicle, money, and disguises in storage units. If arrests are made on the street and the suspect has a storage unit receipt on his person or in his vehicle, this should be explored further. A narcotic canine team can be requested to conduct an examination of the storage unit which the subject is renting. An interview of storage unit staff may be conducted to ascertain if any suspicious activity by the renter has been observed, and how long the individual has had the storage unit. A consent search of the unit based on other factors can be requested from the subject.

## Drug Canine Capabilities

It is imperative that investigators who initiate this type of program and other interdiction programs become familiar with the capabilities and limitations of dog that is trained in the detection of narcotic odor. This type of program is most successful when a dedicated dog handler and his animal are assigned to the program on a permanent basis. This is not always possible for some police agencies; however, this type of investigation can certainly work effectively, even when a narcotics dog has other duties. These can be dual-purpose dogs such as a police dog who is not only trained in the detection of narcotics, but also to track persons. The common theme throughout this book is that a single-purpose dog, specifically trained in the detection of drugs, is the most effective.

As previously mentioned, there are typically two types of narcotics dogs and how they are trained to alert to the odor of narcotics. One is a passive alert dog; one that sits when it detects the odor of narcotics. The other is an aggressive alert dog, which will scratch at the area. The trained handler can provide you with information as to the type of environment the animal best operates in, as well as the animal's capabilities. The handler, with his dog, should train in a variety of environments to be successful in interdiction operations. Most handlers will indicate that masking agents typically do not deter a dog or mask the odor to a trained narcotics dog. The dog has the ability to discriminate between scents, if properly trained. It is a matter of scent availability. The dog is trained for narcotic odor. If narcotics are packaged or stored in a way that prevents the odor from escaping, the dog will not alert to the odor of narcotics. Quantity or weight is not a factor if the drugs are packaged in a manner that prohibits the scent from escaping. Time is a factor, however, in that eventually the odor will permeate from whatever container the drugs are housed in.

The use of the narcotic dog in storage facilities can produce differing results depending on time of day or night and temperature conditions. Examinations by the canine team should be conducted when the unit has higher temperatures within, which enhances the odor due to the expanding air molecules within the storage unit. In the summer, early morning times are best suited for examinations of units. The air is cooler outside and warmer inside. In the winter, depending on the part of the country, early evening hours are usually the best time to conduct examinations. Training under these conditions is recommended.

There are a number of items of case law with respect to the use of narcotic canines in the United States. The investigator and the canine team should do research to identify case law in their jurisdiction and in the state where they operate. There are a number of items of federal case law which indicate that a narcotics canine examination of a storage unit does not constitute a search. Much of the case law notes that the dog's reliability is a factor; also, that the consent of the storage unit facility manager or staff is required.

## Conclusion

Storage unit investigations can be a successful part of a domestic drug investigation's group. Storage units provide what is perceived by the drug trafficker to be a safe haven for narcotics storage. This program provides law enforcement with an opportunity to explore other investigative options concerning a narcotic investigation.

## Case Law

### U.S. v. Reyes, 908 F.2d 281 (1990) 8th Cir.

No reasonable expectation of privacy after lease term expires.

### Colorado v. Weiser, 796 P.2d 983 (1990) Colo.

Court split: Some justices held dog sniff of rented locker was not search under Federal or State Constitution where dog walked past lockers, while others thought police had reasonable suspicion justifying warrantless dog sniff of locker. (Dissent disputed that access way in-side storage facility complex was "public".)

### U.S. v. Vermouth, (1985) 9th Cir. (unpublished), cert. denied, 475 U.S. 1045 (1986)

Sniff of storage locker held not a search triggering Fourth Amendment protection.

### *State v. Boyce,* 723 P.2d 28 (1986) Wash. App. and *Strout v. State,* 688 S.W. 2d 188 (1985) Tex App.

Sniff of exterior of safe deposit box, reasonable suspicion present in both cases.

### *U.S. v. Venema,* 563 F.2d 1003 (1977) 10th Cir.

Police officer's use of a narcotic detector dog to sniff the air outside of a storage unit locker was not a search, in view of the fact that the area in front of the locker was at least semi-public and officers brought dog on premises with consent of the owner of the storage company.

### *U.S. v. Ayala,* 887 F.2d 62 (1989) 5th Cir.

This evidence linked defendant to, and supported conviction for, conspiracy to possess and distribute marijuana.

Defendant was linked to self-storage facility unit to which narcotics dog alerted to. Agents discovered marijuana in front of the unit. Suitcases stored in the unit were identical to one holding marijuana seized from defendant. The defendant accompanied co-defendant to train station.

### *U.S. v. Lingenfelter,* 997 F.2d 632 (1993) 9th Cir.

Canine sniff outside drug suspect's commercial warehouse storage unit did not constitute a search. The canine sniff alone can provide probable cause necessary for the search warrant if the application for warrant establishes dog's reliability.

### *U.S. v. Mahler,* 141 F.3d 811 (1988) 8th Cir.

Police received a tip that narcotics were stored at a storage unit. A narcotics detector dog sniffed the exterior of the units and gave a positive alert. The search warrants for storage units were supported by probable cause based upon narcotic's canine's positive alert for drugs at the units.

### *U.S. v. Ortega-Jiminez,* 232 F.3d 1325 (2000) 10th Cir.

A narcotics detector dog sniffed the exterior of storage unit. The dog gave a positive alert to one unit. Based upon the alert, a search warrant was obtained for the unit.

## Key Terms

Business watch
Canine scent availability
Canine team
Case law
Climate control facility
Cold vs. tip investigations
Drug nexus
Expectation of privacy
"Eyes and ears"
Indicators
Keypad entry
Letter of commitment

Masking agents
Odor
On-site managers
Partnerships
Personal identification number (PIN)
Portable on-demand storage units (PODS)
Random canine examination
Reward funds
Sign-in and sign-out logs
Surveillance

# Train Interdiction

## 8

In the early 1990s, the Gulf War erupted and security levels at all airports in the United States were elevated to Death Con Charlie; that is, every passenger was asked to show his identification upon checking in at the ticket counter as well as the boarding gate. All luggage was scrutinized by airline employees. Passengers were asked at the ticket counters if their luggage had been in their possession the entire time and if anyone unknown to them had approached them and asked them to carry an item. Security levels in all areas had been elevated due to the conflict in the Middle East.

So what were the drug trafficking organizations going to do now to move their product? Trains were one mode of transportation that would be used. Buses were also used, but we will look at that in Chapter 9. Why would any drug trafficking organization send its drug and money couriers across the country on a train? The trip would definitely take a great deal longer. We will look at some of the reasons drug trafficking organizations chose to use the long distance commercial passenger train system.

A small drug interdiction detail located in Albuquerque, New Mexico was involved monitoring an Amtrak Train with a route through Albuquerque. One of the trains the detail monitored originated in Los Angeles and had a final destination of Chicago. That train traveled through Albuquerque once a day, normally about midday. They monitored the same train that proceeded from Chicago to Los Angeles; that train arrived in Albuquerque around 4:30 p.m.

That drug interdiction detail saw a major increase in drug and money courier activity. The detail was making up to two to three drug seizures a week, accompanied by arrests. This was because of increased airline security; drug trafficking organizations had to use alternate forms of commercial passenger transportation.

September 11, 2001, 8:45 a.m., is a date and time that no American will ever forget. I was getting ready to take my children to school and the morning news announced that an airplane had collided with one of the World Trade

Center buildings in New York City. My middle daughter was watching this on television and came into the bathroom to tell me that another airplane had just crashed into the second World Trade Center tower. I told her that they were probably replaying the first crash. She said to me, "No, Dad, there was a second crash, I just witnessed it live on TV."

A third airplane crashed into the Pentagon Building in Washington, D.C., and a fourth had reportedly crashed in Pennsylvania. Terrorism had struck the United States, and the entire country was brought to a halt. Americans were shocked that this could happen in our homeland. Thousands died, and the recovery went on for months.

Security levels at all airports in the country escalated to Death Con Delta, the highest level of security. All passengers were being scrutinized again. All luggage was being searched not only at the ticket counter when checking luggage in, but all carry-on luggage was also being heavily monitored and searched. No knives of any type were allowed to be carried on board the airplane by any passenger.

The United States Government deployed heavily armed National Guard Troops to our airports until stricter security measures could be in place in the ensuing months. Only ticketed passengers were allowed beyond the secured areas. The National Guard troops were stationed at those security checkpoints to ensure passenger safety.

That same drug interdiction detail in Albuquerque, New Mexico once again experienced an increase in drug and money courier activity. The long distance commercial passenger train system was again being tapped by the drug trafficking organizations to move their illegal product.

As we look at this chapter concerning drug interdiction on trains, especially long-distance commercial passenger trains, we will explore the reasons the drug trafficking organizations choose to move their product and proceeds across the country on a method of travel that can take days instead of hours.

## Officer Safety

*OFFICER SAFETY, OFFICER SAFETY, OFFICER SAFETY, OFFICER SAFETY* — these words will be stressed throughout this chapter. Working commercial passenger train drug interdiction is like working no other form of commercial passenger transportation. We will deal with passengers in a common coach setting as well as passengers in a sleeper compartment or roomette setting. Is there a greater expectation of privacy for a passenger traveling in a sleeper compartment than in the coach section of the train? YES.

What is the common factor in all commercial forms of transportation? The transportation of passengers from point A to point B is the primary factor, and the profit that comes from that service. Understanding the long distance commercial passenger train system is a critical factor in working this area of law enforcement. Being sensitive to the nature of the commercial passenger trail system's goals is very important in having a successful interdiction detail.

We will consider all aspects of the train interdiction detail. We will explore the interdiction detail itself and the personnel that will make up the detail. Cooperation with local prosecutors, whether they are state, county, or federal prosecutors, is very important. The staff that are associated with the operation of long distance commercial passengers trains are an integral part of the success of the detail. As we have seen since September 11, 2001, security and safety is everyone's business.

The Amtrak train system is the only long distance carrier of passengers across the country. There are other shorter, or commuter, trains that also operate in the United States, mainly on the east and west coasts. We will concentrate on the Amtrak train system here.

The Amtrak train system is the only mode of long-distance passenger train transportation that has its own certified law enforcement agency. The Amtrak Police Department is an accredited federal law enforcement agency. Its uniformed officers, detectives, and investigators are stationed throughout the United States. The heaviest concentration of Amtrak police officers, detectives, and criminal investigators is on the east coast.

No other public mode of transportation has its own law enforcement agency. All airports have police departments, but these police departments are responsible for the safety of the entire airport and do not work for a particular airline. The public bus systems that operate in the United States as a rule do not have their own police agencies, although they may have some security agency working in their terminals.

The Amtrak Police Department is very concerned about the safety of their passengers and terminals. They investigate all crimes that occur on their trains, in their terminals, or on their property. The Amtrak Police Department is also very concerned about the fact that drug organizations utilize the Amtrak train system to transport their illegal drugs and illicit proceeds, and Amtrak police are involved in efforts to curb this activity.

In law enforcement, it is essential that we work together in a cohesive partnership. We know that we cannot do this job alone and that we must rely on each other for support and assistance. If train interdiction is a program you and your agency are going to establish, then it is essential that the cooperation and permission from the Amtrak Police Department be obtained. Having their cooperation will help make your program successful. Without the Amtrak Police Department's permission to conduct investigations on their trains, terminal, or property, the job will be much more difficult. Therefore it is imperative that your agency obtain permission from the Amtrak Police Department to conduct drug interdiction investigations on board the Amtrak train system. The Amtrak Police Department knows the inner workings of the Amtrak train system, and their assistance and cooperation are necessary for your program's survival.

We must be sensitive to the passenger train system mission, that is to transport passengers from point A to point B with the least amount of disruption, and to make a profit. If a passenger train drug interdiction program delays the trains, then we will only hurt ourselves. Scheduling is very important due to the amount of train traffic that occurs around the country. Priorities on the train tracks that crisscross our country must be adhered to. There are more freight trains, which use thousands of miles of train track, than the passenger trains in this country. We want to attempt to keep the passenger trains on schedule and not delay them due to our investigations. There have been times when we were in the middle of an encounter on board a train when the train was preparing to depart. We had to have a plan in place for this type of event whereby all investigators in the group were aware of their duties. Who would travel to the next stopping point for the train in order to meet the investigators? This will be discussed in greater detail in the planning stages. Communication devices are also essential in working train interdiction, whether walkie-talkies or cellular telephones with walkie-talkie capabilities. Delaying of the train, of course, is the biggest issue.

There are thousands of miles of railroad tracks that crisscross the United States. The Amtrak train system does not own the tracks on which their trains travel except for a few areas on the east coast, where Amtrak does own the tracks. The majority of the railroad tracks around the country are owned and maintained by larger companies such as Burlington Northern and Santa Fe Railroad. There is a complex system to maintaining order on the railroad tracks that covers which trains, whether they are freight or passenger trains, are given priority. The time schedules that call for trains to be in a certain area at certain time on a certain day is very important to maintaining that order.

Each Amtrak passenger train has a name and a number. It is very important to know the train names and numbers. There are names such as the Southwest Chief, California Zephyr, and Sunset Limited.

Can you think of the biggest reason why drug trafficking organizations use Amtrak to transport their illegal drugs and illicit proceeds? Some of the reasons we will look at have also been addressed by Amtrak since September 11, 2001. We will nonetheless explore the reasons drug trafficking organizations use the Amtrak train system.

How many of us have actually been to an Amtrak train station or ridden on an Amtrak train or any other commercial passenger train? Traveling by train is a very pleasant experience. The different types of accommodations and the areas in which some of these trains travel can be very enjoyable. We think it is essential that having traveled by train will enhance the investigator's experience and knowledge of working train interdiction.

One reason drug organizations use the train system is that there are no magnetometers at stations. Some of the areas that Amtrak services make it impossible to staff an employee there and monitor persons entering the passenger trains. In many areas, especially in the Midwest and the West Coast, there is only a building or small station with no employee where the trains stop and passengers board or disembark. It would virtually be impossible to keep a staffed employee at a station when the train only stops once or twice a day, and often in the early morning hours or middle of the night. Therefore, the possibility of encountering passengers with firearms and other weapons is present. **OFFICER SAFETY** is so important in working train interdiction that it should always be at the forefront. Amtrak does have a firearm policy for passengers to adhere to!

There are no x-ray machines for passengers to pass their luggage through. Drug couriers know this and can place a lot of drugs or illicit proceeds in carry-on luggage. We were involved in many seizures of both drugs and money where the contraband was in carry-on luggage. Because there are no x-ray machines, weapons can also be concealed in carry-on luggage as well as on the passenger's person.

There have been many instances where weapons were located during the search of a passenger's luggage when investigators were looking for narcotics or narcotics proceeds.

### Case Study

One such instance occurred on the eastbound Amtrak Train Number 4 as it was stopped in Albuquerque, New Mexico. The interdiction detail was at the station when the train stopped. I had previously reviewed a passenger name record (PNR) for two passengers traveling from Los Angeles to New York's Penn Station. Investigators observed one of the passengers, a male, disembark from the train. The passenger walked about on the platform among the other passengers and looked at the Native American jewelry vendors' wares. I proceeded to the sleeping car from which the passenger had come, and to the deluxe sleeper room the two passengers had been occupying. I knocked on the door and a second passenger, female, answered. I asked for and received permission to speak to the passenger. Simultaneously, a second investigator had approached the male passenger on the waiting platform.

I engaged in conversation with the female passenger and discovered she was traveling with her husband from Los Angeles, where they had visited with friends. The female advised me that they were traveling back to New York where they lived. I subsequently asked the female passenger for permission to search her luggage, which was contained inside of the room. The female passenger told me that she wanted her husband there when the luggage was searched. At this time, the male passenger and the second investigator entered the train car and proceeded up to the second floor of the train car and to the roomette. I told my partner that the female had given permission to search her luggage and but that she wanted her husband there when the search was conducted. My partner said that he also had received permission from the male passenger to search his luggage. I received permission to enter the room to search the luggage. The two passengers remained standing outside of the room with my partner, where he continued to engage in conversation with them. I searched the luggage that was easily accessible on the floor and bed. The upper sleeper berth was in the "up" position; I lowered the bed and observed a gold suit bag unfolded on the bed. Upon searching the bag I discovered a Thomas submachine gun with two loaded magazines. It was later discovered that the machine gun had been converted to be fully automatic. With this discovery, I immediately notified my partner of the weapon, and the two passengers were searched for additional weapons, but none were found. Through later investigation, the couple was tied to a Russian cocaine smuggling organization that operated out of New York.

Many more occurrences of weapons being located in luggage and concealed on passengers have been reported over the years.

### Case Study

On December 12, 2000, investigators of the Chicago interdiction detail encountered two passengers traveling by train from New Hampshire to Tucson, Arizona. If you have ever been to the Chicago Amtrak station, you are aware of how big the station is and how busy the station can be with passengers. Picture the station at approximately 3:30 p.m., and picture the number of passengers passing through the station, waiting for trains, or changing trains.

The passengers in question were changing trains in Chicago and had a 3-hour layover there. The investigators had reviewed a PNR for the two passengers and observed characteristics common to the method in which drug and money couriers travel and make travel arrangements. The passengers had made a reservation on the day of departure for one-way travel from New Hampshire to Tucson, Arizona. They had booked sleeper compartments. The passengers picked up their tickets at the Amtrak station in New Hampshire just before the train left and had paid cash for their tickets. It was later discovered that the passengers had used fictitious names when they made their reservations.

When the train arrived in Chicago from New Hampshire, three investigators from the Chicago interdiction detail were at the station to meet it. The investigators walked out to the passenger platform and watched as passengers disembarked from the train. After most of the passengers had exited the train, one of the investigators entered the train car and proceeded to the roomette the two passengers were occupying. Through the curtains, the investigator observed the silhouettes of two persons standing up in the room.

The two passengers exited the sleeper car, and the investigators observed two males who were dressed exactly alike with long black leather coats, black denim pants, and black military-style boots. The two males looked at the investigators and continued to walk past them and into the train terminal. The investigators had previously decided that they would encounter the two males inside. Once inside, contact was made with the two males. After asking for and receiving permission to speak to them, conversation ensued about their trip. Train tickets were requested and reviewed, and returned to the passengers. One of the investigators asked one of the passengers if they had any large amounts of currency on them, and the passenger advised that he did. A request was made by the investigator to view the money. As the passenger was preparing to remove the money from his inside coat pocket, one of the other investigators told the passenger that he would remove the money from his pocket. That was done and the passenger's coat remained unzipped. The investigator who had removed the money noticed that the passenger's jacket had become unzipped further, and he saw the butt of a pistol inside the passenger's waistband. That weapon was later identified as a 40-caliber Glock. The investigator yelled "Gun!" to his partners, and the passenger removed the gun from his waistband, grabbed the initiating investigator by the hair, shoved her to the ground, and attempted to shoot the investigator in the head. A struggle ensued with the backup investigator, the initiating investigator, and the passenger over control of the gun.

During this time, the second passenger fled the terminal in the direction from which they had come. The third investigator followed in pursuit of the second passenger and engaged in a gun battle on the train's passenger platform area. The second passenger was also armed with a semiautomatic weapon. After an exchange of gunfire, the second passenger ran back into the terminal to help his partner, who was still struggling with the two investigators over the gun and attempting to shoot them. The second passenger came to his partner's aid and pointed his gun at the head of one of the other investigators involved in the struggle. During this time, one of the investigators involved in the struggle over the weapon had unknowingly pressed the magazine release on the weapon, releasing the fully loaded 40-caliber magazine from the offender's weapon.

The third investigator who had been involved in the gun battle with the second offender reentered the terminal and took aim at the second offender. He was able to shoot the offender in the head and kill him. The investigators involved in the struggle with the first passenger were able to gain control of the weapon, and that passenger was also shot and later died at a Chicago hospital. During the scuffle, the first initiating investigator was shot in the leg, but the wound was not life-threatening. The two passengers were found to be wearing body armor, and each had additional fully loaded 40-caliber magazines on his person.

The two passengers had been involved in other criminal activity before their travel on Amtrak. They had assaulted an individual and had committed a burglary of an antique gun show, where they had stolen numerous weapons. The weapons were loaded into a vehicle and the offenders drove away from the scene but were spotted by a New Hampshire Highway patrol officer who attempted to stop the vehicle; the offenders evaded the officer. The vehicle was later found containing numerous weapons. Information learned from the investigation concluded that the two offenders would not be taken alive and they would shoot law enforcement officers.

What began as a possible investigation of money couriers traveling from the east coast to Tucson turned out to be two passengers armed with semi-automatic weapons, wearing body armor, and having the mind set that they would not be taken alive and would shoot it out with law enforcement. Had it not been for the well-trained investigators being able to recognize the conduct and behavior of the two offenders, and the quick and decisive reactions of the investigators, this incident could have resulted in the tragic loss of the law enforcement officers' lives on December 12, 2000 at the Amtrak train station in Chicago. We give our deepest gratitude to the three interdiction investigators who ultimately saved not only their own lives but possibly the lives of other unsuspecting law enforcement officers the two offenders might have encountered had they not been stopped.

Another safety issue working train interdiction before September 11, 2001 is the fact that no identification was required to purchase a train ticket. The two offenders traveling on the Amtrak train on December 12, 2000, had purchased their tickets under assumed names. It is common for persons involved in criminal activity to disguise their identities. Many drug distribution organizations use couriers, and their train tickets are often purchased under assumed names.

The investigator may have the advantage of detecting nervousness when talking with a passenger who is traveling under an assumed name, particularly if the passenger has not taken time to familiarize himself with the assumed name or learn to spell it, which is often the case. Couriers will often give an excuse as to why the name on the ticket is not their own, such as that a relative purchased the ticket, a friend gave it to them, or that the ticket agent must have spelled the name incorrectly or put the wrong name on the ticket altogether. Since September 11, 2001, Amtrak requires passengers to show identification when purchasing tickets.

## Luggage

One of the most important aspects in identifying drug and money couriers is the luggage they use to transport their products. When traveling by Amtrak, a passenger has three choices about where to store his luggage. Luggage can be checked in at the station upon boarding if the station is a staffed Amtrak station. When a passenger checks his luggage in at a staffed stations he is given a luggage claim tag, which is usually stapled to the Amtrak train ticket folder. The luggage is then stored in a separate train car for checked luggage only; no passengers travel in this car. Baggage handlers and conductors normally have access to this area, and passengers as a norm are not allowed in this area of the train. Passengers cannot check their luggage if the location they are traveling to does not have Amtrak staff manning the station. Therefore, the passenger must carry on his luggage. As previously mentioned, there are many stations around the country that Amtrak does not staff. Many of these stations are in remote areas.

The authors have found that couriers will to check their luggage containing contraband. This allows the passenger to be distanced from the contraband he is carrying. Many large marijuana loads have been located in the luggage car. Having permission from Amtrak management to be on the premises and to have access to the interior of the train will allow an interdiction detail to have a certified narcotic detection canine deployed in this area. The luggage car can be accessed from the outside. Large sliding doors give the Amtrak baggage handlers access to its interior (Figure 8.1). Canine handlers will often deploy their canines in the luggage car immediately upon

**Figure 8.1** (Photograph used with permission of Amtrak.)

the train's arrival in the station. The canine handler can also identify any luggage that is destined for his city before it is removed from the luggage car by looking at the destination tag that is attached to the luggage.

If a canine handler identifies a piece of suspect luggage that his canine has alerted to, the piece of luggage is allowed to be placed by the baggage handlers on the luggage carriers along with the other luggage for that stop. Do not segregate the suspect luggage from other passenger luggage. Allow it to be taken to the passenger pickup area, and wait for the suspect to claim it. Once the passenger has taken possession of the suspect luggage, then a consensual encounter can take place.

If the passenger chooses to carry on his luggage, he can carry on large and small pieces of luggage. Normally upon entering a passenger car, there is a common luggage area (Figure 8.2). This area is normally a shelved section off to the side of the doorway where passengers can store their luggage. There

**Figure 8.2** (Photograph used with permission of Amtrak.)

are different configurations of the common luggage area, depending on the passenger car. This area will normally contain the larger pieces of luggage, but smaller pieces or unusual pieces of luggage may also be found there. This is one of the first locations that interdiction details will examine upon entering a passenger car. Examining the luggage in this area is very important.

An important case to keep in mind is *U.S. v. Bond*, 2000, 10th Circuit Court of Appeals. This case resulted from a bus interdiction investigation in which a law enforcement officer had boarded a commercial passenger bus and was performing interdiction duties. The officer observed a piece of soft-sided luggage in the overhead luggage rack and examined it and touched it. The court determined that the manner in which the law enforcement officer touched, or as they termed it, "manipulated," the bag was intrusive and was considered a search. The court described that the law enforcement officer was able to feel the bag and detect a large brick type item in the bag, and the law enforcement officer was able to describe the dimensions of the brick in his report. The court also mentioned that the bag was manipulated in a manner in which the general public would not have touched it.

Being aware of the findings in this case will determine what is done in the common luggage area. Therefore, moving the luggage from one location to another, which is often done by the normal passenger to fit his luggage into the space, would be permitted. You can also check the luggage claim tags on the handles to see if nametags are filled out. Drug couriers frequently leave luggage claim tags blank so they cannot be identified with their luggage. The use of new luggage is also a very common practice for drug couriers, so you should examine this area and look for new luggage. A courier may have left the brand name tags and price tags on the luggage. The size of the load and the method in which the drugs were originally packaged will dictate the type of luggage that a courier uses to transport the product. Hard- and soft-sided luggage are both used, and we have not seen a distinct pattern of luggage types for different types of drugs. We have seen large marijuana, cocaine, and methamphetamine loads in both soft- and hard-sided luggage, so there is no set type of luggage that is used for a particular product.

Upon examining the luggage area, lift the luggage from the bottom to determine its weight. Smell the zippered area of the luggage (or, in the case of hard-sided luggage, where the two pieces come together) to determine any unusual odors, such as masking agents or the contraband itself. Caution must be taken when doing this because of the danger of illegal narcotics such as PCP. A certified narcotic canine is not normally deployed when this drug is suspected to be in a piece of luggage. Once the canine is brought onto the scene, passengers involved in criminal activity or drug trafficking become aware that a drug interdiction detail is working at the station, so we would have a canine deployed in the common luggage area only if suspect luggage was observed. We have located many loads of drugs in this area.

When a piece of suspect luggage is identified, then the owner must be located, and this is often a difficult task. One method for identifying the owner of a piece of luggage in the common luggage area is to seek the assistance of the train conductor or the train attendant. His assistance will only be minimal and is something that he would do as a part of his normal duty.

All passenger train cars have intercom systems that can be activated by Amtrak train employees. The intercom system can either be centralized to one particular car or for all the passenger cars. Each car has an intercom system and access is limited to Amtrak employees.

If a piece of suspect luggage is identified in the common luggage area of a passenger car and a certified narcotic detection canine has alerted to the luggage, a request to the train conductor or train attendant can be made to help identify the owner. You might ask the train attendant or conductor to make an announcement over the passenger train intercom system such as "Will any person having luggage in the common luggage area of the 411 coach car please come down and identify it." At this time the train attendant will either assist the investigators, or, if he chooses, he can leave the area and take up his normal working position. The train attendant or conductor is not normally apprised of the piece of suspect luggage in order to keep his involvement to a minimum. The investigators will then stand next to the common luggage area, and as passengers arrive in the common luggage area, they are asked to identify their luggage. If a passenger does identify the suspect luggage, he will not be contacted at this time. Once the suspect passenger leaves the common luggage area and returns to his seat, a consensual encounter will be conducted at the seat.

The problem with locating suspect luggage in this area is that the luggage may not be identified by anyone and will be abandoned. In the case of abandoned luggage, the investigators must be sure that all passengers are on the train and present. If a suspect piece of luggage is abandoned, an investigator must allow all the passengers in the car to view the luggage and deny ownership. This is done by removing the suspect luggage from its original position and taking it to the passenger seating area. The luggage is then presented to each passenger in that car, and the passengers are asked if the luggage belongs to them, again allowing all passengers to deny ownership of the luggage. Only when all the passengers have had an opportunity to view the luggage and deny ownership can the suspect piece of luggage be determined abandoned. Once this has been done, law enforcement can open the luggage based on it being abandoned. Once the luggage has been opened and contraband is found, it is now time to identify the owner. Drug

**Figure 8.3** (Photograph used with permission of Amtrak.)

couriers will sometimes fill the bag with "filler items" — clothing or articles that cannot be traced to the owner. Some couriers may go to a clothing drop location for the homeless and pack the suitcase with miscellaneous clothing and articles.

The passenger can also take smaller pieces of luggage to his assigned seat. Above the passenger seats are usually open-style luggage racks (Figure 8.3). Passengers can store their smaller and medium size pieces of luggage or personal items in these racks. We have observed larger pieces of luggage in the overhead luggage racks, even though these larger pieces would fit better in the common luggage areas. Some couriers store large pieces of luggage containing drugs in the overhead luggage rack so they can keep eye on them. In our experience, some of these pieces of luggage have been so heavy that it took at least two people to remove them from the overhead rack.

### Case Study

In one such instance, three couriers working together plus a source were encountered on board a train. The encounter took place due to the luggage in the overhead luggage rack above the couriers' and source's seats. The three couriers and the source had large, new, soft-sided luggage abovetheir seats in the overhead rack. The luggage was sticking out approximately 6 inches over the edge of the luggage rack. Two of the couriers were seated next to each other and the third courier was seated across from them. The couriers were seated near the front of the coach car, and the source was seated at the rear of the same car. The source also had a large piece of new luggage above his seat in the overhead luggage rack.

The backup or scanning officer played a major role in identifying the source and tying the source to the three couriers. When contact was made with the three couriers by interdiction investigators, the backup officer, who was standing at the rear of the coach car, observed the source, a 50-year-old heavy-set gentleman, paying close attention to the encounter between the couriers and the investigators. After watching the encounter for a short time, the source moved to the seat in front of him so that he was not sitting directly underneath the luggage. The three couriers abandoned the three large pieces of luggage above their seats, and each courier identified a small duffel bag that was positioned in the overhead luggage rack above their seats next to each piece of suspect luggage.

The source was also contacted by the backup officer based on the observations of the backup officer and the interest the source had in the encounter between the couriers and the investigators. The source denied knowing the couriers, and he also abandoned the new large piece of luggage in the overhead luggage rack above his original seat. The source also had a small duffel bag containing one days' worth of clothing.

After the four pieces of luggage were determined to be abandoned, they were opened and found to contain 45 kg of cocaine. After further investigation, the three couriers and source were placed in custody. The couriers and source were later convicted in federal court on conspiracy to traffic in cocaine, and all were sentenced to prison.

The overhead luggage rack is an important location for couriers to store and keep watch of the contraband they are carrying. Money couriers, unlike drug couriers, will almost always have the currency close by, either in the overhead luggage rack, on the floor near their feet, or on their person.

## Amtrak's Computer System

Amtrak's main computer system is in California. When we look at the PNR system, this is important to know, because times listed on the PNR will be Pacific Standard time. We will explore this in more depth in the PNR portion.

There are three reservation centers located across the country. The reservation centers are located in relationship to the way Amtrak divides up the country. One reservation center is located in Riverside, California; this center normally handles the West Coast. Another reservation center is in Chicago, Illinois; this center handles the inner city area, and the third reservation center is located in Fort Washington, Pennsylvania; this center handles the East Coast. Therefore, if someone on the West Coast called Amtrak's reservation system, the Riverside reservation center would probably handle the call. If that reservation center is backlogged with calls, then the call would normally be channeled to one of the other two reservation centers.

## Amtrak Personnel

One of the key ingredients of working train interdiction, just like any other program, is liaison with the employees who work in the ticket offices and the employees who are responsible for customers and their satisfaction. As mentioned earlier, it is essential when working train interdiction that you first have cooperation and permission from the Amtrak Police Department to participate in a drug interdiction program on their facilities as well as on their trains. It is also important to have permission and the cooperation of the management of the station where you establish your drug interdiction program. Whether you had permission from the station management to be on their premises and on passenger trains conducting drug interdiction can become a critical issue in a suppression hearing.

You should first communicate your desire to work in this area at your train station with the management or lead ticket agent, whoever is in charge. Call him and set up a meeting to discuss the program. Like so many other programs, you will want to stress the importance of a business watch type program and the need for law enforcement at their station. In many stations around the country there is no law enforcement presence, unless there is an Amtrak Police officer, investigator, or detective assigned to that station. Once permission has been received to work at a particular station, you will want to establish a continued liaison with all the employees who operate at the station, such as area managers, lead ticket agents, ticket agents, and baggage handlers.

We must remember that these people will only act as our "eyes and ears" and have no involvement in our investigations; they will take no action, and you will want to separate any employee who provides you with information from your investigation. Conducting independent investigations will ensure that your program will be a success. The employees with whom you will deal are for the most part law-abiding citizens who happen to work in an area that people involved in criminal activity and drug dealing will utilize for their benefit. You will have a constant liaison with these employees concerning the activities of people involved in criminal activity and drug smuggling. You must stress to them that race, age, gender, and national origin should have bearing on the criteria for what these criminals look like, but that their conduct and behavior will identify them. Basically, if the passenger draws suspicion for whatever reason, then the interdiction program should be the avenue for them to relate their suspicions. The normal passenger patterns that these employees have experience with will not be there in the case of a person involved in criminal activity.

## Ticket Agents

The ticket agent will be the first employee to make observations of the passenger. He will often have the opportunity to view the passenger, luggage, or person dropping off the passenger and may be able to identify any nervous or unusual passenger behavior.

Educating ticket agents about behavior to be aware of in persons involved in criminal activity is very important. The criminal will often show up the day of departure without a reservation and purchase a ticket shortly before the train departs. If the passenger does make a reservation, he will ask to leave as soon as possible. This is due to the way the drug business works, where things are done on what we call "doper time." The drug world has many obstacles to work with when attempting to deliver a product. The courier or the source is always waiting for the product to be delivered or waiting for the product to arrive. The drug courier or source is not going to make a reservation several weeks in advance, because they cannot anticipate the exact date or time the product will arrive or that it will be delivered in a timely manner. The reservation will be made when the product is in hand or when the recipient is ready with the money to pay for the product. When the product does arrive or is delivered, the source or courier will have to travel immediately. In our experience, reservations have been made anywhere from the day of departure to up to 3 days before travel.

We tell the ticket agents that if the suspect passenger did not make a reservation, he might come into their station and inquire as to when the next train is departing or arriving and ask if he can reserve a seat. If a passenger reserves a seat for same-day departure, there probably will not be any good discount prices available. The passenger is not going to argue about the price of the ticket because he does not want to draw any attention to himself and he really does not care about the price; this price will be tacked on to the customer's purchase price for their product.

The passenger will probably book a one-way trip, even if he is from the area. The passenger might not know when he is returning, he might return via another form of transportation so he can keep law enforcement at bay, or the passenger may on occasion book round-trip travel with a quick turnaround time, perhaps only staying a day at his final destination. The reservation may be suspicious if, for instance, the passenger is traveling 3 days to reach a destination, stays for 1 day, and then travels another 3 days to return, traveling 6 days to spend 1 day in a particular place.

The passenger involved in criminal activity, especially narcotics trafficking, normally pays in cash, so that there is no paper trail, and also because the drug trade is conducted in cash. If drug cartels, organizations, sources, couriers and even street-level dealers conducted drug transactions using personal checks or cashiers checks, then these checks could be used to identify drug couriers. If the drug business were conducted with credit cards, then we would look for people paying in credit cards, but because the drug business is conducted in cash, then cash is a primary factor.

Amtrak normally requires that whether a person makes a reservation via their reservation system or in person, a call-back number is requested. This is done in almost all forms of public transportation, especially with air and train travel. The reason for the call-back number is to notify a passenger of a delay or cancellation. Passengers involved in criminal activity often provide a fictitious call-back number so they cannot be traced. The ticket agent might observe some nervousness or unusual behavior by the passenger when he is asked to provide this information.

## Baggage Handlers

Another important group with which to initiate a liaison are the baggage handlers. They play an important part in identifying persons involved in criminal activity or drug trafficking. They will be able to assist law enforcement by providing information on the persons checking in or picking up luggage. Baggage handlers should be educated on the various masking agents used by drug couriers. They should also be educated about the weight of luggage, which may be unusually heavy when couriers are transporting large quantities of marijuana, cocaine, or precursor chemicals for methamphetamine and other controlled substances. Newer pieces of luggage are often used to facilitate the transportation of drugs. Couriers will frequently not fill out the identification tags properly, so they cannot be identified with the product. Any overall suspicion about the passenger that the baggage handler might observe should be reported.

## Conductors and Assistant Conductors

These are the "captains of the ship." Nothing occurs on the train that the conductor is not aware of, when it comes to passengers and the operation of the train. It is important to establish a good working relationship with the conductors. The train does not leave the station until the conductor has notified, usually by radio, the engineers that all passengers are on board and all systems are ready for the train to leave. The conductor is responsible for the safe passage of the passengers and for the on-time operation of the train. He is responsible for collecting tickets from passengers, and he can also sell tickets to passengers on board the train. The conductor can also issue upgrade tickets for passengers who want to upgrade their accommodations from coach to sleeper compartments. They keep all the tickets of passengers on board the train in individual ticket pouches, usually located in the transition car or employee car. There are separate ticket pouches for numbered coach cars and numbered sleeper cars. The conductors maintain control of these ticket pouches. In the event you had a PNR for a passenger who was traveling on board the train and you wanted to verify if in fact the passenger was on the train, you could request to view the tickets for a certain car.

You should let the conductors know that you are there to assist them in any way possible. If it means helping them with an unruly passenger or an intoxicated passenger, you will assist them. Again, unless there is an Amtrak law enforcement officer assigned to their home station or near by, we are the only law enforcement presence. Being helpful in other ways will promote a good working relationship.

The conductor knows which passengers purchased their tickets from him after boarding the train and who upgraded their accommodations while traveling. Why would a passenger bypass a ticket office and purchase his ticket from the conductor on board the train? The main reason is because purchasing the ticket from the conductor without having made a reservation keeps the passenger's name from being on file; there will be no record of the passenger traveling until the train reaches its final destination and all passenger information has been input into the Amtrak computer system.

Because the passenger rail system competes with freight train traffic, it is a very time-conscious endeavor. The conductor is responsible for keeping the passenger train on time. If, in the event you board the train at your station and think you have ample time to conduct encounters on board the train, but in the middle of an encounter the train is preparing to depart, the conductor is ultimately the "captain of the ship" and he makes the decision about departure time.

## Engineers

The engineers are responsible for the operation of the train. They operate the train engines and normally do not have contact with passengers. Their function is basically to drive the train from one location to the next. A liaison with the engineers is also important. Engineers take their commands from the conductors as to when to stop and when to depart. The engineers also have access to a nationwide communication base that tracks all train traffic across the country, like a dispatch center. The communication center advises the engineers of track problems, areas where tracks are being repaired, and of other locomotive traffic on the tracks and which trains have the right of way.

The amount of time that conductors and engineers can be on the train is regulated by the Federal National Transportation Board. They are allowed to operate on the train for no more than 8 to 10 hours at a time, and then they must rest. You will see different conductors and engineers every several days. If you have a station in your area where there is a crew change, then you will meet the engineers who terminate their trips in your area and the engineers who begin their trips in your area. Getting to know the conductors and engineers working both ends of the trip will be an asset. If there is a crew change in your area, the train will probably be there longer than 5 minutes. The train can be in a station for a minimum of 20 minutes, and up to 1 hour depending on their schedules in and out of your area.

## Amtrak Crew Personnel

These people are responsible for the overall comfort of the passengers. The crew or attendants will travel with the passengers for the entire trip. For example, the Southwest Chief, Amtrak Train Number 4 originates in Los Angeles with a final destination of Chicago. The passenger crew that begins the trip in Los Angeles will stay with the train for the entire trip to Chicago. The crew then lays overnight in Chicago and makes the return trip from Chicago to Los Angeles the following day (Southwest Chief, Amtrak Train Number 3). The crew for this particular train works for 6 days and then lays off for approximately 5 days, so you will see the same crew, depending on your area, every 4 to 6 days.

Having a good working relationship with the passenger crew will also assist you in operating a successful train interdiction detail. Following is a breakdown of the crew personnel you will have contact with on a long-distance Amtrak train.

### Chief on Board

This is the supervisor and boss of the crew members. The Chief on Board is responsible for making sure the trip is pleasant and comfortable for the passengers. All the other crew members answer to the Chief on Board. When the train stops in your area, normally the Chief on Board exits the train and makes sure that the passengers do not have any difficulty exiting or entering the train. He is there to make sure that passengers get whatever type of assistance they require.

### Coach Car Attendant

Depending on the time of year, there might be one or two coach car attendants working a train. There is normally an attendant for every passenger car. The coach car attendants are responsible for making sure the trip is comfortable and all passenger needs are met. The coach car attendant is also a vital person with whom to establish rapport.

The attendants are very knowledgeable concerning the passengers they service. They are aware of normal passenger travel patterns. The rapport that is established with the train attendant will greatly enhance the success of your train interdiction detail.

When passengers prepare to board their assigned coach car, the train attendant is the first employee who will greet them. The train attendant at this time will assign seats and ask how many persons are in the party. They will attempt to accommodate the passengers as to seating preference. The attendant is able to view all passengers as well as the luggage that they board with. The attendant will assist passengers with their luggage, either placing it in the common luggage area or assisting them in taking it to their seats. The coach car attendant has a great number of passengers to deal with, but they can still be of assistance to you.

The train attendants also will assist passengers in disembarking from the train when they reach their destinations, assisting them with any luggage needs. You should always make a point to get to know all of the train attendants, whether or not they are supportive of your cause. Make a point of conversing with the train attendants, and furnish any new attendants with your business card. Talking with the train attendants is very important in establishing the liaison. Once a rapport has been established, educate the train attendants on the characteristics common among persons involved in criminal activity. The train attendants might ask what these drug couriers look like. You should stress the importance is not what they look like but what they do and how they act once on the train. Explaining this to the train attendants will almost always bring examples from them of passengers they had seen before that exhibited the characteristics described.

You should always ask the attendant's permission to enter his train car. This is his work area and his area of responsibility. Failure to do this would be like someone coming to your house or your workplace and just walking in or making himself at home without asking you. People should be treated with respect in their work areas. After you work in this area for a while and you have established a liaison, the usual comment from the train attendants is, "you don't have to ask, just come on in." However, as a matter of practice, permission should be asked.

After receiving permission to enter an attendant's train car, ask him how the trip is going and if he is having any problems. Are there any passengers on board who are behaving in an abnormal manner? Again, you are not asking for passengers who look strange, but asking about behavior.

If information from a train attendant was received, that information should be followed up on and you should attempt to inform the train attendant of the outcome. If the information did not lead to anything valuable, giving the attendant some type of feedback is important. Of course, you would not give feedback such as, "Hey, that information you gave me was full of crap;" that type of comment would definitely alienate you from the attendant and any hopes of ever having any cooperation or support from him in the future. Even if the information is useless, let him know that you appreciated the information but that nothing panned out, but if they ever see that type of behavior again to notify you, because in another situation it might prove useful. Always treat the attendants with courtesy and respect if you want them working with you and not against you.

### Sleeper Car Attendant

These employees usually have more seniority and are veteran train attendants. They are responsible for fewer passengers, but they provide more service to their passengers than coach car attendants. When traveling by Amtrak in the sleeper section of the train, these are first-class accommodations, and the class of service is usually first class as well. Passengers pay more for these accommodations. All meals are included with the price of the sleeper. The sleepers can range from the one- to two-person type accommodations, like the economy sleeper compartments, or the deluxe sleeper compartments that can accommodate four to five passengers.

Persons involved in drug trafficking use the sleeper sections as well as the coach section. Many couriers who use the rail system travel via the sleeper sections of the train because they are much more private. The courier can keep all of his luggage containing contraband inside the room without having to worry about being disturbed, having the drugs ripped off, or law enforcement identifying where the luggage with the dope is. We have seen some trends with couriers traveling via the coach section of the train. The time of year dictates whether couriers can travel in sleepers. During the peak seasons such as summer and holidays, the sleeper section can be booked up weeks and months in advance, so it is difficult for couriers to book sleeper compartments at the last minute. An advantage for couriers who travel in the coach section of the train is that they can blend in easier with the general passengers.

The sleeper car train attendant is responsible for making sure his passengers are comfortable and have all the amenities needed for a pleasurable trip. The sleeper car attendant is the first employee the passenger meets when boarding the train. The attendant will direct the passenger to his assigned compartment and will ask for any special requests the passenger might have. He will assist the passenger with his luggage, placing it in the common luggage area or in the passenger's room. The sleeper car attendant can assist you in identifying which luggage belongs to which passenger or whether the passenger maintained all of his luggage in the room. He can tell you how many guests are in the room and if there was any unusual behavior in boarding, or if someone assisted the passenger in boarding the train. The sleeper car attendant is a very valuable source of information. As with other personnel, he should only be used as your eyes and ears and told that he should take no enforcement action or assist you in any way. You should distance the sleeper car attendant from the situation and conduct your own independent investigation from any information provided by him.

### Diner Car Attendants

These attendants are responsible for the dining cars and only have contact with the passengers who come to eat in the diner cars. Most long distance passenger trains have diner cars where hot meals are prepared and served. In a two-level car, the kitchen area is on the lower floor with the seating area for passengers on the second level. The kitchen area is maintained by the chefs and kitchen helpers; they are responsible for preparation of the food. They normally do not have much contact with the passengers. The dining car attendants are responsible for waiting on the passengers when they come into the diner car to eat. The dining car attendants serve all three meals on the train: breakfast, lunch, and dinner. If a guest chooses not to go to the dining car to eat, meals can be delivered to the room. This is normally done by the train attendant for the sleeper or coach car. Dining car attendants can also be valuable sources of information. They might be able to tell you where a particular passenger from the coach or sleeper car section is seated. Dining car attendants also will watch out for which passengers belong in the sleeper car section of the train, and might ask a passenger walking through the dining car towards the sleeper car section if he belongs in the sleeper car section.

### Lounge Car Attendants

Most long distance passenger trains also have what is referred to as a lounge car. This car has no assigned seating and is accessible for all passengers on the train. The configuration of the train, whether it is a single- or double-decker train, determines where the lounge car attendant will be located. On most double-decker trains, the lounge car attendant is on the lower floor. The lounge car attendant sells snacks, soft drinks, and alcoholic drinks.

## The Consensual Encounter on a Train

Knowing the answers to your questions before contacting a person is important in any consensual encounter. How will you know the answers to your questions in train interdiction? We will explore several areas that will help answer that.

One thing that is helpful is to become familiar with the Amtrak Train Reservation System and its codes. Being able to read the PNR system that Amtrak uses will be of great assistance to you. We will discuss the passenger manifests for the entire train and also for the sleeper car section. We will also explore the PNRs and learn how to read them. Conduct and behavior will remain our focus for the passengers we want to contact.

## The PNR

The PNR provides information to help determine passenger conduct and behavior. Drug couriers and people involved in criminal activity have to travel in certain ways, and the PNR will help to identify those. Certain characteristics are common among drug and money couriers. When we read the PNR we will be able to segregate those passengers who fall within the criteria that we will set. Age, race, national origin, and gender play no part in determining which passengers we hope to contact, but the conduct and behavior will separate the legitimate passenger from the passenger involved in criminal activity.

We will be looking at when the reservation was made or the ticket purchased. One-way travel is common among drug couriers, and we want to know how the ticket was purchased. The PNR contains all this information. In our law enforcement training and experience, the date and time the reservation was made are important. In the drug world, "doper time" is often used to determine timing of transactions.

Even the biggest and most sophisticated drug organizations have many obstacles in transporting their illicit products, whether that is the product itself or the proceeds from the sale of that product. Legitimate businesses and companies that distribute legitimate products do not have to worry about law enforcement intercepting their products. In the drug trade, law enforcement is the greatest obstacle that drug organizations have to surpass to distribute their products. There are no set time schedules that are adhered to in the drug business. The time when drugs or proceeds are distributed is when the window of opportunity presents itself. Drugs and proceeds are cautiously transported and distributed. The reality of the drugs or proceeds being intercepted by law enforcement is an everyday obstacle for drug organizations.

The drug organizations cannot preplan when the drugs are going to arrive because of the law enforcement obstacles that exist. They cannot make plans for 3 weeks from now that a certain shipment will arrive or be prepared for shipment. They must act immediately. Whenever the product arrives, that is when the planning begins and they must take advantage of the window of opportunity, for if it is missed, waiting for that opportunity to come again might take hours, days, weeks, or months.

When drugs and proceeds are ready for transportation, planning must be immediate. Therefore, when reviewing an Amtrak train PNR, the time the reservation is made will be in close proximity to the time of travel. In our experience, that time is on the day of actual departure or up to 3 days before departure. It is unlikely that a courier would be told that a shipment of drugs was ready to be transported and that they would be leaving in 3 weeks. It is usually the exact opposite; the courier is told to be ready to leave at any time because when the shipment of drugs arrives plans are made immediately for distribution.

Couriers, even though they know they are going to return, often book a one-way trip. That way, if law enforcement missed them on the way out, they do not want to alert law enforcement to the fact that they are returning. Therefore, one-way travel will be common when reviewing the PNR. When contact is made with the courier, this will elicit the question, "How do you plan to return?" If a round trip is booked, then the time spent at the destination city will be minimal, maybe a day or two. Some couriers will book a round-trip ticket with a stay at the location for several weeks, and reschedule their trip once they arrive to return immediately in order to avoid this type of suspicion. Any changes will be indicated on the PNR.

When reviewing the PNR, the method of payment is important. If someone is involved in criminal activity, that method of payment listed on the PNR will almost always be cash. The drug trade is a cash business, and with cash, there is no paper trail. If a credit card is used, then a law enforcement investigator could conduct a historical investigation of other trips made. Also, it is difficult to use a fictitious name when paying with a check or credit card. When paying with cash and, because of the Amtrak identification policy, a person is able to use a fictitious name.

The PNR will also include a home call-back telephone number for the passenger. As discussed previously, this telephone number is requested in the event of a late train or a cancellation, and many couriers use a false call-back telephone number, a pager, or disconnected number on the PNR, so that law enforcement cannot properly identify them.

The passenger manifests are good sources of information. The first passenger manifest to be reviewed will be the manifest for the entire train. This manifest will include the names of the passengers, their reservation numbers, their origination and destination cities, any call-back telephone numbers listed, the train numbers, and if the passenger is in the coach or sleeper section. This manifest gives us minimal information concerning the passengers, but nonetheless we will still have some information to rely on.

Another passenger manifest to be reviewed is the manifest for passengers traveling in the sleeper section of the train. This manifest can be accessed separately. The information contained in this manifest will be the train number, passenger names and number of passengers in a particular room, the type of sleeper accommodation the passenger is in, and whether it is an economy or deluxe sleeper. The sleeper car passenger manifest will also list the room number the passenger is in, and the passenger's origination and destination cities. Again, this passenger manifest also contains minimal information; from here we will review each passenger PNR individually.

Each PNR will be reviewed individually, though it will only take a few seconds to glance at the information once you become familiar with the information and where to look for it. You will be looking primarily at the time the reservation was made, when the ticket was purchased, and the method of payment. Second, you will look at the origination and destination cities, the number of passengers traveling in the party, and where they are located on the train, coach or sleeper (Figures 8.4 aand b).

This information will assist you in determining which passengers you will attempt to contact based on their conduct and behavior. Each of the characteristics or indicators previously listed in and of themselves are not signs of criminal activity, but based on your law enforcement training and experience, this information will indicate a potential individual to contact. We think this is the most effective manner of separating legitimate passengers from passengers involved in criminal activity. And of course, our job is to identify the persons involved in criminal activity and contact them.

## Ticketing Information

Understanding the Amtrak ticketing system is very important. Unlike many airlines that have different ticketing systems and information, Amtrak's ticketing information is all the same. Whether you are in Los Angeles, Chicago, or Miami, all tickets are the same and the information is in the same location (Figure 8.5). When you approach a passenger who is traveling by Amtrak and you ask for and receive permission to look at his ticket, you want to know where the vital information is located on the ticket. You do not want to spend a lot of time looking for that information or asking the passenger about it. You want to be able to look at the ticket briefly and return it to the passenger, so knowing where to look is the key.

Even if you are doing what is referred to as a "cold encounter," with no prior information or PNR information, you still want to ask questions you know the answers to. The ticket will have all those answers, and by taking a brief moment to review the ticket and return it to the passenger you can still ask those questions and know the answers.

## PASSENGER NAME RECORD (PNR)

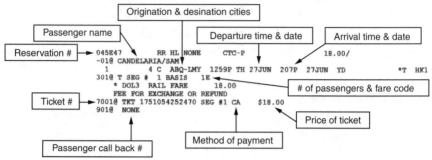

**Figure 8.4a** (Used with permission of Amtrak.)

## HISTORY OF PNR

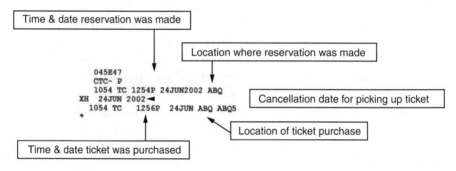

**Figure 8.4b** (Used with permission of Amtrak.)

# Conducting Encounters on the Train

Officer safety always takes precedence in any encounter you do no matter where it is. Conducting consensual encounters on the train is a very dangerous aspect of the job. We are already aware of the safety issues involved with passengers traveling by Amtrak, and we must take into account on every encounter that the potential for the passenger carrying a weapon is very real.

Conducting encounters in the coach section of the train is very much like conducting encounters aboard buses. Never block the passenger in; never block his egress or ingress from the seat.

Take note of where the exits are. More than likely you will have three exits from the car. On the Superliners, double-decker cars mainly seen west of the Mississippi River, there is an exit from the car on either side of the car and one in the middle, where the passenger enters the train car from the outside.

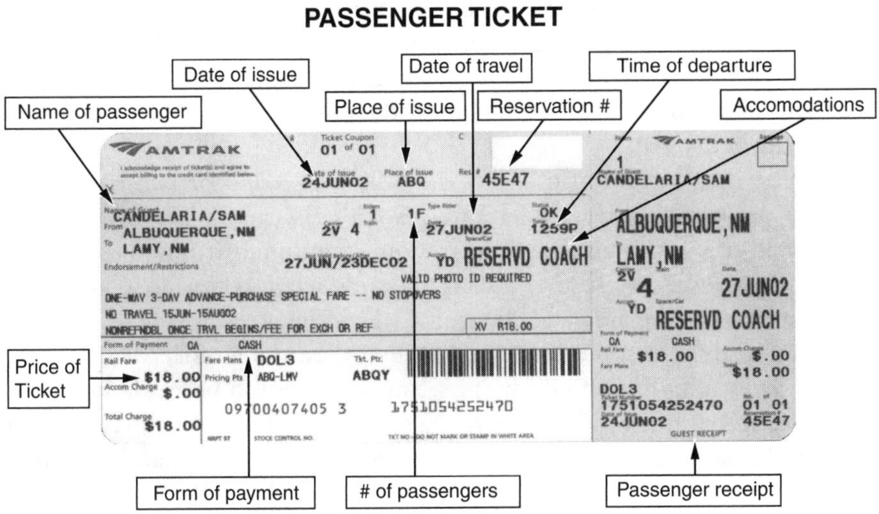

## PASSENGER TICKET

**Figure 8.5** (Used with permission of Amtrak.)

Always stand behind the seat when contacting a passenger; this gives him ample opportunity to exit the seat if he wishes to. As you stand behind the seat, let your backup pick the location he thinks is best for him to assist you. When both of you are ready and in place, then conduct the encounter. Do not conduct the encounter when your partner is not ready or his attention is being distracted.

Displaying your badge of office and identifying yourself is the first aspect of the encounter. Asking for permission to speak is next. What happens when the passenger you are contacting acknowledges you? If you are standing in the aisle and to the rear of his seat, then he must look over his shoulder and look back to acknowledge you. It is important to articulate in your report what the passenger did to acknowledge you.

### *Example*

As Officer Jones approached the seat where the passenger, later identified as Drug Dealer, was seated, Officer Jones remained in the aisle, standing to the rear of Dealer's seat. Officer Jones displayed his badge of office to Dealer and identified himself as a police officer with the Good Town Police Department. Officer Jones then asked Dealer if he had a moment to speak to him. Dealer had to look back over his left shoulder to acknowledge Officer Jones, and when he did, he first looked at Officer Jones' badge and then glanced up at Officer Jones. After making eye contact with Officer Jones, Dealer immediately looked back at Officer Jones badge and stated "Sure, what about?"

In this scenario, it is very important that you articulate where you were standing and what the person did upon your contacting them. In the scenario it is very clear where Officer Jones was standing—to the rear of the passenger's seat and in the aisle, but Officer Jones was not blocking Dealer's egress or ingress from his seat.

This vantage point also allows the officer a second or two of reaction time in the event the passenger emerges with a weapon. The investigating officer should continue the conversation, if granted, from this location, remaining behind the seat. If a search is conducted in this area, again, the tight confines of the area will determine where the investigating officer conducts the search. In some cases the backup or scanning officer will conduct the search; again, this should be preplanned. It should be made known to the passenger at this time that there is a second agent or officer present: "Mr. Dealer, this is my partner Officer Smith, and he is going to stand by while I search your bag." Now if there was any thought in Mr. Dealer's mind that he was going to take you out because he thought you were by yourself, those thoughts have diminished. If there is an open seat across the aisle from the passenger, this is a good place from which to make contact; again, you are not blocking the passenger's egress or ingress from the seat (Figure 8.6).

## Encounters in the Lounge Car

Many encounters are conducted in this area. There is no assigned seating here and passengers in the coach and sleeper car sections of the train have access to the area. In some trains there are separate lounge cars for coach passengers and the sleeper car section. This area will usually have televisions, a snack area, and a bar area. The seating is set up so passengers can converse with each other or so they can look directly out of the windows (Figure 8.7). Take into account where the passenger you wish to contact is seated, and attempt to take up a position behind his seat so you are not blocking his egress or ingress from the seat. If a search is to be conducted, then allow the passenger to lead the way back to his seat. This shows that you are not controlling the passenger and he is not being detained.

## Encounters in the Diner Car

This location can be very dangerous for the investigating officers due to the items such as bottles, knives, forks — that can be used as weapons. If you are looking for a single passenger, there is a possibility he is sitting with someone else. Because of the limited space in the diner car, passengers sit together to eat. You will normally not see a passenger sitting alone, unless there was someone there before who just left (Figure 8.8).

**Figure 8.6** (Photograph used with permission of Amtrak.)

**Figure 8.7** Photograph used with permission of Amtrak.)

**Figure 8.8** (Photograph used with permission of Amtrak.)

The same set of circumstances should be adhered to as in the coach car or lounge car — standing in the aisle behind the passenger's seat when making the contact. Beware of all eating utensils! If the passenger has to go back to his seat or sleeping compartment, allow him to lead the way.

### Encounters in the Sleeper Car

Conducting encounters of passengers in the sleeper car section of the train is unlike conducting an encounter in any other mode of transportation. Because many of the sleeper doors, and of course the windows, are glass, you may look into a person's room through the window or door if they are unobstructed by curtains. Before conducting an encounter in the sleeper car section, you should walk by and conduct a quick visual of the room for passengers and luggage if possible. Allow your scanner or backup to pick a position that is best suited for officer safety. *Remember, the passenger in a sleeper roomette has a greater expectation of privacy than a passenger seated in the coach section of the train.*

If you are standing outside the room and are engaged in conversation with a passenger, unless that passenger exits the room to speak with you he will not see your scanner or backup, and unfortunately your backup cannot see inside the room either, or observe any threat that you might miss.

**Figure 8.9** (Photograph used with permission of Amtrak.)

When conducting a consensual encounter at a roomette, the same procedures should apply as if you were conducting an encounter at a house, apartment, or motel room. You do not stand in the middle of the door and knock. You stand to the side of the doorway even if you can observe inside of the room. Stand to the right or left of the doorway and knock gently: if the person is in the room it is not necessary to knock loudly. Allow the passenger to acknowledge your presence by observing you and opening the door. Then identify yourself verbally and with your credentials or badge of office. Ask the passenger for permission to speak to him.

You will not ask for permission to enter the sleeper room initially; when a search is conducted, you will enter the room. This goes for the smaller economy-type rooms. In the larger deluxe rooms (Figure 8.9), handicap rooms, or family rooms you may initially ask for permission to enter and speak with the passenger, but it is not necessary. Once the passenger has given you permission to speak with him, attempt to remain outside of the room unless you have asked for and received permission to enter.

**Figure 8.10** (Photograph used with permission of Amtrak.)

If you ask for permission to search luggage, depending on the size of the room, search the luggage in a safe manner. You want the passenger to know at this time that your partner will be standing by as you search the luggage. Introduce your partner to the passenger. If you must enter the room, ask the passenger for permission to enter the room, like you would in a house or hotel room. If you conduct a search of luggage in the room, make sure your partner knows you are entering the room and make sure that your partner stays in close proximity to you.

If you are going to search the room, you must also ask the passenger(s) permission to search the room. You cannot receive permission from the train attendant or the chief on board to search the passenger's room.

Many drug and money couriers keep their luggage inside their room so they can maintain control of the luggage. Sometimes the luggage is too big to keep in the room, and the train attendant has probably already suggested placing the luggage in the common luggage area (Figure 8.10).

There are many hiding places in these rooms; in the economy and deluxe rooms there are natural cavities where contraband can be secreted, such as under the seating in the mattresses, and behind the seating cushions.

If you receive permission to search the room, conduct an efficient search. It is always a good idea prior to conducting any type of encounter that you gain experience in the configuration of the room:

- *Are there restrooms and showers?* Yes, in the deluxe rooms.
- *Are there windows that can be escaped from?* Yes, all the windows are emergency type windows, with each window having an emergency pull handle that can be opened for the passenger to escape through.
- *Can the doors be locked from the outside?* No. With many of the rooms, once the passenger has left the room it cannot be locked. The room can be locked from the inside by the passenger but not from the outside.

## Conclusion

Wherever your encounter takes place on the train, be sure to be mindful of all the safety precautions to take, and never forget **officer safety**.

## Case Law

### U.S. v. Thame, 846 F.2d 200 (1988) 3rd Cir.

Agents in the lobby of a train station contacted the defendant. The defendant refused a consent search of his luggage, but did consent to a canine sniff of his luggage. The canine sniff indicated there were drugs in the bag and a search warrant was obtained based upon the alert.

### U.S. v. Whitehead, 849 F.2d 849 (1988) 4th Cir.

A passenger train sleeping compartment is not a "temporary home." Police are not required to have probable cause before they could bring trained dogs into passenger train sleeping compartment to sniff defendant's luggage. Police are required to have reasonable suspicion as to justify conducting the dog sniff, as they did in this case.

### U.S. v. Tartaglia, 864 F.2d 837 (1989) D.C. Cir.

There was probable cause to search a train roomette when a narcotics detector dog indicated an alert at the vent of the door to the roomette. The warrantless search of the roomette was justified under exigent circumstances exception to the warrant requirement.

### U.S. v. Massac, 867 F.2d 174 (1989) 3rd Cir.

Sniff test of luggage by specially trained drug-sniffing dog did not amount to an illegal search because luggage was in the custody of a common carrier (Amtrak).

### U.S. v. Battista, 876 F.2d 201 (1989) D.C. Cir.

Law enforcement officers had sufficient reasonable suspicion when a drug dog alerted outside the defendant's train roomette. The dog was taken down the corridor of the train car and alerted to the door of the roomette.

### U.S. v. Carrasquillo, 877 F.2d 73 (1989) D.C. Cir.

These factors established reasonable suspicion to detain defendant and his luggage temporarily and to have narcotics detection dog sniff bags.

> Defendant was traveling by train from source city.
> Had made a one-way reservation on short notice.
> Changed date only a few minutes before departure.
> Paid cash for ticket.
> Had provided no contact telephone.
> Arrived at the train station shortly prior to departure time.
> Was traveling under assumed name.
> Had used a second assumed name in making first reservation.
> Was visibly nervous.
> Either carrying no luggage or falsely denied bag was his.

After the narcotics detection dog sniffed and alerted to the bag, the bag was searched under the abandonment warrant exception.

### U.S. v. Colyer, 878 F.2d 469 (1989) D.C. Cir.

A canine sniff for narcotics of a train sleeper compartment from a public corridor did not constitute a search. Lawful canine sniff for narcotics of train sleeper compartment from public corridor, that resulted in canine alerting, provided cause for seizure and search of train passenger's bags. Exigent circumstances justify exception to the Fourth Amendment warrant clause.

### U.S. v. Trayer, 898 F.2d 805 (1990) D.C. Cir.

Narcotic detector dog's alert from the corridor of a passenger train to a train roomette gave probable cause to search that roomette. Probable cause that train roomette contained drugs justified search of entire roomette, without bringing dog inside to sniff more directly.

### U.S. v. Edwards, 898 F.2d 1273 (1990) 7th Cir.

These factors established reasonable suspicion to detain defendant and his luggage temporarily and to have a narcotics detection dog sniff bags:

Passenger had arrived from Los Angeles, a major narcotics distribution center.
He repeatedly made eye contact with undercover officers.
He became visibly nervous during questioning.
His story did not match that of separately questioned companion.

The defendant was issued a receipt for his bags and he immediately left on another train. About 15 minutes later, the narcotics detector dog alerted to the bags and a search warrant was obtained.

### U.S. v. Sullivan, 903 F.2d 1093 (1990) 7th Cir.

These factors gave officers reasonable suspicion to detain defendant's luggage for a canine sniff:

Passenger was traveling from source city.
He had purchased a one-way ticket on date of departure.
He paid cash for the ticket.
He carried only one small bag, despite long distance of trip.
He appeared to divert his eyes from those of officers when they followed him.

Detention of his luggage for 45 minutes until dog sniff for narcotics was performed was reasonable. Passenger was informed that inspection could take place in a short period of time, and he not only declined to wait, but also effectively abandoned the bag by declining to accept a receipt.

### U.S. v. Nurse, 916 F.2d 20 (1990) D.C. Cir.

Police officer developed reasonable suspicion of the defendant's illicit drug activity to justify detention of the defendant's bag for canine sniff. Detention of the defendant during the canine sniff of her bag for 20 to 30 minutes was reasonable.

### U.S. v. Ferguson, 935 F.2d 1518 (1991) 7th Cir.

Officers developed reasonable suspicion to detain a train passenger carrying two bags based upon:

Passenger arrived from source city.
He was carrying a bag secured with a padlock.
He was traveling under an assumed name.
He lied about his destination.
He gave conflicting answers about contents of the bag.
He was furtive, nervous, and avoided eye contact.

After refusing consent, the passenger's bag was seized for a canine sniff. The passenger was allowed to leave, a canine alerted to the bag, and a warrant was obtained.

### U.S. v. $639,558.00 U.S. currency, 955 F.2d 712 (1992) D.C. Cir.

A narcotics detector dog "sweeping" the corridor of a train alerted to luggage. The defendant refused consent to his luggage. Police then arrested the defendant. The court ruled that the search of the defendant's luggage could not be justified as incident to arrest.

Discovery of the money in the luggage during an inventory search was not inevitable, the defendant would have been released absent the search of the luggage.

### U.S. v. Ward, 961 F.2d 1526 (1992) 10th Cir.

These factors did not raise reasonable suspicion for an investigative detention:

Suspect paid $600 in cash.
Traveling one-way from Flagstaff to Kansas City.
Had given telephone number from Tucson at time of reservation.
Had reserved the largest private room on train although traveling alone.

As a result of the unlawful detention, the dog sniff resulting in seizure of drugs was illegal.

### U.S. v. Bloom, 975 F.2d 1447 (1992) 10th Cir.

These factors did not raise reasonable suspicion for an investigative detention.

Traveling alone from source city.
Suspect paid cash for one-way ticket.
Stayed in private train compartment.
Kept high quality luggage in compartment.

As a result of the unlawful detention, the dog sniff resulting in seizure of drugs was illegal.

### U.S. v. Hall, 978, F.2d 616 (1992) 10th Cir.

Officers may seize and briefly detain traveler's luggage provided they have reasonable suspicion the luggage contains drugs. Seizure of train passenger's suitcase did not occur when agent first telephoned to secure a narcotics dog to check the suitcase, or when agent lifted suitcase, but when he informed passenger he was detaining her suitcase in order to expose it to a trained narcotics dog, this seizure required reasonable suspicion.

### U.S. v. Robinson, 984 F.2d 911 (1993) 8th Cir.

Defendant at train station was asked to consent to a search of his luggage. The defendant denied consent. Officer's statements to the defendant that he would have a drug sniffing dog sniff the luggage and that would take 30 to 40 minutes to arrive, did not coerce defendant into consenting to search of his luggage. The defendant was not subjected to possible disruption of his travel plans since his travel plans required him to wait in the terminal for over an hour.

### U.S. v. Carter, 985 F.2d 1095 (1993) D.C. Cir.

Officers had reasonable suspicion to detain suspect's bag at the train station for a canine sniff. Upon taking the bag to the dog, the suspect admitted to officers that the bag did in fact contain narcotics. The suspect was placed under arrest. The dog had a positive alert to the bag and the bag was searched incident to the arrest.

### U.S. v. Wynn, 993 F.2d 760 (1993), 10th Cir.

During the time officers question a person on a train to develop reasonable suspicion, no Miranda warnings are required. Officers asked defendant in the coach car of a train permission to conduct a dog sniff of his luggage. The defendant consented. The dog sniffed and gave a positive alert to a box. The officers asked for consent to open the box and the defendant refused. The officers seized the box and left the defendant on the train.

A search warrant was obtained based upon the positive canine alert.

### U.S. v. McCarthur, 6F.3d 1270 (1993) 7th Cir.

Officer's seizure of defendant required reasonable suspicion. Officer's decision to detain defendant's carry-on bag for a canine sniff was justified, where dog would quickly confirm or deny the suspicion the bag contained narcotics. The defendant was told the bag would be detained for 15 minutes for a canine sniff, she was told that she could leave and she was told she did not have to consent to a search.

### U.S. v. Houston, 21 F.3d 1035 (1994) 10th Cir.

Officers may seize and detain train passenger's luggage and subject it to a dog sniff, if they have reasonable suspicion.
    These factors provided reasonable suspicion:

Passenger lied about traveling alone.
Passenger lied about his phone number.
Passenger lied about not having identification.

### U.S. v. Moore, 22F.3d 241 (1994) 10th Cir.

Agents had reasonable suspicion to detain train passenger's luggage for a canine sniff. The bag was seized and the passenger was free to leave. No narcotic detector dog was available at the train station. The bag was driven 5 minutes to where the dog was. The dog alerted and a search warrant was obtained. (It should be noted that the dog was unavailable due to working a security detail for the Vice President of the United States.)

### U.S. v. Garcia, 42 F.3d 604 (1994) 10th Cir.

Dog sniff of luggage in train's baggage car without reasonable suspicion but with authorization of operator of train did not violate the Fourth Amendment. The owner of the luggage had no expectation of privacy of the air space surrounding the luggage.

### U.S. v. Torres, 65 F.3d 1241 (1995) 4th Cir.

Consensual encounter turned into an investigative detention when train passenger refused consent search of carry-on luggage and officers told her that they were seizing her bag for a canine sniff. An investigative detention must be supported by reasonable and articulable suspicion. Drug courier profile, without more, does not create reasonable suspicion.

### U.S. v. Gwinn, 191F.3d 874 (1999) 8th Cir.

No search occurs when an officer briefly moves luggage from the overhead compartment to the aisle in order to facilitate a canine sniff. Passengers have no objective, reasonable expectation of privacy from such action because it is not uncommon for other passengers or employees to move baggage in order to rearrange and maximize use of compartment space. Pushing on sides of a bag to expel air from inside in effort to smell contents is a search.

# Commercial Bus Interdiction

# 9

Officer safety is the most important factor to remember when working bus interdiction. As we have stressed in previous chapters, there is no amount of dope, money, or bad guys out there to justify you, your partner, innocent bystanders, or even the bad guy getting hurt. As in any consensual encounter, approaching the unknown is always a critical factor. Working commercial bus interdiction, this is very evident. This chapter will focus on officer safety within the confines of a crowded bus or in a bus terminal. The people involved in criminal activity such as drug trafficking are fully aware of the lack of safety conditions for commercial bus passengers, and that is why bus travel is so attractive for them. Travel on commercial buses, even if they are chartered or independently owned, is a much more time-consuming method of travel, but it is very popular and is probably the most inexpensive method of travel. Many people who do not want to fly due to the events of September 11, 2001, find bus travel a safe alternative.

In this chapter we will start with the review of the most recent United States Supreme Court decision concerning bus interdiction that was argued on April 16, 2002 and decided on June 17, 2002, allowing law enforcement to continue focusing on bus interdiction and the persons who exploit the security measures to facilitate their criminal activity.

This chapter will also focus on establishing a bus interdiction detail, review of additional case law (specifically *U.S. v. Bostic*), familiarizing yourself with the commercial bus and terminal areas, ticketing system and documents, conducting encounters on board the bus and in the bus terminal, and use of certified narcotic detection canines in this these areas.

## Most Recent United States Supreme Court Decision

### United States v. Christopher Drayton and Clifton Brown, Jr., Cite: 2002 WL 1305729 (U.S.)

The defendants were convicted separately in United States District Court for the Northern District of Florida of conspiracy to distribute cocaine and possession of cocaine with intent to distribute. They each appealed, and their appeals were consolidated. The 11th Circuit Court of Appeals, Justice Carnes, Circuit Judge, 231 F.3d 787, held that defendants' consent to pat-down search was sufficiently free of coercion to serve as valid basis for search, and reversed and remanded. Certiorari was granted. The Supreme Court, Justice Kennedy, held that: first plainclothes police officers did not "seize" passengers on a bus when, as part of routine drug and weapons interdiction effort, they boarded a bus at a rest stop and began asking passengers questions; and that the two passengers' consent to search was voluntary. This case was reversed and remanded.

This case was as follows: the driver of the bus on which Drayton and Brown were traveling allowed three police officers to board the bus as part of a routine drug and weapons interdiction effort. One officer knelt on the driver's seat, facing the rear of the bus, while another officer stayed in the rear, facing forward, Officer Lang worked his way from the back to the front speaking with individual passengers as he went. To avoid blocking the aisle, Officer Lang stood next to or just behind each passenger with whom he spoke. He testified that passengers who declined to cooperate or who chose to exit the bus at any time would have been allowed to do so without argument; that most people are willing to cooperate; that passengers often leave the bus for a cigarette or a snack while officers were on board the bus; and that, although he sometimes informs passengers of their right to refuse to cooperate, he did not do so on the day in question. As Officer Lang approached Drayton and Brown, who were seated together, he held up his badge long enough for them to identify him as an officer. Speaking just loud enough for them to hear, he declared that the police were looking for drugs and weapons. He asked if Drayton or Brown had any bags. When both of them pointed to a bag in the overhead luggage rack, Officer Lang asked if they minded if he checked it. Brown agreed, and a search of the bag revealed no contraband. Officer Lang then asked Brown if he minded if he checked his person and Brown agreed. Officer Lang conducted a pat-down which revealed hard objects similar to drug packages in both thigh areas. Brown was arrested and Lang then asked Drayton if he minded if he checked him. Drayton agreed and a pat-down revealed similar objects to those found on Brown, and Drayton was arrested. A further search revealed that Drayton and Brown had taped cocaine between their shorts. They were charged with federal drug crimes. Drayton and Brown moved to suppress the cocaine on the grounds that their consent to the pat-down searches was invalid. In denying the motions, the District Court determined that the police conduct was not coercive, and Drayton and Brown's consent to search was voluntary. The 11th Circuit Court of Appeals reversed and remanded the case based on prior holdings that bus passengers do not feel free to disregard officers' requests to search absent positive indication that consent may be refused.

It was held: The Fourth Amendment does not require police officers to advise bus passengers of their right not to cooperate and to refuse consent searches.

## *Florida v. Bostick,* Cite as 111 S. Ct. 2382 (1991)

In this case, the Court held that the Fourth Amendment permits officers to approach bus passengers at random to ask questions and request their consent to searches, provided a reasonable person would feel free to decline the requests or otherwise terminate the encounter. The Court identified as "particularly worth noting" the factors that the officer, although obviously armed, did not unholster his gun or use it in a threatening way, and that he advised respondent passenger that he could refuse consent to a search. Relying on this last factor, the 11th Circuit erroneously adopted what is in effect a per se rule that evidence obtained during suspicionless drug interdictions on a bus must be suppressed unless the officers have advised passengers of their right not to cooperate and to refuse consent to a search. Additional case law will be reviewed at the end of this chapter.

The foundation has already been established concerning the case law that allows law enforcement to conduct consensual encounter type investigations on buses and in bus terminals. The recent case just decided by the United States Supreme Court reemphasizes that law enforcement is correct in its investigative opportunities, as long as the law is followed.

Before the Drayton decision, interdiction details relied on the direction from the Terrance Bostick case. The Bostick case, which is another Florida case, concerned a bus passenger by the name of Terrance Bostick.

Facts: In 1989, Bostick had boarded a bus in Miami. Two police officers in Miami boarded the bus during a stopover in Fort Lauderdale and, with articulable suspicion, asked to inspect Bostick's ticket and identification. After finding Bostick's ticket and identification to be in order, the police requested of Bostick to consent to a search of his luggage. Bostick consented to the search, and the police found cocaine in one of Bostick's bags.

Bostick pled guilty to charges of trafficking in cocaine and reserved the right to appeal the trial court's motion to suppress. The District Court of Appeals affirmed the trial court's decision, but certified a question to the

Florida Supreme Court. The Florida Supreme Court reversed the trial court and suppressed the cocaine found during the course of the search.

The issue was, does the rule permitting police officers to randomly approach people in public places to question them and "request consent to search their luggage, as long as a reasonable person would understand that he or she could refuse to cooperate," apply to encounters occurring on a bus?

In reasoning, the United States Supreme Court reversed the Florida Supreme Court, stating that the court had erred in adopting a per se rule that "prohibited the police from randomly boarding buses as a means of drug interdiction." While the court declined to decide whether a seizure occurred in Bostick, the Court did articulate a rule to be used in determining whether a specific encounter with the police constituted a seizure.

Therefore, the Court stated that to determine whether a particular encounter constituted a seizure, a court must consider all the circumstances surrounding the encounter to determine whether the police conduct would have communicated to a reasonable person that he was not free to decline the officer's request or otherwise terminate the encounter.

The court noted that the rule applied to encounters that occur on a bus as it would apply to encounters occurring in other public places.

In reaching its decision, the Court explored a number of cases addressing police encounters and questioning. The court noted that since *Terry*, mere questioning by the police has repeatedly been held to not constitute a seizure. The court rejected Bostick's argument that a police encounter within the confines of a bus is much more intimidating than a normal encounter in a public place. The Court found Bostick's assertion that a reasonable person would not feel free to leave a bus indistinguishable from previous cases permitting such questioning.

## Establishing a Commercial Bus Interdiction Detail

Establishing a commercial bus interdiction detail is paramount to being successful in disrupting the flow of narcotics and illegal proceeds that are transported via commercial buses throughout your community, city, state, and our country. Having your administration's support and backing will greatly increase your success in this endeavor.

You must first ascertain to what extent your administration will allow you to work in this area. Are they dedicated and willing to allow you to contribute 100% to establishing the detail, allowing for manpower and the use of certified narcotic detection canines, and forging the partnerships with the different commercial bus lines? If you are given the opportunity to do this, then your detail will be successful with the support and backing of your administration.

You will also require the support of your local prosecutor, whether your jurisdiction is state of federal or a combination of the two. Meet with your prosecutors to establish a liaison and present your program to them so they will be prepared for the cases that will be initiated in your program. Once you have established a liaison with the prosecutor's office and you have the backing of your administration and support as to manpower and the use of a certified narcotic detection canine, you can forge a partnership with the commercial bus companies in your area.

Research your area for other law enforcement agencies that are actively working bus interdiction. Find out what law enforcement agencies are monitoring the buses on the same line.

Identify which company you want to establish your program with, because you may have several companies in your area. The amount of manpower resources you have at your disposal will determine what companies to establish your program with, and how many. Make sure that the small details have already been worked out, such as:

- Office space with a contact telephone number
- Number of officers or agents that will participate in the detail, and number of outside agencies or federal agencies that want to participate in the detail
- Equipment: canine, cameras, fingerprinting equipment, evidence containers or bags, drug identification test kits, computer equipment, cellular telephones or pagers, luggage keys or Leatherman (folding knife) tools, and leg irons or shackles

Have these things in place before you contact your local bus company to meet with management and establish your commercial bus interdiction program.

## Contacting the Bus Company

The first contact with the bus company can be via telephone or in person to set up a meeting date and time. If contacting the management of the bus company over the telephone, do not discuss any details, but schedule a face-to-face meeting with them.

Once your meeting has been secured, prepare your proposed drug interdiction program for presentation. Rehearse your program before meeting with the management. Are you going to present them with a letter of commitment from your agency and explain the program so they are aware of what to expect and what is expected of them? Some details opt for this type of presentation; others meet with management and verbally describe their program. Either method is valid. The use of a letter of commitment details your plan of action. Examples of letters of commitment can be seen in Chapters 5, 8, and 10.

Explain your mission to the management of the commercial bus company:

- To stem the flow of illegal drugs and currency from reaching the destination points and deter criminal activity
- To seize narcotics, illegal currency, and weapons
- To identify sources of supply
- To establish cooperation between the bus company and law enforcement
- To provide cooperative assistance between law enforcement agencies
- To assist them in any way possible

If you plan to verbally detail your plan of action and the reason for the program, then rehearse your outline and prepare for any questions that management may have. These possible questions have been detailed in other chapters; they are as follows:

- What are the liability issues?
- How will staff and employees participate in the program?
- Will staff and employees be subjected to violent acts from potential violators?
- Will employees be subpoenaed to testify in court?
- Will the premises or business be subjected to acts of violence from potential violators?
- What security measures will the company have to adhere to in order to cooperate with law enforcement?
- Will there be payments made to employees for information?

These are questions that the management may ask during your meeting. Answer all questions honestly and accurately; if you do not have the answer, tell them you will find out and get back to them.

Once you have received permission to implement your program from the management of the commercial bus company, then a meeting with staff and employees is essential. They will be your "eyes and ears." Most companies have some type of bimonthly or weekly meetings. Request permission to attend one of these meetings to present your program to the employees.

Try to schedule the meeting so all members in the detail can attend, so employees and law enforcement personnel can get to know each other. Remember, this is a partnership with the business community and you want all the people involved to have a chance to meet and begin forging working relationships. The size of the bus terminal and the number of buses arriving and departing will dictate the number of employees. Some terminals are small, and only a handful of employees may work in this terminal. Other terminals are large, with a large number of buses arriving and departing and will require a bigger staff.

All employees are your eyes and ears. Training them on the characteristics and indicators of persons who are involved in criminal activity is essential. Employees in a commercial bus terminal may include the following:

- Ticket agents
- Baggage handlers
- Drivers (if there is a driver change at your station, make sure that all personnel in your detail make it a point to meet all drivers)
- Manager
- Bus maintenance personnel
- Custodians
- Parcel handlers

Regardless of the size or location of the terminal, you will need to familiarize yourself with the location. Become familiar with the layout of the terminal.

- Where is your city or location in relationship to source or distribution points? Is your city a source location or distribution point, or both?
- Where do the buses arrive and depart; which doors or gates?
- Are the arriving departing gates the same or are they separate?
- Where are the employee-only access locations, and will you have access to these areas?
- Is there security inside the terminal or outside? Is the security armed?
- Are there restaurants in the terminal?
- Are there locked storage areas in the terminal for public use?
- Where are the public telephones located?
- Where are the restroom facilities and how many are there?
- Does the terminal accept outgoing or incoming parcels or packages?
- What does the parking area look like, and where are the possible concealment areas in the event a passenger flees from you?
- Is there a separate location for taxis to pick up or drop off passengers?
- What are the ticket counters like?
- What does the stored luggage area look like, and will you have access to it?
- Will you be allowed to have a canine in the vicinity?
- Where are the potential escape routes?
- Are buses serviced at this location?

- Do they change drivers at your location?
- Are there bus wash rack facilities?
- Will encounters be conducted on board the bus or in the bus terminal with time permitting?
- Are all passengers required to exit the bus upon arrival?
- What is the frequency of buses and how long do they remain in your terminal?
- What cities do the buses stop at prior to stopping in your city, in either direction?
- What are the next cities the buses stop at in all directions?
- Where is luggage stored or where is checked-in luggage maintained until being placed on a bus or retrieved by a passenger?

Become familiar with the characteristics of buses in your area:

- How many passengers do the buses hold?
- Are all the buses equipped with telephones or communication devices?
- Are there any locations on the bus where a potential contraband can be concealed?
- Some buses use two drivers. Is there an area on the bus for the second driver to sleep?
- Does the bus have a bathroom?
- Are the luggage racks above the seats closed or open?

As you become familiar with your station, more questions may come up.

Some stations have offered office space to interdiction details so the bus company can have closer access to law enforcement.

## Review of Ticketing Information and System

Ask the ticket agents for help in identifying information on the bus tickets. You should become familiar with the ticketing system and be able to review a ticket and itinerary quickly so you do not have to hold onto it for too long (Figures 9.1 and 9.2). The information on the ticket will give you a lot of information about a passenger. Answers to many of the questions we will ask a passenger are available on his ticket.

- What is your name?
- Where are you coming from?
- Where are you going to?

## PASSENGER TICKET

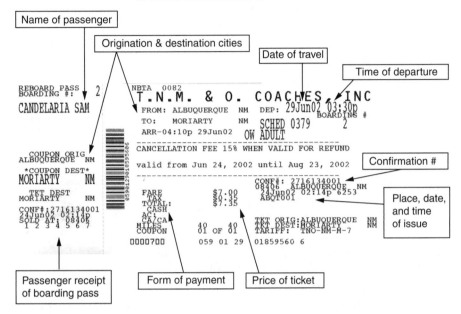

**Figure 9.1** (Used with permission of Greyhound Lines.)

## PASSENGER ITINERARY

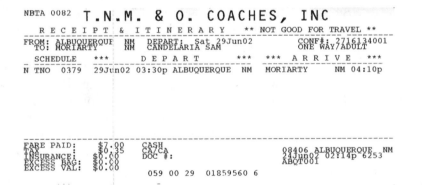

**Figure 9.2** (Used with permission of Greyhound Lines.)

- Where are you from?
- How long have you been planning this trip?
- When did you purchase your ticket?
- How did you purchase your ticket?
- What was the method of payment?
- How long are you staying?

- Is this trip for business or pleasure?
- How many passengers in your party?
- Is this a one-way or round trip?
- How are you going to get back?
- Do you have any luggage?
- Where is your luggage?

These are only a few examples of questions that you will want to ask a passenger, and many of the answers to these questions are provided on the ticket.

## Encounters Conducted on the Bus

The length of time that the buses are in your terminal will determine whether you conduct encounters on the bus, in the terminal, or both. If you have ample time and the bus is in your terminal for ten minutes or more, then you might have time to board the bus and conduct your encounters there. If the time is minimal and only new passengers are boarding and departing passengers are the only ones getting off of the bus, then you will not have time to conduct your encounters on the bus. We must remain sensitive to the goals of the bus company and why they are in business. They are in business to make a profit, and if we delay their buses and cause departure irregularities, then we will not be welcome at the bus terminal.

The Bostick case and other case law concerning consensual encounters on buses should dictate how we conduct encounters on the bus.

Before boarding a bus, you must have the cooperation of your entire unit, whatever the manpower allotment is. If it is just you and your partner, planning is still a major factor prior to entering a bus to conduct consensual encounters. Regardless of manpower, before any encounter you must have a plan worked out. Refer to Chapter 1 on consensual encounters. There will always be a talker and a scanner, and the roles are separate but can be interchanged.

1. Define who is going to do the talking and who is going to do the scanning.
2. What code words or signals have you worked out prior to entering the bus. You should have a signal or code word for discovery of contraband or currency and a code or signal for placing a person under arrest. Will the signal be the same for both activities?
3. Who is going to do the handcuffing, or should both partners be prepared to do so?

4. What happens in the event of multiple couriers associated with each other?
5. What happens if multiple couriers are discovered working separately?
6. Who is going to do the search, the talker or the scanner?
7. Who will take custody of the contraband or the currency?
8. Will the offender be placed in cuffs on board or will they be escorted off of the bus and then placed in cuffs? Cuffing an offender outside of the bus gives him a second chance to consider escaping. If the offender attempts to escape while he has cuffs on, it will be more difficult.
9. Will there be perimeter people involved — other officers or agents?
10. If perimeter people are available, they will contact any passengers that leave the bus while the initial two officers or agents are on board the bus.
11. If there is no perimeter assistance, then it must be determined what to do in the event a passenger gets up and leaves while the officers are on board the bus. The two officers or agents may stay on the bus, or both may leave and attempt to make contact with the passenger that departed the bus.
12. Who will board the bus first? Will the person designated to speak to all passengers be the first officer on the bus, with the scanner following?
13. What is the signal or code for discovery of abandoned luggage on the bus?

It is important to plan for as many different occurrences that you can think of. Practice your entrance onto an empty bus first, walking to the back of the bus and examining the rear bathroom.

When you enter a bus, the first person you will make contact with is the bus driver. The bus driver is the "captain of the ship" and is responsible for all passengers on the bus. He is an essential set of "eyes and ears" for you. He has been with these passengers for the duration of the trip and is aware of any suspicious activity. The bus driver can give you valuable information about the passengers on his bus.

Greeting the driver and establishing a liaison with him will be an asset to your detail and its continued success. What happens if you have a bus driver who cooperates with you only because management instructs him to? You should treat him with the same respect as you would with the more cooperative drivers. Always try to obtain as much information about the passengers as possible: is the bus driver having any problems with any of the passengers? Was there anything suspicious about any of the passengers? Whatever information you obtain from the driver will assist in your investigative efforts.

Once you are satisfied that you have obtained as much information as possible about the passengers, you will enter the bus. There are a number of commercial bus interdiction details around the country, and they may work differently or use specific techniques that they have found work well for them. What might work for an interdiction detail in Kansas City might not work for the interdiction detail in Houston. It will take you time to find the method that works best for you when you enter a bus and conduct interdiction investigations. Whatever method you use, keep it consistent. You may implement new ideas and methods, but attempt to remain consistent with your approach and contact.

Some commercial bus interdiction details will enter a bus with three investigators: two traveling to the back of the bus and then walking from rear to front, contacting passengers, with the third investigator remaining at the front of the bus in the driver's seat so he does not block the aisle or the exit. This was done in the Drayton and Brown case. Other interdiction details will enter the bus with only two investigators, and both investigators will proceed to the rear of the bus and then walk forward and contact passengers. The method you employ will depend on your jurisdiction and the case law in your area.

There are several philosophies on how investigators should identify themselves so there is no doubt about who they are when entering the bus; they are "law enforcement." If the courier or person involved in criminal activity might have suspected there was a law enforcement presence, there will be no doubt once the investigators have entered the bus and identified themselves.

Case law dictates that bus interdiction investigators will be dressed in plain clothes, not uniforms. No weapons, handcuffs, side handle batons, mace, or any other law enforcement tool will be exposed to the passengers. This is so that there can be no claims of coercion or intimidation on behalf of law enforcement. Some investigators wear "police jackets" when they board a bus, but their weapons and law enforcement equipment are concealed. If you do this, make sure you describe your jacket as a police jacket and not a raid jacket; you are not conducting any raid aboard that bus. Some interdiction details choose not to wear police jackets but will be identified by their badge of office that is plainly displayed when they board the bus, again leaving no doubt about who they are when they board the bus. You are not the bus security guard or the neighborhood watch coordinator, you are a law enforcement officer, plain and simple.

Regardless of whether three investigators or two investigators are used, at least two investigators entering the bus will proceed to the rear. The first investigator should walk to the rear slowly, greeting everyone on the bus briefly. During this walk to the rear of the bus, close attention should be paid to body language. Are there any immediate threats? Is someone acting suspicious, attempting to conceal an item or avoiding eye contact? Again, it is difficult for someone who is being spoken to, even if it is a simple "hi," not to respond, unless there is a language barrier, but even then, some type of response will be solicited. The first investigator walks slowly, paying attention to all passenger activity and behavior.

The first location that the first investigator should examine is the bathroom at the left rear of the bus. The investigator needs to make sure that no one is inside the rest room and to see if anyone has attempted to conceal drugs or money in this area.

The first officer should then contact the passengers who are seated on the last bench seat to the right of the bathroom. Attempt to have the passengers identify any luggage in the interior of the bus. If a passenger has no luggage in the interior of the bus, then a request will be made to identify any luggage underneath the bus that was checked in. The main goal of the investigators in making contact with all passengers in the bus is to ascertain and identify all pieces of luggage in the interior of the bus and to make any observations of potential passengers to be engaged in further conversation.

Some interdiction details will proceed to the rear of the bus with the two officers together. Other interdiction details will allow one officer to proceed to the rear of the bus while the second remains at the front of the bus covering the advancing first investigator. Once the first investigator reaches the rear of the bus and the bathroom has been examined, the second investigator can advance to the rear of the bus in the same manner: walking slowly, greeting all passengers, and making observations. Once the second investigator has reached the rear of the bus, whoever was designated as the talker will take the primary role and begin to make his way back to the front of the bus.

The second investigator will either remain at the rear of the bus until the first investigator reaches the front or until the first investigator summons him to assist in an encounter with a passenger. Another method is where the scanner or backup investigator will walk together with the first investigator conducting the contact with passengers. Whichever method is used, be consistent.

When the first investigator or the talker advances forward, he converses with all passengers. He should identify himself as a police officer and ask the passenger if he has any luggage on board the bus, and, if so, if the passenger can please identify his luggage: "Hi. I'm Detective Jones. Do you have any luggage on board the bus today? Could you please point it out for me? Thank you" (Figure 9.3). The officer will then verify the identity of the luggage: "There is a dark green bag in the overhead luggage rack above your seat. Is that your bag? Thank you." The talker should always speak in a conversational

**Figure 9.3** (Used with permission of Greyhound Lines.)

or officer friendly tone of voice, never appearing overbearing, authoritative, coercive, or intimidating. The talker must always be cordial to all passenger.

As the talker addresses a passenger, the talker should remain standing behind the seat of the passenger (Figures 9.4, 9.5, and 9.6) to ensure that the passenger, if he chose to do so, could get up from his seat, walk out into the aisle, and exit the bus without any intervention and without law enforcement blocking his egress from the seat, "therefore being free to leave or terminate the encounter" as stated in *Bostick*.

If the talker decides to engage a passenger in conversation, then he must be standing to the rear of the passenger's seat, not blocking the passenger's egress from the seat or exit from the bus. The talker must have fully identified himself as a law enforcement officer, leaving no doubt in the passenger's mind that the person engaging him in conversation is a law enforcement officer. All aspects of the consensual encounter must be adhered to when engaging a passenger in conversation.

It is up to the backup officer to advance toward the talker as the talker is engaged in conversation with the passenger. With the backup officer remaining to the rear of the talker, there is no blocking of egress or ingress of the passenger from their seat into the aisle and bus exit.

The ultimate goal of the conversation is to obtain permission from the passenger to conduct a search of his luggage. If permission to search is granted, whoever was designated to conduct the search should conduct the search of the luggage immediately without hesitation (Figure 9.7). Using the predetermined code words and signals, if contraband is discovered, arrest of the passenger should not be a major production. The backup officer must be alert and responsive to other passengers in the bus. Just because you and your

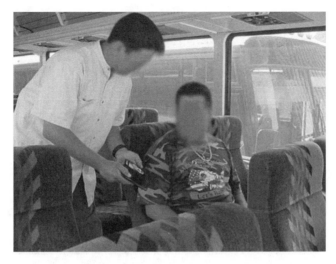

**Figure 9.4** (Used with permission of Greyhound Lines.)

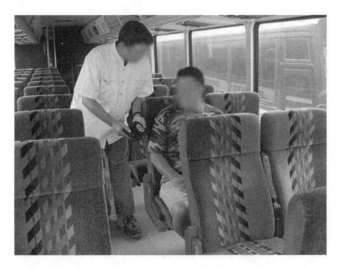

**Figure 9.5** (Used with permission of Greyhound Lines.)

partner are going to arrest a passenger does not mean that the potential for co-conspirators or additional couriers is not there. The backup officer must remain alert. The arrest should be low key, drawing as little attention to the person being arrested as possible. Once the person has been securely placed in handcuffs and is under arrest, attempt to escort him off the bus immediately, keeping in mind that there may be co-conspirators. Make sure that all personal items and belongings of the passenger have been gathered and removed from the bus. Once you have left the bus, the backup officer must remain alert to anyone exiting the bus to assist the offender in an attempt to escape, or cause

**Figure 9.6** (Used with permission of Greyhound Lines.)

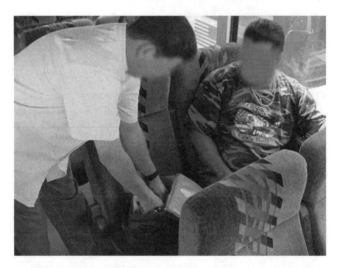

**Figure 9.7** (Used with permission of Greyhound Lines.)

some type of diversion. Be sure that all luggage has been removed, including any luggage from the checked-in luggage area underneath the bus.

In the event that the passenger refuses to give permission to search his luggage, the investigator must rely on reasonable suspicion to seize the luggage for a canine examination. Refer to Chapter 1 on consensual encounters and defining reasonable suspicion. If the investigator seizes the passenger's luggage, keep in mind where the canine handler wants the luggage placed to have it examined.

If the first investigator locates an abandoned piece of luggage, have a code or signal worked out to notify the backup officer that an abandoned piece of luggage has been discovered. If the backup officer is aware of the abandoned luggage, then he must pay close attention to the activity of the passengers in the immediate area of the luggage.

The first officer should inquire of all passengers in the immediate area of the abandoned luggage whether anyone owns the luggage or if anyone knows who owns it. If no response is received as to ownership, the first officer should remove the luggage from its original position (Figure 9.8) and take it to the front of the bus, where it will be presented to all passengers to view. An announcement will be made from the investigator, more likely the talker, inquiring as to ownership of the luggage. If the luggage is determined to be abandoned, then it will be taken outside of the bus and opened and searched. If contraband or currency is located, it is up to the investigator who searched it to associate the luggage to a passenger on the bus. If that cannot be done, then the contraband or currency is tagged into evidence and documented.

Try not to delay the bus for any reason; the driver must attempt to keep his schedule. If the bus must be delayed, assure the driver that all attempts will be made to get the bus on the road as quickly as possible.

If a witness comes forward about an abandoned piece of luggage, do not interview him in front of the potential target, ask either the target or the witness to step off of the bus with you. Do not interview the witness in front of the target (Figure 9.9).

When searching luggage or individuals, do not overlook the obvious concealment areas. Couriers and trafficking organizations may conceal items in obvious locations hoping that you are lazy and will not search the obvious.

Some areas of concealment include:

- Food items
  - Unopened food containers: chips, cookies, boxes of cereal, cans of soda or food
  - Factory-sealed food containers
  - Liquor bottles or beer cans
  - Unusual food items, such as gallon cans of nonperishable foods
- Boxes of electrical equipment and televisions
- Coolers and ice chests
- Gift-wrapped boxes
- Boxes of cigarettes
- Clothing: drugs sewn into lining or secreted into the fabric
- Rugs and furniture
- Toys and stuffed animals

Always suspect the obvious and pursue that area.

**Figure 9.8** (Used with permission of Greyhound Lines.)

**Figure 9.9** (Used with permission of Greyhound Lines.)

## Encounters Conducted inside the Commercial Bus Terminal

As in any commercial transportation setting, conducting surveillance inside of bus terminal areas is another area for identifying potential couriers and people involved in criminal activity. The areas of concern are the terminal area itself, rest rooms, restaurants, and outside the bus terminal, in front or in the parking lots.

Remain in tandem with your backup investigator or scanner, and always work in pairs. Remember, there are no security measures against persons who may be in possession of deadly weapons.

As you observe people in the terminal, you are looking for the courier or person involved in criminal activity; that same person is looking for you and conducting countersurveillance.

Many commercial bus systems also incorporate parcel transportation and delivery operations. Make sure to apply characteristics and indicators from parcel investigations, and investigate this area for potential use by drug couriers.

## Use of a Narcotic Detection Canine

Having the use of a narcotic detection canine is crucial to the success of the commercial bus interdiction detail. The narcotic detection canine is a tool and should be used as such. The canine can be your detail's "ace in the hole." Parading your narcotic detection canine in front of the bus terminal as targeted buses arrive can give the courier or trafficker time to come up with a story concerning the luggage, or give the courier time to abandon the luggage. If the courier or drug trafficker was not previously aware of any law enforcement presence, once the canine has been observed, it is evident that law enforcement is present.

The canine can be used immediately as buses arrive from source locations or it can travel to source locations. At a source location, the canine handler can have the canine examine checked-in luggage that was placed underneath the bus to identify any suspicious luggage destined for your area. Once the canine alerts to a piece of luggage, then you must stay committed to the alert and attempt to identify the owner of the bag.

The courier will often fill out the luggage identification tag with a fictitious name and address so that the luggage cannot be associated with him. Some interdiction details take the luggage that has been alerted to into the bus terminal, and then an announcement is made for the passenger whose name is on the luggage tag to come to the ticket counter. The courier knows the name is fictitious and will not come forward to claim the luggage. Therefore, we now have a bag containing narcotics and no offender. In bus interdiction, this is the nature of the beast.

Since the tragic events of September 11, 2001, the drug trafficking organizations, couriers, and persons involved in criminal activity have been forced to alternative modes of transportation such as trains and buses. These organizations must still operate in an attempt to keep the drugs and currency flowing through our country, state, city, and community.

## Case Law

### *U.S. v. Guapi*, 144 F.3d 1393 (1998) 11th Cir.

When talking with bus passengers inside a bus, officers should inform passengers they can refuse consent of carry-on luggage or that the passengers can simply leave the bus with their luggage.

### *U.S. v. Fulero*, 498 F.2d 748 (1974) D.C. Cir.

Actions of drug-sniffing dog found to be consistently reliable furnished probable cause for issuance of warrant for search of footlockers at bus depot. Action of officers in allowing drug-sniffing dog to sniff air around footlockers in bus depot was not unconstitutional.

### *U.S. v. Viera*, 644 F.2d 509 (1981) 5th Cir.

Use of dogs to sniff exteriors of suitcases outside a bus did not constitute a search, and the light press of hands along the outside of the case was not intrusive.

### *U.S. v. Glover*, 957 F.2d 1004 (1992) 2nd Cir.

Officers who had reasonable suspicion that defendant possessed narcotics, based upon defendant's conduct after exiting bus, did not exceed permissible scope of investigatory detention by detaining defendant with his bags in security office for approximately 30 minutes to verify his identification and to await arrival of narcotics dog. Defendant was told he was free to leave and instead chose to stay. Officer's warrantless seizure of contraband from defendant's bags following narcotics dog's positive sniff test during investigatory detention at bus terminal was proper, where defendant voluntarily consented to search.

### *U.S. v. Harvey*, 961 F. 2d 1361 (1992) 8th Cir.

Canine sniff of luggage on bus was not a search. Initial removal of bus passenger's luggage from overhead baggage area to facilitate canine sniff was not a seizure or search.

### *U.S. v. Graham*, 982 F.2d 273 (1992) 8th Cir.

Removal of suitcase from overhead luggage rack to aisle of bus to facilitate a dog sniff was not a seizure.

### U.S. v. McFarley, 991 F.2d 1188 (1993) 4th Cir.

Police must have reasonable suspicion to justify brief stop of person and detention of luggage for purpose of conducting a dog sniff, although the dog sniff itself is not a search. Detention of defendant's luggage for 38 minutes in order to subject it to a dog sniff did not elevate this investigatory stop into an arrest.

### U.S. v. O'Neal, 17F.3d 239 (1994) 8th Cir.

Without reasonable suspicion officers may not even temporarily seize a person or his luggage. Officers are required to have more than a hunch that a suspect is carrying drugs. Voluntary statement admitting to police officer that one's bag contains drugs is probable cause for a search.

The suspect was at a bus depot when officers seized his carry-on bag for a canine sniff test. An officer asked the suspect if there were drugs in the bag and the suspect said yes. After the dog alerted to the bag, the suspect was arrested and a search warrant was obtained for the bag.

### U.S. v. Guzman, 75 F.3d 1090 (1996) 6th Cir.

Defendant had no reasonable expectation of privacy to the airspace surrounding carry-on luggage, when it was on an open overhead luggage rack of a commercial bus.

### U.S. v. Garzon, 119 F.3d 1446 (1997) 10th Cir.

Defendant bus passenger did not "abandon" his backpacks when he left them on a bus during a layover.

Officer's orders for all passengers to disembark bus during layover with all their personal belongings and to proceed past drug-sniffing dog was unlawful.

Defendant cannot abandon his property by refusing to comply with unlawful order.

### U.S. v. Tugwell, 125 F.3d 600 (1997) 8th Cir.

Officers conducted a canine sniff of checked luggage on a Greyhound bus. The dog had a positive canine alert on one suitcase. The defendant abandoned his suitcase by abruptly departing the bus station after witnessing the dog alert to the suitcase. Officer could then open the suitcase without a warrant.

### U.S. v. Nicholson, 144F.3d 632 (1998) 10th Cir.

Canine sniff is not a search.

Officer conducted a search when without reasonable suspicion or probable cause, removed defendant's carry-on bag from overhead rack of bus and then manipulated bag by pressing its sides with his hands.

### U.S. v. Ward, 144 F.3d 1024 (1998) 7th Cir.

Defendant's bag was not seized when officer handled and removed bag from bus luggage compartment.

Defendant's bag was seized when after removing the bag from the luggage compartment, the officer then decided to hold the bag for a canine sniff, due to the lack of a narcotics dog at the bus station and the bus' imminent departure.

(Officers ended up with reasonable suspicion and abandonment, when no bus passenger claimed the bag.)

### U.S. v. Stephens, 206 F.3d 914 (2000) 9th Cir.

The defendant was seized, rendering his abandonment of a bag involuntarily, when officers boarded a bus and:

Informed passengers that they were free to leave.
Officers did not inform passengers they could remain, but decline to answer officer's questions.
An officer guarded the bus door.
Officers used the P.A. system on the bus.
Officers singled out the defendant by questioning him first.

### Bond v. U.S., 529 U.S. 334, 146i L. Ed. 2d 365 (2000) U.S. Supreme Court

"Physical manipulation" of carry-on luggage violated the defendant's reasonable expectation of privacy.

When a bus passenger places a bag in an overhead bin, he expects that other passengers or bus employees may move it for one reason or another. Thus, a bus passenger clearly expects that his bag may be handled. He does not expect that other passengers or bus employees will, as a matter of course, feel the bag in an exploratory manner. Therefore, physical manipulation of defendant's bag violated the Fourth Amendment.

### U.S. v. Wolohan, 23 Wash., App 813, 598 P2d 421 (1979)

Allowed an indiscriminate, exploratory sniff search of a bus packaging area.

### *U.S. v. Graham*, 982 F.2d 273 (1992) 8th Cir.

Canine reacts with an "air scent" when taken down aisle of bus during refueling stop. Officers properly remove luggage from overhead rack so canine can sniff each bag. Officers obtain search warrant after luggage owner refuses consent, finding 5 kg of cocaine. Officer questioning of suspect about ownership of luggage was proper before arrest.

## Key Terms

Abandoned luggage
Aisle way
Approaching the unknown
Articulable suspicion
Baggage handlers
Belly of bus
Bus maintenance personnel
Bus terminal
Canine alert
Captain of the ship
Carry-on luggage
Checked-in luggage
Co-conspirators
Countersurveillance
Custodians
Distribution point
Drivers
Manager

Mule
Multiple traffickers
Overhead luggage rack
Parcel handlers
Perimeter people
Reasonable person
Scanner
Shorting of ticket
Source
Source cities
Suspicionless
Talker
Ticket agent
Ticket folder
Ticket receipt
Undercover people
*U.S. v. Drayton and Brown*
*U.S. v. Bostick*

# Drug Parcel Systems **10**

Parcel systems — private, commercial, or the U.S. Postal Service — are extremely popular for the transportation of narcotics among drug traffickers. Drug traffickers and drug trafficking organizations have used this method of transportation for a number of years. The transportation of narcotics using various parcel systems has been exploited, and it continues to be a popular method of transportation, because it is relatively safe and inexpensive.

These parcel systems are occasionally monitored by law enforcement, but in most cases, not enough. This type of investigation is difficult to prove and takes extensive investigative effort. This chapter will outline and provide an introduction to parcel investigations as an investigative tool. Parcel task force groups will be explained in detail along with their role in the investigation of organizations using parcel systems. Parcel facilities will be described, as well as instructions for training parcel staff in the detection of individuals using commercial package locations to ship narcotics. Commercial staff will be trained in the behavior and characteristics of criminal activity displayed by traffickers while using the parcel system to facilitate the drug trade. Investigative techniques such as controlled deliveries and the use of tracking devices will be discussed in detail.

## What is Drug Parcel Interdiction?

Drug traffickers and drug trafficking organizations are constantly looking for ways to facilitate their drug trade. One that is relatively safe is the parcel/package system, which they use to ship narcotics from around the globe. Law enforcement agencies throughout the United States have established drug parcel groups to aggressively target and monitor local area shippers and receivers of narcotics through commercial packaging systems. In addition, they monitor outgoing parcels and regularly monitor private parcel systems.

The parcel interdiction group is a team responsible for investigating drug traffickers using commercial and private parcel systems to facilitate drug trafficking. In cooperation with the U.S. Postal Inspector's Office, federal, state, and local law enforcement has partnered with these groups to monitor the flow of narcotics via the U.S. Postal Service and other commercial carriers. Cooperation with management and security personnel (loss prevention) with private parcel shipping companies is essential in establishing and maintaining a successful drug parcel investigative group. A drug parcel investigative group is generally part of an overall interdiction group within a police agency. Branches of federal law enforcement such as the Federal Bureau of Investigation, the Drug Enforcement Administration, and the U.S. Customs Service cooperate with local law enforcement to investigate these types of cases. Historically, there has been a good working relationship between these entities.

## How Do We Get Started?

What can law enforcement do to combat individuals and organizations using the parcel systems to transport and ship narcotics? It is not always easy. Millions of parcels and packages are shipped throughout the world on a daily basis. Trying to segregate those parcels which contain narcotics is a difficult task, to say the least. There are a number of investigative efforts that can be used in this environment.

First and foremost, a properly trained drug canine team needs to be in place to conduct these types of operations. Without such a resource, parcel cases are virtually impossible to make. The drug canine is the ultimate instrument in the development of probable cause for the opening of a suspected drug parcel. The canine should be a single-purpose drug dog whose handler trains in the parcel/package environment.

There are three different types of business which law enforcement should seek out when establishing a parcel interdiction group. First is the commercial private system, such as the United Parcel Service (UPS), Federal Express, Airborne Express, DHL Worldwide Express, and other freight services such as Roadway and Yellow Freight Company. Then there are the independent parcel companies including franchises such as Pac n'Send, Mail Boxes Etc., Zip-N-Ship, and others. The U.S. Postal Service is the third type of parcel business that we will be exploring for suspicious activity.

With respect to the U.S. Postal Service, state and local law enforcement officials must deal with the U.S. Postal Inspector's Office, which has primary jurisdiction over all U.S. mail. The U.S. Postal Inspector's Office works closely with other federal agencies, including the U.S. Customs Service, which inspects parcels and other cargo entering the borders of the United

States. State and local law enforcement, as well as federal authorities, do not have jurisdiction in the investigation of narcotics shipped through the U.S. Postal Service.

The U.S. Postal Inspector has a number of offices located throughout the United States. The Postal Inspector's Service monitors parcels through its system and can provide historical information on previous parcels delivered to a particular location. It also has tracking capabilities of anticipated suspect drug parcels. The U.S. Postal Inspector's Office works closely with state and local law enforcement to conduct joint operations, including controlled deliveries. If a state or local law enforcement does not have a relationship with respect to a drug parcel unit, the Postal Inspector's Service is a good partner that can assist in drug parcel operations. When forming a drug parcel squad, the law enforcement agency should reach out to the Postal Inspector's Office for the purpose of partnering in investigations.

Commercial private systems are typically extremely cooperative with law enforcement in drug parcel investigations. Drug parcel groups should approach company management and the loss prevention officer to initiate a program.

Independent parcel companies, which are franchise companies, generally provide services for small business needs such as packing and shipping, and providing business addresses. These small postal service centers are extremely popular locations for drug traffickers to send and receive drug parcels. Many of these facilities have mailbox rentals available.

## Training Commercial and Independent Parcel Staff

### Commercial Private Parcel Systems

Commercial private parcel systems are familiar with law enforcement's role in investigating narcotics that are shipped through their facilities. These companies are very cooperative in providing law enforcement with the facility and staff to conduct investigations. Concerns of private parcel systems are disruption of business and losing employee service because of criminal court hearings.

Typically, law enforcement will approach the management and loss prevention officer to initiate a cooperative program. As previously noted, commercial private systems are very familiar with investigative interdiction efforts to intercept suspected parcels. If the agency is interested in establishing a proactive program, they will usually deal mostly with the loss prevention officer, who in many cases is a former law enforcement officer.

The investigator should meet with the facility manager and the loss prevention officer and present a letter of commitment (Figure 10.1a). The letter

**Use of Agency Letterhead**

The **Agency Name** is seeking your assistance in establishing a Narcotics Interdiction Program designed to have a direct impact on the commercial package delivery service community.

We are currently living in a very technical society where people are constantly utilizing various methods of distribution/delivery of packages for business and pleasure. The business and general community is the foundation of the commercial packaging business.

Unfortunately, as the general public has become more sophisticated, so has the criminal element within our society. These people have found an alternative method of transporting narcotics or other illicit items utilizing the commercial package delivery systems. By constantly using these methods, it is more difficult for law enforcement to detect and apprehend them. The majority of these individuals are professional criminals who derive most or all of their income through criminal activity. These activities include narcotics trafficking, credit card fraud, stolen property and transportation of weapons, etc. Many will commit any crime of opportunity.

These criminal types directly use the commercial packaging transportation services while conducting their illicit activities. It is the intention of the Narcotics Interdiction Program to make you aware of the problem we face and to enlist the cooperation of our package delivery service community in (**City or County Name**). It is the aim of the Narcotics Interdiction Program to detect and apprehend these subjects through the help of the package delivery community. These people are bad for business and detrimental to the general community.

There are indicators, which will assist you in the detection of potential criminal activity occurring in and around your business.

Notification should be made to law enforcement in the interest of security and with the welfare of your employees in mind. In providing information, you are not acting as a police agent, but a concerned citizen.

Customers who exhibit one or more of the activities listed may or may not be engaged in criminal activity. The **Agency Name** requests that the only action you take is to observe and report those things seen during the course of your normal duties. It is the responsibility of trained law enforcement officers to evaluate your information and take appropriate action.

The investigator presenting this letter can offer a more comprehensive explanation of the Narcotics Interdiction Program.

Your assistance in this matter is greatly appreciated and be assured that any information you provided will be handled in a confidential manner.

Sincerely,

**(Signature of Agency Head)**

## Figure 10.1a

of commitment establishes that the police agency is seeking the assistance of the commercial parcel service in the detection of parcels containing illicit substances. Additionally, a list of indicators (Figure 10.1b) should be attached to the letter of commitment to assist commercial package service employees in the detection of potential criminal activity. With this information, the staff is not acting as an agent of the police, but as a concerned citizen. The letter requests that notification be made to one of the law enforcement personnel

**Confidential**

The attached list of indictors has been prepared to assist commercial postal/package service employees in the detection of potential criminal activity that may occur in or around your business.

In providing information, you are not acting as an agent of **Agency Name**, but as a concerned citizen. Notification should be made to one of the law enforcement personnel listed below in the interest of security and with the welfare of yourselves and the guests in mind.

Your assistance in these endeavors will be greatly appreciated.

**To Report Suspected Criminal Activity** – call **Pager Number**, which is a digital pager. Your call will be returned immediately.

Narcotics Interdiction Unit

> **List Officer names including Office Phone Numbers, Pager Numbers and any other numbers used for contact.**

**Figure 10.1b**

listed on the attachment to report suspected criminal activity. A telephone number, generally a pager number, is provided with the contact list.

The focus of this type of group is access to the facility in order to conduct random examinations of incoming and outgoing parcels. Additionally, law enforcement would like access to parcel tracking information and any other information that a staff member (manager, driver, or loss prevention officer) may have concerning a suspicious package. The investigator should review all police operations with the parcel facility and management with respect to controlled deliveries and using the loss prevention officer. Deployment of a drug canine team should be discussed as well as the expectations of management and law enforcement. An arrangement may be outlined with regard to how the drug canine will be deployed within the facility, or if a suspected parcel is identified, how the drug canine team will operate. All of these areas should be discussed. The 24-hour contact telephone number for parcel management employees shall be provided to the location. Training of staff will be outlined with facility management.

Staff members to be trained should include management, counter clerks, drivers, and loss prevention personnel. Many of the facilities have counter operations where individuals can pick up and drop off parcels for delivery. These facilities typically have meetings either weekly or monthly. This is a good format in which the training can be facilitated.

## Freight Companies

Another source that drug traffickers use to ship narcotics is freight companies. Freight companies typically transport larger quantities of freight that the other commercial facilities may not transfer. Freight companies such as

Roadway and Yellow Freight Company as well as other independent freight companies may be approached to cooperate with law enforcement.

## Independent Franchise Parcel Companies

Independent franchise parcel companies such as Pac n' Send, Mail Boxes Etc., and others are excellent sources for law enforcement in cooperation with other facilities to assist in identifying drug traffickers. Independent parcel companies should be contacted in the same manner as commercial facilities and freight companies. The owner-operator or manager should be provided with information with respect to their cooperation. A letter of commitment can be provided and management and staff should be trained in the process and the indicators of behavior. Franchise meetings are common, and this would be a good time to provide training to the facility as well as other locations. Depending on the police agency's jurisdiction, there may be multiple independent parcel facilities in the area.

These locations typically handle over-the-counter drop-off and pick-up of parcels. Independent facilities provide mailbox rental, packing materials, and other services related to the mailing of packages. Mailbox services are available and are popular among drug traffickers and their organizations due to the anonymity that this affords. This type of service enables drug traffickers to avoid delivery of parcels containing narcotics to their residences.

Once the facilities have been contacted and agree to cooperate with law enforcement, training is scheduled, in which the program is explained in its entirety and staff is asked to be the "eyes and ears" for law enforcement. If the behavior of a subject and suspicious parcel are identified, the staff is asked to observe and report the information to law enforcement, and take no action. Witness testimony is at times unavoidable; however, steps can be taken to avoid it. The staff should be advised to avoid opening suspect parcels. Once a package is opened, it is virtually unavoidable to not use staff as witnesses for testimony. Law enforcement should not direct any staff person from these facilities to open a parcel for them. If they were to do this, they would become an agent of the police; this action should be avoided.

Staff should be provided with parcel indicator guidelines that outline the behavior of an individual who may be sending a parcel containing narcotics. Additionally, the guidelines will provide information about certain characteristics observed on a parcel that might contain contraband or large amounts of currency. It should be explained to parcel staff that no one indicator alone should be considered significant, but if there are several indications observed, these should be reported to law enforcement for further examination. Multiple indicators of the sender or parcel observed should be considered suspect and subject to an examination by the drug canine team.

## Indicators of Possible Criminal Activity

Let us examine some of the possible indicators of criminal activity with respect to parcel investigations. These indicators are not all-inclusive; however, they have been found to be typical of the behavior and conduct of individuals who are using parcel systems to facilitate drug transportation. This behavior is typically identified during a face-to-face encounter at a commercial and independent parcel service. Observation is typically made at the counter when an individual is shipping or receiving parcels. Some of these indicators of possible criminal activity are:

- Sender displays nervous tendencies
- Sender asks many questions as to the details of the delivery of parcel
- Sender information is fictitious
- Receiver address may not be correct; for example, a vacant lot or vacant residence
- Receiver name may be fictitious
- Handwritten or typed airbills
- Handwritten or typed labels; business-to-business labels.
- Sender requests next-day air delivery and will pay a higher rate without question
- New boxes
- Contents are not what is described
- Unusual contents described
- Sender arrives late or very close to closing time to mail parcel
- Sender calls facility to see what time it closes
- Sender is a first-time customer
- Sender has a continuous pattern of suspicious activity
- Mailbox rental receives parcels from source area and no other mail
- Parcel addressed from individual to individual or business to business
- Sender appears rushed and nervous, and provides contradictory information about the parcel
- Strong odor emanating from parcel, possible masking agents
  - Scented dryer sheets
  - Mustard
  - Axle grease
  - Foam insulation
  - Motor oil
- Parcel box flaps heavily glued
- Incorrect zip code
- Surveillance of location by receiver of a parcel
- Cash and corporate labels utilized
- Overall suspicious behavior of sender or receiver

This list of indicators has been compiled to provide the investigator with information about indicators of possible criminal activity. A person may enter a commercial or independent facility to send a suspicious parcel and display a number of these characteristics. The information should be provided to law enforcement by staff for further investigation. Staff must be able to pinpoint and articulate this behavior.

An individual who asks many questions about parcel delivery such as the exact time of delivery may be suspect. Fictitious sender information such as name, address, and telephone number is common because the sender does not want to be identified. Receiver address may not be correct, for example, a vacant lot or an unoccupied residence that may be for sale. The trafficker may be waiting at a vacant residence that is for sale or at a residence that is not theirs that they are just using for a delivery. There may have been surveillance to confirm this. A vacant lot or vacant residence is a common delivery destination, where the delivery driver may drive by and a person would flag him down, asking him if he had a package for that location.

With respect to the airbill or ground bill labels, trends change. Written labels should be examined carefully for fictitious information or other erroneous information. A typed label is suspicious because most commercial parcel systems have label machines for business customers to use. Federal Express has a "power ship label" that can be used by businesses that do a high volume of parcel sending. Investigators should look for parcels sent from independent shipping companies, because many drug traffickers use an address from an independent location but use a fictitious name to send a parcel. A trafficker may send a drug parcel business-to-business, person-to-person, person-to-business, or business-to-person to try to legitimize the package.

Typically, individuals using the parcel system use new boxes, which are common in packaging narcotics. There may be an indication of masking agents. Some common masking agents are scented dryer sheets, axle grease, motor oil, mustard, baby oil, fruit, and peanut butter.

When sending a parcel either through a commercial over-the-counter or independent counter, the drug trafficker may request next-day air delivery at a higher rate. This package typically is guaranteed delivery either at 9:00 a.m. or 10:00 a.m., next-day air. Traffickers may also use ground freight that may take 1 to 2 days. They use different delivery times to confuse law enforcement. Ground freight (1–2 day) has recently become popular. The trafficker may come in late to mail a parcel or call just before the facility closes, so the parcel will not be in the facility for a long period where it could possibly be monitored and examined by law enforcement.

A customer may have a continuous pattern of suspicious activity in sending parcels. He may be coming in weekly or have some other pattern.

A trafficker may be a first time customer and act suspicious. He may appear rushed, nervous, and provide contradictory information about the parcel. The clerk may ask if the customer would like to insure the package. Whether or not the package is insured by the trafficker may indicate that the package contains an item that one would normally not pay a higher rate to send, such as a video or documents, for example. The return address or ZIP code may be incorrect.

If the parcel is a box, the box flaps are often heavily glued. The drug trafficker may feel that this will keep the box from opening easily or breaking during delivery.

In some cases, surveillance by the receiver is conducted either at the facility or a drop location that the parcel is to be delivered to.

It is important that the agency share intelligence with other groups about how trafficking organizations are operating, specific method of operations, and other information that would be helpful.

## Random Examinations of Parcels

Once parcel staff has been trained to conduct operations on sorting facilities and independent operational locations, investigators may utilize a drug canine team to conduct random examinations at these facilities. In the case of independent operations, the canine team may routinely conduct random examinations of parcels. This process can be done quietly in areas away from the public. Typically, when a parcel is received at the facility, it is placed in a routing area with other parcels. The canine team can be deployed to examine parcels at the location. Outgoing and incoming parcels may be examined. In random examinations at sorting facilities such as UPS, Federal Express, and Airborne, investigators may conduct visual examinations of parcels, later segregating those parcels for examination by the canine team. It is not recommended that the drug dog be placed on a sorting belt for examination of parcels. The dog will lose interest if "loaded" parcels (parcels with drugs) are not placed for it to find, or the dog will tire after a time.

Suspicious parcels should be segregated for the canine team to examine. When the canine team advises the investigator that the dog has alerted for the odor of narcotics in a suspected parcel, an investigation commences. An outgoing parcel investigation should be conducted to verify sender information such as name, address, and telephone number. Probable cause necessary to obtain a search warrant for the parcel is developed in this way. It may be necessary for investigators to verify location by driving by the address. A sender address may not exist or may be part of a large apartment complex with no apartment number. The sender name must be verified, and typically is a common name or does not exist as it relates to a particular address and telephone number.

At this time, investigators should notify the law enforcement agency in the jurisdiction the parcel is being sent to, in order to discuss the receiver information in their jurisdiction. Outgoing parcels are typically from source cities or states or from an area from which currency may be sent to purchase drugs. The receiver law enforcement agency should conduct an investigation on the name and address. Typically, the name of the receiver is fictitious or is a variation of the true name of the receiver. The address is generally correct, because the sender wants the package to be delivered. However, the location may be a "drop" location or a residence where the receiver may be waiting for the parcel to be delivered. There may be information from the other law enforcement regarding the location to which the parcel is addressed. Intelligence information or other criminal investigations may reveal the location to be a known drug house.

With a package that is to be delivered from business to business or individual to business, the law enforcement agency should conduct a thorough investigation as to ownership and management of that location. There have been cases where, for example, a clerk at a convenience food store has used that location to receive narcotics via a parcel. The package was addressed to the convenience store, and the employee was awaiting delivery of the parcel.

If law enforcement agencies determine that the information on the sender side is fictitious, coupled with the canine alert on the parcel, probable cause would exist to obtain a search warrant. The local jurisdiction the parcel is located in would prepare a search warrant and have a magistrate or judge sign it for purposes of opening the suspected parcel. Before removing the parcel for the purpose of obtaining a search warrant, a parcel facility should be provided with a receipt for the item. The receipt should include the facility name, location, package type, and the date and time that the parcel was taken into custody, along with a police case number. There should be a description of the parcel or parcels. The receipt should be signed by the person releasing the property and by the investigator. A copy of this property receipt form should be provided to the facility for their records and also be kept as part of the case file.

Parcels from commercial parcel services can be tracked via the Internet or by telephone. With a tracking number, a package can be tracked to its destination and where it is currently located. The package may leave a location to go to a hub area, and be distributed from that location. Management or loss prevention personnel of the facility should be asked to make a computer entry in their system so that if the drug trafficker checks the parcel by tracking number, it is not reflected that the parcel was taken into police custody. This should be discussed, and the tracking may reflect that there was some sort of sorting problem and that the parcel is at a particular location. This is extremely important with overnight parcels, as time is critical in the delivery of the parcel, which makes it very difficult to conduct a controlled delivery in a timely fashion.

Once probable cause is developed and a search warrant is obtained and signed, the parcel may be opened for examination by the law enforcement agency. It should be opened carefully so as to not damage the parcel in its original state. Once the interior of the parcel has been examined for the verification of narcotics, the investigators may take a sample of the contents before delivery in case the parcel is destroyed during the controlled delivery. The parcel should be closed and placed in another parcel, initialed, and dated. It can then be sent through the parcel system to the investigators conducting the controlled delivery in the destination jurisdiction. A copy of the search warrant that was executed on the parcel should be made available to the receiving agency. This will assist in preparing an anticipatory search warrant in preparation for the controlled delivery of the parcel to a residence or business. All investigative documents should be forwarded to the agency as well.

A police agency that has a parcel investigative group in another jurisdiction may contact your agency to ask if you would like to receive a package that has been identified with narcotics. The same steps are taken in preparing for your agency to conduct a controlled delivery in your jurisdiction. Typically, the other law enforcement agency will conduct a thorough investigation and develop probable cause to obtain a search warrant to open the suspected parcel. They may take a sample of the narcotics and then send the parcel with all of the documentation to your agency. Once the incoming parcel is taken into custody at your end, investigators should conduct as thorough an investigation as possible of the individuals who will be taking delivery of the parcel.

## Controlled Deliveries

Once the agency has taken custody of an incoming parcel from another jurisdiction, all documentation should be reviewed including the search warrant and other pertinent information. The parcel group should conduct an investigation including drive-bys of receiver locations to see if there is anyone at the location who can be identified. Information that can be verified from vehicle tag information, residence information, and any other source of information should be explored. Once all of the information has been developed, a controlled delivery is an investigative option.

A controlled delivery is delivery of a parcel, package, or envelope containing narcotics under controlled circumstances that has been sent either via a commercial private parcel company or the U.S. Postal system. The actual physical delivery is typically made by a police officer in an undercover capacity, or by the U.S. Postal Inspector if the parcel is U.S. Mail. Under these controlled circumstances, the objective is to have a law enforcement officer make the delivery of the parcel to the suspect, who will either sign for or take custody of the parcel. The undercover agent will attempt to solicit any statements in which the suspect may admit knowledge of the parcel delivery. The key to any parcel investigation is for law enforcement to prove that the subject had *knowledge* of the parcel's contents. This is critical to the prosecution of the suspect in a parcel investigation. It is virtually impossible to litigate a criminal case without proving knowledge of contents.

The difficulty with controlled deliveries is timeliness. There is limited investigative time if the parcel is sent overnight or express mail. Many traffickers will instruct associates not to accept parcels if they are late. This is a difficult proposition for law enforcement. An officer may attempt to deliver a suspect package but the person will not accept it, because he knows that commercial parcel companies guarantee delivery by a certain time.

Once a decision has been made to conduct a controlled delivery of a parcel, most states allow an anticipatory search warrant to be drafted. An anticipatory search warrant is prepared in anticipation of a controlled delivery of a parcel to a premises. Probable cause, which led the law enforcement agency to the discovery of the parcel, should be included and articulated in the anticipatory search warrant. All fictitious information, type of drugs, examinations, and all other pertinent information should be included in the anticipatory search warrant.

In some jurisdictions, a judge or magistrate will sign the anticipatory search warrant before the controlled delivery of a parcel. In other jurisdictions, the parcel must be delivered and be in the premises before the anticipatory search warrant is signed. In that case, the investigator will be in the presence of a judge and as soon as he is advised that the parcel is in the location, the anticipatory search warrant is signed by the judge. In some jurisdictions, with an anticipatory search warrant, once the parcel that was delivered during the controlled delivery is located, the search must be terminated. In other jurisdictions, investigators may be allowed to include other items as part of the search warrant such as documents related to the parcel activity. This must be discussed with the U.S. Attorney's office, or state or district attorney's office in the particular jurisdiction.

In addition to preparing the anticipatory search warrant, investigators may consider placing an electronic alarm device within the suspect parcel. This court-ordered tracking device emits a tone once placed inside the parcel. When the recipient opens the parcel, the device emits a tone that alerts investigators that the parcel has been opened. The placement and monitoring of this type of electronic device requires issuance of a court order. Application for a court order-authorized mobile tracking device is a separate document from the anticipatory search warrant. The mobile tracking device order should indicate that law enforcement placed the device in a suspected package parcel to track the parcel to its ultimate destination and to alert that the parcel has been opened. No monitoring of conversation is permitted under these circumstances. Typically, the initial tone of the device is a slow beep tone and once the alarm has been triggered, it emits a fast, flowing tone. The criteria for use of an electronic device are the size of the parcel. It is very difficult to place, for example, a device in an overnight envelope. The box should be large enough to house this type of device. Law enforcement agencies can purchase these electronic alarm devices from a variety of vendors. The device is the size of a credit card or smaller, and less than $1/_8$ in thick.

In preparation for the controlled delivery, investigators should conduct pre-surveillance of the targeted location in an attempt to identify any individuals related to the case or any suspicious activity at the location. In a controlled delivery operation, law enforcement should take the same steps as for preparation of any search warrant execution. An operational briefing should be conducted; entry teams and search teams will be assigned with regard to execution of the search warrant.

When conducting a controlled delivery with a commercial private carrier, loss prevention personnel will assist in the delivery. The facility will provide the necessary equipment such as a delivery truck, delivery attire, and necessary documents to accomplish the delivery. In a controlled delivery using U.S. mail, the U.S. Postal Inspector's office will conduct the controlled delivery with the local, state, or other federal agency. The delivery will be conducted by someone wearing U.S. Postal Service attire.

During a controlled delivery, electronic surveillance should be used to secure evidence. Electronic devices such as a body bugs may be used by the investigator making the controlled delivery for the purposes of safety and to obtain any evidentiary conversation with the suspect or suspects. The use of video equipment to conduct electronic surveillance of the controlled delivery is suggested and can be used as evidence in the case. Surveillance teams should be in place for mobile surveillance in case the suspect takes custody of the parcel and departs the location once the delivery has been made. Mobile units as well as air support, if available, with either a fixed-wing plane or a helicopter, is suggested.

The decision to stop or detain the suspects is different in every case. The circumstances will dictate the approach. One of the difficulties in conducting controlled deliveries is the wait — how long it will take the individual to open the parcel after he takes delivery. This goes toward proving knowledge in a parcel case. The electronic alarm device makes this easier. When an alarm device is not feasible due to the size of the parcel, investigators may find themselves playing a guessing game as to how long to give the individual before making entry to a location. If no alarm device is available, investigators must give ample time for the parcel to be opened. Again, circumstances will dictate what occurs. If the suspect departs a location and may have the parcel or the substance contained on his person, a decision may be made to detain the individual.

Experienced traffickers may wait long periods of time, even a number of days, before opening a parcel. The agency must make a decision with respect to how long it will monitor the situation, which will depend on resources and other factors. In many parcel cases, the use of a "drop house" or business is used. A drop house is typically a location designated by the sender and receiver for a parcel to be delivered to. Lower level associates typically staff it. It may be a friend's or relative's home or business or an unknown residence where there is no relationship to the suspect, such as a vacant home that is for sale.

There are advantages to the use of a drop house by drug traffickers. Since it is not the suspect's main residence, the receiver can claim that he had no knowledge of the parcel. The parcel is generally not opened at that location but is picked up by associates and taken to another location where it is opened. The difficulty in all of this is attempting to keep track of the parcel. The parcel may be delivered at the drop house, at which time the appropriate individuals are contacted, and they arrive and take custody of the parcel. If the package is large enough to be seen being removed from the location, investigators may attempt to conduct a surveillance and track the parcel with the tracking alarm device if one is placed. Once the suspected parcel is taken into another location, whether a business or residence, investigators may wait until the alarm is triggered, and then make contact with individuals at the location, securing the residence, and obtaining a search warrant. The law allows for law enforcement to be able to secure a residence and obtain a search warrant based on the circumstances described.

Once an anticipatory search warrant has been executed in a case where a parcel goes into an original location or premises, a number of investigative efforts take place. During the search of a residence, investigators should look for telephone billing information. Any telephone records showing out-of-town telephone numbers may be seized as part of the search warrant. Follow-up efforts can be made by possibly identifying the source sender. This may assist investigators in other jurisdictions with probable cause for warrants or other investigative options. Any documents that may incriminate other individuals in the investigation, such as airline tickets or bills, hotel receipts, credit card receipts, express mail shipping receipts, bank statements, and Western Union Money transfers may assist in the investigation. The suspect's personal property should be examined, such as his wallet (for business cards), personal telephone books, (which may be evidence linking the suspect to the sending source), photographs, and other documents identifying suspects with other associates. If the suspect is wearing a digital pager, the investigators should make contact with their district attorney to see if it is permissible to examine and identify the numbers displayed and saved in the pager. There may be telephone numbers linking the receiver to the source of the narcotics. The packaging should be preserved as much as possible for obtaining latent fingerprints. In many cases, fingerprints on the packaging material have been linked to the sender.

The interview of the receiver suspect should be conducted as soon as possible. The individual may cooperate with law enforcement and enable investigators to use some innovative options to make a case with the sender. In cooperation with law enforcement, the cooperative suspect may contact his source while law enforcement conducts a controlled monitored recorded telephone conversation between the cooperative individual and the source. There may be an opportunity for a delivery of monies that are owed for the narcotics to be made by another jurisdiction, if the suspect cooperates. Attempt to identify the source during the interview of the receiver suspect. Obtain information about where the individual resides; names, telephone numbers, and other pertinent information.

Many agencies that have parcel task force groups have tried an investigative method known as a "reverse knock and talk." This is used where timeliness is a factor and the parcel could not be delivered due to a variety of circumstances, such as resource issues. The reverse knock and talk is when investigators contact the individuals at the address on the label of the parcel containing the drugs. Generally, the name will be fictitious. The agents ask if they can speak with the party and ask if he has knowledge of a parcel being delivered at his location. Many will deny any knowledge of the parcel. Others will admit to having knowledge of the contents and will provide details about the package and its delivery. The individual may cooperate and assist in follow-up operations. Nothing ventured, nothing gained is the motto here. Why not take a shot at trying to further the investigation, unless other information is developed and a long-term operation is warranted.

Follow-up efforts may include trash or garbage pulls from the suspect residence to determine what activity may be occurring. Trash pulls are permissible from a residence or business if the trash is put out to the curb for collection. Investigators should not take trash from the residence if it is near the home such as by the garage; it must be clearly left on the curb for collection, where there is no expectation by the owner that it will not be taken. Trash should be examined for remnants or trace amounts of drugs, evidence of parcel activity such as discarded packaging from parcels received, and other evidence of narcotic activity. Investigators have found trace amounts of drugs in discarded packages. All of this evidence can be used if there is a pattern to track parcels being delivered at the location as well as build probable cause for a search warrant for the premises. These are all options that the investigator may take into consideration.

## U.S. Postal Inspection Service Role

The U.S. Postal Inspection Service is the investigative arm of the U.S. Postal Service. Postal inspectors are federal law enforcement officers who enforce over 200 federal laws in investigations of crime to include controlled substances. Under U.S. Code 21, U.S. C841, 843, and 844, postal inspectors initiate investigations related to transportation and distribution of narcotics through the U.S. Mail or other postal facilities. The U.S. Postal Inspection Service cooperates with local, state, and other federal law enforcement agencies in controlled substance operations. These joint investigative efforts with local authorities are part of parcel interdiction groups around the country. The postal inspectors investigate individuals who utilize the U.S. Postal system to facilitate the transportation of narcotics. The postal inspector's office does perform the controlled deliveries of suspected parcels with the assistance of local, state, and other federal authorities. The U.S. Postal Inspector is typically the individual who makes a controlled delivery of U.S. mail. Federal search warrants are only used in searching U.S. mail. State search warrants are not valid in the searching of U.S. mail.

The U.S. Postal Inspection Service can also assist local law enforcement in identifying patterns of activity, through what is known as "mail watch." With a mail watch, investigators can identify patterns of incoming and outgoing mail by an individual. Correspondence with the suspect of incoming mail only is known as a "mail cover." Investigators can identify correspondence with the suspect from other individuals. The U.S. Postal Inspection Service can also conduct a historical search of mail being delivered to a particular location.

## U.S. Customs Service

Working hand in hand with the U.S. Postal Inspection Service is the U.S. Customs Service. The U.S. Customs Service has the authority to inspect all outgoing and incoming mail entering or leaving the borders of the United States. A Customs inspector or agent can examine the parcels without a warrant. In many cases, contraband is located during inspection of inbound mail in the United States from foreign countries. Once U.S. mail has been searched and contraband is located, the U.S. Customs Service contacts the U.S. Postal Inspection Service, who takes custody of the parcel. The next contact is typically with the local authorities to initiate further investigation and possibly conduct a controlled delivery.

## Freight Companies

Freight companies have become a popular transportation method for drug traffickers in conjunction with other parcel services. Freight cargo companies transport larger freight. Standard ground freight and temperature-controlled vehicles are some of the services available. Much of the coverage area is within the continental United States, Canada, and Mexico, although there can be shipments to other countries as well. Some of the concealment methods for narcotics in the utilization of freight companies are common items such as water heaters, washers, and dryers. Traffickers gut out the internal mechanisms and fill the items with substances such as cocaine and cannabis. Other items used to transport controlled substances are wooden or steel crates. The delivery process is not as rapid as the traditional commercial type services; however, trafficking organizations do use these systems.

There are a number of ways traffickers obtain the freight once it is delivered. The freight can be delivered to a particular location or to the loading dock of the freight company. The trafficker would then arrive at the freight company and pick up the package. This is known as a "dock pickup." The receiver can pick up the items directly from the freight company.

Parcel interdiction groups should contact freight companies and make them aware that their businesses can be used as transportation systems for narcotics. Investigators can enlist their cooperation in dealing with drug trafficking activities. Freight companies should be briefed and trained about the same indicators that commercial parcel systems are trained to recognize. The freight company staff should be alerted to items used in concealing narcotics such as those previously suggested — in common appliances and other packaging. The question to ask is why would an individual pay several hundred dollars to have a water heater, washer, or dryer delivered from a remote location when it could be purchased locally at a much lower price?

## Other Common Practices

Parcel delivery systems of all types attract other criminal activity as well as narcotics. These systems can be used in a variety of criminal activities, such as the dealing and transportation of stolen property. Investigators should be aware that they may receive information concerning other activities that are occurring.

Drug trafficking organizations sometimes use multiple services including the U.S. Postal Service, Federal Express, Airborne Express, and United Parcel Service, in order to elude law enforcement, so that their parcels may not be identified. In this fashion, they do what is known as "splitting loads." Narcotics are sent in several packages instead of one large package. The theory is that several parcels may go through the system and others may be intercepted.

Drug traffickers also send "test parcels", which they intentionally contaminate. Investigators may see a heavy parcel in which a drug canine alerts to the odor of narcotics and, when it is opened it may contain other items, such as books, and no narcotics. This is done to see if the parcel is going to be intercepted, and the trafficker may then decide to use another method of transportation.

Commercial bus systems also provide parcel service through their bus lines. Greyhound bus lines in all parts of the country have this service. An individual can walk into any Greyhound bus terminal and send a package.

Another delivery service called Package Express is utilized by drug traffickers in many parts of the United States. It is another popular transportation method.

Common among commercial and independent parcel facilities is the sale of new boxes for shipping. Investigators should make a practice of asking staff if they have any individuals buying new boxes on a regular basis. If there is a pattern of a person buying boxes, that individual may be buying them to send drugs. This is also common at storage unit facilities, where boxes are sold for moving purposes. A person may indicate he is moving or doing other things with the boxes. Most of us do not move but a few times in our lifetimes; these people claim they move frequently. If it appears suspicious, a closer examination may be warranted. Drug traffickers go to a variety of places to buy boxes. If interdiction programs exist in a jurisdiction, that information will be revealed.

Another indicator is parcels being sent from independent facilities in source cities or states, such as California, Florida, or Texas. A drug trafficker typically will walk into an independent store (pack-and-ship type) in a source area and mail a package to a receiver in another part of the country. The label will be the independent store's label, using their address, and the sender will use a fictitious name. This way the sender cannot be tracked because he is not using his address. An indicator that investigators look for is a person sending a parcel through an independent company.

Another common practice is sending a package to oneself. Individuals will travel to a source state or city, procure the drugs, and then send them through a parcel service to a location that is either their business or home, or a drop location such as a relative or friend's home. They can also use post office boxes, mailbox rentals at storage facilities, or independent facilities. In some cases, individuals travel to foreign countries and obtain narcotics, and send the items back using a parcel service.

### Case Study

In a case in Florida, an individual traveled to Amsterdam, Holland and purchased a quantity of hashish. In Amsterdam, many drugs can be purchased legally. This particular individual, before leaving for Amsterdam from the United States, told eight of his friends to anticipate receiving a letter from Amsterdam. They were instructed not to open the letters and to provide them to him when he returned to the United States. In Amsterdam, the person purchased the hashish, placed small amounts in eight envelopes, and sent them to his friends in the United States. The U.S. Customs Service noticed that the envelopes were identical. They opened several of them and discovered the hashish. The U.S. Postal Inspector's Office was contacted, which contacted local law enforcement, and controlled deliveries were made to the eight locations. The investigation revealed that the common denominator for all eight individuals was their association with the person who traveled to Amsterdam. A criminal case was made when the subject returned from Amsterdam.

Hotels are a popular receiving point for parcel deliveries that contain narcotics. As outlined in Chapter 5, investigators should be mindful of parcels delivered to hotels and motels.

### Case Study

A case in west central Florida revealed an individual using a hotel to accept delivery of a parcel from a Central American country. In this case, U.S. Customs Service Inspectors seized a package inbound from the Central American country. Examination of the interior of the box revealed a number of clothing items, including shirts and pants. The customs inspector found that cocaine had been secreted in the interior seam of the waistline area of the pants and the seam was resewn. In addition, several woman's hair barrettes had been taken apart and cocaine was secreted in the hair barrettes, which were then placed back into their original state. The parcel was destined for a small hotel, addressed to a subject who was staying at the hotel for a number of weeks. The person left the motel and left instructions with the owner/manager to contact him if a parcel arrived for him. The name, as it turned out, was a fictitious name. The person did leave a telephone number. The U.S. Postal Inspector's Office took custody of the parcel and contacted the local police agency to attempt a controlled delivery. The postal inspector, in an undercover capacity posing as a postman, made contact with the manager of the hotel, who indicated that he was given instructions to contact the person when the package arrived. The postal inspector directed the hotel manager to have the receiver contact the local post office, at which time the package would be held at that location.

The suspect made contact with the local post office, at which time he was asked to pick up the parcel from that location. The suspect and his girlfriend arrived at the location, picked up the box, and traveled to a nearby residence. Entry was made to the residence, which was secured, for a search warrant. It was discovered that the suspect had opened the package and had used a razor blade to open the seams on the interior waistline area of the pants as well as the hair barrettes. Much of the cocaine had been extracted from those areas and was observed on the coffee table when investigators made entry. The person was convicted in circuit court for trafficking cocaine. There were approximately 10 ounces of cocaine secreted in these items.

Many other types of containers are used to transport narcotics through various parcel systems, including Igloo coolers with foam insulation or crates, wooden or steel type, to house and secrete narcotics, from marijuana to cocaine.

Internet activity is popular for procuring narcotics such as steroids from many European countries and Mexico. Many individuals not only use the Internet for steroid procurement, but also travel to Mexico and buy steroids at local pharmacies and send the items to themselves via a parcel system instead of carrying them over the border. Many agencies have made controlled deliveries of steroids from a variety of sources, in which the person used the Internet to purchase the items. Steroids and other controlled substances are available via the Internet.

Parcels can be tracked via the Internet. Tracking by airbill number is available with the majority of the larger commercial parcel services. Individuals can log on to the web site of the parcel service and access their tracking page. Multiple tracking numbers can be loaded, so that a trafficker is able to trace his parcel's progress through the packaging system.

# Conclusion

The use of parcel systems to facilitate the transportation of drugs is extremely popular worldwide. This global phenomenon has exploded in the past several years, and there is no end in sight. Parcel task force groups in police jurisdictions nationwide are busy trying to keep up with this transportation method. Trafficking organizations, gang members, and individuals alike use the parcel/package systems as part of their drug trafficking activities. Other methods are also used to complement the parcel movement. Drug trafficking organizations use not only parcel systems but other methods such as commercial bus, train, and commercial air to move their product.

# Case Law

### *Wisconsin v. Gordon*, 964 N.W. 2d 91 (1990) Wis. App.

Detention of package from private dormitory for 52 hours was permissible on reasonable suspicion it contained narcotics; police acted with due diligence to transport package to closest location where drug-sniffing dog available.

### *New York v. Offen*, 558, N.Y.S. 2d 415 (1990) N.Y.D.

Few hours' delay in delivering UPS package, to submit to dog sniff and x-ray, upheld on reasonable suspicion.

### *State v. Daly*, 47 CRL 1099 (1990) Kan. Ct. App.

Suspicion apparently based on package being sealed with duct tape; no delay delivering.

### *State v. Snitkin*, 681 P.2d 980 (1984) Hawaii

Random sniffing.

### *U.S. v. Fulero*, 498 F.2d 748 (1974) D.C. Cir.

Footlocker shipped via Greyhound; prior suspicion.

### *U.S. v. Dillon*, 810 F. Supp. 57 (1992) WDNY

Search warrant for UPS parcels and residence of addressee was valid based on canine sniff, which was not a search.

### U.S. v. Pono, 746 F. Supp. 220 (1990) D. Me

Detaining express mail package for sniff did not delay normal delivery time for the package, so no interference with possessory interest.

### U.S. v. Van Leewen, 397 U.S. 249, (1970) 90 S. Ct. 1029

Detention of packages for 30 hours based on reasonable suspicion the packages contained stolen coins was proper.

### U.S. v. Aldaz, 921 F.2d 227 (1990) 9th Cir.

Reasonable suspicion justifies detention and rerouting postal mail from normal route to a special location for dog sniff is proper.

### U.S. v. England, 971 F.2d 419 (1992) 9th Cir.

Post office diversion of suspect mail for dog sniff was not a seizure (Jacobsen) because no delay in normal delivery schedule occurred.

## Key Terms

Airbill tracking
Alarm device
Anticipatory search warrants
Commercial parcel companies
Controlled deliveries
Court-ordered tracking device
Dock pickup
Drop houses
Electronic surveillance
"Eyes and ears"
Freight companies
Independent parcel service
Indicators
Internet access
Latent fingerprints
Letter of commitment

Mail cover
Mail watch
Over-the-counter operations
Parcel systems
Probable cause
Pulls
Random examinations
Reverse knock and talk
Shotgun effect
Splitting loads
Test parcels
Trash
U.S. Customs Service
U.S. Postal Inspector's Office
U.S. Postal Service

# Rental Vehicle Investigations

# 11

The vehicle, whether an automobile, truck, or recreation vehicle, is the most important means of personal transportation for millions of Americans. Individuals depend on their vehicles to travel from one place to another, travel to work, visit friends, run errands, and to go on vacations.

The rental vehicle industry has been in existence since the early 1900s. In the years of the Model T, vehicle rental businesses were starting to generate revenues. In the earliest years, rental car companies became associated with criminal activity. During the prohibition era, bootleggers, bank robbers, and prostitutes often used rental cars to facilitate criminal activity. When the 18th Amendment was repealed in 1933, the industry was able to regain a respectable reputation in the business community.

After World War II, the car rental industry grew rapidly. This growth was closely linked with the boom in the airline industry and was attributed to the Hertz Rental Company, which developed the "fly drive" car rental concept. Hertz opened franchises at airports in Milwaukee, Wisconsin, and Atlanta, Georgia. The industry has been extremely competitive since the 1960s and enjoys the patronage of business travelers and vacationers. National franchises as well as local rental companies exist in many communities.

Rental vehicles are used extensively by drug trafficking organizations and drug couriers to transport narcotics. What is the attraction to the criminal element of renting vehicles? This allows them to keep their anonymity by using rental vehicles rather than their personal vehicles. They can avoid civil forfeiture where a personal vehicle can be seized when used in a commission of a felony such as drug trafficking. Detection by law enforcement can be avoided due to inconsistent monitoring of rental vehicle agencies by law enforcement. Unfortunately, there is little investigation of drug traffickers using rental vehicles for the transportation of drugs. This can be changed by law enforcement agencies interested in instituting a proactive program specifically targeting drug traffickers who use rental vehicles to facilitate their drug trade. There are a wealth of investigative opportunities. These are uncharted waters for many police agencies.

## Purpose of a Rental Vehicle Program

Initiating a rental vehicle program provides law enforcement with the opportunity to monitor rental vehicle facilities for use of their vehicles by drug traffickers, drug organizations, drug couriers, or local dealers to transport or facilitate drug deals. This type of program will enhance the law enforcement agency's capability of monitoring such activity by networking with rental vehicle management and staff. The behavior and conduct of the person renting a car for these purposes will be a factor in identifying these individuals. A rental vehicle program will complement other interdiction programs that the agency has in place, either in a narcotics group or other parts of the department.

We are all familiar with the larger rental vehicle agencies throughout the United States and the world. Rental agencies such as Avis, Hertz, National, Alamo, Budget, Dollar, Enterprise, and Thrifty are the larger, more competitive rental vehicle companies. There are also many smaller local companies in all parts of the United States, as well as car dealerships, which frequently rent vehicles.

Not only does this program concentrate efforts on the traditional rental vehicle agencies, but also truck and recreational vehicle (RV) rentals. Rental truck agencies such as U-Haul, Ryder, and others should be examined for illicit activity by drug traffickers. The RV business and truck rental facilities are other avenues for law enforcement to monitor with respect to transportation of narcotics.

Individuals can rent a vehicle in person or via the Internet, which has become a popular method for renting a vehicle. Rental vehicle locations are typically found at airports and standard rental agency locations in towns and cities. Some hotels house vehicle rental agencies. Investigators who have existing interdiction groups or who want to commence this program should determine which locations to approach for the program.

## Contacting Management

As with all domestic interdiction programs, the premise is essentially the same — to elicit legitimate businesses to cooperate in partnership with law enforcement. Once the vehicle rental facilities have been identified to implement the program, an appointment can be scheduled with management to explain and initiate the program. Investigators may contact management by telephone or in person, explaining that they would like their participation in a new program in cooperation with rental vehicle facilities. When an appointment has been scheduled, investigators travel to the vehicle rental facility and make contact with management. It is suggested that the program not be explained in detail over the telephone; a face-to-face meeting with management staff is much more effective.

At the first meeting, the purpose of the program should be explained to the management in detail, providing them with an opportunity to ask questions about the program and your intent. It should be made clear how investigators will initiate inquiries on suspect renters, and that they will seek access to computer and rental agreements to make investigative decisions. Along with access to information, investigators will want to be able to examine returned vehicles for possible manipulation. Examination of vehicles by a canine team to identify possible residue on returns in areas in which drugs were secreted in a vehicle will be part of the program. It should be made clear that the program is strictly voluntary and that law enforcement is seeking their cooperation in providing information when suspicious behavior is observed, such as frequent renters who have established patterns of conduct.

A letter of commitment is presented to management at that time. The letter of commitment, similar to the ones in Chapters 5 and 7, should outline the purpose of the program. In combination with the letter of commitment, a list of contact names and telephone numbers for investigators should be included. A list containing indicators of possible criminal activity should given as well. The investigator presenting the letter can offer further explanation of the program. After the program has been explained to management, a training date for staff should be scheduled.

As with the other interdiction programs, investigators should anticipate questions concerning liability, mostly concerning access to renter information from rental agreements and other sources. Management should be assured that much like hotel registration cards, there appears to be no expectation of privacy to information provided to a third party, in this case the rental agency. The manager should be told that inquiries and possible subsequent investigations of renters are rooted in case law, with respect to what can be conducted on premises and information retrieved as result of law enforcement inquires with this program.

Like many of these businesses, they typically have weekly or biweekly staff meetings. This would be an excellent opportunity to conduct training for staff. If they are not available at that time, investigators could conduct individual training to provide information regarding characteristics and behavior of an individual who may be renting a vehicle to conduct illicit activity. Once the meeting has been scheduled, investigators may ask to do a "walk through" of the facility to view the site in order to examine the entrance and exit locations as well as the environment for possible surveillance operations. An interior walk through should be conducted as well, including the counter areas and return areas where return crews would be operating.

Concentration of training for rental facility staff should be: management, counter clerks, and return crews or clean-up crews. Typically, this staff will have contact with the individual renter and access to the rental vehicles. At the training session, investigators should provide staff with the letter of commitment and telephone numbers to contact investigators once information has been developed. In addition, the indicators of possible criminal behavior should be provided and explained in detail. A telephone sticker with contact information may be provided to place on telephones behind the counter areas of the vehicle rental location as well as the locations of the return crew. The staff should be told that investigators are requesting their assistance in identifying individuals who may be renting vehicles for the purpose of transporting narcotics. An explanation should be provided to the staff that law enforcement is requesting that they only observe and report the information they see and not to take any action other than to be the "eyes and ears" for the police. Witness testimony can be avoided when possible if the staff acts only as a reporter and concerned citizen.

As with many of the programs in domestic interdiction, staff will ask if they have to testify in court regarding what they observed. Typically, if the information is collaborated with respect to the activity that the renter may be displaying, witness testimony can be avoided. However, there may be times, depending on the discovery process in certain states, that an individual may be called to testify on behalf of the government or state. Reward funds for information from employees of rental agencies may be available if the individual police agency policy permits it. Monetary funds may be paid for information. Once a case has been developed, the individual agency may elect to pay monies for information provided. The amount of funds would vary depending on the complexity of the operation and the participation of the individual of the vehicle rental staff.

During the training process, staff should be solicited for information they can provide about observations made that would lead them to believe that renters recently or in the past have aroused their suspicion in any way. Many staff members will share their impressions about certain behavior of a renter. Some may provide information about a current renter who has a pattern of conduct that is suspicious. Suspicious behavior should be followed up for potential investigation by investigators. Permitting rental staff to express themselves and ask questions will start the networking process for future working relationships. The more they see the investigators, the more comfortable they will be in relating information. It's all about putting a human touch to professional relationships and partnerships with business staff. It really works!

Many people will be concerned about their personal safety if they participate in the program. Inevitably the question is asked, "Will these guys come back and hurt me if I give you information about them?" The honest answer is always, that can happen; however, it is unlikely. It is rare that a suspect would go to a rental facility and cause harm to an employee.

## Indicators of Possible Criminal Activity

An indicator is described as the behavior or conduct of an individual which law enforcement can identify as possible criminal activity based on law enforcement training and experience. An individual who is not trained and has not developed the experience may not recognize this behavior. In training vehicle rental staff, law enforcement enjoys having a competitive edge in identifying individuals who may be using rental vehicles to conduct narcotics trafficking.

Typically investigators find that once they train staff in this area, there almost always seems to be a story concerning an individual or individuals who rent vehicles that displayed the behavior described. They may have always felt suspicious about an individual, but were not certain that this person was involved in criminal activity. Additionally, they had no outlet to provide the information to law enforcement, which they now have. The liaison with law enforcement enables them to provide information about suspicious conduct.

Some of the indicators that an individual renting a vehicle for the purpose of narcotics trafficking may be display are as follows:

- Pattern of rental
  - Weekly
  - Monthly
  - Same individual
- Very High or very low mileage upon return of vehicle
- No reservation, walk-up
- Renting multiple vehicles
- Renting of vehicle by one person and returned by another

- Evasive as to travel
- Request cash payment for rental
  - High deposit
  - No questions asked
- Asks for certain vehicle color, style, or model
- Individual utilizing multiple rental agencies to rent cars
- Removes keys from agency holder and places with own keys
- Vehicle manipulation noted upon return
  - Trunk area
  - Door panels
  - Gas tank
  - Vehicle tag area
  - Other areas
- Odor of narcotics emitting from vehicle
  - Trunk area
- Narcotic residue present in vehicle
  - Trunk or other area
- Strong odor of cleaning agents emitting from vehicle upon return
- Consistent pattern of missing rental cars from lot for short periods of time (possible employee participation)
- Individuals renting vehicles from source cities or states
- Overall suspicious behavior of renter

Breaking down each of the indicators will show how an individual may display certain suspicious behavior. He or she may be compelled to act a certain way based on the criminal activity in which they are engaged.

Typically an individual who utilizes a rental vehicle to conduct illegal drug activity will have some type of rental pattern, whether it is weekly, monthly, or some other rental pattern. The renter typically has this pattern of activity based on the type of narcotic activity that he is engaged in. Drug traffickers who, for example, may be traveling to a source area (city or state) weekly, biweekly, or monthly to procure narcotics and then return, have a consistent pattern. Instead of using their personal vehicle, they use a rental vehicle. The rental vehicle staff may see the same individual renting a vehicle with this particular pattern. They may see the same individual bringing other people to rent a vehicle for him while he stands nearby. This is common when the individual wants to keep his anonymity. The person may wait outside of the rental location or come in with the other individual to rent the vehicle.

Staff may see high or very low mileage upon the return of the rental vehicle. High mileage coupled with a short rental period may be indicative of continuous travel to a location to obtain drugs and doing a quick turnaround. This is popular where there is a source city near or several hundred miles away from the location in your jurisdiction. There may a vehicle rented for 1 day that is returned with, for example, 600 miles on the odometer. The renter may have traveled to a source location and returned quickly the same day, dropping off the vehicle. On the other hand, staff may see that there was very little mileage upon the return of the vehicle. This can be attributed to a possible local transaction. The vehicle may have been rented for the purpose of conducting a transaction in the area, but the trafficker does not want to be identified in his or her own vehicle. The vehicle may be returned with limited mileage such as 30 to 50 miles. The vehicle was possibly used solely for the purpose of making an exchange and then returned within the day or within several hours of rental.

There may be instances of vehicle "dumping" by the renter. This is when the renter leaves the vehicle somewhere after its use and does not return it. This may be an individual or group who is not concerned about the car being returned. One reason for this may be that the renter is from out of the area and has come in to do a transaction, and did not want to bother with the return because he may not be coming back to the area.

A vehicle may have been taken from the rental lot by an employee who is assisting drug traffickers, or by the traffickers themselves by an employee leaving the keys in the vehicle for that specific purpose. That employee is compensated for doing this.

A renter may request a certain vehicle color, style, or model. The reason for this may be superstition, or sometimes traffickers believe that certain vehicle colors appear more suspicious than others to law enforcement. Many traffickers will not rent a vehicle that is a bright color, such as red. They may request vehicle colors such as white or beige; a car that does not attract attention and blends in.

Traffickers may ask for a particular style or model of vehicle. Some styles or models of vehicle have what are known as "natural cavities" within the vehicle. These cavities are areas in the vehicle that have not been manipulated in any fashion but are part of the vehicle makeup during the manufacturing process. These parts of the car are frequently utilized to secrete drugs. Additionally, there are some vehicles that can be manipulated in various ways to accommodate the secretion of drugs. Some foreign and domestic vehicles have natural cavities in the trunk area, under the hood, and in the interior compartment of the vehicle, such as under the dash.

### Case Study

A case in central Florida revealed a marijuana drug trafficking organization that was renting a specific make and style of vehicle. They would rent Ford products, specifically Ford Explorer SUV and other Ford models. The organization would rent vehicles and remove the gas tank. They created a hidden compartment within the gas tank to secrete and transport marijuana. The fuel line was also altered in a bypassing fashion to work with the altered gas tank. In this case, there was a specific pattern of rental by the same individuals. The process of removing the gas tank and welding and loading the marijuana into the tank was a long and tedious operation. The group was traveling to Texas, loading the gas tank with the marijuana, and returning to Florida, where the substance was distributed. They did this to several vehicles, later returning them to the facility (Figure 11.1). The gas tanks were discovered when the vehicles were cleaned and rented to innocent renters, who indicated that there was a problem with the fuel gauge and that they had to fill their vehicle with fuel much more often. An examination of the undercarriage of the vehicle revealed the altered gas tank and fuel line. The gas tanks on the vehicles were removed and examined further where it was discovered that they had inserted the compartments (Figure 11.2). Not only did they ask for a particular model, the drug traffickers also requested a certain color, typically white.

This organization was transporting large quantities of marijuana from south Texas to Florida. It was discovered that each of the gas tanks could hold 50 to 80 pounds of marijuana. It was subsequently learned that the organization also requested Ford products the majority of the time. It appeared that it was easier for the organization to manipulate and alter the fuel line and remove the gas tank on rental vehicles than their own vehicles (Figure 11.3). With a rental vehicle interdiction group in place, this type of activity can be identified and investigated. Law enforcement was able to liaison with the rental facility to further the investigation regarding the drug trafficking organization.

Renters who are involved in criminal activity may be evasive as to where they will be traveling or how long they are going to rent the vehicle. They may ask questions about extended rental of the vehicle. They may not have a reservation and walk-up to rent a vehicle. They may rent the vehicle via the Internet. Some of the smaller local vehicle rental locations accept cash rather than a credit card. It is difficult to rent a vehicle without a credit card with most of the larger agencies; however, they may take a high deposit with no questions asked if the amount is high enough. Individuals may walk in and ask the clerk if they would take cash instead of a credit card. They will offer a significant cash deposit for consideration of a rental by cash. Drug trafficking is a cash business, and many traffickers do not have credit cards in their name. This is why having another individual rent a car for the trafficker is a popular approach. They will use someone who has a credit card and pay him or her cash for renting the car.

**Figure 11.1**

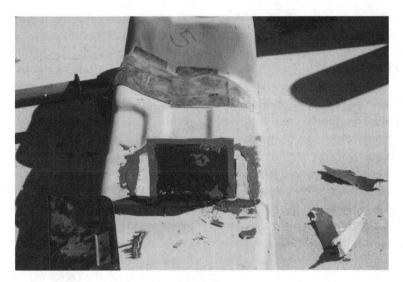

**Figure 11.2**

Drug trafficking organizations and individuals may rent multiple vehicles from the same rental company. They may do what is known as "rental hopping" and go to several agencies to rent single cars or multiple vehicles at different times. They may use Avis one time and go to Hertz another. If a rental program is in place, investigators should be able to capture this information and identify a pattern of activity. In these situations, there may be a "load" car, in which the drugs are secreted, and "lookout"

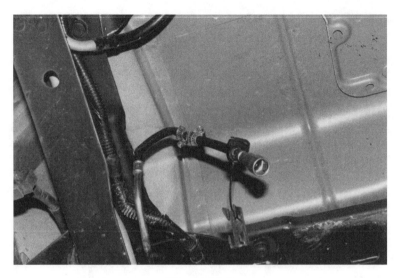

**Figure 11.3**

vehicles. In this situation, the group will travel with one vehicle in front of the load car and one behind it. The lookout vehicles may be decoys or may serve as counter surveillance for the loaded vehicle. They may use walkie-talkies or cellular telephones to communicate with each other if they see suspicious activity. When renting multiple vehicles, the renters may ask for a specific vehicle, style, model, and color. A vehicle may be rented by one person and returned by another. The individual who returns the vehicle may not be listed as another driver. The renter may remove the rental key vehicles from the agency holder and place them with his own keys. This is in preparation for being stopped by the police. They do not want to show that they are holding rental car vehicle keys. There may be an overall nervousness about the renter. The behavior of the person must be articulated to describe the conduct. The investigator must debrief the staff member to have him articulate what nervous tendencies the renter may be displaying.

When a vehicle is returned, cleaning crews and return crews may notice visual signs of vehicle manipulation. The trunk and trunk panel areas may be loose where there is an indication that they were taken apart from their normal setting and position. In addition, the door panels and other natural compartments of the vehicle may have been manipulated. The vehicle tag area may have been manipulated and the screws on the tag may have been removed and returned. The car tag may be loose, which may indicate that another tag was used and the vehicle rental tag was hastily placed back on the vehicle. Other tags may have been used during transportation of drugs or during drug deals or negotiations. Other areas such as the interior of the vehicle behind the steering wheel area or behind the forward compartment of the vehicle may have been manipulated as well. The engine compartment, with other cavities where narcotics can be stored, may have also been used.

The cleaning crew may indicate that there is an odor of narcotics emanating from the vehicle in the areas that were discussed. Large quantities of drugs, specifically marijuana, leave a pungent odor that may last for a period of time and may embed itself into the fabric layer of the trunk area. Narcotic residue may also be present in the vehicle. Cleaning crews may see seeds, stalks, or small marijuana leaves that have been left behind when the vehicle was loaded and unloaded with the substance. Crews may find a white powdery substance in the vehicle, which may be identified as cocaine or other similar substance. There may be a strong smell of cleaning agents, such as Pine-Sol or Lysol, emanating from the vehicle upon its return. There may have been an effort by the drug traffickers to clean the vehicle thoroughly before returning it to remove any evidence of the drug they had in the vehicle.

In some of the larger vehicle rental facilities, there may be a pattern of missing rental vehicles from the lot for short periods. This may be indicative of employee participation, where employees who work for the rental agency may also be operating with the drug trafficking organization. Many employees have access to the vehicles and keys. They will either provide the keys to a confidante to remove the car from the lot and return it in several hours or days. Since some rental agencies have large quantities of vehicles in the lots, such as an airport area, it is difficult to track vehicles. This would require an internal investigation using the vehicle agency's loss prevention specialist in cooperation with law enforcement to investigate and possibly conduct surveillance to identify the employee if this is occurring.

## Investigative Techniques

As with many domestic interdiction programs, law enforcement relies on staff of the business they are working with to provide information about suspicious activity occurring there. Staff and management are trained to be the "eyes and ears" for law enforcement and report the information. There are typically two types of investigations done in this setting. They are *cold* versus tip investigations. As explained in other chapters, cold investigations are proactive, self-initiated investigations in which law enforcement maintains constant contact with the staff and asking them if they may have a suspicious renter. Cold investigations seem to work well, and the continuous liaison with employees can be very fruitful for law enforcement.

A "tip" or information from a staff member with information of suspicious activity initiates tip investigations. This can be through a telephone call or in person when the investigator visits the facility. The staff person might be a counter clerk, crew person, or management. The employee outlines the activity that appears suspicious and provides law enforcement with the name and other pertinent information.

Investigators subsequently make contact with the staff person and initiate an inquiry. In cold proactive investigations, investigators make contact with vehicle rental staff on a continuous basis. This contact should be made several times a week by the same investigator if possible, to create a relationship between staff and law enforcement. The staff feels comfortable with the same investigator.

Once the investigator makes contact with staff, management, if available, or the shift manager in charge of the location at that time, should be contacted. The investigator should ask the manager if he would consent on this date to have investigators examine the facility's computer and renter information. Most of the larger vehicle rental agencies have a computer-generated list that can be examined by the investigator. While doing this, the officer should speak with counter personnel to ask if they have had a suspicious renter either on that day or the day before. If there is another investigator available, he can speak with the cleanup and return crews to ask them if they have had a vehicle that appeared suspicious. One would think that a staff person would contact the investigator if a suspicious renter were encountered, after all of the staff has been trained. This is not always the case. Investigators will learn that employees may not always call them because of a number of perceived notions. They may say that they didn't want to bother you or that they felt the suspicious activity was not exactly what the officer was looking for. A staff member may not necessarily agree with the philosophy of the program, and so does not call if activity is observed. These are circumstances that are unavoidable, and investigators must do what is necessary to uphold the program. Every time an officer makes contact with rental staff on a routine basis, they should be asked if they have any suspicious activity to report.

While examining the computer-generated list of renters, investigators should be looking for individuals they may know as local drug traffickers in the area. Once an individual has been identified, either by a staff member or investigator, investigators should conduct a background investigation to include criminal history, any intelligence inquiries, whether federal, state or local, and conduct a rental history inquiry. This may show a pattern of vehicle rentals by that person or any associates that may be identified. Not only should that particular rental agency be examined for the information, inquiries should be made with other rental agencies as well. There may a case of rental-hopping by the traffickers.

There are a number of ways to proceed with the investigation from this point. Investigators may ask staff to contact them when the subject returns his or her vehicle. The purpose of this is for investigators to examine the vehicle for any manipulation that may have occurred or items that may have been left in the vehicle. A drug canine team can examine the vehicle for the odor of narcotics. Depending on the time factor, there may be a residual odor emanating from somewhere in the vehicle; this is likely if there was a sizable quantity of drugs in the vehicle for a time. This will give the investigators an indication as to how to proceed the next time the person rents a vehicle, and will give them other investigative avenues to pursue. There may be items in the returned vehicle that are indicative of drug trafficking, such as firearms, notations on paper or other documents with names telephone numbers, maps, or directions to a location later found to be involved in narcotics trafficking. These items may lead investigators to believe that there is drug trafficking or other criminal activity occurring, and can be seized as evidence. Once the renter releases the vehicle back to the agency, there is no expectation of privacy by the renter.

There have been many cases initiated by a vehicle rental investigation program in which major drug trafficking organizations have been identified. Documents were left behind, such as hand-written notations, telephone numbers of other individuals involved in the organization. Remnants of narcotics trafficking such as small portions of drugs, marijuana seeds, stalks, and stems have also been found. One would be surprised what is left behind in rental vehicles. Conversely, a vehicle that has been thoroughly cleaned with Pine-Sol, Lysol, or bleach may be indicative of drug traffickers using rental vehicles. They want to clean the vehicle of everything so as not to alert anyone of the car being loaded with an illicit substance, such as marijuana, which has a strong odor. The investigator should pay attention to manipulation such as the removal of any panels in the vehicle. He should examine the gas tank area and other areas of the vehicle. If a pattern of renting can be developed, a surveillance team should be considered to conduct surveillance of the suspect when he returns to rent another vehicle. Surveillance operations are beneficial in identifying other associates of an organization or individual drug couriers and traffickers. The surveillance team may see an exchange of narcotics, or meetings or negotiations with associates, such as sources of supply and other individuals involved in drug trafficking.

Reasonable suspicion, even probable cause, may be developed based on what is observed during the surveillance. Law enforcement may be in a position to conduct vehicle stops based on their observations, or may approach individuals based on reasonable suspicion or a consensual encounter situation. Investigators may also initiate "spin-off" investigations from vehicle rental investigations. A spin-off investigation involves separate operations or investigations whose information was developed from the particular rental vehicle investigation.

With regard to tip investigations, staff members will contact an investigator with information concerning a renter that displays certain conduct or indicators, which they were trained to be alert for. A tip may come from a counter person or some of the cleaning crew. Generally the counter personnel will provide the bulk of the information for law enforcement. The staff at the counter has the most contact with the potential renter, and will recognize this person if he has a pattern of rental. They can provide information concerning this person's behavior. Additionally, they will be able to provide information concerning other possible associates, other vehicles that may be observed when the renter is dropped off, and other relevant information concerning the renter.

Once a tip has been received from a staff member, it is incumbent upon the investigator, as with a cold investigation, to conduct a background check of the renter to examine any potential intelligence and history of narcotics trafficking. An inquiry of his personal rental history should be conducted as well. Debrief the staff person as thoroughly as possible to obtain information concerning the overall suspicion of the renter(s). There should be an investigative plan of action in place for the interdiction group, depending at what stage the rental is made. There should be pre-rental and post-rental investigation plans in place.

In the pre-rental investigation, initiating surveillance is an option. Surveillance of the renter can be conducted to observe any possible suspicious activity such as exchanges made or other observations. Locations of sources of supply and stash houses have been identified during surveillance operations. If investigators anticipate that the renter will be traveling to a location to rent a vehicle, undercover investigators may be conducting counter monitoring to listen to the conversation between the staff member and the suspicious renter. A commitment to surveillance is the key factor in conducting pre-rental investigations. An investigative decision can then be made as to what course of action to take. A consensual encounter may be in order, or reasonable suspicion or probable cause may be developed.

A post-rental investigation is where the examination of the vehicle is conducted; it is important to debrief the rental employee regarding what they observed. Law enforcement should examine the vehicles themselves when possible, and initiate a surveillance of the renter during the next rental. During the post-rental investigation, the canine team may be requested to examine the vehicle further, to examine other areas which the investigator was not able to examine. There have been cases where drug traffickers have forgotten to remove a large quantity of an illicit substance in the vehicle. There have been cases where investigators have found a kilogram of cocaine hidden in a natural compartment of a vehicle.

If investigators discover a quantity of narcotics, whether through examination by the investigator or the canine team, it should be treated as evidence and processed for latent fingerprints or other evidence that may be extracted from the substance. Law enforcement may be able to later identify individuals directly related to the substance.

## Canine Team

As with any interdiction group, a rental vehicle program requires that a narcotics canine team be part of the program. The team's functions include the examination of returned rental vehicles from renters who display certain suspicious conduct. The canine can also be used during a vehicle stop of the rental by investigators after reasonable suspicion or other circumstances. An opportunity may present itself during surveillance where a canine can be used to examine the vehicle for narcotics. We cannot stress enough how important a canine team is to the overall operation and success of the program.

## Other Information

Law enforcement should consult with their federal or state prosecutors concerning the intention of the agency to start a rental vehicle investigation program. The prosecutor should be asked to research case law relating to such activities by law enforcement in that particular jurisdiction. It is an advantage to advise the prosecutors of the program so they may be prepared to prosecute these cases in criminal court. As always, investigators should be familiar with search and seizure and be well versed with the Fourth Amendment.

Once an investigation is initiated, it is incumbent upon the investigator to clearly and concisely document all investigative efforts and actions taken. All of the conduct observed during the investigation, including activity during the rental process, during surveillance, and during return of the vehicle. If the vehicle is found to have been manipulated in any fashion, this will be documented, as well as remnants of drugs found in the vehicle upon return.

Other investigative avenues related to rental vehicles are truck rental facilities such as U-Haul, Ryder, and others as well as RV rentals. Rental trucks in a variety of sizes are popular methods for narcotic traffickers to transport illicit narcotics. Investigators can make contact with rental truck agencies and elicit their cooperation to participate in a vehicle rental program. The contact and training of the staff is the same as the vehicle rental program. The investigative process is essentially the same. RV rental is another popular method which drug traffickers use to transport narcotics. Large quantities of narcotics can be transported in a rented RV. There are many compartments within RVs. Many police agencies have had success in all three of the vehicle rental programs.

Other indicators to be mindful of are renters who drop off a vehicle, whether it is a truck, RV, or other conveyance, abruptly from other source areas of the country. Drug traffickers may load rental vehicles with the drugs from a source state, travel to another area of the state or country, and drop off the vehicle after the narcotics have been removed. There are several factors related to this. One is when the trafficker does not return the vehicle to its original rental facility, and will drop it off in an area where the narcotics are to be transported; there is typically a "drop-off" fee associated with this. The trafficker will pay this fee to avoid suspicion. The traffickers may cite mechanical problems, or say that other circumstances have arisen where they cannot return the vehicle to its original rental location. In this case, staff should be alerted and trained to contact the interdiction group to examine the circumstances and the vehicle further for evidence of drug trafficking. The trafficker may use other means of transportation to return to his or her home, such as commercial airlines, Amtrak train, or a vehicle from a different rental facility.

## Conclusion

Drug traffickers continue to use a variety of transportation methods to transport narcotics from one point to another. The vehicle rental is a popular and relatively secure method for couriers to utilize. With this type of investigative program in place, law enforcement has another avenue to combat drug transportation and trafficking. The partnering of the rental vehicle business and law enforcement is an excellent opportunity to explore other investigative avenues. This program gives the police agency the advantage in this arena.

## Key Terms

Behavior and conduct
Cold versus TIP investigations
Clean-up crews
Counter clerks
Drop-off fee
"Eyes and ears" concept
Indicators
Letter of commitment
Load vehicle
Look-out vehicle
Management and staff

Natural cavities
Partnerships
Pre- and post-rental investigations
Rental hopping
Return crews
Surveillance
Telephone sticker
Vehicle dumping
Vehicle manipulation

# Currency Seizures 12

Is there anything illegal about being in possession of a large amount of U.S currency? Of course not; there is no crime against carrying a large amount of U.S. currency, such as $10,000, $50,000, $200,000, or even $1,200,000. If we encounter an individual carrying money in these amounts, what gives us the right to seize this money, and once we seize it, how will we be able to have that currency forfeited?

Currency seizure investigations have become much more difficult than they were in the past, and the laws concerning the seizure of money have put greater restrictions on law enforcement. We must overcome many obstacles when seizing money and having that money forfeited. Investigations can be complex; we must be exact about the reason for seizing the money, and we must have proof of a drug nexus to show that the currency was either the proceeds of illegal activity, for example, drug trafficking, or was going to be used to purchase narcotics.

In this chapter, we will explore several cases where money was seized, and look at the reasons for the contact, the discovery of the currency, and what led to seizure of the currency.

Working in an interdiction arena, we have a small window of opportunity, once an individual has been encountered and money has been discovered, to determine if the currency is in fact illegal proceeds of drug activity or is going to be used for the purchase of drugs. We cannot detain these individuals for long to conduct our investigation.

In the majority of currency seizure cases, there will not be any narcotics with the currency, making it harder to prove the illegality of the currency. Currency couriers may have been contracted to transport just the currency, or they may have just dropped of the dope load and had to wait for the currency to be delivered. The organizations contracting these couriers will not mix the dope and the money. They may use the same couriers, but the money will almost always be separate from the dope.

We have encountered individuals who went out to pick up a quantity of narcotics and, if the entire load was not ready, they may have picked up only a partial load, and are returning with the partial load and whatever money was left over. These are the occasions where we will find currency together with dope.

For many of our encounters, we will have either the drug courier or the money courier.

The activity we observe in the money couriers is the same conduct and behavior that we will observe with the drug couriers and, in many instances, they are the same people. The conduct and behavior observed will be that of someone conducting illegal business. Many money couriers know they will not be arrested for being in possession of a large amount of U.S. currency, even though their conduct and behavior will be the same as that of a drug courier.

When money is discovered and seized, that activity is usually followed through in a civil proceeding. The burden of proof to seize money is not as great as if you were attempting to convict that same person of a drug offense. We only need a "preponderance of evidence" to win the seizure of currency and have it forfeited.

What must be done to make sure that our encounter, discovery of currency, and ultimate seizing of the currency will result in the forfeiture of the currency? The same standards apply as to any type of police–citizen contact. Many of our contacts with citizens in these investigations will commence with the consensual encounter. No reasonable suspicion, probable cause, or articulatable facts are necessary to encounter a person. Once the encounter has legally been conducted and the person has consented to the encounter and consented to the search of the item, room, house, or motel room, we will conduct the search of the item or location. So now we search and discover a large amount of U.S. currency — the window of opportunity has presented itself and we must take advantage of it. A lengthy interview should follow once the currency has been discovered, because this is going to determine the seizure of the currency, and we have to lock the individual into a story concerning the currency. This is our window!

### Case Study

On February 3, 2001, Detective Smith reviewed a Passenger Name Record (PNR) for a passenger who was traveling on the westbound Amtrak Train number 3 from Kansas City, Missouri to Flagstaff, Arizona. The passenger had booked a reservation for travel under the name of Johnny Doe. The PNR indicated that the passenger had made the reservation for travel on February 2, 2001 and had purchased the ticket approximately 3 hours before travel to begin on February 3, 2001. The PNR indicated that the passenger had reserved an economy sleeper compartment in sleeper car number 331, room number 13. The PNR also listed a home call-back telephone number for the passenger Johnny Doe. The telephone number (816) 123–4567 was noted. That telephone number was called by Detective Smith on February 3, 2001, and the person who answered the telephone told Detective Smith that there was no Johnny Doe living at that residence.

Members of the interdiction detail were there to meet the westbound Amtrak Train Number 3 in Small Town, USA. Detective Smith was positioned at the north end of the passenger waiting platform, and when the train came to a stop, he was in a position to observe as passengers disembarked from the 331 sleeper car. After passengers had exited the train, Detective Smith made contact with the train attendant for that car. Detective Smith asked the train attendant if he had a passenger in room number 13; the train attendant advised that he did, and Detective Smith asked the train attendant if the passenger's name was Johnny Doe. The train attendant advised that it was. Detective Smith asked the train attendant to describe Johnny Doe, which the train attendant did. Detective Smith asked the train attendant if Johnny Doe had any luggage with him, and he advised he did, and that all of Johnny Doe's luggage was in his room. Detective Smith asked the train attendant if he remembered what type of luggage Johnny Doe had, and the train attendant replied that he had two pieces of luggage — both small black soft-sided suitcases on wheels, the flight attendant type. The train attendant advised that Johnny Doe had the two pieces of luggage in his room.

Detective Smith asked the train attendant if there was anything unusual about the passenger. The train attendant told Detective Smith that the passenger had not been out of his room except to eat, and that the passenger had the curtains closed to his room the entire trip. Detective Smith asked the train attendant if there were any other passengers with Johnny Doe, and the train attendant stated that Johnny Doe had been by himself. The train attendant volunteered the fact that when the train attendant had attempted to tidy things up in the room, Johnny Doe would not leave the room and remained there during the time that the train attendant cleaned the room.

Detective Smith asked the train attendant on car number 331 for permission to board the train, and permission was granted. Detective Smith and his partner proceeded to room number 13, and as they walked to it, they observed an individual who they believed was passenger Johnny Doe, preparing to exit the room. Detective Smith and his partner continued walking through the sleeper car and into the next car, where they exited the train. As Detective Smith and his partner exited sleeper car number 331, they observed that Johnny Doe had also exited sleeper compartment number 13 and was now standing on the passenger waiting platform just to the right of the door to car number 331.

Detective Smith observed Doe as he stood smoking a cigarette. Doe appeared to be smoking the cigarette rapidly, taking quick puffs and exhaling the smoke. Detective Smith observed Doe remove a pack of cigarettes from his shirt pocket and remove another cigarette from the pack. Doe still had a lit cigarette in his mouth, and he was inhaling and exhaling the smoke from the cigarette. Doe returned the pack of cigarettes to his shirt pocket and with his right hand he removed the lit cigarette from his mouth, and with his left hand he placed the unlit cigarette into his mouth. Doe then used the lit cigarette in his right hand to light the cigarette in his mouth. Doe then threw the half-smoked cigarette on the ground, and extinguished it with his foot. Detective Smith observed that Doe repeated this same activity three times during the ten minutes that Doe remained outside of the sleeper car and stood on the passenger waiting platform.

Detective Smith noted that Doe was continuously looking around in all directions, watching other passengers as they walked past him, and continuing to watch them after they passed. Detective Smith observed that Doe would converse only with the train attendant, who was also standing out on the passenger waiting platform next to the sleeper car entrance. Detective Smith observed that Doe could not remain still, but paced in short strides, taking a few steps in different directions, but always staying close to the door of sleeper car number 331.

Detective Smith approached Doe, who was now standing approximately 3 feet to the left of the outside entrance to sleeper car number 331. Doe was looking out over the parking lot to the train station and puffing on his fourth cigarette in a rapid fashion. Detective Smith stepped to the right side of Doe, not blocking his forward movement, and stood approximately 2 feet away from Doe, also facing the train station parking lot. Detective Smith greeted Doe and stated, "Hi, how are you?" Doe looked in Detective Smith's direction and stated, "Okay." Detective Smith removed his police badge from his pocket and showed Smith the badge and identified himself as a police officer of the Small Town Police Department. Detective Smith noticed that Doe stop puffing on the cigarette momentarily and looked down at Detective Smith's badge. Doe then looked up at Detective Smith, and Detective Smith noticed that Doe had his mouth slightly open with the cigarette clinging to his bottom lip. Detective Smith asked Doe, "Sir, may I please speak with you?" Several seconds passed before Doe answered, and he stated, "Ya, ya, go ahead." Detective Smith noticed that Doe's mouth remained slightly open and he had not taken a puff from the lit cigarette still in his mouth.

Detective Smith asked Doe if he was a passenger on the train, and Doe replied that he was. Detective Smith asked Doe where was he traveling from, and Doe stated that he was traveling from Kansas City, Missouri. Detective Smith noticed that Doe had not removed the cigarette from his mouth, and a long ash stem was beginning to form at the end of the cigarette. Detective Smith asked Doe where was he traveling to, and Doe stated he was traveling to Flagstaff, Arizona to an antique convention. Detective Smith asked Doe if he was on a pleasure trip or business trip, and Doe stated he was on business. Detective Smith noticed that Doe had removed the cigarette pack from his shirt pocket again and had removed a cigarette from the pack. Doe returned the cigarette pack to his shirt pocket, removed the lit cigarette from his mouth and replaced it with the unlit cigarette. Doe then used the lit cigarette to light the unlit one, and threw the half-smoked cigarette to the ground where four other half-smoked cigarettes had been stomped out. This took about one minute to complete.

Detective Smith asked Doe if he was traveling in the coach or the sleeper section of the train. Doe then looked at the train car he was standing in front of and hesitated, then stated, "Ah, ah, I think I'm in the sleeper section." Detective Smith asked Doe if he had been planning the trip for a long time, and Doe stated that he had and that he was just coming from another antique show in Springfield, Illinois. Detective Smith asked Doe what type of antiques he dealt with, and Doe stated that he bought, sold, and repaired old slot machines. Doe then took a long puff off the cigarette and asked Detective Smith if there was anything wrong. Detective Smith advised Doe that nothing was wrong; that he worked at the train station and spoke to people every day who traveled on the train, making sure they were having a safe trip. Doe responded that he felt much safer knowing that there were cops along the route.

Detective Smith noticed that while Doe would move his right hand up to retrieve the cigarette from his lips that the hand trembled, and he would take a quick puff from the cigarette and then remove it from his lips. Detective Smith noticed that Doe kept his left hand in his left front pants pocket and appeared to be toying with coins in his pocket.

Detective Smith asked Doe if he had a train ticket that Detective Smith could look at, and Doe said, "Sure," and began padding his pockets in search of his train ticket. Doe told Detective Smith that he thought he had left his ticket in his room. Detective Smith asked if it would be okay with him if Detective Smith looked at it, and Doe said that he would have to go to his room and get it. Doe then told Detective Smith to wait on the platform and he would go up to his room and bring the ticket back down to Detective Smith. Detective Smith asked Doe if it was okay with him if he followed him to his room and looked at the ticket there, so Doe would not have to come back down again. Doe responded that it would be okay.

Doe then entered the 331 sleeper car and walked down the aisle way to room number 13, and Detective Smith followed him to his room. Detective Smith's partner, Detective Right, took up a position on the opposite side of the entrance to the sleeper car, thus not blocking the aisle way or exit from the train car. Doe approached room number 13, opened the door, and moved the curtain aside in order to enter the room. Detective Smith noticed that the upper sleeper berth was in the down position, with a small black soft-sided suitcase laying on top of the bed. Doe used his right hand to slide the suitcase to the other side of the bed and then used a pillow in an attempt to conceal the suitcase. Doe had a second suitcase on the left side seat that was similar to the one on the upper sleeper berth. The suitcase was open, and through the window Detective Smith could observe clothing, toiletry items, and personal items. Doe removed a train ticket folder from the suitcase, stepped outside of the room in the aisle way, and handed Detective Smith the ticket folder.

Detective Smith opened the ticket folder, removed the ticket and ticket receipt from the folder, and reviewed the ticket. Detective Smith observed that the ticket was in the name of John Doe, with one-way travel from Kansas City, Missouri to Flagstaff, Arizona; the ticket indicated that the price was $338. Detective Smith handed the ticket back to Doe immediately. Detective Smith asked Doe if he had any identification on him that Detective Smith might be able to look at, and Doe said he did, and reached into his left rear pocket and removed an Illinois driver's license and handed it to Detective Smith. Detective Smith looked at the driver's license and observed that it was in the name of John Doe, with a picture of Doe on the license. The license listed an address of Naperville, Illinois. Detective Smith handed the license back to Doe, and Doe returned the license to his wallet.

Detective Smith pointed to the luggage in the room and to the suitcase on the upper bed and asked Doe if that was all his luggage and if he had any more on the train. Doe advised that it was his luggage and that it was all he had.

Detective Smith advised Doe that he worked an interdiction detail at the train station and that he spoke with people every day. Detective Smith asked Doe if he would voluntarily consent to a search of his luggage. Doe asked Detective Smith for what reason, and Detective Smith advised that he was looking for criminal activity and contraband. Doe asked Detective Smith what was he looking for again, and Detective Smith advised him that he was looking for contraband. Doe then replied, "Ya, that'll be fine." Detective Smith waved for his partner, Detective Right, to step up. Detective Smith advised Doe that Detective Smith's partner was also present and would assist in the search. Detective Smith began a search of the bag on the left side seat. Detective Right began to converse with Doe as Detective Smith searched through the black carry-on suitcase, and Detective Smith did not locate any contraband or illegal items. Detective Smith returned the first suitcase to Doe, and Doe placed it back in his room. Detective Smith asked Doe if he could search the small black soft-sided suitcase that was laying atop the upper sleeper berth. Doe turned around to look at the suitcase. He glanced at it briefly and turned around to face Detective Smith and said, "Ya that'll be okay." Doe removed the suitcase from the upper sleeper berth and handed it to Detective Smith, placing the suitcase on the floor outside of the room. Detective Smith unzipped the case and immediately observed a white plastic store bag that contained several magazines and other items. Upon looking through the white plastic store bag, Detective Smith noticed that there were rubber bands surrounding the magazines. Detective Smith looked in between one of the magazines and observed several bundles of what appeared to be U.S currency. He looked through another magazine that also had rubber bands surrounding it, and that magazine also contained several bundles of U.S. currency. A total of five magazines were in the white store bag, along with some toiletry items, and all of the magazines were identical, with rubber bands surrounding them and containing several bundles of U.S. currency.

Detective Smith asked Doe whose money was in the magazines, and Doe hesitated briefly and stated that the money had been given to him by an antique broker in Springfield, Illinois, and that he was taking the money to Flagstaff to purchase slot machines. Detective Smith asked Doe if he knew how much money was in the magazines, and Doe stated about $15,000 to $20,000. Detective Smith asked Doe who gave him the money, and Doe advised it was an antique broker. Detective Smith asked Doe for the antique broker's name, and Doe again hesitated momentarily and stated that he did not know the name. Detective Smith stated to Doe that it was unusual that someone gave him $15,000 to $20,0000 and that Doe did not know his name. Doe advised that the broker worked for a large antique brokering company called Argon Limited.

Detective Smith asked Doe how he met this antique broker, and Doe advised that he met him several days ago at the antique show in Springfield, where he had been showing some of his slot machines. Detective Smith asked Doe if he had ever seen this antique broker before, and he advised he had not. Detective Smith asked Doe if he was knew anything about the antique brokering company, and Doe advised that it was a large company that dealt in antiques throughout the Midwest. Detective Smith asked Doe if he had a business card from the broker or the company, and Doe stated he did not. Detective Smith asked Doe how the broker asked him to take the money to Flagstaff for him. Doe advised that they had been talking at the antique show and Doe had mentioned to the broker that he was traveling to Flagstaff to purchase some antique slot machines, and the broker asked Doe if he would purchase some for him if he gave him money, and Doe stated that he said he would. Detective Smith asked Doe why the antique broker did not give him a cashier's check, and Doe advised that it was common to deal in cash at most antique shows. Detective Smith asked Doe when the antique dealer gave him the cash, and Doe stated right after the antique show was over. Detective Smith asked Doe how the money was given to him, and Doe stated that it had been given to him in a bag. Detective Smith asked Doe if the money was bundled up in rubber bands in between the magazines as it now was, and Doe advised that the money was given to him bundled up in rubber bands, but that he had placed it between the magazines to transport it more safely.

Detective Smith asked Doe how many slot machines was he supposed to purchase with the money given to him by the antique broker, and Doe stated that antique slot machines were usually sold for $3000 to $5000 per machine.

At this time, Doe reached into his shirt pocket and removed the pack of cigarettes, and removed a cigarette from the pack and placed it in his mouth. Detective Smith noticed that Doe was biting down on the filtered end and Doe's hand was trembling as he held onto the cigarette.

Detective Smith asked Doe if he had a telephone number for the antique broker in the event there was an emergency or if he was unable to make it to the antique show. Doe advised that he did not have a telephone number for him, and that he was supposed to just go to the antique show and another representative from Argon Limited would be there to meet him and pick up the slot machines. Detective Smith asked Doe who from Argon Limited was he supposed to meet at the antique show, and Doe advised that the broker did not give him a name but said that a representative from Argon Limited would meet him there.

Detective Smith asked Doe if he had ever traveled to Flagstaff to purchase antique slot machines, and Doe responded that he had not, and that this was the first time. Detective Smith asked Doe where the antique show was going to be held, and Doe advised that he did not know but that he would find out when he arrived in Flagstaff. Detective Smith asked Doe if he knew the name of the antique show, and Doe advised that he did not. Detective Smith asked Doe if the antique show had only antique slot machines, and Doe advised he did not know anything about this particular antique show.

Detective Smith then asked Doe if he could remove some of the money from the rubber-banded magazines, and Doe said "Sure." Detective Smith removed the magazines from the bag, and there were a total of four magazines: two travel magazines and two magazines about cooking. Detective Smith noticed that there was an address label on the magazines; it appeared the magazines were subscription magazines and not magazines that had been purchased at a store. Detective Smith repeated the name on the address label to Doe and asked Doe if he knew the person, and Doe and advised he did not. Detective Smith asked Doe if he was familiar with the address on the address labels, and Doe advised he was not.

Detective Smith removed the currency from two of the magazines and examined it. Each magazine had a total of three bundles of U.S. currency. Detective Smith noticed that each bundle was bound by one large rubber band to keep all the currency together, and that each bundle contained five separate bundles that were bound by two rubber bands each. Detective Smith had seen U.S. currency wrapped in the same manner on previous occasions. Detective Smith quickly leafed through one of the large bundles and noted that there was approximately $5000 in the bundle. Detective Smith noted that the denomination of bills contained in the bundles was small: $20s, $10s, and $5s.

Detective Smith asked Doe again how much money was in the bag, and Doe changed the amount he had earlier stated, of $15,000–$20,000, to $35,000–$40,000. Detective Smith asked Doe if all the money belonged to Argon Limited, and Doe stated "No." Doe advised Detective Smith that some of the money was his, because he was also going to purchase some slot machines. Detective Smith asked Doe how much of the money was his and he stated "About $15,000." Detective Smith asked Doe if this was the manner in which he had received the money from the antique broker, and

Doe advised that it was. Detective Smith asked Doe if he also transported his money in this manner, and Doe responded that he thought it was a good idea so he repeated the same fashion of bundling the money. Detective Smith asked Doe if he knew which magazine contained his money, and Doe advised he could not remember which magazine contained his money, but it was about $15,000.

Detective Smith removed all of the money from the four magazines and placed it out on the right passenger seat in Doe's room. Detective Smith counted 10 bundles of U.S. currency, and each bundle appeared to contain the same number of smaller bundles inside of one larger rubber-banded bundle. Detective Smith made a comment to Doe that it appeared there was more than the last figure Doe had stated of $35,000 to $40,000. Detective Smith noticed that Doe still had the cigarette in his mouth and that he had bitten through the filtered end. Doe then reached into his pocket and removed a pack of matches, and was preparing to light the cigarette when Detective Smith reminded Doe that there was no smoking in the train. Doe removed the cigarette from his mouth and threw it on the floor.

Doe responded to Detective Smith's question concerning the amount of U.S. currency. He stated that he thought there could be $60,000. Detective Smith asked Doe how much currency he really thought there was in the bag and quoted the earlier amounts that Doe had mentioned of $15,000–$20,000, $35,000–$40,000, and $60,000, and Doe said he thought it might be closer to $60,000. Doe stated that he thought Detective Smith's early question about how much money was there was a question about his own personal money of $15,000.

Detective Smith asked Doe if dealing in antiques was his only source of income, and Doe stated that it was, and that he helped a friend of his at home remodel apartments and houses. Doe stated that he once worked in the construction field. Detective Smith asked Doe about how much money he made annually, and Smith stated around $35,000 a year in a good year. Doe advised that some years did not bring in as much. Detective Smith asked Doe if he did his banking at a particular bank in his hometown of Peoria, and Doe advised he did not like using banks, and because of the cash business of antiques, he always kept his money at home. Detective Smith asked Doe if he had a checking or savings account, and Doe advised he did not. Detective Smith asked Doe if he owned his own home, and Doe stated that he did not; that he lived in one of his friend's apartments that he had refurbished.

Detective Smith asked Doe if he had ever been arrested, and Doe advised that he had once been arrested for simple possession of marijuana and that he had several traffic citations. Detective Smith asked him about the marijuana arrest, and Doe responded that he was traveling in a car with some people and that the marijuana was not his, but he was arrested anyway.

Detective Smith asked Doe if he would allow Detective Smith to have the money examined by a narcotic detection canine, and Doe stated "Ya, go ahead." He further stated that he did not use drugs and was totally against it. Detective Smith advised Doe that Detective Smith was going to replace the money back into the magazine and back into the store bag. Detective Smith placed the store bag into the suitcase and closed the suitcase. The suitcase was left in the room on the right side seat.

Detective Smith made a request for canine officer Bill, who was standing by near the train, to bring his certified narcotic detection canine "Blue" up to the train. Detective Smith then asked the train attendant for permission to bring "Blue" inside of the train, and permission was granted.

Detective Smith asked Doe if it would be okay with him if he stepped a few feet away from the room when the canine was brought in, and Doe stated "No problem at all." Officer Bill entered the train car and had "Blue" examine the luggage in the common luggage area as well as the area in front of the doors of all the first-floor rooms. Officer Bill concluded his examination of the area and asked to speak with Detective Smith. Officer Bill advised that "Blue" had alerted to room number 13 and to the black suitcase that was on the right side seat inside of room number 13.

Detective Smith returned to where Doe was standing and asked Doe if the U.S. currency had recently been around any drugs. Doe immediately reached into his upper shirt pocket and removed the pack of cigarettes, and was going to remove a cigarette from the pack and noticed that the pack was empty. Doe then looked to the floor and stated that his money had not been around any drugs  and that he did not like drugs. Doe stated that he did not know about the money that was given to him by the antique broker. Doe would not look up at Detective Smith but continued to look at the black suitcase that contained the money.

Detective Smith asked Doe if he knew where the money had come from, and Doe stated that he had received it from the antique broker. Detective Smith asked Doe if the antique broker had told him where the money had come from, and Doe stated "No." Detective Smith asked Doe if he knew if the money was the proceeds of any type of narcotic trafficking, and Doe stuttered and said "I don't think so," still looking down at the floor. Detective Smith asked Doe if he knew if the money was going to be used to purchase drugs, and Doe hesitated in answering and stated as far as he knew the money was going to be used to purchase slot machines. Detective Smith asked Doe if Flagstaff was a popular location for purchasing antiques, particularly slot machines. Doe stated that he had never been to Flagstaff to purchase antique slot machines and that he did not know.

At this point is there enough reasoning for Detective Smith to seize the currency? Were all the appropriate questions asked, and were the answers consistent with someone involved in a legitimate antique business? Was the conduct and behavior displayed by Doe consistent with that of someone who was traveling for legitimate business, or did his conduct show signs of deception, dishonesty, evasiveness, and untruthfulness? We will analyze the encounter and determine whether there was enough reason for Detective Smith to seize the money.

As in any consensual encounter, all the same standards must apply in determining the validity of the encounter and the seizure. Once the standard has been met for the validity of the encounter, Detective Smith must also be able to articulate the seizure of the money. Does he have "probable cause" to seize the currency? Detective Smith is also going to rely on his training and law enforcement experience. The number of years he has been employed as a law enforcement officer, how many times he has conducted seizures of currency, how many times he has seen U.S. currency wrapped, packaged, and transported in this manner all come into play. Was the area from which Doe was traveling considered a drug distribution point or source location? Was the area that Doe was traveling to, Flagstaff, Arizona, considered a source location for drugs? How far are Phoenix and Tucson located from Flagstaff, and are those areas source locations for drugs?

Detective Smith did conduct a lengthy interview with Doe, and the window of opportunity  presented itself and was taken advantage of. Of course, there will be follow-up investigations, but for Detective Smith to seize the currency, he must be able to articulate that he had enough reason to do so. He must be able to show that there was a *"drug nexus"* associated with the money or that the currency was the proceeds of other criminal activity or was going to be used to facilitate other criminal activity.

## Establishing Ownership

One of the first things to do is to establish ownership of the money. Initially Doe had responded that the money had come from an antique broker — for whom he did not have a name, business card, or telephone number — someone that Doe had just met days earlier and who trusted Doe enough to give him more than $45,000 in U.S. currency. Remember, Doe had mentioned that $15,000 of the currency was his. Detective Smith made inquires into Doe's financial background, which is very important; you want to establish if the person who has the currency has the resources and opportunity to be in control of this amount of currency. The subject's financial status is a key factor: what does he do for a living and how much money does he make; what are living expenses like; does he own or rent a house or a car; where does he bank; what is the name and location of the bank, does the subject have any documentation to support the banking institution such as a check-book, savings book, or bank receipts for deposits or withdrawals; does he have a checking or savings account; how much money does he have in his accounts at the present time; how much time did it take him to accumulate this amount of money; and so on.

If other parties are involved and also have ownership of the currency, who are they? What is the relationship to the person who is in possession of the money? Are they co-owners or business associates? What type of business are they involved in, and where do they conduct their business? What are their names and addresses, both street address and city where they reside? What are their telephone numbers, and can they be contacted at this minute to verify the transportation of the currency? If the other parties are family, what are their names and where do they live, street addresses and city. What is the family relationship — mother, father, sister, brother, aunt, uncle, or cousins? When did the business associate or family member give the subject the currency and where and how was it obtained? Where did they meet; at whose house or apartment did he pick up the currency? How often does the subject see this person, and when was the last time he saw the person before picking up the money?

Does the person who owns the currency always transport his money in the same manner and fashion? Is this something that is typically done in this type of business? Remember, the person transporting the money is probably making up the story as he goes along; he does not know if you are familiar with his particular business.

If the person who is in possession of the currency is transporting it for someone else, then we must attempt to identify the person to whom the money belongs. If the person who is in possession of the currency does not know who owns the money and was given it by someone else, as in the case study, we must still attempt to do all we can at that moment to identify an owner or at least show the evasiveness of the person transporting the currency. If the money was received from multiple parties, then we must establish the percentage of money for each person that participated. Was the money received in total or did each person provide the courier with the money separately?

If the person in possession of the currency claims the money belongs to him, ask what he does for a living and how long it took him to accumulate this amount of money. Was the money in a banking institution before travel? If so, what is the name of the banking institution, and what is the physical address of the bank, and what city is it in? Is the banking institution close to where the subject lives? Whose name is the account in, and is the account shared by more than one person; if so, what is the other person's name, and what type of account is it? Does the person know the telephone number for the bank, or does he know the name of the bank teller or bank officer who waited on him? Does the subject have any receipts or banking documents to verify the transaction or previous banking transactions?

If the subject claims that the money was a gift or inheritance, ask the nature of the gift and who the gift giver was. If inheritance, what type was it, and who was the family member or friend from whom the subject inherited the money? When did the person die? When did the subject pick up the currency and where from — was it from a lawyer's office, did they meet at a bank, did he first receive a check and then cash it in?

If the subject claims he won the money gambling at a casino, the gambling industry and casinos keep some of the best records, and these records can be accessed via subpoena. Casinos do not allow someone to win a large amount of money from them without keeping records on the amount won, where it was won (at what gambling venue), how much money was played, how long the person was there, how much money the person spent, and whether the person was a frequent gambler at their casino. Records reflect how long they played at that particular casino and how long it took them to win the money. All this information is accessible via subpoena, and most casinos are cooperative with law enforcement in providing this information.

## Origin of the Currency

Where did the money come from, how was it gained, and by what means? For instance, Doe said he was given the money at the antique auction by the antique broker. Doe was asked when and where he received the money and how it was packaged. You should ask as many questions as possible concerning the money's origin. How often has the person seen the business associate, family, or friend with this amount of currency? If the person with the money states it is his money, then how often does he have this amount of money, or how long did it take him to accumulate the money?

It is very important to pin down where the money was obtained. Was it obtained by the courier at a residence? If so, whose residence was it? Where is the residence and what does it look like? If the money was obtained at an apartment, whose apartment was it, where is it located, what was the apartment number, and who was present? If the money was obtained from an individual at a meeting place such as a parking lot, a bar, or restaurant, ask who was there and what type of vehicles were seen. Who was the person from whom the money was received? Did the subject know the person; how long did he know him; had he ever seen him with this amount of money before? Had the person ever been to this location or had he ever received currency from this person before at the same location? Ask how soon before travel the currency was obtained: date, day of the week, and approximate time.

If the person is a courier, how many other times has he transported money for the person(s) or organization? Couriers are often hesitant for fear of harm. How much money were they going to receive for transporting the money? What instructions did they receive for transferring the money to a third party: day, date, time of day, and location where the money was going to be transferred. Was the courier instructed to wait and bring back a product or contraband?

## Purpose of the Currency

Was Detective Smith able to pinpoint the reasoning for the amount and what was going to be done with the money? Ask the subject what reason he has for transporting a large amount of currency and if this is a method that he always adheres to. Ask how often he transports money in this manner. Ask what the money was going to be used for. If the courier claims farm equipment, cars, restaurant equipment, or appliances, then ask him about the locations where he plans to purchase these items. Does he have references or business cards for these locations? Does he have telephone numbers for businesses, or names of salespersons? Ask about the equipment to be purchased and his knowledge of the equipment and its use. Is his employment related to the equipment to be purchased?

Ask if the money is going to be used to purchase drugs or other illegal contraband. Remember, we are dealing with a civil, not a criminal case. If there is just currency involved and no drugs, as in many cases (because the courier will have one or the other), then the case will probably be a civil action. If this is a civil action, must we advise him of the *Miranda* warning? Can we ask these questions? Can we ask if he is a drug dealer? Unless you plan to take some type of enforcement action, this is the question you need to ask yourself. Can we ask if the money was the proceeds from drug trafficking or other illegal activity?

## Packaging and Transportation

During Detective Smith's interview of Doe, did Doe provide a reasonable answer for the way the money was wrapped, packaged, and transported in the manner in which Detective Smith discovered it? You need to ascertain the reasoning for the packaging of the currency. Was the currency received in this manner, or did the person wrap or package the money in this manner after receiving it, and for what reason? Does the person always package his money in this manner? Was there a masking odor and, if so, why was a masking agent used?

Inquire about the reason for transporting the money in this fashion. Does the subject always do this with his money, or was he instructed to transport the money in this manner? Was there an opportunity to obtain cashier's check or money transfers from one banking institution to another? How many other times has the courier transported currency, and was it always in this manner and fashion?

## Use of a Canine

Will a certified narcotic detection canine alerting to the currency give us more reason for seizing it? Some jurisdictions require that the money be subjected to examination by a trained and certified narcotic detection canine. What happens if the canine does not alert to the currency — will that hurt the seizure of the money? Again, each jurisdiction has its own guidelines concerning the use of canines to examine currency, and this will determine the importance of the canine alert. Will a trained and certified narcotic detection canine alert to all currency, and is all currency contaminated with drug residue? Refer to Chapter 4 for more information.

Your observations, knowledge of the person in possession of the currency, interview with this person, and method of packaging and transportation of the currency will be your determining factors in seizing it. The alert by a certified narcotic detection canine may or may not give you additional grounds to seize currency.

## Decision to Seize the Currency

Before making the decision to seize the currency, the law enforcement officers or agents must be satisfied that they have explored all possible reasoning for the person to have the currency. Are the officers or agents satisfied with the answers to their questions? Confer with your partner(s) and make sure all questions have been asked and answered, whether the answers were lies or not. Again, this is your "window of opportunity" to tie the subject to his story concerning the currency.

Once the decision has been made, explain to the individual what is going to happen. "Mr. Doe, at this time we have reason to believe that this money was either the proceeds of illegal activity such as drug trafficking or that this currency was going to be used to purchase drugs or other illegal contraband, and therefore we are going to seize the currency."

What happens if the person refuses? You will inform him that any interference or obstruction concerning seizure of the currency will result in a criminal action. Tell him that he is not under arrest but that you are going to seize the money. If the person persists in obstructing you or interfering with seizure of the currency, then take whatever action you deem is necessary to place him under arrest for interfering with a police officer or obstructing a police officer — whatever type of misdemeanor offense your jurisdiction allows.

Explain to the subject what is going to happen to the currency. Every agency has different policies concerning seizure of currency; adhere to your policy.

Will the currency be counted in front of the subject before leaving the scene? Adhere to your policy. If the money is counted in front of the subject, verify its amount to the best of your ability. You do not want to count the money in front of the subject and then come up with a different amount when the money is placed in your asset seizure account, especially if there is a shortage of the money.

A good policy is to conduct one count of the currency at a bank, where a cashier's check can be issued for the amount of the seizure. Therefore, when the money is counted in front of the subject, the number of bundles is all that is listed on the receipt, e.g., 4 bundles of U.S. currency, or 30 bundles of U.S. currency, with each bundle separately bound in rubber bands. If the subject states an amount, that amount should be written on the receipt, in quotation marks, e.g., the subject stated "I have $15,000 total." That is not necessarily the amount that was actually seized from the subject, but the amount that the subject stated he had.

Explain to the subject your department's policy on contesting the seizure of the money and tell him what type of documentation he will receive. Give him time frames on these issues. Allow him to ask any questions or voice any concerns as far as the seizure is concerned.

Make sure a receipt is provided for the currency. Make sure you have fully identified the person from whom you are seizing the money. The receipt should be made out to the person or persons from whom the currency is being seized. Write in full detail what is being seized and, depending on your agency's policies, how much or what denominations are being seized. Refer to your department or agency's policies for this.

Obtain a correct mailing address from the person from whom the money is being seized. Let him know this is very important if he wishes to contest the seizure of the money. If the subject is just a courier, the person for whom he is working will want this documentation.

Provide a way for the subject to contact you or your asset seizure personnel. Give him your business card.

If the subject chooses to disclaim ownership of the money, can we allow him to do this? Yes, if that is his choice, then we cannot force him into claiming the money belongs to him. Make sure you have disclaimer forms if your agency or department allows for these documents. If there is more than one person involved and they disclaim knowledge or ownership of the currency, then have all parties involved sign a disclaimer form. Make sure you have the disclaimer form in the appropriate languages for your area: English, Spanish, Italian, French, Japanese, Chinese, or whatever is the ethnic makeup of your area.

Ask the subject if he would consent to have a picture taken. Let him know if he contests and wins the seizure of the currency, that you want to make sure the money is retrieved by him and not by someone else. Make sure you have recorded all identification documents, whether they are false or not.


## Have We Forgotten Anything?

Confer with your partners to make sure all the appropriate documents have been signed and issued to the person from whom the money was seized. Were all the appropriate questions asked? Does the person have any questions for you? Is there a possibility of a controlled delivery being conducted, and what other type of cooperation or assistance will the subject provide to you? Will the subject give a statement concerning the money and his involvement with it? Now the fun part of documenting your seizure is ahead, which is one of the most critical aspects of your case.


## Case Law

### *United States v. $639,558 in U.S. Currency,* 955 F.2d 712 (1992) D.C. Cir.

A narcotics dog alerted to suitcases on a train. Inside was $639,558. During a civil forfeiture action, the court ruled that the dog alerted to cocaine adhering to the cash. The defendant's expert testified that 90% of all cash in the United States contains sufficient quantities of cocaine to alert a trained dog. This expert also testified that bills may contain as little as a millionth of a gram of cocaine, but that is many times more cocaine than is needed for a dog to alert. The handler testified that the number was lower, near 70%.

There is one study indicating that up to 97% of all bills in circulation in the country are contaminated by cocaine, with an average of 7.3 µg of cocaine per bill.

### *United States v. $506,231 U.S. Currency,* 125 F.3d 600 (1998) 7th Cir.

A trained drug dog identified traces of narcotics on currency. The court held that this was insufficient to establish probable cause for forfeiture.

Even the government admits that no one can place much stock in the results of dog sniffs on currency because at least one third of the currency in the United States is contaminated with cocaine. Therefore, the court is unwilling to take seriously the evidence of the post-seizure dog sniff.

### *United States v. $22,474 U.S. Currency,* 246F.3d 1212 (2001) 9th Cir.

In a civil forfeiture action, there was probable cause to connect currency to drug trafficking due to:

> Sophisticated dog sniff indicated presence of narcotics on currency
> Defendant was carrying large amount of cash
> He had given conflicting statement regarding amount of cash and its origin
> He had given conflicting statements about his reasons for visiting city
> He admitted having prior drug trafficking conviction

Here the government presented evidence that the dog would not alert to cocaine residue found on circulated currency. Rather, the dog was trained to, and would only alert to, the odor of cocaine. Moreover, the government presented evidence that unless the currency had recently been in the proximity of cocaine, the dog would not alert to it. That evidence was not disputed.

## Key Terms

| | |
|---|---|
| Agency polices | Disclaimer forms |
| Banking institutions | Drug money |
| Bundles of currency | Drug nexus |
| Business cards | Drug trafficking |
| Canine alert | Forfeiture |
| Canine examination | Illegal money |
| Canine handler | Illicit proceeds |
| Contesting the seizure | Interdiction arena |
| Currency seizure | Interview |
| Department receipts | Jurisdiction |

# Report Writing and Courtroom Testimony

# 13

The topics of report writing and courtroom testimony follow hand in hand. How well you document your interdiction case will be an important factor in the outcome of your case. The authors have over 40 years of combined law enforcement experience and have prepared police reports for prosecution in state and federal courts. We have spent numerous hours testifying in detention and probable cause hearings, suppression hearings, and jury trials, and wish to relay our experiences, both positive and negative, so that you can be proficient in both report writing and courtroom testimony. We all want to win our cases, whether they plead out or are decided by a judge or jury.

One of the most important aspects of your case will be how well you described the events that transpired. An old saying that many of us in law enforcement have heard, but should never use, is the saying "less is more." How many of you, when you were starting out in law enforcement, were trained by officers or agents who told you that the less information you put in your report, the harder it would be for a defense attorney to attack you, and the more you included, the more ammunition you were giving the defense attorney. This approach is incorrect. You should document everything that occurred, including before your contact with the offender and any information that you had before your encounter, and any follow-up investigation that you produced.

It is extremely important to document everything that occurs in the events during a consensual encounter case. In many jurisdictions, because of the backlog of cases, going to court on a case might take months, or even years if the defendant is a fugitive. Will you remember everything that occurred during your encounter, months or years from now when you are subpoenaed to testify in your case? What do you remember? If the case happened long ago and you did not document all aspects of the case precisely, your memory may be vague and you may not be sure of everything that transpired. As you confer with the prosecutor, who is supposed to walk you through the events of the case in a court of law, you may not be able to relate the events if you did not document them correctly.

In law enforcement, we all know that one of our greatest assets is our credibility; once we have lost that or it comes into question, we might as well look for another career. If a judge finds your credibility questionable during a case, the defense attorney will make it known to the rest of the defense attorney community in your area, and whenever you go before that same judge or any defense attorney, no matter how well you are prepared, the question of your integrity and credibility will be an issue.

To overcome this issue of questionable credibility, you must be proficient at preparing concise, articulate, and accurate reports and being able to properly and truthfully testify to the events in a professional and appropriate manner.

What we do is not a secret. Where did we gain our law enforcement experience concerning the operations of drug and money trafficking organizations? Since the mid-1970s, when airport groups around the country began operating in the attempt to stop the flow of drugs and money, and began to identify the conduct and behavior of drug traffickers. These law enforcement groups noted certain characteristics or indicators that were consistent with this type of criminal activity. They began documenting the conduct and behavior in their reports, and they testified to this conduct and behavior in court proceedings. The United States Supreme Court also noted this conduct and behavior, set forth guidelines in case law, and dictated to law enforcement what was appropriate and legal.

Do you think that since the 1970s the drug and money trafficking organizations that were dealt severe blows by the early pioneers in drug interdiction changed their methods of operation because law enforcement had become aware of how they operated? Of course not; their methods of conducting business were conducive to their illicit activity: flooding the United States with illegal drugs and money. These organizations have to operate in a certain manner regardless of the fact that law enforcement is aware of it. They might change the venues, using all the methods of commercial transportation and areas where the general public conduct their business — hotels, storage units, and public and private parcel locations. They might change packaging methods, concealment areas, and masking odors, but one thing that will remain consistent is the conduct and behavior involved with timing. When the time is right, or when they think it is right, is when business is conducted. The biggest obstacle for drug trafficking business, unlike legitimate business, is law enforcement. All the documentation in police reports and all the expert and police officer testimony in courts of law will not change how the drug business operates.

## Report Writing

One of the most important aspects of your professional law enforcement career is being able to properly articulate in a police document all events that transpired during a law enforcement action — whether that action was the seizure of drugs and arrest of the traffickers, or the seizure of illicit currency from a mule and the successful forfeiture of that asset.

In interdiction type cases, it is especially important to properly document all the events that transpired. Documentation should begin with prior information that you might have uncovered before making contact. The United States Supreme Courts holds that we do not need probable cause, reasonable suspicion, or even articulatable facts to approach or encounter a person and engage him in conversation, as long as the person consents to the encounter.

It is not our goal to approach everyone in a setting such as in an airport terminal, bus terminal, aboard a passenger train, or at a motel. We want to narrow it down to the person or persons most likely involved in criminal activity. We will conduct our approach and encounter based on their conduct and behavior. You will rely on your training and experience coupled with the conduct and behavior of the subject to decide who to approach.

You should be able to document all information before making contact. If necessary, record the information or actions as they occur. Keep a notebook detailing dates, days of the week, and time of day for a particular incident, and save all notes or documentation of events you have witnessed or discovered.

### Report Examples

As you prepare your report, remember, you are attempting to describe the events and paint a picture for a third party who has no experience in drug interdiction and has never been in the area you are describing, such as your bus station and inside its terminal. The persons who must read your report — your supervisor, prosecutor, and defense attorney —have probably never been to your bus station (with the exception of your supervisor) and are not familiar with its layout. As they read your report, if they close their eyes they should be able to visualize the entire setting you are describing. Articulating your observations and your actions, and the actions of the courier, are critical to the success of your case.

You cannot record too much information on your report; remember you have to testify on this case, and testimony should be consistent with the information contained in the report. There should be no questions left unanswered as to what occurred in your case. Articulate every detail as well as the actions of the person(s) you are contacting and the sequence of the events that transpire. The courts will be concerned with all your actions. Pay close attention to detail. Document both verbal and nonverbal responses to your questions.

In Example 2 below, you will see that Detective Jones has gone the extra step in preparing his initial observations of passenger Doper, who has just arrived in his city via bus. You are familiar with the setting of your area; if you are working bus interdiction, you would be familiar with the number of passengers on a bus. Detective Jones does not need a reason to approach Doper, and if Detective Jones chose to, he could talk with every passenger who exited that bus, but that is not his goal. Detective Jones is there to separate the legitimate passengers from the passengers involved in criminal activity. Even though it is not necessary, Detective Jones will describe in great detail the actions of Doper even before Detective Jones contacted him. Compare Examples 1 and 2.

### Example 1

Detective Jones, of the New City Police Department, while working at his local bus station observed activity from a bus passenger who had just arrived from Los Angeles.

Detective Jones observed Doper walk through the bus terminal, walk into the restaurant and sit down at a table.

Detective Jones entered the bus terminal restaurant and began a conversation with Doper.

Detective Jones asked for and received permission from Doper to search his luggage. Detective Jones subsequently searched the backpack and discovered drugs, and Doper was placed under arrest.

### Example 2

On Monday, January 23, 2002 at approximately 10:00 a.m., Detective Bob Jones of the New City Police Department was working at the local bus station when the eastbound bus from Tucson, Arizona arrived in New City. The bus pulled into bus stall number 3, and Detective Jones remained standing inside the terminal just to the right of the door to terminal 3. Detective Jones observed as passengers began to exit from the bus. The baggage handler was removing checked-in luggage from underneath the luggage storage area of the bus and began placing the luggage into a cart to be taken back into the station. After approximately 15 people had exited from the bus, Detective Jones stepped outside and continued to observe as passengers exited from the bus.

Detective Jones observed a passenger, later identified as John Doper, exit from the bus. Doper stepped off of the bus and Detective Jones noticed that he was clutching a black backpack. Detective Jones noted the manner in which Doper was clutching the bag — very tightly and close to his body. Detective Jones noticed that Doper's right hand knuckles were white from clutching the bag so tightly. Doper stepped onto the ground and stepped two feet to the right of the bus door and stopped, even though additional people were exiting from the bus. Doper stopped and began to slowly conduct what Detective Jones recognized as countersurveillance of the passengers in and around the bus as well as other passengers entering and exiting through door 3 of the bus terminal. Doper looked all around and even looked back at some of the passengers that were still exiting from the bus.

Doper slowly walked toward door 3 and looked back over his left shoulder at the bus and the passengers who were still exiting from the bus. Doper stopped walking just outside of door 3 and again turned around to look back at the passengers mingling around the bus. Doper then continued and entered the bus terminal through door 3.

Detective Jones noticed as Doper walked into the bus terminal through door 3 that Doper took approximately five steps into the terminal and turned around to watch the other passengers as they also entered the terminal through door 3. Doper watched several passengers as they entered the bus terminal. Doper then turned back toward the main area of the bus terminal and took a slow scan of all persons who were inside of the bus terminal; looking toward his left, Doper looked out through the terminal and continued his watch of passengers as his gaze continued to the right toward the ticket counter. Doper watched several passengers at the ticket counter and then abruptly looked toward the side door exits when he observed two persons entering the terminal and talking in a loud tone of voice. Doper watched the two people as they proceeded toward the ticket counter. Detective Jones noticed that Doper was still clutching the black backpack close to his body.

Detective Jones observed Doper as he walked straight across the bus terminal to the other side of the terminal and then began to walk west through the terminal. Before reaching the other side of the terminal, Doper looked over his left shoulder two separate times, and each time he did this, Doper looked back at door 3 and at the passengers who were entering the terminal through door 3.

Detective Jones observed Doper reach the north end of the terminal and Doper stopped and turned around to face the area in front of bus stall 3. Doper continued to watch the passengers entering the bus terminal from this door and watched as passengers approached the ticket counter and mingled in the bus terminal. After several minutes of watching passengers,

Doper, still clutching the black backpack, began walking west through the bus terminal near the north wall. As Doper walked, he watched intently as passengers passed by him, turning around to look at people who had walked past him.

Detective Jones had taken up a position near the west end of the terminal to watch the activity of Doper as well as his reactions as he watched people walking near and past him.

Doper stopped walking approximately halfway through the terminal and abruptly sat down on one of the chairs against the north wall. Doper continued to scan the entire terminal, looking in all directions from left to right, and his head would turn immediately toward any person who was approaching him or walking past him. Doper would continue to watch the person as they continued walking. During this time, another person sat down in a set of chairs one seat over from Doper. Doper looked quickly at the person and then stared straight ahead for approximately several minutes. Detective Jones observed as Doper's eyes would look to his left where the person was seated, but his head would remain still. Doper remained seated in this manner for another 5 minutes until the person got up from his seat and walked to the ticket counter. Doper watched the person as he walked and did not take his eyes off the person.

Detective Jones observed Doper get up from his seat and begin to walk slowly west through the terminal. Doper stopped walking after several steps to turn and look toward the ticket counter at the person who had sat down near him. Doper then continued walking west through the terminal toward the bus terminal restaurant. Doper stopped just outside of the bus terminal restaurant and watched the people inside the restaurant. Doper looked back over his left should again to scan the passengers. Detective Jones observed as Doper looked from left to right, watching all the passengers. Doper then entered the restaurant area, walked to the rear of the restaurant, and sat down at a table near the back.

Detective Jones observed as Doper released his grasp on the black backpack and placed it between his feet. Doper continued to watch the people in the restaurant as well as the passengers walking around in the terminal. Detective Jones continued to observe Doper, who did not purchase anything to eat or drink but just sat at the table watching all the passengers.

Detective Jones motioned to his partner that he was going to approach and contact Doper. Detective Jones waited until his partner was in a position to observe Doper and Detective Jones.

Detective Jones entered the bus terminal restaurant area and began to walk in the direction of Doper. Detective Jones observed as Doper looked up at him, and Detective Jones and Doper made eye contact. Doper watched intently as Detective Jones neared the table where Doper was seated. Detective

Jones sat down on a chair at the table next to Doper. Detective Jones did not obstruct Doper from getting out of his seat and did not impede Doper's forward movement from his chair. Detective Jones greeted Doper by saying "Hi," and Doper responded with "Hey." Detective Jones displayed his badge of office to Doper and at that time Detective Jones identified himself as a police officer and asked Doper for permission to speak to him. Doper glanced down at Detective Jones's badge and then looked up at Detective Jones Doper, had his mouth open and did not say anything, but nodded his head in an up-and-down affirmative motion. Detective Jones confirmed the gesture and told Doper "I see you've nodded your head affirmatively. Are you giving me permission to speak to you?" Doper verbally answered "Ya."

Detective Jones noticed that Doper tucked his legs farther underneath toward the back of his seat, with the black backpack still between his feet. Detective Jones asked Doper if he was traveling on the bus, and Doper stated that he was, and was coming from Tucson, Arizona. Detective Smith asked Doper where he was traveling to and Doper stated that he was traveling to Chicago. Detective Smith asked Doper if he was from Tucson or Chicago, and Doper told Detective Smith that he was actually from Calexico, California. Detective Jones asked Doper if he was traveling for business or pleasure, and Doper said he was going to see his sister, who lived in Chicago. Detective Jones asked Doper how long he was going to stay in Chicago, and Doper advised about a week. Detective Jones asked Doper if he had ever been to Chicago, and Doper responded that he had never been there and this would be his first time. Detective Jones noticed that Doper remained seated with his legs tucked underneath his seat. Detective Jones observed that Doper's left leg was trembling, and Doper placed his left hand on his left thigh to keep it from trembling.

Detective Jones asked Doper how long had he been planning his trip and Doper stated about a month, that he had received some vacation time at work and he had about a week off. Detective Jones asked Doper what he did for a living, and Doper looked down at the floor and hesitated, and said he did odd jobs and that it was slow right now. Detective Jones asked Doper if he worked for someone, and Doper stated he was self-employed.

Detective Jones asked Doper if he had a bus ticket that Detective Jones could see, and Doper said "Ya" and reached into his right rear pocket and removed a bus ticket folder and handed it to Detective Jones. Detective Jones reviewed the ticket and noted that the ticket was in the name of J. Doper, with one-way travel from Tucson to Chicago. The ticket indicated that it was purchased on the day of departure from Tucson, Arizona, Monday, January 23, 2002. The ticket also indicated that the method of payment was cash, for a total price of $110. After reviewing the bus ticket for a brief moment, Detective Jones handed it back to Doper.

Detective Jones asked Doper if he had any identification with him that Detective Jones could see, and Doper padded his front pants pocket and then he padded his rear pants pockets, and he then looked away from Detective Jones and stated that he did not have identification. Detective Jones asked Doper if he had to have identification to board the bus and Doper stated, "No." Detective Jones asked Doper how he spelled his name and Doper hesitated and stated "What, spell my name? You know how to spell my name." Detective Jones asked Doper if he could spell his name for Detective Jones, and Doper again hesitated and said in a slow manner "J-O-H-N D-O-O-P-E-R." Detective Jones did not confront Doper with the misspelling. Detective Jones asked Doper where he lived in Calexico, California, and Doper told Detective Jones that he lived in an apartment at 415 Well St. Detective Jones asked what apartment, and Doper stated he couldn't remember; that he had just moved in.

Detective Jones asked Doper how he got to Tucson from Calexico, and Doper said that a friend had given him a ride as far as Tucson. Detective Jones asked Doper what his friend's name was and Doper stated "Anthony." Detective Jones told Doper that Detective Jones had noted that he had a one-way ticket from Tucson to Chicago, and asked how he was going to get back to Tucson. Doper told Detective Jones that he did not know how he was getting back — that he had not decided yet, maybe flying or taking the train.

Detective Jones asked Doper if he had any luggage, and Doper stated that he had a blue duffel bag on the bus. Detective Jones then pointed to the black backpack and asked if the black backpack was his, and Doper looked underneath his chair and then looked back up at Detective Jones and stated, "This backpack?" Detective Jones said "Yes." Doper stated that the backpack was his.

Detective Jones explained to Doper what Detective Jones' duties were at the bus station. Detective Jones told Doper that he worked a bus interdiction detail and that they spoke to passengers traveling in and out of their area.

Detective Jones pointed to the black duffel bag that was still tucked underneath Doper's seat, in between his feet. Detective Jones then asked Doper if he would voluntarily consent for Detective Jones to search his black backpack. Doper asked Detective Jones what was he looking for, and Detective Jones told Doper that there was a problem with passengers transporting illegal narcotics, guns, and U.S. currency. Doper told Detective Jones that he was totally against drugs and violence. Detective Jones told Doper that there should be more people who shared his attitude. Detective Jones then asked Doper again if he would allow Detective Jones to search his backpack, and Doper said "Ya, go ahead."

Detective Jones then motioned for his partner to come forward. At this time, Detective Jones' partner approached Doper and Detective Jones as they conversed. Detective Jones introduced his partner to Doper and told Doper that his partner was going to stand by while he searched Doper's backpack.

Detective Jones' partner began to converse with Doper while Detective Jones removed the black backpack from underneath Doper's chair. Doper then reached out to take the bag, and Detective Jones advised Doper that Detective Jones would search the bag, and this was for safety reasons. Detective Jones then stated "Man, I'm hungry. Is it lunch time yet?" This phrase was a predetermined code phrase that was familiar to the detectives in Detective Jones' detail. All members knew this phrase meant "arrest or seizure." Detective Jones asked Doper to stand up and turn around to face Detective Jones' partner. Doper stood up, and Detective Jones placed Doper in handcuffs, and Doper was advised he was under arrest.

## Preparation for Court and Courtroom Testimony

"Integrity, honesty, truthfulness, and professionalism" is what law enforcement officers have to hang their hats on when it comes to being a witness on the stand. If our integrity is in question, or if our integrity has faltered, then it is time for us to pick a different career because when we walk into that courtroom, this is all we carry with us. Being truthful on the stand will never be undercut, even if your answer is "I don't know," which for many law enforcement officers is hard to admit. Your professionalism as a police officer will be noted when you walk into the courtroom, and everyone will take notice — the judge, prosecutor, defense attorney, and jury.

If your experience in front of a judge or jury is minimal, then it is a good idea to learn from the experts in this field. Who are the experts? Are they your partners who have been conducting these types of cases for years, the prosecutors who have experience in prosecuting these types of cases, the defense attorneys who get paid, either by the court or by the defendant, to defend the person charged, or the judge who will preside and pass judgment or give instructions to a jury to decide whether the defendant is guilty? It is a combination of all persons involved in the court and trial system, the judges, juries, prosecutors, and defense attorneys. You can learn from all these people to better prepare yourself as a witness in a court hearing.

Sometimes losing a case can be your best lesson, because your mistakes will be brought out in court by the defense council. If you repeat your mistakes at the next hearing, then you did not learn from them. You want to be able to leave each hearing or trial learning something from it that you can bring to your next case. There is nothing better than a law enforcement officer having a reputation as a professional, of being honest and truthful on the stand, and having the highest integrity, and hearing this praise coming from a defense attorney. You know you have reached your best when defense attorneys see your name on the reports for a case and ask "What can my client plead to?"

## Observation of a Trial

The authors have spent many hours on the stand testifying in hundreds of interdiction cases. We did not testify in our first case without some assistance from fellow officers and prosecutors, and we hope that our experiences in the state and federal court systems will help you to perform better in court.

If you have never testified in court or have minimal experience, then it is a good idea to spend some time observing trials. Find out when one of your partners has a hearing, regardless of the type. Sitting in on any type of hearing is valuable learning experience.

At an initial hearing to determine probable cause, you will see firsthand what testimony the court will allow, how long this hearing will take, and what type of evidence is presented. This is one of the first hearings for many cases. At this hearing, only probable cause is determined, and the final decision as to whether or not probable cause is present in order to proceed on the case is usually made by a judge.

Suppression hearings are another excellent type of case to sit in on and learn from the experts. Similar to a full hearing, the judge again is the one who makes the decision as to whether the evidence in the case is to be allowed or suppressed. Decisions made here can make it difficult for your case and the prosecution's to proceed. Evidence is presented so that the prosecutor can convince a judge that your lawful actions and the actions of your partners did not violate the defendant's Fourth Amendment rights. If the judge agrees, then the evidence in your case will stand and be allowed to be introduced at a later hearing. The defense council will attempt to show that your actions did in fact violate his client's Fourth Amendment rights, and if he can succeed in convincing the trial judge of this, then the judge can choose to suppress the evidence in your case, which means you have no evidence to introduce at trial.

These cases can take several days, but never take as long as a full trial. Sitting in on these cases is very helpful, and you will learn a lot by listening to the prosecutors and the defense council ask questions, and seeing how the judges make their decisions based on the evidence presented in the hearing.

## Pretrial Interview

This is an important aspect of your case. This is your case; you are the one who is testifying in court and you are the one who will be on the stand. Always find out which prosecutor is handling your case. If it is a new prosecutor, make sure to meet with him before the court date. Make sure all documents, reports, and statements have been submitted with regard to your case. Make sure all the information you have in your working case file is what the prosecutor has. Take the time to meet with the prosecutor, and take your case file so you can make sure that his file is a duplicate of yours. It is going to be a partnership between you and the prosecutor, and you must work together to achieve a favorable outcome for your case.

Find out which judge will hear your case. If the opportunity arises, sit in on some of the judge's trials or court proceedings. Get a firsthand look at how this particular judge conducts his court and note possible items that he concentrates on.

Find out who the defense council is. This will also help you in preparing for your court proceedings. If the defense attorney is someone you are not familiar with, ask your colleagues if any of them have been in court before him. What kind of defense attorney is he? Does he do homework on the case; is he proficient and professional? As we all know, there are some defense attorneys who play by the rules and some who do not. Some defense attorneys have a history of always coming after the officer or agent personally. If they cannot break your case on its merits, many defense attorneys will opt to try and discredit you or make you look unprofessional. We all know which defense attorneys use this tactic on their cases, whether your case is solid or not. And we know which defense attorneys are going to attack your case and not you.

Many defense attorneys attack the officer on the stand personally in an attempt to show that the officer is lying. If that is something you have done, than you will have to deal with its consequences. This tactic is becoming more and more common, and is referred to as the "cops are lying" (CAL) defense. If a defense attorney can accomplish this, then you might lose your case on this tactic and not on the merits of the case. Truthfulness and honesty are your assets when testifying in court. If you do not know the answer to a question, a simple "I don't know" is better than trying to make something up. For law enforcement officers and agents, saying "I don't know" can be the hardest answer to give, but what can the defense attorney do with that answer? He might follow up with additional questions in an attempt to show that you are not sure of a particular aspect in your case, but you have to deal with it. Being truthful on the stand will overcome this, and the judge or jury will see that your answers are honest and to the best of your knowledge.

We know where law enforcement officers and agents always want to be — out looking for the drug or money courier in an attempt to initiate another case. But you must handle the case at hand, and the pretrial interview is essential to achieving a favorable outcome. Meet with your prosecutor and take your time, especially with a new prosecutor. Sit down with him and rehearse preparing yourself with the questions that will be asked. Make sure that you and the prosecutor have gone over all the questions, and if questions are missing from your testimony, suggest to the prosecutor areas that you know from your experience have worked.

Of course, if the prosecutor is someone you have worked with before, many of the questions will already be prepared, and you know what to expect. However, you still want to have a pretrial meeting with that familiar prosecutor to discuss any new developments or evidence in your case. Make sure, even with a prosecutor with whom you have worked extensively in the past, that all possible questions are brought to the table. If the prosecutor is not aware of your background, make sure this is brought up, because your training and law enforcement experience are critical to your case. Make sure questions will be asked during your testimony that will establish your training and law enforcement experience. These questions may seem obvious, and you might believe they are going to be asked, but you do not want to overlook them, so prepare for this by bringing them up at pretrial. Questions that should be asked are:

- Name
- Employer, department or agency
- Law enforcement experience and areas worked
- Present position and number of years spent in position
- Other positions you have had that are critical to your experience in this case
- Training you have received
  - Number of hours and course titles
  - Who presented this training (DEA, FBI, your department)
  - Any specialized training

You want to establish your credibility in this area so when you testify to something that is based on your training and law enforcement experience, the judge or jury are aware of your training and law enforcement record, as they are now part of the record in your case.

We expect the prosecutor to be aware of any new court decisions or opinions, but there is no harm in asking. Make sure you are aware of any new court decisions or opinions, and make sure you have copies of them.

Make sure all evidence has been reviewed and included in your testimony. Any and all documents should be reviewed, and any key material that is to be brought out during your testimony should be discussed. Make sure any graphs or photographs that are to be used have been reviewed, and key points examined.

Have all the witnesses in your case been contacted, and have they been through pretrial interviews as well? What assistance can you lend in identifying or locating witnesses? Remember, this is your case! All witnesses in your case are equally important, whether that witness is a civilian or another law enforcement agent.

## Testimony Preparation

Review your case file and all documents and reports that have been prepared, whether they have been prepared by you or by other officers or law enforcement professionals. Be familiar with all aspects of your case, including any scientific analysis that was conducted. Even though you are not going to testify in these matters, it is essential that you are aware of them. Go over your testimony, make sure you have reviewed the reports you initiated and prepared in the case. If you discover an item or an aspect of your case that was not discussed or brought out during pretrial, contact your prosecutor and discuss the issue. Do not wait until trial day to bring it up.

## Your Professionalism

How you present yourself in the court is critical to your case. Your attire when in the courtroom should be appropriate for the arena which you are in. Coat and tie are suggested. What is your demeanor like when you are inside or outside the courtroom waiting to testify? Be aware of persons around you, and do not talk about your case openly. Be cordial to the defense attorneys but avoid any contact with defense witnesses or defendants.

## Testifying

If you do not have a great deal of experience in this area, the only way to learn is to listen to other officers or agents testify, or to gain the experience by doing it yourself. The only way to gain experience at testifying is by doing it. Keep the following things in mind:

- Sit up straight on the stand.
- Attempt to maintain eye contact with the judge, or in a jury trial, with the jurors.
- Avoid sarcasm.
- Make sure you know who the defendant is and can identify him or her.
- Know where the defendant is seated at the defense table if your identification of him or her is needed.
- Take your time in answering questions.
- Do not volunteer more information than is asked of you.
- Listen carefully to the questions being asked.
- If you cannot understand the question, ask that it be repeated.
- Always attempt to maintain eye contact with the prosecutor and the defense attorney when they are asking questions.
- When you respond, attempt eye contact with the judge or jury in your case; they are the decision makers.
- If documents are presented to you, take your time in reviewing them, especially when presented by the defense attorney.
- When articles of evidence are presented to you, take your time and review them.
- If the defense attorney becomes irritated with you, remain calm.
- If the defense attorney becomes sarcastic with you during questioning, remain professional.
- If the defense attorney raises his voice at you, take your time and remain calm. He will be the one to appear unprofessional.
- Avoid stares or glares with the defendant.
- Once you have been excused by the judge from the witness stand, look at judge and say "Thank you, your honor," and leave the courtroom, unless you are seated at the prosecution table.

Some defense attorneys make a practice of asking two-pronged questions. Be aware of this.

> *Question*: Officer Jones, when you stopped my client, he was very cooperative with you, and he even agreed to speak with you and gave you permission to search his backpack, isn't that right?"
> *Response*: Sir, I did not stop your client. (End of answer. Now wait for defense attorney to respond. After response from defense attorney, wait for the remainder of that question to be asked again.)

Answer one question at a time.
*Response*: In response to the first part of the question ...

You are in a fishbowl when you are on the witness stand; the judge and jury will take notice of everything you do and say. It's okay to be nervous, especially if you do not have a lot of experience on the stand. It will become easier as you gain more experience and time in court. The trial is the final outcome of your case if the defendant did not plead guilty to the charge. This is your arena, so become proficient at it and learn from the prosecutors, your colleagues, and, more importantly, from the defense attorneys who will handle the majority of the drug cases you will present for prosecution. Always remember, you are a professional.

## Key Terms

| | |
|---|---|
| Articulable | Judge |
| Articulate | Jury |
| Baggage | Law enforcement |
| Baggage handler | Law enforcement experience |
| Civilian witness | Partner |
| Conduct and behavior | Pretrial |
| Cops are lying (CAL) | Probable cause |
| Countersurveillance | Professionalism |
| Courtroom testimony | Prosecution table |
| Credibility | Prosecution |
| Defense council | Prosecutor |
| Defense council table | Questionable credibility |
| Department policy | Reasonable suspicion |
| Detention | Reports |
| Detention hearing | State court |
| Documentation | State jurisdiction |
| Documents | Suppression hearing |
| Doper | Talker scanner |
| Drug trafficking | Testifying |
| Evidence | Ticket |
| Expert witness | Ticket folder |
| Federal court | Training experience |
| Federal jurisdiction | Trial |
| Forms | Trial preparation |
| Honesty | Truthful |
| Initial hearing | Truthfulness |
| Integrity | Witness stand |

# Role of the Interdiction Supervisor

# 14

What is the role of an interdiction group supervisor? What should he bring to the table with respect to knowledge, training, people skills, and administrative skills? As with all supervision, he or she should play the role of mentor, facilitator, and leader, and set good solid examples for his personnel. The first line supervisor, whether a sergeant or group supervisor, should play a significant role in supervising a domestic interdiction group. This work presents a unique set of circumstances that differs from traditional narcotic enforcement. The programs that have been outlined here provide readers with a glimpse of what it takes to implement strategies and training, along with the partnering of a variety of businesses and companies and using innovative techniques to combat the drug problem in their communities.

We have found that the most successful interdiction supervisor is the one who actually participates in the interdiction process. One who performs with the investigators, gets on a Greyhound bus or an Amtrak train, and goes through the operation. The sergeant who meets business owners and managers and trains with his or her staff, including the drug canine team, is the one who is the most prepared to deal with potential problems. A successful supervisor believes in the interdiction philosophy and is able to deal effectively with the administration in the agency.

## Instituting the Interdiction Program

When a police agency decides to institute a domestic drug interdiction group, there are many things to take into consideration. Whether it is a large urban police department or a smaller rural police agency, it is critical to the success of the program to make a number of key choices in the area of personnel.

The canine handler and trained narcotic dog (canine team), the programs to institute in a particular jurisdiction, and the supervisor who will coordinate the efforts in a successful program are all important choices. It is imperative to choose a supervisor who has the right temperament for this type of role. The supervisor should have a good working knowledge of search and seizure, and a good foundation in case law relating to drug interdiction. As we have stated, the most successful supervisor in an interdiction group historically has been the one who becomes involved in daily operations with the group.

Traditional narcotic investigations are different from domestic drug investigations, and the potential supervisor for the group should be aware of this. It is certainly an advantage for the supervisor to have a narcotics enforcement background; however, it is not critical. Once a manager has been selected for this supervisory role, it is important that the he be part of the personnel selection process.

Other considerations by the supervisor are resources, equipment, overtime, and preparation for all personnel involved for what is known as a "roller coaster" type program. What we mean by this is that interdiction is a type of drug enforcement that one day could be extremely busy and on other days nothing seems to be happening. Consequently, one of the criteria for selecting personnel to work in this environment is patience. The instant gratification of making an undercover buy from a drug dealer does not happen every day in interdiction; however, we can tell you that many interdiction groups seize more narcotics than the typical drug enforcement group. Undercover operations, search warrants, and other traditional narcotic enforcement arenas may work months or even years to seize the quantity of drugs that an interdiction group may seize in a day.

During the selection process of investigators who have an interest in working domestic interdiction, certain factors should be taken into consideration. The person must be flexible, creative, and patient. There may be hours of surveillance involved in interdiction cases. Creativity is needed in each type of case, whether a hotel investigation or a parcel case. The investigator must be able to be creative in his interactions with individuals in a consensual encounter setting, where he is asking consent to search a person's items, person, or residence. An investigator must be flexible during operations and working hours. Several days of surveillance of a drug trafficker may be necessary, and adjustments often have to be made in plans during an investigation.

An investigator must have the ability to communicate with people. He or she must have good interview skills in a variety of environments. The officer should have a good demeanor. He is generally a self-starter; an assertive type of personality works best in the interdiction environment.

Knowledge of search and seizure and case law is imperative. The agent must know the law and how to proceed in any given situation.

In the majority of interdiction cases, the investigator does not have the luxury of time. Time is not always on our side, and we have to make investigative decisions on the spot. We do not have the luxury of saying to the drug trafficker "Can you wait a minute while I contact my prosecutor?" Decisions have to be made concerning consent searches and other issues on a daily basis. This is why it is important for the investigator to have a good foundation of search and seizure and case law. Good surveillance techniques are important in the domestic interdiction environment. Agents must be able to blend into the background when conducting surveillance. An individual who needs minimal supervision will be the most successful.

The supervisor's role may be to select a dog handler and a trained narcotics canine. If a trained canine is not available within the agency, a decision must be made to purchase a trained dog or train the animal if local training is available. Many agencies already have existing drug dogs working in the agency. The most prevalent type of dog is a dual-purpose dog that is used by patrol officers for bite and tracking purposes and is also trained in drugs or bomb detection. However, the most successful handler and dog for a drug interdiction group is the single-purpose type of animal. In this case, the drug dog is trained strictly on the odor of narcotics and is not trained in other areas. The dog can be a passive or aggressive alert dog (see Chapter 4 for more information on this subject).

In the selection of a dog handler, experience is preferred. This gives an edge in maintaining the conditioning of the dog and its adaptability to expanding areas of deployment of the canine team. The canine team (the handler and the dog) should meet and exceed national standards of proficiency as set by organizations such as the United States Police Canine Association, the North American Work Dog Association, and the National Narcotic Detector Dog Association. The supervisor must be aware of how the canine team trains and how it maintains training records. A supervisor of an interdiction group may be called to the stand in a criminal trial to testify about all aspects of the canine team.

The supervisor is also responsible for equipment availability to the interdiction group. Electronic surveillance equipment includes video and listening devices, body bugs, and alarm systems for drug parcel/package operations. Typically, an alarm system would be placed in a parcel package to alert surveillance teams that a package has been opened. This keeps the investigators from approaching the trafficker prematurely before he opens the parcel.

A marked police vehicle is suggested as part of the interdiction group, which should be available for the purpose of making vehicle stops when appropriate. Investigators sometimes need to make a vehicle stop during an operation, based on reasonable suspicion or probable cause. An interdiction investigator is much more effective in making the vehicle stop in a marked police car than a regular patrol unit, who may not be aware of the details and nuances of the case. A uniformed officer of some sort should be available so that there is no mistake in the identity of the officer. The interdiction officer can ask the right questions because of his knowledge of the case. Taking an officer off of the street to make a vehicle stop and having him ask certain questions puts him in a difficult position since he does not have a thorough knowledge of the case.

Part of instituting an interdiction program is choosing which programs to initiate in a particular jurisdiction. The supervisor must first look at the resources available, and make a decision about what investigative avenues the agency wants to take. Typically, a smaller interdiction group may only be involved in one or a small number of interdiction efforts, such as hotels, commercial bus lines, or parcel packages. The supervisor must look at his particular environment and choose the appropriate programs. The key is not to overextend your resources. This creates a "burnout" factor for personnel, and is detrimental to the program.

## Administrative Matters

The interdiction supervisor is a significant part of the success of the group. It is also important that police administrators and higher command staff be apprised of the interdiction efforts of their agency. There is no question that interdiction efforts can be controversial in nature. We are supported by the courts with respect to interdiction efforts; however, we want the administrative staff to be prepared to address issues such as interdiction techniques and operations.

The administrative staff must also meet the needs of the interdiction group regarding personnel and resources. Selling the program to administrators is easy once they realize the benefit and success of this technique. The key to the success of these programs certainly is the community business partnerships that are formed. Without the cooperation of the business community (the hotel/motel community, the commercial bus system, commercial train system, and others), this type of program could not exist. An important role for the supervisor is to initiate business community contacts to explain the program and establish partnerships.

The supervisor and designated staff should approach the District, State, or U.S. Attorney's Office to make them aware of the police agency intent to start an interdiction program in their jurisdiction. Ultimately, their prosecutors will be litigating the cases. Interdiction cases are different from traditional drug cases such as undercover, wiretap, and conspiracy cases. Prosecutors should be educated and encouraged to research case law related to interdiction operations.

## Training

Interdiction groups must be prepared to deal with the challenges that face them on a daily basis, not only concerning the law, but also safety. Investigators who participate in domestic drug investigations must be properly trained in the legal issues and case law. Supervisors should support and participate in training whenever possible. Training should be provided to investigators in interdiction techniques, new case law, and maintaining tactical awareness using a variety of tactical techniques and equipment. Equipment that all investigators should be provided with includes a ballistic vest, flashlight, handcuffs, and communications with portable radios.

Investigators should train in the environments in which they will be working, such as bus terminals, hotels and motels, and trains. They should be trained in consensual encounter approaches with individuals. If an officer becomes engaged in a situation where he needs to use his tactical skills, it is important to train in the settings where he will be using them. Techniques to be trained in should include voice commands, cover and contact, and maintaining a two-to-one or higher ratio when coming in contact with individuals. Tactical techniques such as limited penetration, quick peeks, button hooks, the tactical L position, and not flagging your weapon should be practiced. Investigators should be trained in building and room clearing for conducting and executing search warrants when a tactical team is not used.

Tactical training should be conducted in the areas of linear dangers, attention scanning 360 degrees, security, perimeter considerations, and a tactical retreat and escape route. Investigators should be taught never to pass a danger zone to get to another danger zone, never to pass an unclear area, and never divide the team if the team is together in a particular situation. Training should be conducted in handcuffing techniques, and weapon and firing positioning during operations. Circumstances will dictate how an interdiction officer will react. Preparation and training will reduce the risk.

## Operational Briefings

When executing search warrants and conducting controlled delivery operations, the responsibility of the interdiction supervisor increases. He must prepare his team to execute the operation in a manner with the least risk possible. Briefing operations are essential to inform investigators and other participants in how the operation is to be executed. This is the time when everyone should be on the same page. Briefings should be conducted in a serious manner and in a suitable location. There are times, however, when circumstances dictate an impromptu briefing. There may not be time to wait to conduct a detailed briefing; this is why training is imperative.

An operational briefing should be initiated by providing a summary of the case to participants in the operation. Whether it is an execution of a search warrant, a controlled delivery, or surveillance, each member should clearly know his or her role in the operation. An operational briefing should include a case synopsis of the type of operation, the location, additional staging areas, suspect information, suspect vehicle information, and photographs of the subject and associates, if available. A photograph of any suspect vehicles should also be included. The supervising agent should designate assignments. Radio protocol should be established, and other components of the agency (the flight section, canine unit, and patrol units) should be briefed in totality. If a supervisor or team members are not thoroughly prepared, it could be detrimental to the operation, its members, and the agency. Any questions should be addressed in the briefing to alleviate issues in the field during the operation. Never compromise safety and the safety of your staff.

## Controlled Deliveries

Interdiction supervisors will have the task of supervising controlled delivery operations (see Chapter 10). Essentially, a controlled delivery is the actual physical delivery of the drug package or parcel by law enforcement acting in an undercover capacity. Controlled deliveries typically are time-consuming, time-sensitive, and require a number of resources to accomplish.

When conducting briefing operations regarding controlled deliveries, the interdiction supervisor should stress that this operation should be no different from a traditional search warrant operation. Resources should be available such as a surveillance team to monitor the undercover officer making the controlled delivery, air support (helicopter or fixed-wing aircraft) if available, to assist in conducting surveillance of the suspect if the parcel becomes mobile in a vehicle. A spotter should be utilized in the aircraft to provide information to surveillance units. The entry team that will enter the residence or business in which the parcel has been delivered should be briefed, and the same team should be used on every controlled delivery. In a high-risk situation, for example one in which weapons might be involved, a police agency may use a SWAT or TAC team to make entry. As with any briefing, an operational briefing sheet should be provided to all officers involved. The briefing should include possible locations, suspect information, photographs of the suspect, associated photographs, and any photographs or video of the location to which the delivery is to be made. A diagram of the interior of the delivery location, if available, is extremely useful. Aerial photographs are of great value to an entry team. Many agencies have adopted a search warrant checklist to be completed by the interdiction supervisor or the case agent involved in the operation.

## Preparing for the Execution of Search Warrants

Domestic drug interdiction groups will have to draft and execute search warrants, such as in a controlled delivery of a parcel or package containing contraband, as discussed above, and in circumstances where probable cause is established in a hotel/motel investigation (where a search warrant may be executed on the actual room, suspect's bags or luggage, suspect's vehicle). A search warrant may be necessary in other environments such as bus, train, or airport investigations as well.

The role of the interdiction supervisor is to provide guidance and to prepare for the execution of these court orders. Once probable cause has been established to draft and execute a search warrant, the supervisor should review all search warrants and search warrant affidavits before they are presented either to the district or state attorney and ultimately to a magistrate or judge. An important factor in reviewing a search warrant is that the supervisor becomes familiar with the investigation and the probable cause. Any additional documentation that may be necessary in the affidavit should be brought to the attention of the case agent by the supervisor. Coordination with the prosecutor, who may review the search warrant, is necessary in order to have a successful prosecution in the case. In preparing for the execution of a search warrant, presurveillance should be done at the location where the search warrant is to be executed.

A search warrant checklist may be used by the case agent and supervisor. Typically what is included in a search warrant checklist is general information such as the case agent, case number, the contraband involved, location of the execution of the search warrant, and a recommended staging area once a briefing has been conducted. Checklists should also include information regarding the doors, windows, alarms, or obstacles that may be involved.

The location or structure, whether a dwelling or business, should be examined prior to the search warrant. Exterior photographs, aerial photographs, video, map of the area, and exterior and/or interior diagrams, if available, are all helpful. The doors of the location, front, back, or others should be examined to determine if they are fortified, if they open in or out, or any other pertinent details which will provide the entry team with critical information needed to breach the door to execute the search warrant. Any information about windows that may be fortified, porch area, alarms, censored lights, or booby trap information, are essential to an entry team.

It should be ascertained whether there are any weapons in the residence, hazardous materials (such as in a clandestine laboratory operation), known hiding places for narcotics or weapons, or animals that may be in the residence or the exterior (such as guard dogs). The exterior of the location should be well documented during the checklist protocol. A description of fences, obstacles, landscape, and foliage should be noted, and whether there is a swimming pool at the location. These are critical factors once an approach has been made.

The checklist should also include suspect and associate information, such as how many individuals may be involved, and if there are any younger children, elderly, or handicapped individuals in the location. The names and descriptions of the suspects should be provided, along with information about any criminal charges that may be pending before the search warrant. Each suspect and associate should have a background inquiry made through a local, state, and national database for criminal history, photograph, warrant checks, or any weapon or violent tendency information.

Information should be included regarding the approach to the location, and it should be decided who will have the entry tools, if necessary, such as a battering ram or halogen tool. Who will knock and announce at the location and determine the order of the entry element? The primary entry point should be identified as well as alternate entries. Search teams should be assigned to the location. A search team for each area (room) of the premises or business should be designated.

There is some flexibility in all operations, but being prepared is the ultimate goal. Once an entry has been made into a residence or business, the search warrant teams begin the process of conducting their search. Once any type of contraband is located, it is important to document how it was found. The proper way to document is to photograph or video the items the way they were found, using a forensic science team. Processing the scene is recommended in order for those photographs to be used later in the prosecution of the case. Any items that may require latent fingerprint processing should be collected and processed.

## Conclusion

Training, knowledge, and preparation are the key elements in the success of any domestic drug investigation program. The role of the interdiction supervisor is to properly execute all of those elements. Participation in domestic drug investigations is one of the most rewarding and frustrating counter-drug efforts that an investigator can be involved in. An interdiction supervisor is the glue that holds the interdiction group together.

Train, prepare, and stay safe!

## Key Terms

Aerial photographs
Alarm systems ·
Anticipatory search warrant
Assertive
Body bugs
Canine team
Canine training records
Case law
Case synopsis
Court-ordered tracking device
Creative
Diagrams
District, State, U.S. Attorney's Office
Dual-purpose dog
Electronic surveillance equipment
Entry team
Equipment
Flexible
Flight section
Forensic science team
Interdiction supervisor

Marked police vehicle
NAPWDA
NNDA
Operational briefing
Overtime considerations
Passive versus aggressive alert dog
Patient
Radio protocol
Resources
"Roller coaster" ride
Search and seizure
Search warrant checklist
Self-starter
Single-purpose dog
Staging areas
Surveillance
Tactical awareness
Tactical retreat
Tactical skills
Training
USPCA
Video

# Index

## V

## W